The Lag of 21st Century Democratic Elections: In the African Union Member States

The Lag of 21st Century Democratic Elections: In the African Union Member States

Carl W. Dundas

authorHOUSE®

AuthorHouse™
1663 Liberty Drive
Bloomington, IN 47403
www.authorhouse.com
Phone: 1-800-839-8640

First published by AuthorHouse   11/02/2011

ISBN: 978-1-4567-9706-5 (sc)
ISBN: 978-1-4567-9707-2 (ebk)

Printed in the United States of America

Contents

Chapter XIII Electoral Training in the Member States of the African Union for the 21st Century............................278

Election Case Studies:

Foreword

The Lag in 21st Century Democratic Elections: **In** African Union Member States.

The relationship between development in the Third World and democratic processes, transparency, corruption and human rights has assumed a central place in development literature in the last decades of the twentieth and the first decade of the twenty first centuries. The African Union has received specific focus because of the monumental efforts being made to achieve development on the one hand and democracy and good governance on the other. Mr. Carl Dundas' work,—the Lag in 21st Century Democratic Elections: **In** African Union Member States, has made a significant contribution to this literature. It evaluates the performance of democratic elections in the member states of the African Union during the first decade of the 21st century.

Mr. Dundas brings to the work the perspective of a participant observer, with a well established expertise in the conduct of elections throughout the Commonwealth and in Africa in particular. For this reason his analysis, recommendations and conclusions are refreshing and credible. In a comprehensive look at elections detailing topics such as the African Union Foundation for Democratic Elections, Election Observation in the African Union, Overview of the Democratic Deficits in the Union, Electoral Management Bodies of the African Union, The Role of Political Parties in Democratic Elections, Civil Society Organisations' Potential to Contribute to the Democratic Elections in the African Union, Election Education and Electoral Disputes Resolution Within the African Union, one gets a close-up and revealing look at the democratic processes within the Union. The general observations are given specific application by the election case studies in Kenya, Zimbabwe and Malawi.

On the basis of these detailed analyses the author suggests "the big challenge of the 21st century for the member states of the African Union is to develop and consolidate good practices in electoral organisation and conduct and make them as attractive as possible to as many member states as practical". The challenge is a huge one, given the history of failure of democratic processes in many of the countries and the continuing deficits that exist. While the 1990s saw the abandonment of one party regimes, the demise of apartheid and checks on the growth of military regimes in Africa, multi-party elections were slow to take root in many of the complex national societies which have been beset by ethnic and religious loyalties historically.

The author is optimistic that improvements in electoral management bodies, the constructive role of political parties and the potential contribution of civil society organizations, improved electoral education of the electoral officers and the establishment of appropriate electoral disputes mechanisms could see significant improvements in the next decades. Perhaps the major contribution of the work is the effort being made at the continental level through the African Union and its partners in the international community to establish practices that would be internationally acceptable.

The author is to be commended for the measured but insightful commentaries that are made on each of the topics covered in the book. For those interested in the current status of democratic election processes in the African Union the work is highly recommended. Furthermore, though focused on the African Union and the member states, the work draws upon literature from other jurisdictions thereby establishing criteria by which all of these efforts can be evaluated in the future.

Sir Kenneth Hall

Former Governor General of Jamaica and Distinguished Research Fellow—University of the West Indies.

Preface

This work aims at looking closely at the performance of democratic elections in the Member States of the African Union during the first decade of the 21st Century. The progress towards organizing credible democratic elections for most of the Member States was almost imperceptible, but on the whole, the Union can take comfort from the fact that some Member States did organize credible democratic elections. In the process of evaluating the achievement of the Member States individually and collectively some attention was paid to the extent, if any, that good electoral practice was fostered along the way.

The conversation about democratic election development in the Member States of the African Union during the first decade of the 21st Century also explored the dimensions that the impact of the Member States' progress towards improved methods of organizing democratic elections had on the African Union's ability to influence the process. There has been a keen awareness on the part of the departments of the central entity, the African Union Commission (AUC) that regional integration bodies such as the Regional Economic Communities (RECs) and other institutions like the Pan-African Parliament would not like to see too much concentration of influence in the field of election with the AUC in Addis Ababa in Ethiopia. Notwithstanding this keen awareness, the AUC, through its Department of Political Affairs (DPA) and its Democracy and Electoral Assistance Unit (DEAU) made substantial contributions in the promotion of more credible election observation missions' reports, training of AU observers, and engagement of national electoral management bodies (NEMBs) to improve standards.

The challenges that await the fledgling democracies of the Union need to be clearly identified by the respective NEMBs and assistance sought where necessary. The many Member States that are struggling to accommodate sound democratic elections need to be assisted at all stages of preparation, including laying the foundation with appropriate electoral system and sound electoral legislative schemes.

The African Union has began the process of strengthening the African Union Commission's ability, during the decade under review, to help the process of development along through the establishment of a Unit dedicated to improving the standard of conducting election processes at the national electoral management level by Member States. The DEAU and the accompanying fund, the Democracy and Electoral Assistance Fund (DEAF) are both charged with conducting electoral activities designed to improve the organization and conduct of democratic elections in the Union. The DEAU is also charged with the responsibility of improving the quality of the African Union's election observation. The DEAF is charged with the task of mobilizing funds to finance the electoral activities undertaken by the DEAU.

This work, it is hoped, will lay the foundation for further interest in recording incremental progress in raising standards in conducting electoral processes by election management bodies (EMBs) in the African Union.

Carl W. Dundas

Abuja, Nigeria, August, 2011.

Dedicated to my sons, Carl Jr. and Dean.

Acronyms and Abbreviations

AAEA	Association of Asian of Election Authorities
AAUW	American Association of University Women
ACEEEO	Association of Central and Eastern European Electoral Officials
ACEO	Association of Caribbean Electoral Organizations
AEA	Association of Election Administrators
ACDEG	African Charter on Democracy, Elections & Governance
AEC	Africa Economic Community
AFTZ	Africa Free Trade Zone
AIPA	Africa Institute Analysis and Economic Integration
ANC	African National Congress
APRM	African Peer Review Mechanism
AU	African Union
AV	Alternative Vote
BEAT	Basic Electoral Administration Training
BDP	Botswana Democratic Party
BRIDGE	Building Resources in Democracy, Governance and Elections
CAPEL	Center for Electoral Promotion and Assistance
CBO	Community-based organizations
CDD	Centre for Democratic Development
CEN-SAD	Community of Sahel-Saharan States
CEPA	Centre for Economic Policy Analysis
CEPGL	Economic Community of the Great Lakes States
COMESA	Common Market for Eastern and Southern Africa
CoP	Chief of Party
COPAX	Council for Peace and Security in Central Africa
CPDRM	Cameroon People's Democratic Movement
CRM	Country Review Mission
CSOs	Civil society organizations
DEAF	Democracy and Electoral Assistance Fund

DEAU	Democracy and Electoral Assistance Unit
EAC	East African Community
EALA	East African Legislative Assembly
ECCAS	Economic Community of Central African States
ECK	Economic Commission of Kenya
ECOSOCC	Economic, Social and Cultural Council
ECOWAS	Economic Community of West African States
EMB	Electoral Management body
ESCC	Economic, Social, and Cultural Council
EU	European Union
FBO	Faith-based organizations
FPTP	First past the post
FOMAC	Multinational force in Central Africa
IACREOT	International Association of Clerks, Recorders, Election Officials & Treasurers
IFES	International Foundation for Electoral Systems
IGAD	Inter-Governmental Authority for Development
IRI	International Republican Institute
ISSER	Institute for Statistical, Social and Economic Research
KANU	Kenyan African National Union
LGA	Local Government Area
LRO	Lead Research Organizations
MARAC	Early Warning Mechanism of Central Africa
MDC-M	Movement for Democratic Change-Mutambara
MDC-T	Movement for Democratic Change-Tsvangirai
MINATD	Ministry of Territorial Administration & Decentralization
MMP	Mixed Member Proportional
MMPZ	Media Monitoring Project of Zimbabwe
NARC	National Rainbow Coalition
NBS	National Bureau of Statistics
NCERC	New Citizen Education and Research Centre
NCS	National Coordinating Structure
NEMB	National electoral management body
NEPAD	New Partners for Africa's Development

NEO	National Elections Observatory
NDI	National Democratic Institute
NESC	National Economic and Social Council
NGC	National Governing Council
NGO	Non-governmental organization
NRM-O	National Resistance Movement—Organization
NOA	National Orientation Agency
NPO	Non-profit organization
NPOA	National Plan of Action
NSC	National Steering Committee
OAS	Organization of American States
OAU	Organization of African Unity
PAD	Political Affairs Department
PAP	Pan-African Parliament
PBV	Party bloc vote
PEF	Private Enterprise Foundation
PIANZEA	Pacific Islands, Australia & New Zealand Electoral Association
PRC	Permanent Representative Committee
REC	Regional Economic Community
REPAC	Network of Parliamentarians of Central Africa
SADC	Southern African Development Community
SDF	Social Democratic Front
SNTV	Single non-transferable vote
SSGS	Secretaries of State Governments
TRS	Two-round system
TRTs	Technical Research Institutes
UDEAC	Central African Customs & Economic Union
Union	The African Union
UNIORE	Inter-American Union of Electoral Organizations
ZANU-PF	Zimbabwe African National Union-Patriotic Front
ZEC	Zimbabwe Electoral Commission
ZESN	Zimbabwe Election Support Network

Note about the Author

Carl W. Dundas, LL.B, LL.M (Lon.), Barrister-at-law (Gray's Inn) is an Election Expert and Maritime Delimitation Consultant. Mr. Dundas is also experienced in governance, democratic development, election organisation and Law of the Sea matters.

Before joining the Commonwealth Secretariat in November 1980, Mr. Dundas was a member of the Attorney-General's Department in Jamaica. In 1973, he was appointed to the post of Legal Counsel and Director of the Legal Division of the Caribbean Community (CARICOM) to oversee the implementation of the Treaty Establishing the Caribbean Community, of which he was a leading negotiator. As Principal Legal Advisor, he drafted legal instruments in respect of, *inter alia,* rules of origin, common external tariff, a harmonised scheme for fiscal incentive to industry, regional laboratory service, a regional shipping service, regional food corporation and regional agriculture research and development institute.

While in the service of Jamaica, Mr. Dundas, as the Technical Adviser to a Joint Select Committee of both Houses of Parliament, which dealt with constitutional and electoral reform, eventually became the first Director of Elections 1979-80. His extensive experience in constitution drafting, particularly the provisions relating to election management bodies and his wide experience in drafting legislative frameworks for petroleum and hard rock mineral exploration, gave rise to service in many countries of the Commonwealth, including Barbados, Botswana, Guyana, Kenya, Malawi, Samoa, Seychelles, Solomon Islands, Vanuatu, and Cook Islands.

He has given technical assistance in electoral matters in many countries, including Aceh, (Indonesia), Antigua & Barbuda, Botswana, Cayman Islands, Guyana, Kenya, Lesotho, Liberia, Malawi, Mozambique, Nigeria, Sierra Leone, South Africa, Tanzania/Zanzibar, and Zambia; and has been assigned to observe elections in many countries, including Bangladesh, Guyana, Kenya, Liberia, Malaysia, Malawi, Pakistan, Mozambique, South Africa, Tanzania/Zanzibar, and Zambia. He has also advised on election organization and management in Jamaica, Kenya, Liberia, Malawi, Mozambique, Nigeria, South Africa, and Sierra Leone.

Mr. Dundas led Commonwealth Secretariat's electoral technical assistance missions to Guyana, Kenya, Malawi, Namibia, Nigeria, Sierra Leone, South Africa, Tanzania/Zanzibar, and Zambia. He carried out assignments in areas such as designing electoral frameworks for a neutral and impartial electoral management body, the establishment of instruments for the transition from a military one-party to a multiparty system, and has organised capacity-building seminars and workshops.

Constitutional reform, particularly relating to the fundamental provisions dealing with election legislative schemes, is a focal area of his specialization. Consequently, he has undertaken assignments in this area in Guyana, Lesotho, Malawi, South Africa, Tanzania (Zanzibar) and has advised on electoral legislation in Antigua & Barbuda, Cayman Islands, Jamaica, Kenya, Lesotho, Liberia, Malawi, Nigeria, and Sierra Leone.

Mr. Dundas has led the Support Team to the Commonwealth Observer Missions to elections in Malaysia (1990), Zambia (1991), Kenya (1992), Guyana (1992 & 97), Malawi (1994), Mozambique (1994), Tanzania (1995), Zanzibar (Tanzania), Trinidad & Tobago (2000). He also served as technical adviser to the Commonwealth pre-election Observation Group to Namibia in 1989 and to the Commonwealth Observer Group to South Africa in 1994.

Mr. Dundas was Chairman of the Electoral Boundary Delimitation Commission of the Cayman Islands in 2003 and again in 2010. As an Election Legal Consultant from 2001 to 2006, Mr. Dundas advised many election management bodies (EMBs) on reform and modernisation, including Aceh (Indonesia), Antigua & Barbuda, Botswana, Cayman Islands, Guyana, Lesotho, Liberia, Nigeria, and Tanzania.

In 2006, Mr. Dundas took up an appointment as the Chief of Party of the International Foundation for Electoral Systems' (IFES') African Union

Support Program (funded by USAID) to advise the African Union on the establishment of a Democracy and Electoral Assistance Unit (DEAU). The DEAU was established in May 2008 and I remained its adviser at the African Union in Addis Ababa until 2010.

GENERAL INTRODUCTION

The first decade of the 21st Century has ended with an apparent overall lag in democratic elections in African Union Member States and so it is appropriate to take stock of the health of democratic elections in these States. There are fifty-three States in the African Union the majority of which are committed to multiparty democracy. Indeed the African Union boasts of multiparty democracy as among its shared values of its Member States. However, some of the Member States of the Union are less committed to the ideals of true multiparty democracy than others. The big challenge of the 21st Century for the Member States of the African Union is to develop and consolidate good practices in electoral organization and conduct and make them as attractive as possible to as many Member States as practicable.

The focus of this book is on the performance of democratic elections in the Member States of the AU during the first decade of the 21st Century. This period is interesting for a number of reasons, particularly as the AU had seen off colonialism, apartheid, and one-party regimes. Notwithstanding these positive developments, there were at the time of writing a few lingering military regimes in the Union (Madagascar, for example) and a few electorally unsettled country environments, such as Kenya, Côte d'Ivoire, Guinea and Zimbabwe.

The underlying goal of this work is to throw light on the actual or potential influence of the African Union, as the central body, on its Member States in strengthening the performance of the national EMBs' ability to organize credible democratic elections.

The early part of the first decade started off well. The Organization of African Unity which soon ceded its powers to the African Union bequeathed a number of concepts and rules relating to good governance and democratic elections. Some of these instruments will be discussed in chapter 1 and subsequently. They sought not only to articulate the principles of democratic elections, but also to lay down guidelines by which democratic elections may be conducted, as well as how such election might be properly observed by domestic and international groups that specialize in election observation. These instruments which were formulated in the early part of this century were not standing by themselves, as they sought to build on relevant resolutions preceding them. However, while the instruments and procedures for election observers met international standards, not enough emphasis was placed on electoral justice and on improving the standard of election management bodies' (EMBs') organization of the electoral process as a whole, or with respect to particular election processes. Thus by the end of the first decade of the present century some EMBs have not grasped the knack of organizing proper democratic elections, although the managers thereof will insist that their goal is to deliver free and fair elections to the electorate.

The work which the OAU did in the 1990s and subsequently which the AU continued with respect to election observation in this decade did not achieve recognition for credibility. The Democracy and Electoral Assistance Unit (DEAU) was conceived about the time when the AU succeeded to the OAU's responsibilities, but did not come on stream until 2008. The DEAU is charged with the responsibility of improving all aspects of election observations by AU observers and hence enhancing the credibility of AU's election observation missions' reports. The DEAU was also mandated to assist national EMBs' ability to organize and conduct credible democratic elections.

The DEAU had a funding arm, Democracy and Electoral Assistance Fund (DEAF) which is aimed at mobilizing financial resources for the DEAU's electoral activities. Funds were raised from partners and from Member States which were slow to contribute initially.

Bakary Report and the DEAU

The essential role of the DEAU was to spearhead the drive from the centre of the AU Commission to improve the quality and credibility of election observation mission reports, as well as head a proactive programme of assistance to national EMBs designed to upgrade the organization of democratic elections in Member States. The provisions contained in the instrument dealing with guidelines for AU election observation and monitoring, though not perfect, provided an adequate platform for the DEAU to introduce its reforms.

The Department of Political Affairs (DPA) was not unaware that AU election observer missions' reports were falling short of their expected performance under the AU election observation guidelines and so in 2007 it engaged the services of a consultant, Prof. Tessy Bakary, to undertake a study of the election observation mission reports of the AU covering the period from the OAU (1992) to 2006. The focus of the study was on the extent to which the DPA was implementing the provisions of the AU Guidelines on Electoral Observation. On this important issue, the Bakary findings were clear; large chunks of the Guidelines were not being implemented, particularly the dispatch of exploratory teams preceding the sending of election observation missions. The Bakary Report made many useful recommendations which in essence pointed to the urgent need for the AU observation guidelines to be implemented. The AU Guidelines for Election Observers and Monitors are discussed in chapter 2 and the DEAU's approach is examined in chapter 3.

Deficits regarding Democratic Elections in the AU

When analysing the shortcomings of democratic elections in the first decade of the 21st Century in AU Member States, it is appropriate to examine, even briefly, the democratic changes that took place in the preceding decade in the last century. The 1990s saw the abandonment of one-party regimes, the demise of apartheid, and checks on the growth of military regimes in Africa. While the end of the cold war triggered the drive towards democracy, the majority of the people in African countries had grown tired of dictatorial regimes of one sort or another. Unfortunately, the popular wave of crave for the riddance of dictatorial regimes did not usher in an era of genuine democracy, as the dominant party syndrome soon replaced the one-party or military regimes. Multiparty elections were slow to take root in many of the complex national societies which have been beset by ethnic and religious loyalties historically.

Most of the foregoing shortcomings were carried over from the previous decade into the first decade of the 21st Century and the AU tried to deal with those deficits so far as democratic elections were concerned. The first task in tackling the democratic deficits regarding elections was to identify what they were and then formulate appropriate remedies. The task of identifying election deficit is difficult but fascinating; for to begin with some eliminations, for example, Libya, an important Member State of the AU, does not support democratic elections; Swaziland does not allow the existence of political parties to contest elections; Algeria, Tunisia, and Rwanda revel in the ruling party garnering more than 90% of the vote in national elections; Zimbabwe tolerate a farcical multiparty system; Côte d'Ivoire and Guinea emerged from disputed multiparty elections at the very end of the decade; Madagascar was still under unclear military-backed rule at the end of the decade. The democratic deficits in the AU and the attribution there for are discussed in chapters IV and V within.

Electoral Management Bodies of the African Union

Electoral management bodies (EMBs) of Member States of the African Union are fascinating because formally they belong to three categories, namely, independent model, mixed model and government model, but in practice few of the EMBs in Member States of the Union were independent of the influence of the ruling party and government, regardless of the category of their classification. There are notable exceptions, but unfortunately the general perception, particularly among the erstwhile colonial European Powers is that only a few EMBs can withstand the influence of the incumbent regimes, coupled with past colonial ties. However, there has been steady improvement in the performance of some EMBs which have shown independence from the influence of government, the ruling party and other outside entities in particular jurisdictions, during the first decade of the 21st Century. These developments have been analysed and their potential impact on the future of democratic elections in other Member States, as well as on the African Union, assessed

Electoral management bodies of Member States of the African Union receive generous assistance from partners, particularly European and American through bi-lateral and affiliated agency aid for governance and elections. International agencies, primarily the UN and its in-country arms, also contribute generously to EMBs of the AU. The principal electoral fields for attracting funding include technical assistance for national EMBs, voter education, voter registration, training of electoral staff and the conduct of polling.

This work looks at some general issues that EMBs in Member States of the AU should be concerned with in particular, relations with the executive (while avoiding improper influence); the path to good practices; proper internal democracy; transparency, efficiency and professionalism; and the secretariat of the EMB.

Political Parties and Electoral Campaign in the Member States of the AU

Healthy and strong political parties form the competitive base for democratic elections. Such political parties need to have access to adequate financial resources and proper internal democratic structure in order to function smoothly. In most Member States of the AU, opposition political parties struggle to survive due to inadequate financial resources and hostile political and electoral environment. It has been an uncomfortable fact that to a large extent the one-party and military regimes of the pre-1990s era had given way to the era of 'dominant' political parties which form the incumbent party in many Member States of the Union, from Botswana to Cameroon, Congo, Gabon, Nigeria, Rwanda, South Africa and Tanzania to name a few of these countries. The growth of the dominant parties in the first decade of the 21st Century was due to a combination of factors, the principal ones being affiliation to the dominant ethnic group within the particular country; access to state (public) resources; or superior political party organization, coupled in some cases with fraudulent electoral practices.

The general unhealthy state of opposition political parties in the Member States of the AU made it difficult for them to mount serious election campaign contests against the dominant parties. Dominant parties had all the electoral advantages in a disproportionate manner stocked in their favour, in particular, unfair access to resources, public and private. The publicly owned media which dominated the air waves and the print media in most Member States often fell under the influence of the incumbent party. The impartial stakeholders in many Member States complained about the perception of EMBs field staff acting in a partisan manner in favour of incumbents. Often times, EMBs failed to rise to the level of creating a level playing field during election campaigns between the contesting candidates.

The lack of traditional tolerance and courtesy that the letter and spirit democracy entail was extended between political parties and candidates and codes of conduct, where they existed were often ignored by the supporter of all sides. Hate speeches and similar inflammable language aimed at political opponents at rallies became a popular occurrence in Kenya in 2007 campaign and in Zimbabwe in the 2008 election campaign. The upshot had been the characteristic intimidation and violence which accompanied many elections, for example, post-election in Kenya in 2007, pre-run off election in Zimbabwe in June 2008, and post run-off election in Guinea in November 2010 when a state of emergency had to be declared.

Rise of Civil Society in Election Organization in the AU Member States

During the last decade of the 20th Century, civil society organizations (CSOs) played a prominent role in the preparation for the elections of 1994 and 1995 (local elections) in South Africa and in Nigeria in 1998-99 in the series of elections that ushered in civilian rule in place of the out-going military regime. At the beginning of the first decade of this century, CSOs continued their electoral activities and even increased them with the generous assistance with international partners through government agencies and international CSOs. Many CSOs played a part in the restoration of democratic elections to post-conflict Liberia and Sierra Leone during the first half of the first decade of the 21st Century.

The story of CSOs assistance to national EMBs was not all success during the period. Governments like Zimbabwe's in 2008 and there after denied freedom of operation within its territory to both local and foreign CSOs dealing with electoral issues. In a similar vein, the Government of Ethiopia, which had expelled a number of foreign-based CSOs after the 2005 elections, remained less than enthusiastic to welcome foreign-based CSOs and had enacted legislation 2009 which many CSOs claimed restricted their sphere of operation within the jurisdiction of Ethiopia.

Notwithstanding the actions of individual governments against CSOs assistance with elections, the prognosis is positive for the AU as a whole. The African Union's initiative with respect to interaction with civil society entities through the Economic, Social & Cultural Council (ECOSOCC) stood up during this period. The contribution of CSOs to democratic elections during the decade and their potential to contribute in the future is assessed in chapter IX.

Regional Economic Communities

The Regional Economic Communities (RECs) of the African Union are charged with economic development within their respective regions. However, as so often happened in the African Union, institutions created for a particular purpose stealthily spread their portfolio to embrace and gradually takeover related fields. Thus some of the RECs ventured into the fields of governance and issues related to democratic elections. The book deals with the nature and short description of the structure of each of the eight RECs, and assesses their contribution, if any, to democratic elections in the member states of their region.

The vexed issue of rationalization of regional institutions in the AU is discussed. There are 14 regional integration institutions of which 8 had been granted RECs status. Many of the RECs (as well as the other non-RECs integration institutions) have overlapping membership of member states. Repeated attempts throughout the decade to rationalize the membership of these RECs to eliminate overlapping membership failed. The five regions into which the AU is officially divided are discussed in chapter X, but these regions had not been able to assimilate the 8 RECs by the end of the decade.

Other entities which are believed to have a bearing on democratic elections in the context of the AU, such as the Pan-African Parliament, the African Peer Review Mechanism (APRM), and the African Charter on Democracy, Elections and Governance, are also discussed in chapter X.

The APRM concept was an off-shoot of the New Partnership for Africa's Development (NEPAD) which was concerned with economic development program for the AU and which was adopted in Lusaka,

Zambia, in July 2001. The APRM was a voluntary mechanism under which the member states of NEPAD who joined subjected their respective governments to full evaluation of performance against a stipulated set of criteria. The general concept of the APRM found favour with some EMBs and electoral experts. Thus at an African conference on elections, democracy and governance held in Pretoria, South Africa, in April 2003 issued a statement in which it proposed that EMBs forum should establish a committee to look at the criteria and a mechanism for peer review of elections. In a series of short case studies of peer reviews undertaken under the APRM an attempt is made in this book to examine the success of the peer reviews under the APRM and the appropriateness of establishing an APRM-type mechanism among EMBs.

Election Education in the AU Member States.

Any discussion on election education in the African Union rightly tends to point to the fact that there has been too little of it in too many Member States. The main reasons for inadequate depth and reach of election education in the AU during the decade under review was due to insufficient allocation of resources, the multiplicity of ethnicity giving rise to many languages and dialects, as well as the failure to address the urgent need to target the political personnel, such as party officials, candidates, representatives of parties and candidates, and party agents at registration and polling centres for targeted exposure to election education.

The respective stakeholders in an election need to be given as much relevant election information as would enable them to make an informed choice on polling day. Political parties' functionaries and candidates should be facilitated to become familiar with the election rules governing the electoral process, particularly the campaign rules, including financial campaign regulations. Most important is that the voters should be thoroughly trained to apply the voting procedure properly and efficiently. The role of the media, private and public, should be clearly articulated; and where appropriate both arms of the media should be encouraged and facilitated to play an objective role in election education.

Electoral Disputes Resolution in the Member States of the AU.

Electoral disputes mechanisms in the Member States of the African Union had varying levels of credibility, because the dispute settlement mechanisms employed vary widely and often lacked the confidence of the stakeholders. The dispute resolution mechanisms range from the EMBs in some jurisdictions to the ordinary court systems, or electoral tribunals, or special electoral or constitutional courts or even the legislature in a few instances. Further more, some electoral legislative schemes allow non-judicial procedures, such as conciliation, mediation, negotiation, fact-finding commission of inquiries, brokered agreements, to be used to resolve electoral disputes. By way of a faint comparison with the absence of proper electoral dispute resolution structures, a very brief reference to the problems China experienced with their village elections due to lack of defined mechanisms to hear and determine electoral disputes.

The existence of a proper mechanism to hear and dispose of electoral disputes in the legislative scheme of a country is indispensable to confidence building in a country's democratic electoral process. However such mechanisms should be independent of the incumbent party and government should be efficient and be governed by clear transparent procedures that are consistent with best practices. Many of the court and special electoral tribunal systems which existed in many Member States of the AU during the past decade were believed to be under the influence of the government and ruling party of the day.

Training Electoral Officers in the AU for the 21st Century

Training of electoral staff in the rules and procedures with respect to electoral processes is necessary to ensure that electoral rules and procedures are properly applied at stages of election organization. Proper training should also focus on the orientation of staff, particularly field staffs that interface with stakeholders almost daily in preparation for and during polling, regarding the culture of fairness, non-partisanship and impartiality in dealing with political parties and candidates. Courtesy and helpfulness to all stakeholders should also be emphasized as a part of the training routine.

Despite considerable efforts by national EMBs of the Member States of the AU, assisted generously by international partners, the progress exhibited in the quality of election organization and conduct by national EMBs during the decade in question was generally below international standard, with a few exceptions. Perhaps the main reason for this failure to respond more positively to the training made available was that there was not nearly enough of it to reach all the EMBs in need. The nature and type of training made available was inadequate in that they tend to focus on level of professional training, for example, the Basic Election Administration Training (BEAT), and Building Resources in Democracy, Governance and Elections (BRIDGE), while too little effort, as a general rule, went towards the people who actually conduct polling (and compile the register in some cases).

The Members States of the AU, individually or regionally where possible, need to develop units or cadres of dedicated certified trainers of electoral field officers who conduct polling and counting of votes.

Cases Studies: Elections

The election case studies are intended to illustrate some of the problems that attended election organization and conduct in some Member States of the AU during the past decade. The cases of Kenya and Zimbabwe stood out because of the extreme nature of the intimidation and violence touching elections occurring so close to each other, although it was not unusual to have violence accompanying election campaigns or post-election violence in Member States of the African Union. Malawi's case illustrated a classical example of the battle to control party succession to leadership which created such animosity between two men that full tale would be outside of the scope of this work. However, suffice to say that a successful outcome for the 2009 elections was largely due to the repeated quiet intervention by the AU Commission.

Case Studies: African Peer Review Mechanism (APRM)

The APRM case studies offered an opportunity to gauge the relevance or otherwise of applying those principles to EMBs' performance in election conduct.

Discourse: Compact Agreements

The Discourse on compact agreements is aimed at examining the relevance of compact arrangements between governments and national (or regional) CSOs in election matters with a view to seeing whether or not they could work successfully in the Member States of African Union. It drew inspiration from the Deakin Report in the United Kingdom in 1996 which explored the potential for partnerships between the voluntary sector and public authorities.

Chapter 1

African Union's Foundation
for Democratic Elections

Introduction

At the time of its creation in 1963, the Organization of African Unity (OAU) was not known for its outstanding democratic credentials. However, as time went by the OAU became more conscious of the key role that sound democratic credentials in its Member States could play in its development generally. Shortly before transforming itself into the African Union (AU) a number of steps were taken to lay the foundation for the development of democracy through the conduct of regular periodic elections in each Member State. In the early nineteen nineties, the OAU began to observe elections in member states with a view to enabling national election management bodies (EMBs) to improve and strengthen their capability to organize credible democratic elections. A number of declarations followed which sought to give guidance with respect to holding credible democratic elections and to set formal guidance to African Union election observers.

The OAU began to show much interest in the spread of democracy and the holding of democratic elections throughout the continent, as time went by. A number of instruments and declarations were approved by the OAU. These included the Algiers Decision of July 1999 and the Lomé Declaration of July 2000 on the approach by the OAU to unconstitutional changes of government in Member States of the Organization. In this context, mention may be made of the African Charter on Human and

Peoples' Rights, adopted in Kenya in 1981 which recognized the right of every citizen to participate freely in the government of his or her country whether directly or through democratically elected representatives. By the Declaration in Addis Ababa in 1990, Member States undertook to continue with the democratization of African societies and the consolidation of democratic institutions.

The Constitutive Act of the African Union of 11 July 2000 has, as one of its objectives, promotion of democratic principles and institutions, popular participation and good governance (Article 3 (g)). Also one of the principles of the Constitutive Act is the 'condemnation and rejection of unconstitutional changes of governments' of the Union, (Article 4 (p)).

Declaration of Principles Governing Democratic Elections

The Declaration on the Principles Governing Democratic Elections in Africa which came out of the38th Ordinary Session of the Assembly of the OAU on 20 February 2002 was a key element in the foundation on which the African Union would launch its drive to develop democratic elections. The Declaration set out the principles of democratic elections. It stated that democratic elections were the basis of the authority of any representative government. It called for regular elections which were key elements of the democratization process. The Declaration cited the holding of elections as an important dimension in conflict prevention, management and resolution. It listed the main elements of democratic elections as: election being conducted free and fair manner; under democratic constitutions supported by legal instruments; within the framework of a system of separation of powers with an independent judiciary; at regular intervals; and by impartial and accountable electoral institutions.

The Declaration contained responsibilities for the Member States of the OAU to which those States subscribed as follows, to:

(a) take measures to implement the principles contained in the Declaration;
(b) establish, where none existed, appropriate institutions where issues such as codes of conduct, citizenship, residency, age requirements for eligible voters, compilation of voters' registers, would be addressed;

(c)   establish impartial, all-inclusive, competent and accountable national electoral bodies staffed by qualified personnel, as well as competent legal entities, including effective constitutional courts to arbitrate in the event of dispute arising from the conduct of elections;

(d)   safeguard the human and civil liberties of all citizens, including freedom of movement, assembly, association, expression, and campaigning as well as access to the media by all stakeholders, during the electoral process;

(e)   promote civic and voters' education on the democratic principles and values in close cooperation with the civil society groups and other relevant stakeholders;

(f)   take all necessary measures and precautions to prevent the perpetration of fraud, rigging or any other illegal practices throughout the whole electoral process, in order to maintain peace and security;

(g)   ensure the availability of adequate logistics and resources for carrying out democratic elections, as well as ensure that adequate provision of funding for all registered political parties to enable them to organize their work, including participation in the electoral process;

(h)   ensure that adequate security is provided to all parties participating in elections;

(i)   ensure the transparency and integrity of the entire electoral process by facilitating the deployment of representatives of political parties and individual candidates at polling and counting stations and by accrediting national and other observers or monitors; and

(j)   encourage the participation of African women in all aspects of the electoral process in accordance with the national laws.

The Declaration set out rights and obligations relating to democratic elections as follows:

(a)   every citizen shall have the right to participate freely in the government of his or her country, either directly or through freely elected representatives in accordance with the provisions of the law;

(b)   every citizen has the right to fully participate in the electoral processes of the country, including the right to vote or be voted for, according to the laws of the country and as guaranteed by the Constitution, without any kind of discrimination;

(c) every citizen shall have the right to free association and assembly in accordance with the law;

(d) every citizen shall have the freedom to establish or to be a member of a political party or organization in accordance with the law;

(e) individual or political parties shall have the right to appeal and to obtain timely hearing against all proven electoral malpractices to the competent judicial authorities in accordance with the electoral laws of the country;

(f) candidates or political parties shall have the right to be represented at polling and counting stations by duly designated agents or representatives;

(g) No individual or political party shall engage in any act that may lead to violence or deprive others of their constitutional rights and freedoms. Hence all stakeholders should refrain from, among others, using abusive language and/or incitement to hate or defamatory allegations and provocative language. These acts should be sanctioned by designated electoral authorities;

(h) All stakeholders in electoral contests shall publicly renounce the practice of granting favours to the voting public for the purpose of influencing the outcome of elections;

(i) in covering the electoral process, the media should maintain impartiality and refrain from broadcasting and publishing abusive language, incitement to hate, and other forms of provocative language that may lead to violence;

(j) every candidate and political party shall respect the impartiality of the public media by undertaking to refrain from any act which might constrain or limit their electoral adversaries from using the facilities and resources of the public media to air their campaign messages;

(k) every individual and political party participating in elections shall recognize the authority of the electoral commission or any statutory body empowered to oversee the electoral process and accordingly render full cooperation to such a commission/body in order to facilitate their duties; and

(l)   every citizen and political party shall accept the results of elections proclaimed to have been free and fair by the competent national bodies as provided for in the Constitution and the electoral laws and accordingly respect the final decision of competent electoral authorities or, challenge the result appropriately according to law.

This Declaration also dealt with election observation by the OAU and the role of the OAU's Secretariat but those aspects will be dealt with later.

The OAU's Declaration on the Principles Governing Democratic Elections in Africa was a bold and prudent step, coming at a time when there were few mechanisms within the OAU to oversee or enforce its various operative provisions. However, as will be shown below, the Heads of State and Government of the OAU meeting at the same 38th Session of the Assembly of the OAU went on to lay the foundation for the creation of mechanisms and detailed guidelines to deal with the strengthening of electoral organization and election observation within the OAU.

Initiation of Sustained Action

At about the same time when the OAU Declaration on the Principles Governing Democratic Elections in Africa was being contemplated, the OAU Council of Ministers, during the 78th ordinary session held in Durban, South Africa, June 28th to 6th July 2002 decided to establish an administrative unit to follow-up and to observe elections assisting the Commissioner in charge of the Political Affairs Department of the AUC, which was responsible for the co-ordination and organization of the OAU's participation in the observation of elections, in collaboration with the official authorities of the concerned countries.[1] This Ministerial action was followed by the Heads of State at their Summit in Durban on the 8th and 9th of July 2002 to request the Secretary-General of the OAU to take all necessary measures to ensure the implementation of the Declaration while committing to undertake to launch a feasibility study on the creation, within the General Secretariat of the OAU, of a unit responsible for issues of good government.[2]

---

[1]   See CM/Dec. (LXXVI).

[2]   See AHG/Decl.1.(XXXVIII)

Subsequently, discussion was initiated in various forums for the need to establish an electoral assistance fund, and a document on 'Prospects for Establishment of an Electoral Assistance Fund[3]' was circulated to promote discussion on the concept of an election fund.

Feasibility Studies

In response to the request of the Heads of State at its Durban Summit in 2002, the Political Affairs Department of the Commission appointed a consultant to undertake a feasibility study into the requirements of creating an electoral assistance unit. The terms of reference were brief, namely, to assist in the establishment and operation of an electoral unit with specific program lines as guidelines, as well as helping in the capacity building of the unit.

The raison d'etre for the establishment of a Democracy and Electoral Assistance Unit was the need for the Commission of the African Union to implement its program on the subject of the advancement of democracy and democratic elections on the continent.

The feasibility study identified three broad areas in which the unit might be engaged, namely, election observations; election monitoring; and support to all other aspects of democracy.

The feasibility study on the elections unit summarized its findings and recommendations as follows:

(a)   the mandate of the unit was to implement all activities of the Commission aimed at promoting democracy and democratic elections in Africa;

(b)   to observe and monitor elections;

(c)   to offer electoral assistance; and to support other aspects of democracy.

---

[3]   See Annex III of the Report of the Interim Chairperson on the Proceedings of the African Conference on Elections, Democracy and Good Governance, for the Executive Council at its Third Ordinary Session in Maputo, Mozambique 2003.

With respect to AU election observation missions, the Unit would undertake the following tasks (i) prepare elections observation and monitoring missions; electoral observation training; publish and dissemination of documents; proposals for establishing regional structure for electoral observation and coordination of regional mechanisms; and follow up with African Union partners on election observation.

With respect to the provision of electoral support, the Unit would develop a framework document for electoral assistance which would, among other things, determine the form of assistance as well as the categories of beneficiaries; coordinate administrative processing of requests for electoral assistance; strengthen capacities of national electoral institutions through training; exchange of human and material resources; and promote a continental forum of these institutions.

Regarding the support to other aspects of democracy, the Unit would be responsible for implementing the program of the Commission on Constitutions and constitutional processes, as well as designing and implementing a program for the promotion of a culture of democracy on the continent. The Unit would also have the responsibility to design and develop cross-cutting projects that affect the sectors within its scope, for example, fundraising and managing support funds for democracy and electoral assistance, consolidating the Resource Center in the Department and launching an African Union website for publication of important documents on democracy and elections or setting up an experts' database.

The conclusion reached by the study was that the project to set up a support unit for democracy and electoral assistance was fully justified and was feasible.

The movement to develop the democratic process in Africa stimulated the need to explore ways and means to better fund electoral activities. Specific attention was directed at funding the activities of the proposed Democracy and Electoral Assistance Unit and the AU Commission was asked also to undertake a feasibility study to follow up on a paper which explored the prospects of establishment of a trust fund for the purpose. An electoral trust fund was thought to have many advantages, in particular,

(a)   quick response to request for technical assistance;
(b)   provides untied funding from different sources;
(c)   allows flexibility to the AU to allocate resources and coordinate assistance to recipients according to the assessed democracy and electoral priorities;
(d)   facilitates effective coordination between the AU, sub-regional and national organizations leading to more effective use of resources.

The purpose of the Trust Fund was to enhance the capacity of the African Union to support national and regional initiatives to build and sustain democratic processes, entrench government accountability and promotes the transparency and accountability of state institutions; support and enhance national electoral processes that contribute to holding of regular, free and fair elections in accordance with internationally recognized standards; and support regional and national capacity building of electoral management bodies, regional forums and networks to manage and oversee, democratic electoral processes and electoral processes and electoral observation missions.

The study postulated that the trust fund might be used for the following purposes:

(a)   organizing or supporting courses, workshops, seminars, meetings and roundtables for the role players in the democratic processes arena;
(b)   support national and regional bodies composed of members of civil society to develop the capacity to undertake non-partisan electoral observation;
(c)   promote the adoption of democratic constitutions in conformity with generally accepted principles;
(d)   encourage civil society in member states to support the process of democratization;
(e)   Strengthen institutions that sustain and support democracy;
(f)   promote the recognition of democratic change, political pluralism and the role of the opposition;
(g)   support freedom of expression and freedom of the press; and
(h)   encourage minority and women participation and representation in the electoral process.

The report on the study set out the following salient points:

(a)   The Democracy and Electoral Fund will be a specific fund established to support exclusively African Union operational activities relating to the promotion and establishment of democracy and the conduct of democratic elections in member countries;

(b)   The Focal Point for the Fund will be the Commissioner for Political Affairs;

(c)   The fund will be developed on a flexible co-financing framework based on the work program of a unit established under the Political Affairs Department;

(d)   Contribution will be made to the fund from the regular budget, voluntary contributions from member states, AU international partners, and donor agencies and from private sources. Although contributors to the fund will have the flexibility of specifying how the funds contributed will be used, contributors to the fund will be encouraged as far as possible to provide non-earmarked funds to support the priorities set by the Political Affairs Department;

(e)   The fund will be distributed according to the priorities set by Political Affairs Department. A trust forum that will provide expert opinion on activities and programs to be considered by the unit will assist the Department;

(f)   The fund will be managed by the AU's Finance, Budget and Administrative Department (responsible for management of other AU funds), the implementation of the activities supported by the fund will rest with a newly established unit within the Political Affairs Department;

(g)   The fund will be managed under the financial and administrative rules of the AU. If contributors to the fund require separate auditing outside the AU financial framework, this requirement should be incorporated in the Grant Agreement that they may have made with the fund. Guidelines set for the financial management of the fund should be rigorously followed. The guidelines set out clearly what expenditures should be charged and the responsibilities of the implementing office, DEU, and the Finance Department in respect of the management of the fund.

(h)   To establish accountability of the fund to member countries and donors, stringent reporting mechanism will be established and adhered to. The responsibility of providing narrative reports will reside with the Democracy and Electoral Assistance Unit that will be established, while the financial reporting will be the responsibility of the Finance and Budget Office;

(i)   Established African Union procedures for monitoring and evaluation will be applicable for all activities sponsored by the fund. While approval of proposals will be expedited and funds disbursed as quickly as the situation demands, accountability of funds received will be ensured by vigorous reporting and the standard African Union auditing procedures.

The feasibility study report proposed that a strong unit under the Political Affairs Department be created to operate and manage the fund. Such a unit should be staffed with highly skilled personnel; and it endorsed the structure of the unit and the staff profiles which were contained in the feasibility study relating to the establishment of the Democracy and Electoral Assistance Unit.

Subject to the guidelines adopted with respect there to, the feasibility study of the fund proposed that the following entities might have access to the fund after its creation:

(a)   Member States of the African Union;

(b)   National electoral management bodies (NEMBs);

(c)   Regional bodies such as ECOWAS and SADC;

(d)   Continental and regional electoral networks, forums and democracy organizations;

(e)   Government agencies like the judiciary and security forces;

(f)   Independent NGOs not affiliated to any political parties and are involved in the promotion of democracy and elections and the media particularly where voter education is being promoted;

(g)   The African Union for the organization and conduct of an electoral process and for the fielding of election observer and monitoring missions;

(h)   The African Union for the management of activities supported by the fund.

Further recommendations which were made in the feasibility study relating to the fund included proposals that the democracy and electoral assistance unit when established should develop a standard request form to ensure consistency of approach, and each request should be in clear terms, accompanied by a comprehensive budget and timelines for financial reporting.

Consideration of the Reports of the Feasibility Studies

The African Union Commission has a very careful approach to dealing with commissioned studies. The procedure is to subject such studies to two tiers of scrutiny before they are submitted to the primary bodies of the AU for consideration and approval. The first tier is a meeting of independent experts and the second tier is a meeting of experts drawn from the representatives of Governments. With respect to the first tier, objectives are to make an independent and critical appraisal of the study in order to make improvements, and to validate the study before it is presented to the Government experts (second tier) meeting and then to the meeting of the policy organs of the African Union.

The First Tier
Meeting of Independent Experts

The meeting of independent experts was chaired by Dr Brigalia Bam and the rapporteur was Dr. Julien Nimubona. Professor Gerard Niyumgeko, the consultant responsible for the Feasibility Study on the Establishment of a Democracy and Electoral Assistance Unit (DEAU), gave a summary of the findings and recommendations contained in the report. The other consultant, Mr. Abdou Jahna, who dealt with the Feasibility Study into the Establishment of a Democracy and Electoral Assistance Fund (DEAF), then gave a summary of his findings and recommendations.

In considering the summary with respect to the DEAU, the meeting concluded that in dealing with the link between democracy and elections, the study placed too much emphasis on elections to the detriment of other aspects of democracy. After discussions on the matter, the experts felt that the concepts of observation and follow-up (the latter being understood in the sense of formulation of recommendations for the future) were appropriate. Particular emphasis was on the three observation phases, namely, pre-election, election and post-election observation. The meeting set up a committee which looked at the structure of the Unit proposed by the study and approved the study's recommendations that the Unit should be placed in the Political Affairs Department.

The independent experts reinforced the study regarding the functions of the Unit with respect to electoral assistance and the consolidation of democracy. The experts emphasized the election observation should be carried out in three phases, namely, pre-election, election and post-election phases, and that each phase should be carried out on request or otherwise in cooperation with the Member States concerned. They recommended that each phase should be covered by a timely report, including recommendations. They stated that election observation missions' reports should be as objective as possible, reflecting the negative and positive points so as to create a balanced judgment and enable the Union to make well-informed and well-advised declarations and recommendations. The experts also recommended the strengthening of professionalism of institutions, organizations and networks involved in election management and observation, and that observation mission teams should be inter or multidisciplinary so as to ensure wider informed inputs during observation and drafting of reports. The meeting recommended that programmes should be designed and developed to train officers in the management of electoral disputes for the benefit of election management and observation institutions, organizations and networks. It also proposed that partnerships should be established and strengthened at national, regional and international levels so as to pool resources and share experiences. Further the meeting recommended that civil society organizations involved with elections should be strengthened in capacity, and that a data bank of experts and professionals in election observation and management should be established in order to facilitate the mobilization of resources, as well as building and consolidating partnerships.

The meeting of independent experts made the following recommendations regarding the DEAU:

(a)   that the Unit (DEAU) ensures that concrete implementation and promotion of African Union's legal and political instruments regarding democracy and elections be promoted among member states as well as national and regional non-governmental organizations;

(b)   that the development and promotion of African democracy indicators as may be identified through research work recommended in the feasibility study on the DEAU;

(c)   that the DEAU conduct and promote activities for monitoring the status of democracy in Africa according to these indicators;

(d)   organization of forums for civil society organizations concerned with the democratization process and election observation; and

(e)   development of civic education programmes.

With respect to the structure of the DEAU, the meeting of independent experts proposed that the criteria of skills and professionalism should be given priority in the advertisement of posts, and that partnerships with regional and national organizations could strengthen the capacity of the DEAU.

The meeting of independent experts considered the report of the feasibility study on the Fund (DEAF) and made the following recommendations:

(a)   the mechanism for establishment of the Fund, its statutes and management modalities should be inspired by previous achievements, innovations should not be ruled out;

(b)   that the mechanisms and modalities relating to the financing, management and or eligibility to access the Fund were not sufficiently clear;

(c)   the area or category of beneficiaries should be better defined in order to avoid the risks of excesses and confusion resulting in lack of credibility of the Fund;

(d)   that the efficiency in mobilizing funds and the credibility of the Fund itself depended on the administrative framework and management mechanisms (especially the procedural manual) that are put in place.

The meeting of independent experts recommended that the two studies should be merged to form a single project document comprising two parts: part one on the Feasibility Study on the Setting up of a Democracy and Electoral Assistance Unit, and part two on the Feasibility of the Establishment of a Democracy and Electoral Support Trust Fund.

Second Tier
Government Experts Meeting

The meeting of government experts was convened in Brazzaville, Congo, from 5 to 6 June 2006. The Bureau for the meeting was elected as follows: Republic of Congo was elected to the Chair, with Uganda elected as 1st Vice Chair, South Africa as 2nd Vice Chair, Saharawi Arab Democratic Republic as 3rd Vice Chair, while Senegal provided the Rapporteur for the meeting.

The respective Rapporteurs of the meeting of Independent Experts, Dr Julien Nimubona, gave a summary of the recommendations made at that meeting with respect to the findings and recommendations in respect of the feasibility studies regarding the Unit and the Fund. The respective consultants, Professor Gerard Niyumgeko for the feasibility study on the Unit, and Mr. Abdou Jahna, for the Trust Fund, made short presentations to the meeting of Government experts.

The report of the meeting of Government experts showed that some delegations were concerned about the sustainability and viability of the Unit and the Fund, in particular, the operational costs of the Unit and the likelihood of duplication of the existing Division within the Political Affairs Department which deals with election issues. Other delegations favored the merging of the two studies as recommended by the independent experts.

Having considered the matter, the Meeting of Government Experts made the following recommendations:

(a)   That the mandate of the Unit should be the coordination of all actions of the Commission aimed at enhancing democracy and democratic elections in Africa;

(b)   The missions devolving upon the Unit as a result of the general mandate should be the enhancement of democracy in general, election observation and monitoring as well as electoral assistance;

(c)   The Unit should be directly under the Political Affairs Department, and should be appropriately staffed starting with a small structure, with progressive recruitment of staff;

(d)   The capacity of the Political Affairs Department should be strengthened to enable it to implement the programme of the Commission in the area of democracy and elections;

(e)   The Unit operation costs should financed by the regular budget of the Union, while its operations and programmes will be implemented from the Fund.

Specific recommendations regarding the Fund were:

(a)   The purpose of the Fund should be to support activities of the Unit;

(b)   The administration of the Fund should be the responsibility of the Unit within the Department of Political Affairs, with the Finance Department managing its finances in accordance with the Financial Rules and Regulations of the Union;

(c)   The primary beneficiaries of the Fund should be the Member States as well as other institutions, such as national electoral institutions, civil society organizations, political parties, the media and other stakeholders in democratic processes, according to the activities conducted by the Unit;

(d)   The Commission should define procedures for access to the Fund as well as evaluation and performance mechanisms which derive from supervision and evaluation procedures of the African Union;

(e)   The Commission should design sustainable strategies for mobilizing and replenishing the necessary resources for the Fund, to address the problems of financing the Fund's activities; and

(f)   The Fund, while remaining open to receive external resources from the African Union's partners, should be an exclusively African instrument for enhancement of democracy and electoral assistance in the continent.

The Meeting of Government Experts made two general recommendations, namely, that the two studies should be merged into a two-part document, with the first part on the Unit and the second part on the Fund; and that the recommendations from the Government Experts' Meeting be submitted to the competent organs of the Union, in accordance with the standard procedure.

Decision Establishing the Democracy and Electoral Assistance Unit and Fund

In Banjul, Gambia, in June 2006, the Executive Council noted the Report of the meeting of Government Experts on the Unit and the Fund and the recommendations contained therein and decided as follows:[4]

(a) To set up a 'Democracy and Electoral Assistance Unit' within the Political Affairs Department of the African Union Commission;

(b) The Unit shall be responsible for coordinating and implementing all African Union Commission actions aimed at promoting democracy and democratic elections in Africa; the duties of the Unit shall include the promotion of democracy in general, observation and monitoring of elections and electoral assistance;

(c) The Unit shall be financed by the African Union ordinary budget and the Democracy and Electoral Assistance Special Fund; and

(d) The Commission is hereby authorized to take the necessary measures to set up and make the Democracy and Electoral Assistance Unit operational as soon as possible.

The Decision of the Executive Council extended to the Fund as follows:

(a) To set up a 'Democracy and Electoral Assistance Special Fund' within the African Union;

(b) The purpose of the Fund is to lend support to the activities of the Democracy and Electoral Assistance Unit;

(c) The Fund shall be resourced from the ordinary budget of the Union, voluntary contributions from Member States, including the private sector, civil society and individuals, as well as fund-raising activities;

(d) The Fund shall be managed, administratively by the Democracy and Electoral Assistance Unit within the Political Affairs Department

---

[4] EX.CL/Dec.300(IX)

and financially by the Finance Directorate. The Financial Rules and Regulations of the Union shall govern the operations of the Fund;

(e)   The Fund shall benefit national elections and the Electoral Assistance Unit;

(f)   The Commission shall lay down the procedures for accessing the Fund and also mechanisms for the evaluation and performance of programmes financed by the Fund; and

(g)   The Commission is hereby authorized to take all the necessary measures to set up and make operational the Democracy and Electoral Assistance Fund.

Operational Structure of the Unit (DEAU) and the Fund (DEAF)

The Decision of the Executive Council did not expressly endorse any operational structure for the DEAU and the DEAF. The Feasibility Study of the DEAU did propose and indicate an initial structure for it which would place the Head of the DEAU at P5 level and the Electoral and Democracy Officers at P3 level. However, the rules of the Commission reserved issues of structure for any new entity to be first dealt with by a Sub-Committee of the Permanent Representatives Committee (PRC) which made recommendations on structures to the PRC. The Sub-Committee on Structures did not meet until June 2007 and recommended only one post, that of Head of Unit, at P3 level. The matter was then taken up by the PRC in Accra, Ghana, during the week of the Summit and two other posts of Election Officers were approved at P2 level. Since the Experts Meetings had recommended the merger of the DEAU and the DEAF, the Head of DEAU and the two Election Officers, were responsible to make operational both entities, DEAU and DEAF.[5]

---

5   The intention of the approval of the two officers in Accra was that one would be responsible for the DEAU and the other for the DEAF under the supervision of the Head of DEAU. However, at the critical time when the terms of reference for the role were being prepared, there was disagreement between the respective officers in the Political Affairs Department (PAD) and the Administrative Human Resources Department. The PAD representative who was in Accra when the matter was dealt with maintained that one of the two officers was required to focus on election financing, but that was

As was to be expected, the recruitment of staff was a slow process. The terms of reference of each post had to be translated into the four working languages, namely, Arabic, English, French and Portuguese. In the case of the recruitment of the DEAU's staff, the Chairman of the Commission approved a 'fast track' procedure, and to expedite matters further, IFES-USAID secured the translation through free-lance translators, thus saving a couple of weeks. Although the fast track procedure worked and interviews were conducted in November 2007, the successful candidates were not able to assume duties until towards the end of April 2008.

The DEAU and the DEAF became operational in May 2008 after departmental induction courses in the Political Affairs Department and orientation sessions with the International Foundation for Electoral Systems (IFES) Chief of Party who was the adviser to the DEAU.[6] The DEAU then turned to preparation of a work plan for 2008 and then for 2009. The work plan for 2008 encompassed six main issues, namely, election observation, convening a continental meeting of African election management bodies, training of election observers, improving electoral processes standards, assistance to national election management bodies (EMBs), a master database, accompanied by a number of auxiliary databases, and mobilization of funds under the auspices of DEAF. The election observation missions occupied the greater part of the early attention of the DEAU. The DEAU was assisted by the IFES Chief of Party who had prepared many draft papers dealing with the initial work plan. The Carter Center and the Electoral Institute of Southern Africa (EISA) were partners of IFES in the programme of support to the DEAU and dealt with training of election observers and the creation of master and auxiliary databases.

---

not included in the terms of reference. As it turned out the representative of PAD was correct. The two officers who were recruited neither wished to deal with the financial aspects and so the Head of the DEAU along with the help of the IFES COP had to take on the task initially.

[6]   The Chief of Party of IFES at the time was the author.

Assessment of the New Approach

The OAU had almost four decades of dealing with elections in its Member States. With the rapid movement toward multiparty elections during the 1990s, it clearly felt that something had to be done centrally within the Organization to aide the forward movement of democratic elections. Strategically, this contemplation of forward movement came at good time when the OAU was about to give way to a 'deepening' of collaboration among the Member States in the form of the African Union. The new Union inherited the mixed experience of democratic elections in Member States and set a path to seek to strengthen the democratic practice.

The OAU, the AU's predecessor organization, was conscious of the adverse effects of the frequent unconstitutional change of governments since its founding in 1963 had on politics and democratic elections in the Member States. It was necessary for the OAU, and it's Member States, to reaffirm their commitment to the principle of democracy and democratic elections, because there had been frequent military takeovers from civilian regimes during the four decades of OAU existent. The prominence given to AU election observation signified over emphasis on observation as a manner of clothing democratic elections in Member States with undeserved credibility, rather than offering technical assistance to particular national EMBs to improve their ability to organize elections in accordance with good practices. However, as will be shown in chapter II below, election observation offered the OAU and subsequently the AU the opportunity to bring to bear an AU-wide perspective on election preparation and conduct in Member States and making recommendations for improvements to national EMBs.

Chapter II

Election Observation in African Union

Introduction

Electoral observation and monitoring formed an integral part of the democratic and electoral processes in Africa during the first decade of the 21st Century. Election observation by international, regional and national observers became an acceptable mechanism with respect to strengthening the transparency and credibility of elections and democratic governance in the Member States of the African Union. It also helped to facilitate the acceptance of election results throughout the continent. Electoral observation was widely credited with the potential ability to diminish conflicts prior to, during and after elections. African countries made commendable progress in institutionalizing democratic elections during the 1990s; nevertheless considerable challenges were yet to be overcome, including electoral campaign violence, polling day and post-polling conflicts. Major challenges lay in improving the integrity of the electoral processes, and it was believed that in this quest election observation had a significant role to play.

To the extent that election observation could be perceived as a tool to measure the improvement in the organization and conduct of democratic elections, the OAU and its successor organization, the AU, elevated observation as their chief means of intervention in the conduct of elections in Member States. The contribution of AU election observation to the improvement of the quality of democratic elections in Member States in the first decade of the 21st Century is difficult to assess, as observer mission reports did not enjoy a high level of credibility among most stakeholders and there was no reliable mechanism in the AU Commission to assist national EMBs to implement recommendations of missions' reports to rectify weaknesses.[7]

For the purposes of the African Union's election observation and monitoring guidelines, 'election observation' is defined as 'gathering information and making an informed judgment'; while 'election monitoring' is defined as 'the authority to observe an election process and to intervene in that process if relevant laws or standard procedures are being violated or ignored'. The guidelines aimed at covering the pre-election, election, and post-election phases of the electoral process.

The African Union Guidelines for Elections Observation and Monitoring Missions

These Guidelines were formulated to strengthen the democratization and governance processes which were taking place in the Member States of the African Union.

The first rule for African Union election observers and monitors was that they shall be guided by the guidelines of the AU Commission which were based on the OAU Declaration of Principles Governing Democratic Elections. The Commission was required to keep an up-to-date election calendar in the Union. The Guidelines required that the country organizing an election should send a formal invitation to the AU pursuant to the sub-paragraphs V (i) and V (3) of the OAU Declaration on Principles Governing Democratic Elections in Africa (2002) either through the National Electoral Commission (NEC), or electoral authority, or the government. The Guidelines indicated that the AU, upon receiving the invitation to observe an election, should ensure that adequate lead-time for preparation was available; that access to essential planning information was secured; that there was access to professional expertise; and that there were sufficient financial and other resources to undertake election observations and related activities.

---

[7] The DEAU had plans to offer such assistance to national EMBs in the future.

A key stipulation in the Guidelines was the requirement that upon receiving an invitation to observe an election, the AU should expeditiously dispatch an election assessment team to the country planning for the election. The assessment team should establish whether or not conditions existed in the country for organizing credible, legitimate, free and fair elections in accordance with the Durban Declaration. The Head of the Assessment Team should advise the AU Commission whether the necessary conditions and environment existed for a free and fair election as provided for in the AU principles governing democratic elections, had been met. The Chairman of the Commission should confirm the findings of the Assessment Team in a public statement.

An AU electoral assessment team should address relevant issues to its terms of reference, including the following:

(i)   Whether or not the constitution and legal framework guaranteed fundamental freedoms and human rights;

(ii)   Whether or not the electoral system was premised on the right to freedom of association, and enables people to advance this right through the formation of political parties for the purposes of electoral competition;

(iii)   Whether or not there was an independent and impartial electoral commission which exercises its powers and performs its function without fear, favour or prejudice;

(iv)   Whether or not the rights of observers were guaranteed;

(v)   Whether or not the security forces would maintain a neutral role in the provision of election security;

(vi)   Whether or not the situation in the country is generally peaceful or was there political violence? If there was violence, would the government's security measures provide an environment provide for a free election campaign or were there substantial restrictions on the freedom of expression, association and assembly?

(vii)   Whether or not there were clear rules relating to political party funding applicable to all parties and candidates;

(viii) Whether or not voter education was provided on a non-partisan, independent and coordinated manner throughout the country;

(ix)   Whether or not there was equitable use or access to public resources for election campaigning;

(x) Whether or not registration of voters was undertaken without prejudice or discrimination on the basis of gender, race, religion, region or ethnicity;

(xi) Whether or not there existed an independent media authority responsible for monitoring and regulating the media to allow equitable access to the media

The Guidelines required that prior to sending an observer mission to a member country a preliminary assessment should be made of the country's social, economic, political and constitutional arrangements. Recognition of the differing levels of organizational capacity, financial and human resources, infrastructural development—especially road, telecommunication and technological infrastructure—had an impact on the way elections were organized across the continent. However, the Guidelines stated that such factors should not compromise the conduct of free, fair and transparent elections.

The Guidelines required every electoral assessment team to advise the DEAU on whether or not to undertake an AU election observation mission. Where it was decided that an AU observation or monitoring mission should be sent, the Assessment Team should advise the AU on the nature of the mission that is, whether an observation, technical assistance, monitoring or supervision—should be undertaken. There could be a combination of the available options; the Guidelines stated that the recommended mix of mandate should avoid conflict of interest. If the decision was not to send an observation or monitoring mission because of the prevailing unsatisfactory conditions in the country, the Guidelines suggested possible intermediate responses. The one option could be a technical team or supervisory team to remedy the situation through working with the national electoral commission, if the host country agreed. The other approach, if the unsatisfactory conditions deteriorated, and the host country was not prepared to accept outside assistance, the AU could decide against sending a mission and could refer the matter to the appropriate organs of the Union.

The Guidelines conferred flexibility on the AU to arrange prior understanding with the host country that it reserved the right not to send or withdraw observers in certain circumstances when the conditions in the country did not meet the AU guiding principles for organizing free and fair elections. They required that the Regional Economic Communities (RECs) should be involved actively in elections observation and monitoring. The RECs should complement continental electoral assistance efforts of the African Union and ensure mutual sharing of experience and resources.

If an assessment team decided that the necessary conditions existed for genuine elections to take place and all stakeholders welcomed the AU, the assessment team should recommend the size, duration and mandate of the mission to be deployed. The rights accorded to observers and monitors were as follows:

(i)   Freedom of movement within the host country;

(ii)   Accreditation as election observers or monitors on a non-discriminatory basis;

(iii)   Communicate freely with all competing political parties, candidates, other political associations and organizations, and civil society organizations;

(iv)   Communicate freely with voters except when the electoral law reasonably proscribes such communication in order to protect the secrecy of the vote;

(v)   Unhindered access to and communicate freely with the media;

(vi)   Communicate with and have unimpeded access to the National Election Commission or appropriate electoral authority and all other election administrators;

(vii)   Communicate and seek the collaborate of the Judiciary, the National Assembly or Parliament, security personnel, and all other appropriate government departments and agencies involved in the election process;

(viii) Free access to all legislation and regulations governing the electoral process and environment;

(ix)   Free access to all electoral registers or voters' list; and

(x)   Unimpeded access to all polling stations and counting centres, including those used by the military or other specific groups.

The Guidelines required an assessment team to decide the scope or mandate of the electoral mission which may be:

(i)   Observation, which involves gathering information and making an informed judgment;

(ii)   Monitoring, which involves the authority to observe an election process and to intervene in that process if the relevant laws or standard procedures are being violated or ignored;

(iii)   Mediation, that is third-party intervention in electoral disputes, directed at assisting disputants to find mutually acceptable outcomes and solutions to electoral disputes;

(iv)   Technical Assistance, which generally takes the form of technical support and advice to the Electoral Commission; and

(v)   Supervision and Audit, which involves certifying the validity of all or some of the steps in the election process either prior to or after the election has taken place.

The Guidelines allowed an assessment team to make recommendations on the duration of the observation or monitoring mission and the nature of deployment of the observers. The assessment team should also take account of available financial and human resources. The Guidelines stated that the AU is committed to the deployment of long—and short-term observers. It is recommended that AU election observation missions issue a statement on the electoral environment, process and outcome on a timely basis after the announcement of the election result.

The Guidelines recommended that an assessment mission should make recommendations on the number of personnel required to fulfill the mandate of the mission. They state that the terms of reference, scope of work, and mandate of each mission should be clearly defined and include the designation of the Head of the Mission who would represent the AU. The Head of Mission would be responsible for any statement made on the conduct of the election on behalf of the AU. The Guidelines provided that in some circumstances, the head of mission might conduct on-going assessments and management roles throughout the mission, while a suitably qualified deputy head supervise the work of the rest of the mission.

The Guidelines dealt with assessment teams' recommendations concerning long-term observation or monitoring missions. Concerning the deployment of long-term observation, an assessment mission could recommend the number of personnel required. The assessment team could also recommend, by way of example, that specialist personnel be deployed to assess the legal framework and any disputes that might arise, monitoring media, or evaluation of the electoral registers. The experts envisaged to be co-opted for these assignments were expected to be kept on a roster kept by the AU of suitably qualified personnel from across the continent.

The medium to long-term missions envisaged that the AU observation or monitoring team would be deployed throughout the country to deal with the pre-election, election, and post-election processes. The Guidelines envisaged that an assessment team when dealing with the deployment of medium or long-term observers, needed to take account of the following:

(i)   The number of electoral or administrative units across the country;
(ii)   The infrastructure and geography of the host country;
(iii)   Problematic or 'hot spot' areas which were likely to be highly contested, had in the past experienced tension, disputes or violence;
(iv)   The human and financial resources available; and
(v)   The deployment of other national or international observers.

Post-Election Review

The Guidelines proposed that such a review be undertaken, through an evaluation by the observation team or an independent consultant agreed upon by the AU. The post-election review should have a clearly defined time-frame and concentrate on the performance and administration of the entire observation mission. The aim of the evaluation is to improve the deployment of future observation missions. The Guidelines recommended that AU should explore the possibilities for election observation and monitoring outside the continent with a view to sharing experiences with other parts of the world with respect to elections and democracy.[8]

Code of Conduct for AU Election Observers and Monitors

The Guidelines contained a binding code of conduct for AU election observers and monitors. Any observer or monitor who committed a breach of the code of conduct could be subject to disciplinary action, including being sent home. The Code of Conduct provided as follows, observers shall:

(i)   Abide by and comply with all national laws and regulations as well as respect the culture of the host country;

(ii)   Maintain strict impartiality in the conduct of their duties, and shall at no time express any bias or preference in relation to national authorities, parties and candidates in contention in the election process. Furthermore, they will not display or wear any partisan symbols, colours or banners;

(iii) Neither accept nor attempt to procure any gifts, favours or inducements from a candidate, their agent, the parties or any other organization or person involved in the electoral process;

(iv)   Immediately disclose to the AU any relationship that could lead to a conflict of interest with their duties or with the process of the observation and assessment of the elections;

(v)   Base all reports and conclusions on well documented, factual, and verifiable evidence from multiple number of credible sources as well as their own eye witness accounts;

(vi)   Seek a response from the person or organization concerned before treating any unsubstantiated allegation as valid;

(vii) Identify in their reports the exact information and sources of the information they have gathered and used as a basis for their assessment of the electoral process or environment;

(viii) Report all information gathered or witnessed by them honestly and accurately;

---

8   In 2007, the AU had a joint observation mission with the OAS. The AU sent one election observer to elections in Colombia; and a reciprocal mission from the OAS observed the elections in Angola in September 2008.

(ix)   When meeting election officials, relevant state authorities and public officials, parties, candidates and their agents inform them of the aims and objectives of the AU Electoral Mission;

(x)   Bring irregularities to the attention of the local election officials, but they must never give instructions or countermand decisions of the elections officials;

(xi)   Carry any prescribed identification issued at all times, and will identify themselves to any interested authority upon request;

(xii) Undertake their duties in an unobtrusive manner, and will not interfere with the election process, polling day procedures, or the vote count;

(xiii) Refrain from making personal or premature comments or judgments about their observations to the media or any other interested persons, and will limit any remarks to general information about the nature of their activity as observers;

(xiv) Participate in the briefings/training provided by the AU Electoral Mission;

(xv)   Provide their reports on time to their supervisors and attend any debriefings as required; and

(xvi) Work harmoniously with each other and with observers from other organizations in their area of deployment.

The Bakary Report

It was well known that the mission reports of AU observers enjoyed a low level of credibility inside and outside of the African Union. The Department of Political Affairs (DPA) became aware of this and decided to look into the matter. The DPA engaged Professor Tessy Bakary[9] to do a study of the African Union's election observation missions' reports from 1990—2006. The purpose of the study was to:

(a)   Define pertinent criteria for a critical analysis of the African Union's election observation activity;

---

[9]   Professor Tessy Bakary was from the Political Science Department of Université Laval, Québec.

(b)   Prepare an appropriate questionnaire designed for the major stakeholders in the electoral process (electoral institutions, political parties, civil society organizations, etc,.) in Member States;

(c)   Carry out surveys with the African Union Commission personnel involved in elections observation, or former members of the Organization of African Unity and African Union observer missions;

(d)   Critically examine all OAU/AU observation reports with a view to gathering all elements relevant to the evaluation as highlighted in these documents;

(e)   Prepared a detailed report on the African Union elections observation activity in the light of all relevant information obtained from the survey and from the analysis of the reports of observer missions;

(f)   Put forward proposals and recommendations to improve African Union election observation activities, highlighting the recommendations that could be incorporated into the Observers' Manual; and

(g)   Present the report to a group of experts for critical evaluation and validation. The consultant will take into account comments, reactions and inputs from the group of experts, for inclusion in the final version of the study.

The Bakary Report was important for a couple of reasons, namely, it was the first comprehensive report of its kind on the assessment of AU Election Observers' reports, and when it was presented to a group of experts in 2007, it had preceded the constitution of the DEAU by nearly six months. Among the main findings of the Report were the following:

(a)   The OAU-AU had observed 133 elections in 47 countries during the period 1990 to 2006 out of the total number of 284 elections organized during that period;

(b)   That during the years 1990 to 2000, the approach to election observation was largely political and diplomatic, as was seen in the composition of observation missions then;

(c)   The procedural requirement of AU receiving at least two months invitation prior to the election should be changed to allow AU the automatic right to observe;

(d)   After 2000, a greater mix of technicians (election experts) began to appear;

(e)   Contrary to the requirements of the provisions of the AU Guidelines for Elections Observation and Monitoring Missions, electoral observation missions were not preceded by assessment missions;

(f)   The limited geographic coverage of the host country's territory;

(g)   Inadequate thematic coverage of election processes;

(h)   Failure by the Political Affairs Department to follow up on the recommendations of observers reports directed at the host EMB; and

(i)   Inadequate use of election professionals.

Recommendations by Bakary Report

Among the more important recommendations in the Bakary Report were the following:

(a)   Standing invitation from Member States, AU should obtain a permanent invitation from its Member States and if that could not be obtained, the period for invitation should be extended from two to three months;

(b)   No observation mission should be fielded to any country without assessment mission;

(c)   There should be appropriate mechanisms to follow up the recommendations of observation missions, firm commitment should be had from the host country implementing the recommendations;

(d)   The AU should encourage 'electoral professionalism' through training leading to a certificate (a Masters Degree or Certificate in specialized graduate studies) within the framework of a university programme;

(e)   There should be regional followed by general harmonization of electoral practices;

(f)   The AU should intensify, systemize and diversify its collaboration with Regional Economic Communities (RECs);

(g)   AU should rely heavily on country NGOs in Member States;

(h)   Partnership with other organizations, intergovernmental and international NGOs;

(i)   The AU should on regular basis, every two to three years, conduct comprehensive assessment of the observer missions deployed in Member States;

(j)   Greater flexibility in decision on the nature of elections to be observed, including local and regional elections, as well as constitutional referenda;

(k)   Enhancing the institutional capacity of the Elections Unit, that is the Democracy and Electoral Assistance Unit;

(l)   Renew the composition of observer missions with particular focus on women, higher proportion of election specialists and NGO members, example of proportional distribution of mission members as 50% election specialists, 25% civil society and 25% elected persons;

(m)   AU should build observer database;

(n)   In order to improve visibility and transparency AU should post observer reports on its Website, and reports should be available in electronic gadgets such as floppy disks, USB flash and internet;

(o)   The institutional memory of the DEAU should be saved electronically (the report pointed out that only eleven of the AU 133 missions undertaken during the period under review were saved electronically);

(p)   The 'road map' of observers—the checklist of observers for use at polling stations should be modified to ensure that all relevant phases are covered in particular—opening of polling stations; voting operations; closing of polling stations and vote counting; and communication, centralization and collation of results in the appropriate structures;

(q)   The checklist for polling stations should cover a wide range of thematic electoral issues, for example, gender, minority, disabled persons, etc,;

(r)   The checklist should be user-friendly to follow and fill out;

(s)   The content of the briefing book should be reviewed and include the broader thematic coverage of election issues;

(t)   The DEAU should consider calling for applications with a view to filling such technical positions in observation missions as—legal and electoral dispute expert; constitutional law expert; media analyst; country expert political analyst; and security specialist;

(u) There should be more co-ordination of local and international observations;

(v) Attention should be paid to issues such as individual rights; gender, minorities; disabled persons; and prisoners.

The expert group, which considered Prof. Bakary's work in Brazzaville, Congo, in 2007, endorsed the major recommendations contained in the report.

In its first six months of operation, the DEAU began implementing much of the recommendations contained in the Bakary report.

Declaration of Principles for International Election Observation

This Declaration was commemorated at the United Nations in New York on October 27 2005. The African Union endorsed it and so had many international organizations. The principles stated in this Declaration were not dissimilar to those set out in the AU Guidelines on Election Observation and Monitoring enunciated some three years earlier. The intergovernmental and international nongovernmental organizations which endorsed the Declaration (including the African Union) and the accompanying Code of Conduct for International Election Observers joined in the declaration, see Annex 2.

Assessment and Way Ahead for AU Election Observation

The inability of the DPA to properly implement the AU Guidelines on election observation was due in part to the slow pace of getting the DEAU (discussed in chapter III below) operational. The Bakary Report found that failure to implement essential provisions of the AU election guidelines contributed to the low credibility attached to AU observation mission reports.

The Guidelines for AU Election Observation and Monitoring, accompanied by the Code of Conduct for Election Observers agreed and issued in 2002 were largely in accord with good practice, although the Guidelines were not implemented in important respects and the credibility of the AU's observation missions' report never achieved the credibility that they should have. The African Union endorsed in 2005 the Declaration of Principles for International Election Observation and the accompanying Code of Conduct for International Election Observers, which was commemorated at the United Nations in October 2005 and endorsed by some 23 intergovernmental and international nongovernmental organizations. The AU's endorsement rekindled interest and the Department of Political Affairs commissioned a study with respect to the AU election missions' reports in 2007[10] and undertook to implement the findings and recommendations with a view to strengthen and improve AU's election observation missions' reports.

It was against that background that the DEAU placed AU's election observation at the top of its agenda when it became operational in May 2008. Its initial approach was to revisit the AU's Guidelines on Election Observation and Monitoring and the recommendations of the Bakary Report of AU Election Observation Missions' Reports, which in essence exhorted the AU to take steps to ensure that election observation was organized and conducted in accordance with the Guidelines.

---

[10]   The Bakary Report.

Chapter III

The DEAU Mechanism

Introduction

The Democracy and Electoral Assistance Unit (DEAU) commenced work as a unit within the Department of Political Affairs in the Commission of the African Union, while the accompanying Fund, the Democracy and Electoral Assistance Fund (DEAF) became operational in June 2008. The electoral landscape in the Department, though not exactly non-existent, lay in an under-developed condition, despite the fact that in the case of election observation the AU and its predecessor, the Organization of African Unity (OAU), had dispatched approximately one hundred and sixty observation missions between 1990 and the end of the first decade of the 21st Century. The records of the organization and performance of the observation missions were patchy and many records were unavailable making it difficult to present a complete factual picture of the institutional accomplishment in this area. Indeed, a good deal of the institutional memory in this field in the Department could not be readily identified. This state of affairs did not make the task of the fledgling Electoral Unit any easier.

Though it came late in the decade under review, the establishment of the DEAU backed by its funding arm, the DEAF, was the first significant central structure in the AU Commission dedicated to democratic electoral development. It demonstrated the determination of the AU to assist the national EMBs to improve their ability to organize democratic elections. At the outset, the DEAU's preoccupation was with upgrading AU's election observation with a view to raising the quality of missions' reports and enhance their perceived credibility. The DEAU was the mechanism by which the AU intended to get a better handle on the development of democratic elections in its Member States.

The new officers of the DEAU started out familiarizing themselves with the Political Affairs Department and how it worked. The Department offered induction courses and the IFES consultant who was advising the Department on the establishment of the Unit offered a series of orientation courses on election administration and organization.

'House-Keeping' Matters

The first 'port of call' as it were for the DEAU's new staff was to identify the 'house-keeping' matters that were essential to provide a sound early start. Such matters included the constitutive instruments of the AU and the various declarations that the OAU and AU made relating to the principles of democratic elections and good governance. In particular, the Guidelines for Election Observers and Monitors were highlighted for special familiarization. Other 'house-keeping' matters included the Departmental budget and the AU's operational budget relating to elections for 2008-09. The DEAU's attention was drawn to the structure of the Department and the level of its staff members in the organizational structure.

The Work Plan

In a quirk of fate, the DEAU began its operation at an infelicitous time in elections development in the Member States of the African Union, for the Kenyan elections in December 2007 ended in a disastrous post-election conflict which claimed more than a thousand lives, and Zimbabwe was undergoing murderous election violence. At the same time, the challenge was clear to be seen and the DEAU had to rise to the occasion. The Kenyan post-election developments had put the Political Affairs Department in the spotlight as it did not recommend an AU election observer mission to Kenya for the December 2007 elections because the invitation to observe the elections came several days late that is, outside the time period (at least two months before the election) stipulated by the Guidelines of the AU. One consequence of not sending an observer mission to Kenya in 2007 was that the AU had no authentic report of its own as to how the violence started and quickly got out of control. In May 2008 when the DEAU stood up, the focus in the AU was on election observation and DEAU was constrained to make it a priority. Mobilization of resources for the DEAF was an on-going exercise which fell to the Head of Unit and the IFES Chief of Party who continued to advise the DEAU after it became operational.

The DEAU and AU Election Observation

Election observation, though perhaps not the most important aspect of the work plan, was certainly the most compelling because of Kenya and Zimbabwe. The DEAU was asked to take over election observation just at the time when the Zimbabwean Electoral Commission had announced (on May 2 2008) an election run-off for the presidential election on 27 June 2008. The DEAU quickly decided, in line with the AU Guidelines for Election Observers and Monitors, and the Bakary Report recommendations, to send an Assessment Mission to Zimbabwe. It was like a novice swimmer jumping in a pool at the deep end. Unfortunately, before the election took place the opposition presidential candidate was force to withdraw from the race due to unprecedented violence which was allegedly unleashed by the incumbent President and the ruling party leaving only the incumbent to contest the run-off election. In short, the presidential run-off election was a farce and not a genuine competitive election and it was not difficult for the AU mission to so find. That was not an election that tested the judgment of the mission. The challenge for the DEAU did not go away with the flawed run-off election of Zimbabwe, indeed it was just beginning. The real challenge to be overcome was the rather low level of credibility that AU's election observer missions attracted. With that in mind, the DEAU undertook to review all the procedures and administrative instruments in order to take over 'ownership' of such procedures which were revised to ensure that they were consistent with acceptable standards. The review included the terms of reference for pre-elections assessment teams and for election observation missions. The observers' brief, profiles of countries which were holding elections and the list of things to look for on polling day at polling stations. A similar review was done with respect to the counting of the votes and the tabulation. A concerted effort was made to improve election observer mission reports, but the exercise was made much more difficult as it was the custom of AU observer missions to write their reports without much assistance from the AU coordinating team and there was considerable resistance to changing that approach. That resistance to change also had implications for the quality and contents of the missions' reports.

The work plan with respect to election observation had some other dimensions aimed at improving the nature and quality of AU election observation mission performance. The DEAU work plan encompassed a comprehensive training programme for AU election observers to be executed with the support of partners, including the Carter Center and the Electoral Institute of Southern Africa (EISA). There were joint observation missions planned with the European Union and the Organization of American States (OAS).

Training of AU Election Observers

During 2009, the Carter Center and EISA formally joined IFES in the Elections Support Program for the AU. The Carter Center produced a series of training modules for election observers and a toolkit. EISA produced an administrative manual for the DEAU. The partnership of IFES, Carter Center and EISA, together with the DEAU organized the first orientation course for AU Observers in Nairobi, Kenya, in September 2009. There were about 30 attendees from the East Africa Region of the AU. The participants indicated that the course was useful. A second orientation course was held in February 2010 in Dakar for AU Observers from the West African Region of the AU.

Continental Meeting of EMBs

The DEAU knew that the key to improvement of election organization in the AU was strengthening the competence and capacity of national EMBs. Thus the DEAU's work plan provided, as a matter of urgency, for a continental meeting of EMBs to forge greater contacts and consider mechanisms such as a Network of EMBs of the AU and to seek their cooperation in completing a questionnaire which would aide the creation of a master database on national EMBs (NEMBs) in the AU. The continental meeting was envisaged as an ideal forum to discuss two other activities which would revolve around national EMBs, namely, raising standards of election processes and offering of technical assistance to NEMBs. The DEAU had developed a procedural mechanism to deal with the prioritization of requests for technical assistance but that instrument was not put for discussion at the continental meeting.

After much delay for a variety of reasons which were largely administrative, the continental meeting of EMBs was held in Accra, Ghana, on December 17-19 2009. The attendance was 29 representatives from 23 countries, somewhat less than was expected. Nevertheless, there were interesting presentations by selected EMBs from each of the five Regions of the AU. In addition, a few papers were presented on selected topics, namely, of the funding of EMBs; the problems facing EMBs; and EMBs' relationship with stakeholders. The instruments designed to promote greater inter-EMBs relations, the Facilitation Mechanism, and the Prioritization of Request for Technical Assistance, were merely mentioned as work in progress, since the Department of Political Affairs (DPA) had not yet approved the working drafts.

The EMB meeting agreed to make the continental meeting an annual event. It made a series of recommendations which the DPA through the DEAU undertook to implement.

Raising Standards in Electoral Organization within the African Union

The great challenge for the DEAU was to identify the ways and means to improve standards in election organization by national EMBs. In the area of election observation, the DEAU quickly identified deficiencies, such as lack of credibility in the observation missions' reports due to lack of adequate objectivity, poor visibility, weak treatment of core issues, and insufficient attention to relevant issues such as gender, disability, the role of publicly owned media and treatment of nomadic and ethnic issues.

With respect to the organization and conduct of elections, except for a very limited number of EMBs, the general perception of stakeholders and election observers was that there was an urgent need to raise the standard of preparation and conduct of electoral processes in the Member States of the Union. In this regard, the DEAU identified several areas, including review of electoral systems, delimitation of electoral districts, compiling and maintenance of voters' register, election campaign, settlement of election disputes, management of election logistics, and polling and counting of votes, for discussion at seminars and workshops with EMBs, to be followed by technical assistance where requested. At the same time, the DEAU resolved to assist Member States in which the AU had observed elections to implement the recommendations, if any, made by election observation missions in their reports.

The DEAU launched the raising of standards activity towards the end of 2009 with the selection of two consultants from the SADC Region to undertake a study in five countries each with respect to election disputes resolution mechanisms. Each study would be accompanied by a report with recommendations which would be discussed at a seminar convened for that purpose and recommendations which were endorsed at the seminar would be submitted to the SADC member states and their respective EMBs for consideration and implementation with the assistance of DEAU.

Technical Assistance

The DEAU felt that notwithstanding that historically the OAU and the AU had placed considerable emphasis on getting election observation going in the Union on a proper footing, offering support to national election management bodies to enable them to improve the quality of election organization was equally important. Consequently, the DEAU formulated a programme of technical assistance to national election management bodies (NEMBs) based on requests which would be considered on the basis of prioritization as set out by the DEAU and agreed to by the EMBs. The prioritization methodology was necessary because of the number of potential Member States involved-over 50. The formula would give preference to requests coming to the DEAU from States experiencing conflict situations, or were emerging from conflict, States that were in a fragile situation because of economic or natural disaster, and so on—(see Annex 3 for a draft specimen of Prioritization Procedure).

Creation of AU Database

The DEAU database was created during 2009. Some materials for the database were provided by EISA, the IFES AU Office and DEAU. The database was designed by Mr. Amidou Baa, a United Nations Expert in consultation with Carl Dundas, IFES' Chief of Party in the AUC's Office in Addis Ababa. The database has four sections, namely, EMBs, African election experts, AU election observers, and African civil society organizations (CSOs) involved with elections. At the time of writing, approximately 1025 election observers were entered in database, with less than 100 had undergone the AU's observers' orientation course. There were approximately 343 African election experts were in the database and about 43 EMBs. African CSOs involved in elections would be selected using criteria similar to those used for the membership of CSOs in the ECOSOCC body, and in addition to being involved in elections; CSOs must have had less than 50% foreign funding.

The DEAF—Mobilization of Resources for the DEAU

The DEAF was established to finance the election activities of the DEAU. The DEAF is governed by the Financial Regulations of the AUC and has its own account. It is committed to regular reporting to contributors and full accounting with respect any conditions stipulated regarding particular contributions. During the first two years, the DEAF received pledges of over five million US dollars from six contributors, namely, France, Italy, Denmark, European Union, Algeria and Sweden. Canada[11] made a pledge but subsequently withdrew it. Other potential partners contacted early to contribute to the DEAF were Spain, Finland, Germany, the UK, India, Brazil and The Netherlands. The DEAU discussed the procedures which governed the contribution to the DEAF and placed them on the AU's Website and also published a brochure with those procedures as well as relevant information concerning the DEAF and the DEAU.

---

[11] Canada made an early pledge, but for reasons which were not made clear, the pledge was withdrawn.

Role of Early Partners

The partners to the IFES-USAID African Union Support Program were the Carter Center and the Electoral Institute of Southern Africa (EISA) which came on stream in November 2008. Their role was to assist the DEAU with the training of election observers and the creation of a master database on EMBs in the AU. Their work plan entailed that they first prepared a toolkit for the training of election observers before the actual training took place.

The Electoral Assistance Division (EAD) of the United Nations offered a short–term consultant for four months from October 2008 to February 2009 to assist with capacity building of the DEAU.

International Institute for Democracy and Electoral Assistance (International IDEA), as a part of its Joint Activity Plan (JAP) with the African Union, provided two sections aimed at supporting the DEAU—

a. Support to the Electoral Assistance Unit in the implementation of the observation mandate to the amount EUR 1 million;
b. Support to the Electoral Assistance Unit to provide technical assistance to election management bodies (EMBs)—Bridge Capacity Building Training—budget EUR 2.1 million.

The co-operative arrangement between the DEAU and IDEA was closely monitored to measure the level of success of the implementation of the ear-marked funds for the stipulated activities.

Early Detection of Potential Hurdles

The initial structure of the DEAU did not correspond to that recommended in the feasibility study, particularly that the level of the Head of Unit should be P5 and that the other officers should be at P3 level. That recommendation of feasibility study was endorsed by the two expert groups, the independent experts and the experts from governments. Further, the staff levels of the Unit as recommended by the feasibility study was accepted by the Department of Political Affairs and was also endorsed by the IFES Chief of Party as adviser to the Unit. However, the

Sub-Committee on Structures[12] whose task it is to approve staff numbers and levels in the AU set the level of the Unit Head at P3 and the officers at P2. The reasons for the scaling down of the levels were not clear, but it was blamed in part on unavailability of resources. Some interested persons believed that the representatives on the Sub-Committee on Structures from Member States who were keen on the development of democracy in the Union did not win the argument. The decision of the Sub-Committee on Structure was perhaps a misunderstanding of the role of the Unit or to limit the influence of the Unit on the democratic development in the Union.

It may very well be that the scaling down of the levels of the grades of the Unit impacted adversely on its operation within the Department of Political Affairs and hence in the AU Commission. Election organization has a certain measure of political content that may spill over into controversy and conflict. This requires an election unit within any large bureaucracy, such as the United Nations, European Union, and Commonwealth Secretariat, to be closely linked structurally or administratively to the decision-making authority to facilitate quick decisions as warranted in given cases. The DEAU, in terms of its status, is located some five-tiers down from the Executive and was not favourably placed to offer speedy advice and recommendation to the AU Commission.

Other hurdles which had to be navigated in the early life of the DEAU included the usual human problem of those who were dealing with elections, particularly election observation, found it uncomfortable to let go, and so it took the DEAU longer than anticipated to claim full ownership electoral activities in the Department.

During the first two years of the DEAU's existence, the effects of the Kenya post-election conflict which started in December 2007 was still fresh in the minds of stakeholders and others in the AU, the aftermath of the run-off presidential elections in Zimbabwe still remained unsettled as the power-sharing arrangement was in place, but there was uneasiness between the two main partners, and, as if to complete the period on an

---

[12] The Structures Sub-Committee is a sub-committee of the Permanent Representatives Committee of the African Union.

even dimmer note, post-local election violence erupted in religious and communal areas of the city of Jos in Nigeria in 2008 claiming more than three hundred lives.

Some of the foregoing problems were to be expected and would be corrected over time. Nevertheless, the DEAU quickly learned that in a bureaucracy it is advisable to work with the resources that are at its disposal. In the first months, the DEAU had much to do to lay the foundation on which to build sound democratic institutions, particularly strong electoral management bodies.

Assessment

The AU is an inter-governmental organization with 53 Member States and with potentially 53 EMBs (a few Member States like Eritrea, Libya and Swaziland do not have proper EMBs) had to be treated with great care. The DEAU had to ensure that national EMBs were comfortable with its work plans and overall programmes. The DEAU had to win over national EMBs to buy into its programmes of raising electoral processes standards and implementation of recommendations in AU election missions' reports. By the end of the first decade of the 21st Century, the DEAU had been operating for 31 months and was still a work in progress, nevertheless, as seen form the fore-going initial work plan and the actual tasks undertaken during the past decade, it displayed considerable potential to influence the quality of national EMBs' election organization and gave the centre, the AUC, a voice in continental-wide election observation and organization.

Chapter IV

Analysis Of The Democratic Deficits
In The Union

Introduction

An analysis of the deficits of democratic elections in the Member States of the African Union during the first decade of the 21st Century began with the constitutional environment. Many of the constitutional instruments in the Member States were transplants or modified versions of the inherited instruments upon the achievement of independence after years of colonial rule. In most of the Member States, the electoral framework was set out in the constitution in which the provisions governing, among other things, the structure of the election management, the electoral system, electoral districts (where applicable), and eligibility to vote, were set out. Many of the inherited constitutions changed when political regimes were changed through unconstitutional means, while others were changed by consensus to meet new circumstances.

Constitutions and Elections

Often changes to a particular country's Constitution had implications for elections, as was the case when the term of office of a Head of State was extended from two to three terms. However, this 'third term' issue was largely political and with much less electoral significance. Of much more significance were changes to the constitutional provisions relating to the election management body and its terms of reference. Though there were instances of election management bodies (EMBs) being created by statutory means, there were many cases where EMBs were created by the Constitution, and the limits of their mandate set thereby. The trend in new and emerging democracies was to embed the clauses dealing with fundamental electoral provisions in the constitution to give greater protection against the government of the day changing such provisions hurriedly for expediency. On the other hand, when clauses relating to elections were entrenched in the constitution, it made electoral reform more difficult at times.

It is easy to generalize in discussing the weaknesses of Constitutions in the Member States of the African Union regarding the foundations for democratic elections. But scouring election reports, election observer missions reports, domestic, regional and international, along with commissioned post-election audits, studies and commentaries of electoral experts, there was little doubt that there was an urgent need to review the constitutional provisions relating to election organization and administration in most Member States of the Union. Such a review in a Union of more than 50 countries would need to be selective, but should include countries from each of the five regions and have regard to language and demographic and geographic size. The review should be undertaken under the auspices of the AU's Democratic and Electoral Assistance Unit (DEAU) and should focus on, among other things, EMBs' mandate, status, appointment formula and removal of members, tenure of office, and appointment of staff. The review should cover other aspects of the constitutional provisions relating to elections, for example, the electoral system, delimitation of constituencies/electoral districts, qualification to vote, and qualification to register as a candidate to contest elections.

Electoral Management Systems in the African Union.

Electoral management bodies of the African Union operated under different systems and were structurally dissimilar. Some national EMBs (NEMBs) were established by the constitution as autonomous bodies independent of the influence of the political directorate and other outside authorities the particular Member State of the AU. Examples are Benin, Botswana, Ghana, Lesotho, Liberia, Seychelles, Sierra Leone, and South Africa. Other EMBs were structurally connected to a government Ministry or department, like Cameroon and some other Francophonie related countries. Other EMBs, like Kenya's, Nigeria's, and Zimbabwe's, whatever their formal constitutional status of independence, by their behaviour and performance, were perceived as being under the influence of the government and ruling party of the day.

Some NEMBs were fragmented having multi-bodied entities, for example, a supervisory commission, a boundary delimitation commission, an entity dealing with voter registration, and a body which organized preparation for and conduct of polling. In addition, other bodies which performed tasks relating to elections such as issuing national identity cards, the possession of which was a condition precedent to registering as a voter, and the registering of political parties, was sometimes carried out by yet other entities.

Electoral management bodies, whatever their structure or form, were the key factor in the organization and conduct of multiparty democratic elections in Member States of the African Union, during the period under review. Where they were structurally weak, or otherwise flawed, the elections which they organized could hardly be expected to be credible. A number of deficits could be laid against many of the NEMBs of the Union. The size of the membership of some EMBs should be reviewed with a view to reducing the number of members. Although too much emphasis should not be placed on size as an inevitable defect, when the number of commissioners reaches 21 as in Kenya in 2007, cost and unwieldiness come into focus. To put this issue in perspective, India with nearly 700 million voters has an EMB of three and Canada with an electorate of comparative size to the average, or even larger than the average, NEMB of the Union has one Chief Electoral Officer in charge.

The issue of appointment of the chairperson and members of most EMBs had been a hotly contested matter since often the Head of State, who was also leader of the ruling party, had the sole discretion to appoint the chairperson and members of the commission without consultation with opposition parties or other stakeholders. There were some notable exceptions that worked, like South Africa's, and others that had not worked smoothly as was intended, like Namibia's and Botswana's. Yet other EMBs' members were appointed by the Head of State upon consultation of the Council of State, as in Lesotho and Ghana or the second Chamber, as in Nigeria, in these cases the results of consultation did not necessarily produce non-partisanship.

The quality of election organization and conduct depended largely on the EMB in question in three particular areas of management, namely, the quality and training of field staff recruited; non-partisanship EMB's members and staff, and the transparency of the decisions and actions.

The field staffs of an EMB were the ones who interfaced with stakeholders throughout the country. In short they ran the elections. The recruitment process should ensure that field staff were competent, not politically partisan, and above all were thoroughly trained before commencing any election task. Their training should impart the overwhelming need to understand the culture of impartiality, fairness and political neutrality in carrying out their election tasks. These standards were not achieved by the majority of NEMBs during the decade under review.

In the context of organizing democratic elections, the management and individual members should set the tone for the staff, including field staff, of complete non-partisanship. Political parties, independent candidates, political party sponsored candidates, as well as other stakeholders should be treated fairly and courteously at all stages of election preparation and conduct by the EMB and its staff. Election complaints and disputes should be treated with care and seriousness, and be looked into in a timely manner. These practices were not achieved by many NEMBs during the period under review.

Transparency by the EMB and staff with respect to decisions taken and implemented should flow through the conduct of the affairs of the EMB, except where there was genuine need for confidentiality, as in dealing with certain aspects of ballot paper design. Transparency entails informing stakeholders and the general public on a timely basis, information on the progress of the preparation for and commencement of any election process. It means that the EMB should operate internal democratic procedures respecting its members and inform, on a timely basis, its staff, including field staff, of decisions that affect them. Transparency means keeping the parties, candidates, and media informed on a timely basis of developments of interest to them. Many NEMBs fell far short of the transparency standard stated herein during the decade under review.

The foregoing issues have been focused upon because they hold the key to improving the quality of electoral organization and conduct in the Union, but there were other actions that were necessary for the EMBs to be able to deliver improved electoral services to their respective electorates. For example, the need to formulate and implement relevant and comprehensive election/voter/civic education programmes with respect to voters' registration and polling. Also, as will be discussed below, the need to regulated electoral campaigns to ensure that peace and security was maintained, and campaign financial rules (if any) were observed.

Electoral Systems in the African Union

A review of constitutional provisions relating to elections should cover electoral systems in the countries in which such a review was carried out. However, in any event, it would be useful to reinforce the importance of reviewing the electoral system inherited in order to ensure that the system in place produced fair and balanced distribution of seats in relation to votes in the National Assembly. Stakeholders in many Member States complained about systems that threw up disproportionate results, especially in Lesotho and Mauritius. Lesotho changed the inherited first past the post to a mixed proportional (MMP) system in the late 1990s, consisting of both first past the post and the mixed proportional representation. In the case of Mauritius, a Commission of Inquiry did recommend a change in the electoral system, but that had not happened at the time of writing. There were many Member States where a review of the electoral system was recommended by election experts or called for by stakeholders. For example, in Botswana, an Election Audit Report on the 2004 elections suggested that electoral system should be reviewed, in Liberia many stakeholders called for the two-round system for all elective positions should be modified, in Nigeria and South Africa some stakeholders have been pressing for a review of the electoral systems in the respective countries.

Delimitation of Electoral Districts/Constituencies

Multiparty democratic elections require that electoral districts or constituencies are constructed fairly and be reviewed periodically to ensure that the distribution of voters be done according to a stipulated formula. In many Member States of the Union during the decade under review electoral districts were criticized for lack of fairness, either because the process of delimitation was not transparent or participatory, or that a review of the boundaries had not been carried out in accordance with the legal requirement. Delimitation or lack of it had come under scrutiny repeatedly in recent elections in Cameroon, Kenya, Liberia, Nigeria, and Zimbabwe. There was a need for the Member States of the Union to be assisted to undertake a systematic review of their electoral districts/constituencies.

Compiling Registers of Voters

Not unlike most emerging democratic States the state of the voters' register gave most cause for concern regarding whether or not an election would be free and fair. The matter became complicated because numerous checks and balances were frequently built into the procedures to prevent election fraud, while not making the procedures too onerous as to prevent qualified persons seeking registration in a voluntary system. Voters' register should be accurate, complete and current. It does matter what system was used for its compilation. A register may be compiled under a voluntary or a compulsory system of voter registration. A compulsory system means that a qualified person must ensure that he/she was registered as a voter, failing which that person may be fined or sent to prison, whereas under the voluntary system a person may refuse to register without fear of being fined or imprisoned for not registering as a voter.

Voters' registration may be carried out periodically—annually, or continuously, and in some jurisdictions voter registration will only take place if the qualified person can produce a national identification card. The voters' register may be compiled from data contained in a civil registry where a national database was kept for various national purposes, or qualified persons may give their particulars to enumerators who conducted house-to-house visits for the specific purposes, or the qualified person may be required to go to a specified centre to register his/her particulars.

Registration of voters required accurate identification of individuals who present themselves as a particular individual. This was important to avoid multiple registration of a particular individual. For the purposes of voter identification, a person's photograph, finger prints, or bio-metric features—eyes, face or other features, may be captured and stored on the computer for comparative use on polling day.

In a voluntary system, every qualified person should be given a fair opportunity to register or be registered and to check, during a period of public display of the preliminary list of voters, if his or her name was on that list.

There had been situations where the national identity card (ID card) was issued by a different body from the NEMB and the non-issuance of the national ID card to a qualified person deprived him/her of the right to register as a voter where the possession of a national ID card was a condition precedent to voter registration.

There was a growing number of EMBs that were using modern election technology in voter registration, ranging from improved voter identification means to scanning of data of registered persons and full computerization of the process and storage of the register. The level of the use of technology in voter registration varied considerably through out the Member States of the Union, and so was the quality of the organization of voter registration exercise. This was due to a variety of factors such as inability to afford improved election technology, inadequate training of voter registration staff, insufficient registration awareness programmes, and weak safeguards against multiple registrations. Specific problems identified in some regions included lack of mechanisms to deal with nomadic persons, insufficient rules to determine age qualification, as well as the rules which determine permanent residence. There were instances where the period of the publication, or as the Liberians called it 'the exhibition', of the preliminary voters' register was much too short and the purpose and fact of publication were not conveyed clearly to stakeholders.

The cost of organizing elections and in particular registration of voters needed to be studied throughout the Member States of the Union and urgent steps taken to make election organization more cost-effective. Stakeholders had occasion in South Africa in 1995 to complain about the high cost of voter registration, and in Nigeria post-election 1998-99 voter registration cost, and in Kenya about the cost of the pre-election reforms of 2006-7. A methodological study in selected countries of the Union would be helpful in promoting measures to reduce the cost of organizing elections in the Member States of the Union.

Registration of Political Parties

The registration of political parties had a special recent history in the African Union as the last four decades saw a movement away from a semblance of multiparty democracy gained at the achievement of independence to one-party regime until the 1990s when a return to multi-party system became once again fashionable. Some countries like Malawi in 1993 and Uganda, as late as 2005, held referenda to return to multiparty politics, others like Kenya and Zambia, grudgingly amended their respective Constitution to allow parties, other than the ruling parties, to contest elections.

Many countries of the Union shed the one-party status reluctantly and relatively suddenly and there was no real attempt to create a proper framework for the creation, and no mechanism for the registration, of new political parties. The upshot of this development was that in some countries independent candidates were not recognized for the purposes of contesting elections, and more importantly, the registration of political parties were not brought under the EMB's supervision and control. Many political parties sprung from voluntary associations which were governed by a law and that law was used to regulate the evolution from voluntary association into a political party. That approach quickly came under close scrutiny and aggrieved stakeholders complained of lack of objectivity in dealing with application to form and register political parties. The trend had clearly been to vest the political parties' formation and registration in the NEMB with the necessary regulatory powers to campaign matters such as financing and general behaviour through a code of conduct.

Registration of Political Parties and Candidates to Contest Elections

This relatively simple election process was normally without much scope for rigging, although from time to time irregularities did occur as in the OAU before it and the AU, as in Uganda in 1980 and Kenya in 1992 when 17 and 16 candidates from the ruling party respectively were returned unopposed through abductions, violence and intimidations against prospective opposition candidates. Although serious incidents regarding this process remained few, there was need for a review in some Member States like Nigeria generally, and in specific areas such as the qualification for candidature, deposit to be paid, declaration of assets,[13] and the time frame for registration (nomination) papers to be received and processed, as well as pre-election redress in the court for aggrieved prospective candidates whose application was refused.

Management of Election Logistics & Polling Preparation

Perhaps second only to the voters' register in election organization weakness, during the period under review, was the management of election logistics. In the broader sense, election logistics encompassed recruitment and training of field staff to run an election, acquisition, storage and distribution of election equipment, materials and supplies, identifying and equipping polling stations, and distributing the correct amounts of materials, including ballot papers and ballot boxes, to polling stations in a timely manner for the opening of the polls.

Many elections in Member States of the Union failed in their genuine quest to provide proper management of election logistics, sometimes in several areas of that vital phase of election preparation. Much too often there was failure to recruit and train competent and non-partisan field staff who actually interfaced with the electorate and conducted the polling. While there had been discernible improvement in some jurisdictions, the constant stream of complaints from stakeholders and election observers, domestic and international, was a reminder that there was yet much more work to be done in this area. With respect to the acquisition of election materials, particularly ballot papers, often times the acquisition process started late causing unnecessary pressure on the logistics management system. One of the main deficits in election management of logistics was the persistent shortfall of critical election materials supplied to polling

---

[13] For example, Liberia required prospective candidates to declare assets and liabilities at the time of nomination.

stations. Shortfalls frequently occurred with ballot papers, ballot boxes, seals and sealing wax, and sometimes even envelopes.

The choice of polling station location can make a difference between poor quality and very poor quality service offered to electors. Except in exceptional cases, polling stations should be relatively near to the voters who reside at the greatest distance from the station. The location should be user-friendly to disabled voters and be equipped with sufficient chairs and benches to accommodate candidates' and parties' agents, as well as observers.

Adequate transportation means should be available to deliver and retrieve election materials, equipment and supplies to and from polling stations

Election Campaign Regulations

The regulation of electoral campaigns throughout the Member States of the African Union during the decade under review varied considerably. While there was little merit in trying to harmonize practices in this area, there was a strong case for having clear rules for candidates and political parties to follow, and such rules should be consistent with democratic elections. There should be a designated period for the campaign with a stipulated commencement and ending date. There should be a code of conduct for candidates, parties and their agents throughout the period. The code of conduct should be backed by sanctions where breaches occurred. The code of conduct should extend to supporters attending rallies, and should pronounce against violence and intimidation against supporters of opposition parties. While in essence election campaign was about contestants in a political campaign putting their parties' policies to the electorate and so free speech, movement and association were necessary, 'hate' speeches and incitement to violence should not be countenanced at rallies.[14]

---

[14]   Many stakeholders in Kenya in 2007 and Zimbabwe in 2008 elections respectively attributed in part the election and post-election intimidation and violence to 'hate' speeches during the campaigns.

Allocation of the continent's scarce resources towards public funding
of election campaigns for political parties was topical throughout the
decade under review and was supported by some countries, including
Mozambique, Namibia, Seychelles and South Africa. A problem faced
by many Member States was the unfair advantage gained by incumbent
governments and ruling parties from the improper use of public resources
for party purposes, including the publicly owned media. This problem
should be dealt with through regulations.

Many Member States of the Union had laws and regulations in place to
deal with balanced conduct during campaign reporting. The quest to have
equitable treatment meted out to all contestants by the publicly owned
media should be backed by regulations. The privately owned media should
also be required to offer balanced and accurate reporting if they chose to
report on election campaigns.

Campaign Financing

Campaign financing was slowly taking hold on the continent during the
decade being reviewed, although it was still a discussion topic in many
countries which were unable to afford public financing of political parties.
Public funding of political parties and or candidates had been put forward
as a possible solution to campaign financing. The formula for giving public
funding to political parties or candidates was not standardized. Formulae
which were used in some countries like Cameroon and Namibia drew
criticisms from stakeholders on the grounds that the dominant party in
the House of Assembly got the lion share and opposition and new parties
got very little public assistance. In Mozambique, Seychelles and South
Africa public funding worked relatively well.

Campaign financing went much further than making funds available
to candidates or political parties; it covered private funding through
contributions by companies or individuals. In order to bring such funding
under control, there needed to be full disclosure of the amount contributed
by a company or an individual to the political campaign of candidates and
parties. There may also be a limit on the amount of money or goods in kind
that a company or individual may give to a political party or candidate. The
amounts received by a political party or candidate from public or private,

funding should be accounted for and the accounts should be audited by a reputable firm of auditors. Parties and candidates, successful or otherwise should be held to account for any monies received during the campaign period[15] while contesting an election. The regulations and forms dealing with campaign finance should be simple and user-friendly.[16] The true aim of a properly regulated campaign finance scheme is to prevent 'money politics' from distorting the influence of a party or candidate.

Election/Civic/Voter Education

Voter education (sometimes called civic education, may also be called election education) is an indispensable aspect of creating awareness of the electorate how to use the voting procedure correctly in order to ensure that the vote is cast correctly. Voter education has taken on a wider scope in modern democratic practices and encompasses the reasons why turning out to vote is an act of citizenship. Voter education invariably involved aspects of being able to identify persons with leadership potential. Voter education extends to voter registration and registration of candidates and political parties to contest an election. Ideally, the EMB is the entity best placed to be primarily responsible for voter education; however, during the decade under review, some EMBs did not have it as one of their functions.[17] It is submitted that voter education should be a primary responsibility of the NEMBs. The dimension of election education has a wider connotation which targets the election contestants and their agents and representatives with the emphasis on campaign and polling procedures. This aspect of election education was often deemphasized inadvertently during the period under review in many Member States of the African Union and many reports from election observers and stakeholders in many countries of the Union showed that there was critical need to educate parties,

---

15   See chapter VIII within.

16   The campaign finance regulations and forms introduced in Liberia for the 2005 elections drew heavy criticisms from stakeholders as being too complicated and sophisticated for Liberia.

17   For some time after military rule ended in Nigeria, voter education remained with the National Orientation Agency (NOA) which was established by the military regime.

candidates and their representatives in the subtle ways that democratic elections work.

Resolution of Election Complaints and Disputes

Election complaints should be dealt with expeditiously and transparently. By this process confidence in the electoral process grows among stakeholders. Swift, competent and transparent consideration and disposal of election complaints may prevent any grievance from developing into larger disputes with potentially grave consequences. Most election disputes can be determined administratively within the structure of the EMB concerned. However there are many potential election disputes that may need to be resolved by outside bodies, either by the ordinary court system or by a special election court or tribunal system. In a post-conflict situation or a situation of or akin to apartheid, a special election tribunal system may be contemplated, as in the Namibian and South African cases in 1989 and 1994 respectively where the opposition had no confidence in the apartheid court system. In Liberia in 2004-5 it was hotly debated whether the court system that survived the civil wars had sufficient integrity to deal with election disputes. In the end the ordinary court system was retained for election cases and it dealt with several election cases with mixed results.[18]

In examining the needs of the Union in this area, a distinction may be made between election disputes that can be determined before polling day and those that may be more conveniently heard after polling day. Matters relating to registration of voters and political parties and many campaign issues can be heard and disposed of prior to polling day. Other issues like registration of candidates or parties to contest an election may be heard either before or after polling day. For example, in Malawi, Pakistan and Trinidad & Tobago, cases involving an aggrieved prospective candidate are heard and disposed of before polling day, while in many other countries like Botswana and Kenya, these cases can only be heard by way of election petition after polling day.

---

[18] Ironically, the court system was kept for election cases in order to enhance the confidence of the post-conflict Liberia in one of the premier democratic institutions, the judiciary.

The issue of election petition has been seldom examined with a view to improving its application. Election petitions are important as they are responsible for more than fifty percent of the election disputes filed. There are several deficits in the election petitions' procedure; firstly, in many jurisdictions the petition procedure is extremely slow, and the petition list is known to have lasted from one national election to the calling of another without the petition list being exhausted. Secondly, from Nigeria to Lesotho to Kenya, election petitions have been known to be dismissed on the grounds of technicality because the procedure to be followed was not well known, or counsel appearing for the EMB did not have sufficient training in election petition matters. Thirdly, election petition cases are not published on a timely basis to assist EMB lawyers.[19] Please see chapter XII within for a fuller account of electoral disputes resolution within the AU Member States.

Announcement of Election Results

The delay in the announcement of the presidential election results in a timely manner by NEMBS during the decade under review, for example, in Kenya in December 2007 and in Zimbabwe in March 2008 caused untold damage to the democratic credentials of both countries and caused disturbances and loss of lives. This is an area that can be improved with clear procedural guidelines and transparency of action by the counting officers, tabulation officers and the authorities making the election announcements. The proceedings regarding the counting of the votes should be open to parties' and candidates' agents, as well as to domestic and international election observers. This openness should follow through at the tabulation stages up to the point of the announcement of election results. In addition, transparency may be strengthened by the presiding officer at the polling station, or the counting officer at the centre, as the case may be, attesting the statement of the count-by whatever name called—in the presence of agents of parties and candidates and giving each agent a copy there of. Further, transparency would be enhanced by the presiding officer at the polling station, or counting officer at the counting

---

[19]   The Legal Department of the Independent National Electoral Commission had plans a few years back to publish election petitions reports in Nigeria, but it is unclear if it got enough funds for the project.

centre, posting up a copy of the statement of the poll with the results on the premises.

Run-off Elections

Run-off elections are necessary parts of the process to complete the election process where the two-round system applies and no candidate gained 50% plus one vote to constitute an absolute majority in the first round. The date of the run-off election should be carefully set out in the legislation or regulation so that there is time to set up the election machinery after the first round in order to accommodate the run-off election. In 2008, the EMB of Zimbabwe and the EMB of Guinea in 2010 had to adjust the date of the run-off election, because they could not meet the existing stipulated time frame. Although the 2008 Zimbabwe, as well as the Guinea 2010, experiences were abnormal, they did illustrate some of the pitfalls in the two-round electoral system. There in Zimbabwe, the leader (Mr. Robert Mugabe) and the ruling party allegedly unleashed such intimidation and violence, leading to death of opposition supporters and destruction and their property that the presidential candidate of the opposition had to withdraw from the run-off election.

Brokered Peace Agreements

Brokered peace arrangements between parties to a civil conflict or between political parties between which relations have broken down have been widely and successfully used in the Member States of the Union and elsewhere in recent times. Examples may be found in Côte d'Ivoire, Kenya, Lesotho, Liberia, Sierra Leone, and Zimbabwe with little success, in the African Union, (and beyond in Fiji Islands and Guyana.) When a brokered agreement leads to democratic elections as in the case of Liberia in 2005 that's good, but when the goal is an immediate interim power-sharing arrangement to put a temporary end to the disputed results of national elections, the question rightly may be asked whether a brokered arrangement can ever be a substitute for ascertaining the proper results of the elections in question. The situation may be clearer where the brokered arrangement entailed an election audit by impartial election experts (as in Guyana post-election 1997) or constitutional reform and review of the electoral system, as in Lesotho. The situation in Kenya, post-election

2007 and Zimbabwe (post-election 2008) was being tracked to see how successful those brokered power-sharing arrangements will be.

Reducing the Deficits of Electoral Organization

The key factor in reducing the deficits in electoral organization in the Member States of the African Union is strengthening the national EMBs. This will require considerable financial resources to equip these institutions with the minimum up-to-date election technology and trained staff to organize credible election. Each EMB of the Union ought to accept the principle that the organization of democratic elections requires that its members and staff, particularly field staffs, should be imbued with the culture of non-partisanship, fairness and impartiality.

The virtue of thorough training of staff, especially field staff charged with the responsibility of running elections, should be at the top of the agenda of every EMB. Special attention should be paid to the proper training of relatively large numbers of field staff managing polling stations and counting centres, even in a small country, so that adequate time and resources can be allocated for these purposes. The basic competence of persons recruited to do field work in election organization, voters' registration, polling and counting of votes, should not be over looked, as each election task must be completed competently. Moreover, electoral field staffs, doing both voters' registration and polling, are interfacing with the public and good confident and courteous performance will enhance the general confidence in the electoral process.

The transparent operation of an EMB and its field staffs will enhance confidence in their operation. Transparency entails the timely release of relevant developments concerning electoral preparation to stakeholders, including all political parties and the media, and regularly sharing information that is not confidential with all stakeholders, including civil societies organizations involved with elections. Transparency also means granting accreditation in a timely manner to election observers, domestic and international to observe the preparatory processes, as well as polling and counting of the votes, including the various levels of tabulation of results and the announcement of final results.

Transparency also extends to the internal democracy of the EMBs themselves. They should observe the usual rules and practice of good governance whereby the dates and times of meetings should be announced in a timely manner. The rules relating to quorum and decision-making should be followed. Decisions of EMBs should be circulated to staff members who are involved in their implementation, and be published if they are not confidential.

EMBs and their staff should be independent of outside influence of government, the ruling party and the opposition party, or any other entity. Decisions and recommendations of EMB should be made by the members uninfluenced by any outside authority. Equally important is that an EMB should not be passive or inactive in circumstances in which stakeholders would expect positive action, such as in cases of the unlawful use of public resources by the governing party, or any other party, for political party purposes. EMBs should ensure that their vulnerability to the dependence on government funding does not compromise their independence. They should be formal channels established to achieve adequate election budget and that both formal and practical lines of communications should be opened to get disbursements in a timely manner.

Consistent with good governance in organizing democratic elections, EMBs should be confident to recommend a review of the existing electoral system, if they feel that a review might be beneficial to the electoral process. A similar routine approach could be undertaken where post-election audit or evaluation recommends changes to the election law. Areas such as the working of electoral campaign rules, including campaign finance rules, and codes of conduct for political parties and the media, should be reviewed by the EMBs on their own accord.

Deficits listed with respect to other aspects of election organization including delimitation of electoral districts, registration of voters, formation and registration of political parties, registration of candidates and political parties to contest elections, managing election logistics, and preparation for polling and counting of votes, are well within the scope of the management of the EMB.

Election/voter/civic education programmes are sometimes of a slightly broader dimension, since civil society organizations are often co-opted to assist EMBs. Nevertheless, EMBs are responsible not only to coordinate all election/voter education and civic education programmes, but should approve the content and form of all such programmes.

Chapter V

Attribution of Democratic Deficits in the Member States of the African Union

Introduction

The attribution of modern democratic deficits in the African Union has been ascribed generally to colonialism, and more particularly to the widespread introduction of the first past the post (FPTP) and its variant, the two-round electoral system, both of which espoused the winner-takes-all form of governance. African constitution scholars often begin conversations on African constitutionalism by recalling pre-colonial palaver and its equivalent systems of traditional consultation of the people.[20] Colonial rulers introduce indirect and selected forms of consultation, often based on ethnicity and or geography, and put an end to direct consultation for the purposes of good governance. Most African countries were given a form of democratic governance upon the achievement of independence, but in most it proved to be short lived, being superseded by a military regime or a one-party system of governance. This chapter is aimed at exploring the reasons why societies which had been so deeply rooted historically in 'people consultation' suddenly displayed highly partisanship behaviour in managing state power and resources.

---

[20] At an African Union workshop on African constitutionalism the argument led by Prof. El Hadj Mbodj pointed to the lack of internalization of African constitutions and the need to make African constitutions more user-friendly. It was pointed out that colonial constitutions were transplanted without any modifications to meet local suitability-workshop held in Brazzaville, Congo, in November 2007.

It is true to state that the traditional palaver consultation was not practiced in the context of modern states as existed today, but one would have thought that the roots of 'people participation' in governance were deep and strong enough to have lingered on. Perhaps the search for answers as to why the inherited constitution and electoral systems at the time of independence did not survive and thrive lay in the weakness of the inherited systems. Some analysts put the blame on the electoral systems that were bequeathed, namely, the first past the post (in the case of the British) and the two-round, an offshoot of the FPTP, (in the case of the French) system, both of which embrace the concept of 'winner-takes-all.

There is no doubt that the tradition of sharing limited resources, even though often along ethnic lines, dies hard when the impact of the concept of 'winner-takes-all' is played out in the modern states with artificial borders, as far as many local tribes are concerned. It has been mooted that the frequent military coups d'état in West African States 1980s, 90s and 2000s were to spread the national spoils around different ethnic groups[21] Even if some of these prevalent perceptions were not correct, understanding the failure of multiparty democracy in many AU Member States may offer lessons for the renewed drive by the AU to rekindle the quest for democratic governance. Since the blame for democratic development in the AU has often been placed on the FPTP and its off-shoot, the two-round (TR) system, it is appropriate to explore these two electoral systems and other relevant ones to see the extent to which, if any, the blame can stand up to scrutiny.

In addition to constitutions and electoral systems in AU Member States, the causes of flaws in electoral activities, such as electoral management structures; delimitation of electoral districts; compiling voters' register; campaign regulations; election/voter education; resolution of electoral

---

21   See, for example, article entitled "Africa: The Ontology of Failed States" page 9, By Franklyne Ogbunwezeh 2005, http://www.dawodu.com/ ogbunwezeh1.htm. Also A. Adeyan, "Africa records 78 coups in 30 years", The Guardian, Lagos, 9 February 1997; see also Paul Collier: Wars, Guns and Votes, chapter 7 'Melt down in Côte d'Ivoire' p.155, Vintage 2010; see also note 184 below.

disputes; logistics management; announcement of election results; and run-off elections will be explored in this chapter.

Have FPTP and the TR Electoral Systems Failed African States?

It is possible to argue that it was the failure of the existing electoral systems which were dominated by the FPTP and the TR systems that caused the demise of those systems and gave rise to the one-party or the military regimes of the late 1960s through to the 1990s The harsh disproportional distribution of seats to vote gained coupled with the winner-takes-all concept that accompanied the FPTP and the TR systems were used to discredit multiparty democratic elections. It was no surprise that many ruling parties, including those of Kenya, Malawi, Seychelles and Zambia, only grudgingly accepted the return to multiparty democracy from the then prevailing one-party regime that existed in their respective states until the early 1990s. Indeed, up to the eve of polling in the 1992 elections in Kenya, President Moi was protesting to the Commonwealth observer group in Nkuru that he did not believe in multiparty elections, and that when he saw others from outside campaigning in his area, he considered it to be provocation. Nevertheless, the tide was already turning against one-party regimes and military interventions in Africa. In the almost two decades since President Moi expressed his distaste for multiparty democratic elections, there has been mixed developments in the outcomes of democratic elections in the Member States of the Union. There have been relatively successful first and second national elections held in countries such as Benin and Zambia in 1991, Mali in 1992, South Africa in 1994, 99 and 2004, Malawi in 1994, Ghana and Senegal in 2000, Kenya in 2002, Liberia in 2005 and Sierra Leone in 2007. Many of these elections, particularly the initial multiparty ones, were heavily assisted by outside agencies, for example, South Africa and Malawi in 1994, and Liberia in 2005. Other countries of the Union that have developed a relatively good, if short, track record are Botswana, Cape Verde Islands, Mauritius, Mozambique, Namibia and Seychelles. Kenya in 2007, Zimbabwe in 2008, and Nigeria in 2007 have demonstrated how difficult it is to measure progress in organizing credible multiparty elections in the Union.

There have been some significant departure from the FPTP and TR systems, notably, Namibia, Mozambique, Seychelles and South Africa, but there are many countries of the Union which have not reviewed their electoral system to see if there is a better one or a combination of systems that would be more advantageous. Indeed, a survey of the electoral systems in the Member States of the African Union showed that at the National Assembly level, the electoral systems used were distributed as follows: first past the post were used in thirteen countries,[22] all of which, except for Ethiopia, had a Commonwealth background. There are fourteen countries which use the List PR system to elect their National Assembly.[23] There are eleven countries which use the mixed system which varies from a combination of the FPTP and List PR, or List PR and TRS, or the parallel system of the PBV and the List PR.[24] There are nine countries which use the two-round system to elect their National Assembly.[25] Two countries of the Union use the Party Bloc Vote (PBV) system.[26]

The assertion that the use of the first past the post and the two-round systems bourn the greatest responsibility for Africa's democratic deficits is not supported by the record, at least at the level of National Assembly elections. Indeed these two electoral systems are used by less than fifty percent of the AU countries to elect their National Assemblies. The countries that use direct election for the presidency, the predominant

---

[22]   Namely, Botswana, Ethiopia, Gambia, Ghana, Kenya, Malawi, Nigeria, Sierra Leone, Swaziland, Tanzania, Uganda, Zambia, and Zimbabwe.

[23]   These are Algeria, Angola, Benin, Burkina Faso, Burundi, Cape Verde, Democratic Republic of Congo, Equatorial Guinea, Guinea Bissau, Mozambique, Namibia, Rwanda, Sao Tome & Principe, and South Africa.

[24]   These are Cameroon, Chad, Côte d'Ivoire, Guinea (Conakry), Lesotho, Madagascar, Niger, Senegal, Seychelles, Sudan, and Tunisia.

[25]   These are Central African Republic, Comoros, Congo (Brazzaville), Egypt, Gabon, Liberia, Mali, Mauritania and Togo.

[26]   These are Djibouti and Mauritius.

number, some thirty-four,[27] use the TRS, while only six use the FPTP.[28] Thus while there may be little doubt that the choice of electoral systems has contributed to the democratic deficits in some AU countries, the key to reducing the relatively high levels of deficits may lie in a number of factors only one of which is the electoral system. Nevertheless, it is appropriate to look closely at the electoral systems that are widely used throughout the Union. During the decade under review, there had been few changes in electoral systems of note in Member States except for a short change from FPTP to List PR and back to FPTP in Sierra Leone due to conflict and the introduction of the mixed member proportional (MMP) at the beginning of the decade under review in Lesotho.

FPTP

The FPTP boasts of much strength which no doubt attract many countries to it. For example, it is characterized as simple to apply, produces clear results and thus enhances government stability, and as a by-product also produces strong opposition, militates against parliamentary splinter groups, provide strong links with constituents, allows of independent candidates, and provides for choice between candidates and not between parties.

The more prominent weaknesses have been listed as denying fair representation to minority parties, facilitates unfair delimitation of electoral districts, encourages dominance of representation based on ethnicity in given localities, and generates wasted votes. In the context of facilitating the spread of democracy or otherwise in the Union, the relatively poor track record of the FPTP electoral system in dealing effectively with the ethnicity issue and the tendency to espouse the winner-takes-all concept do not commend it to many African critics.

---

[27] These are Algeria, Angola, Benin, Burkina Faso, Cape Verde, Central African Republic, Chad, Congo (Brazzaville), Congo (DR), Côte d'Ivoire, Djibouti, Gabon, Gambia, Ghana, Guinea (Conakry), Guinea Bissau, Kenya, Liberia, Madagascar, Mali, Mauritania, Mozambique, Namibia, Niger, Nigeria, Sao tome & Principe, Senegal, Seychelles, Sierra Leone, Sudan, Tanzania, Togo, Uganda and Zimbabwe.

[28] Cameroon, Equatorial Guinea, Malawi, Rwanda, Tunisia and Zambia.

TRS

The TR system requires a candidate to obtain 50 per cent plus one vote of the total valid votes cast in order to be elected[29]. Where no candidate receives an absolute majority, a second round of voting is held. Some would argue that the substratum of the TR system is its ability to lift the level of legitimacy of the winning candidate. However, other commentators place emphasis on the breathing space afforded to the voters to reflect on the first round voting and to change their mind if they see fit.[30]

The main disadvantages are the cost in conducting a run-off election where no candidate obtained an absolute majority at the first round. The TR system places a great deal of pressure on electoral staff, particularly those who manage the election logistics to procure and distribute the electoral materials to polling stations in the correct amounts. There is the potential for uncertainty between the voting rounds.[31] The TR system, being a variant of the FPTP system, does not produce proportionate results.

List PR

The List Proportional Representation is well known in the African Union. Under this system each political party presents a list of candidates to the electorate. Voters vote for a party, and the parties receive seats in proportion to their overall share of the national vote. Normally, the winning candidates are taken from the lists in order of their position on

---

[29]   Sierra Leone requires a presidential candidate to receive 55% in the first round in order to be elected.

[30]   See for example, Electoral System Design: The New International IDEA Handbook, paragraph 98, page 53.

[31]   This is what happened in Angola in 1992 when during the first round of voting the opposition leader came second, he (Jonas Savimbi) called off the second round and resumed fighting which went on for another decade. A not dissimilar situation arose in 1993 in Congo (Brazzaville) where the prospects of victory by the governing party prompted the opposition to boycott the second round and took up arms. Also in 1992 in Algeria, when the candidate of the Islamic Salvation Front led in the first round, the military intervened and cancelled the second round.

the lists. The advantages of this system are that it converts votes into seats won in such a manner that there are few 'wasted' votes, and at the same time by its nature facilitates minority parties' access to fair representation. In a similar vein, the List PR system allows parties to present socially diverse lists of candidates, including minority groups and women.

The main disadvantages are the tendency to produce weak coalition governments; at times it leads to the fragmentation of political parties, while it may allow extremists into Parliament; it often creates a weak link between representatives and constituents; and because it has the potential to vest concentration of power in the party leadership, it works best in societies that have a developed party structure.

Mixed Systems

The mixed electoral systems seek to combine the more acceptable attributes of the plurality and majority system with the proportional representation systems. Under the mixed systems, two electoral systems are linked using different formulae. The voter casts two votes using both systems. There are different types of mixed systems. Eleven countries of the African Union use a type of mixed electoral system.[32] Two that are closely related are the mixed member proportional and the parallel.

Mixed Member Proportional

The mixed member proportional (MMP) entails the linking of two types of elections—the PR and the majority/plurality types. Seat allocations at the PR level are dependent on the outcome of the constituency seats and compensation for any disproportionate results that arose in the constituency seats. The proportional representation results yield seats that are awarded in a manner to be seen as compensation for any disproportionate effects produced by the constituency results.

---

[32] See note 19 above.

The Alternative Vote

The alternative vote (AV) electoral system is not well known in the AU countries and it may offer another system to be considered in any review of electoral systems from a functional point of view. The AV system works best in single member constituencies. It gives the voter a number of options when marking the ballot paper in that the voter may be required to rank the candidates in the order of their choice numerically, for example 1, 2,3, and so on. The preferential choice of candidates has earned the label of 'preferential voting' in some countries. The AV system allows a candidate who gains an absolute majority, that is, 50% plus 1 vote, or more of the valid first preference votes is the winner. Where no candidate is the winner, the candidate with the lowest number of first preference votes is eliminated from the count and those ballots are examined for their second preferences. Each of those ballots is then transferred to the remaining candidate who has the highest preference in the order marked on the ballot paper. The process is repeated until one candidate gains an absolute majority, and is declared duly elected. Some variation of the AV system requires all the candidates on the ballot paper to be graded.

The strength of the AV system is that it forces candidates who are not strong enough to win in their ethnic group to campaign on issues that may be of interest to others outside their ethnicity in order to gain second or later preferences in other groups. The AV system often allows for preference swapping whereby large parties bargain with smaller ones for second or later preference votes. The absolute majority requirement of the AV gives some legitimacy to the winner.

Perhaps the absence of the AV system in the AU is due in part to the relatively complex grading of candidates. It is also not known for its proportional outcomes in the same way as the PR systems. The experiences of Papua New Guinea and Fiji Islands with FPTP and AV are instructive. At the time when Papua New Guinea achieved its independence from Australia in 1975 it changed from the AV electoral system to FPTP. However, the FPTP did not work to the expectation of the stakeholders of Papua New Guinea and in 2003 a change to the electoral system was made back to the AV, a limited form of preferential voting. The main reason for the disillusionment with the FPTP came about because candidates from the large clans were able to win seats without the votes from others as was the case when an absolute majority was required under the AV system. Stakeholders complained that electoral violence was on the rise because, instead of campaigning to gain votes, some candidates were given to embarking on campaigns to stop voters voting for opponents.[33]

In the case of Fiji which underwent a series of military interventions largely motivated by racial differences, the electoral system was changed from FPTP to AV in 1997, but unfortunately the change did not prevent subsequent military interventions.

Weakness in Management Structures

During the decade under review, many EMBs in Member States of the African Union failed to gain the confidence of the electoral stakeholders due to poor performance in preparing for and conducting elections. Poor performance was often blamed on partisanship, but also on flawed appointment formulae with respect to the chairperson and members of EMBs. During the past decade, it was still the case that in many Member States of the AU, the President had the sole discretion to appoint the chairperson and members of electoral commission in particular Member States. Although such actions accorded with the respective constitutions, it was often conceived as a way of dispensing patronage by the incumbent government of the day. Stakeholders often complained that because of the appointment formulae in respect of EMBs in some Member States, the members and staff became partisan and frequently failed to create a level playing field for contestants in election campaigns.

Many EMBs in Member States of the AU lacked the ability to recruit their own staff and relied on the civil servants to assist in managing the preparations for elections. This was a cost-effective way to organize elections and was used by respected democracies as India, but some EMBs' in Member States of the AU pointed out that the practice inhibited their

---

[33] See Case Study: Papua New Guinea, page 50-51, Electoral System Design: The New International IDEA Handbook, International Institute for Democracy and Electoral Assistance 2005.

training programmes for electoral and voter education officers. Chapter VI examines in some detail the EMBs of the AU.

Delimitation of Electoral districts

The electoral system used in many Member States of the AU required constituency boundaries to be delimited in accordance with good practices. The inability of some Member States of the AU to carry out timely, transparent and fair review of the boundaries of constituency boundaries had attracted complaints by stakeholders in countries like Cameroon, Kenya, Nigeria and Zimbabwe to name a few cases by way of examples. The problem seemed to be lack of awareness of the importance of fair boundaries of electoral districts to democratic elections. In the case of Nigeria, for example, several national elections were held in the decade in question without a thorough review of constituency and electoral districts boundaries, largely through failure by the INEC to undertake the tasks on a timely basis. International election observers had reported evidence of gerrymandering of electoral boundaries in the 2007 and 2008 in Kenya and Zimbabwe respectively.

Compiling Voters' Registers

The compilation of current, complete and accurate voters' registers was always a challenge in new and emerging democracies. It had been possible to identify some specific causes of the frequent flawed voters' registers in Member States of the AU. Lack of adequate training of registration officers, coupled with partisanship, impacted adversely on meeting the requirements of good practices in voters' registration. The requirement to possess a national identity card as a condition precedent to registering to vote exposed qualified persons to a condition that may not be necessary for them to prove their eligibility. Furthermore, the inability of the government authorities in question to issue the national ID cards, whether through intent or otherwise, often denied many qualified persons the right to register. Lack of up-to-date registration equipment and procedures also accounted for low registration numbers in many jurisdictions.

Election Campaigns

In general, election campaigns were not as properly conducted as they could. The matter was left to the particular Member States concerned. Codes of conduct for political parties, despite the provisions of the code in the AU principles of democracy, were not always followed. Hate speeches uttered during election campaigns in Kenya in 2007 and in Zimbabwe in 2008 drew widespread condemnation throughout the AU and beyond. Those speeches were believed to contribute to the incitement of intimidation and violence in those countries.

Campaign finance regulations, whether by setting limits on contributions or expenditure with respect to political parties and or candidates had not been placed on a proper footing. Liberia, with the help of partners in the election campaign for the 2005 elections, introduced a campaign finance regime focusing on reporting on contributions to parties and reporting on expenditures, but the regime was not properly enforced and quickly became shambolic, as it was considered to be complex and sophisticated for a small country emerging from conflict. Some Member States of the AU had some form of state funding of election campaigns, for example, Cameroon, Mozambique, Nigeria, Namibia, Seychelles and South Africa (see chapter VIII for a fuller analysis).

Political Parties

The growth of opposition parties in most Member States of the AU remained stunted through the first decade of the 21st Century due largely to the rise of the dominant political party syndrome and the often improper use of public resources by incumbent regimes. This situation stymied the desire of struggling opposition parties to participate fully in the democratic process. The lack of enthusiasm to contribute to democratic elections may be illustrated by the reluctance of opposition political parties to subscribe to code of conduct for political parties prior to the 2003 Nigerian elections, while the ruling party had given its commitment to participate. The opposition parties did not believe that codes of conduct would change the way the electoral process worked and they did not believe that the ruling party would observe the provisions of the code.[34] Chapter VII deals with the strengths and weaknesses of political parties generally throughout the AU.

Election/Voter Education

Election or voter or civic education with respect to elections in the Member States of the AU often attracted adverse comments by election observers, domestic and international alike. The negative findings were often blamed on lack of resources to produce sufficient relevant training materials and to train personnel to impart the messages and apply the materials effectively. Frequently, voter education programmes were late in starting up and not sufficiently monitored to enable a change in programme design if the feedback indicated that the programme was ineffective.

Voter education programmes had proven to be less effective than they could be because they were often conceived in too narrow a framework for the purposes of the needs of the Member States of the AU. In strict electoral parlance, voter education was educating the electorate in the voting procedures in the voting station. Indeed, some EMBs in the Member States of the AU (see chapter VI) were not mandated to deal with voter education. Some jurisdictions of the AU Member States also developed separate institutions to deal with civic education. The wider embrace of election education, encompassing both voter and relevant aspects of civic education, as well as including uncovered areas of educating politicians, namely, political parties' functionaries, candidates, agents and representatives, in their rights and obligations respecting the electoral process was not covered. Taking all these considerations into account, and the fact that electoral justice demands that an important principle of democratic elections is the availability of relevant information[35] to the electorate and other stakeholders, programmes in this area should be labeled 'election, civic and voter education'.

---

[34]   The author interviewed several opposition party leaders prior to the 2003 elections, as well as senior members of the ruling party.

[35]   See for example Denis Thompson, "Just Elections" p.87, University of Chicago Press 2002

Electoral Disputes Resolution in AU Member States

The perceived lack of credibility in the mechanisms to resolve electoral disputes in the Member States of the AU was due to the belief that those mechanisms were not independent of the government and ruling party in a particular Member State. The inability of the dispute settlement mechanisms to dispose of electoral actions in a timely and transparent manner during the decade under review did nothing to enhance their credibility. The training of officials and judges to deal expeditiously with electoral cases in AU Member States was limited during the period under review.[36] Election cases were not routinely published nationally or circulated continental-wide for general information.

The DEAU's programme on raising electoral processes standards, which started with a study of electoral resolution mechanisms in AU Member States toward the end of the first decade of the 21st Century, was aimed at enhancing the role of electoral dispute resolution mechanisms in Member States of the AU. That intervention by the AUC, through the DEAU, will eventually give the AUC an enhanced role in improving the quality of dispute resolution mechanisms in the Member States of the AU.

Electoral Logistics Management

Many flawed elections in AU Member States during the first decade of the 21st Century could be traced back to inadequate or perhaps more accurately the absence of proper management of election logistics, whether through intent, or innocence of its importance. This deficiency led to defect in election planning and execution ranging from selection of poor polling sites, to inaccurate calculation of polling materials, such as ballot boxes, ballot papers, and other polling items; selection of partisan electoral field officers; and inadequately trained field officers. A similar list of shortcomings with respect to arrangements for the counting of votes and the announcement of election results could be made; and so could be done for inadequate arrangement to protect the secrecy of the ballot.

---

[36] Certain American-based CSOs offered training to officials judges in Liberian electoral matters in mid-2000s

Many of these defects in planning and organizing democratic elections in the Member States of the AU may be overcome by focusing on logistics and putting a proper programme in place to correct past deficiencies, as Mainland Tanzania did in 1996, after serious logistics breakdown in Dar es Salaam in the 1995 elections. The elections in all 7 constituencies in Dar es Salaam had to be re-run.[37]

Election Results Announcements

The manipulation of announcement of election results in some Member States of the AU had caused uneasiness among AU election watchers for a long time.[38] According to the Kriegler Report, the flawed procedure of relaying the election results from the field to the tallying centres led to errors and created suspicions about the credibility of the results of the 2007 Kenyan elections. The procedure lacked transparency. It was also believed to aggravate ethnic tension by reporting first districts in which the incumbent President had the lead in the polls. The EMBs in many Member States of the AU had not worked out a proper procedure to ensure transparency with the use of computers in managing the tallying process. Indeed, many international observer groups had commented adversely on the level of transparency achieved with the computerized vote tallying processes in some Member States.

Run-off Elections

The majority of electoral systems in Member States of the AU require a run-off election if the first round of election did not produce a winning candidate with fifty percent plus one of the valid votes cast. Throughout

---

[37]   The author was instrumental in securing Commonwealth Secretariat technical assistance to place Dr. Afari-Gyan, Chairman of the Ghanaian Electoral Commission to review Tanzanian electoral logistics management and since Mainland Tanzania's electoral logistics management improved significantly.

[38]   Chief Anyaoku, a former Secretary-General of the Commonwealth expressed the fear that the 'parallel count' procedure could trigger premature ethnic tension, if the findings got out too soon or were inaccurate, and so he was not an enthusiastic supporter of that procedure.

the decade the run-off elections created much attention in many Member States of the AU. The excitement triggered by run-off elections in Liberia in 2005, Sierra Leone 2007, and Ghana 2008-9 were controlled, the same could not be said of Zimbabwe in June 2008 and Guinea 2010. A part of the problem seemed to be due to ethnicity which appeared to trigger greater aggressiveness in run-off elections than during first-round elections.

Chapter VI

Electoral Management Bodies of the African Union

Introduction

Many election commentators would probably argue justifiably that the AU Commission could have done more to help some of the less equipped EMBs in the more economically disadvantaged Member States to organize more credible elections during the past decade. This point of view would not only be tenable, but also logical, since the AU Commission would have enhanced its ability to influence the direction of democratic elections in the inter-governmental organization.

Nonetheless, many of the EMBs of Member States of the AU improved on their capacity to organize credible elections with the application of professional training staffs and field officers. Also through greater awareness stemming from interaction through election workshops and conferences, a growing number of EMBs' adopted good practices in election organization, including non-partisanship, transparency, improved internal democracy, greater efficiency and higher levels of professionalism.

Many EMBs in Member States of the AU complained that their funding was not on a proper footing as even when election budgets were approved, the disbursement of funds would be untimely resulting in delays to important electoral activities on their election calendar.

Some EMBs had not established efficient secretariats or directorates (by whatever name called) to administer the affairs of the commission. An efficiently run EMB needs to be supported by a professional secretariat which ensures that support staffs in particular perform to expectation.

Types of EMBs in the AU

Most electoral management bodies (EMBs) in the Member States of the AU consist of the independent model. Indeed, some thirty-three of the EMBs in the Member States of the AU are of this type.[39] Four of the AU Member States' EMBs may be classified as governmental[40] and the rest, fourteen, fall into the mixed model.[41]

The Independent Model

The formal description of an independent EMB is that it is institutionally independent and autonomous from the executive branch of government and which manages its own budget. As its name suggests, the independent model is expected to exhibit certain attributes of functional autonomy, but that is exactly where weaknesses usually appear. Many independent EMBs are structured in such a way that policy making decisions are conferred on the commissioners and the operations are vested in the Directorate or Secretariat. The key to good governance by an EMB lies with the strict adherence to this structural format. For when the commissioners fail to make policy according to their best judgment and allow outside influence to seep in and or when the policy makers begin to interfere in the operations problems are likely to arise.

The Governmental Model

The government model of electoral management is not widely used in the AU Member States and the trend against its use in emerging democracies

---

[39] They include Angola, Benin, Botswana, Burkina Faso, Comoros, Congo (DR), Eritrea, Ethiopia, Gambia, Ghana, Guinea (Conakry), Guinea-Bissau, Kenya, Lesotho, Liberia, Malawi, Mauritius, Mauritania, Mauritius, Mozambique, Namibia, Niger, Nigeria, Rwanda, Seychelles, Sierra Leone, Somalia, South Africa, Sudan, Swaziland, Tanzania, Uganda, Zambia and Zimbabwe.

[40] These are Algeria, Egypt, Sao Tome and Principe, and Tunisia.

[41] Burundi, Cameroon, Cape Verde, Central African Republic, Chad, Congo (Brazzaville), Côte d'Ivoire, Djibouti, Equatorial Guinea, Gabon, Madagascar, Mali, Senegal, and Togo.

is strong. Perhaps it is because the very appearance of elections being organized and managed by or through the executive branch, a ministry of government, or through the local authorities, triggers fear of interference by the incumbents for their advantage. Often the EMBs under the governmental model are controlled by a minister or civil servant who is answerable to the Cabinet. Such EMBs are not managed by members and are funded from the budget of a ministry or local authorities.

Mixed Model of Electoral Management

The nature of the mixed model of electoral management is a combination of an operating or implementing arm usually undertaken by the executive branch of government, and a policy, or monitoring or supervisory arm independent of the executive branch of government. The organization of elections is usually carried out by the governmental EMB and the independent arm of the EMB undertakes the oversight or supervisor role. The strength of the independent EMB component versus the governmental EMB may vary in different countries, but generally the governmental component of the mixed models is the more influential of the two components.

The General Characteristics of the Three Models

The Independent Model in the Member States of the African Union

The independent model of electoral management bodies exhibits an appearance of independence from the executive branch of government, and has a measure of control over its budget. Typically, an independent EMB may be accountable to the legislature or the head of state, but not to a government ministry or department. Although in practice, the level of autonomy may vary considerably and the resolve to pursue the full potential of the institutional and functional independence may be diminished by partisan inclinations, the EMBs of the African Union are overwhelmingly attracted to the independent model of electoral management, (see note 31 above). In some cases, independent EMBs are vested with regulatory powers. The members of the EMBs and their senior functionaries are outside of the executive branch of government.

The members of independent EMBs often enjoy security of tenure of office consistent with the status of the institution. An independent EMB has the potential to take full responsibility for the implementation of a programme that will lead to the delivery of free and fair elections. In the implementation of such a programme, the EMB should be free to act in accordance with good governance practices and act in its sole discretion uninfluenced by any outside entity in formulating its policies. The independent EMBs should have the ability to determine their staff requirements, rules, policies, and in particular to discipline and or dismiss staff. This legal ability to deal with staffing independently is not widely enjoyed in practice in the African Union, as many EMBs co-opt their staff from the civil service and in a manner which does not enable freedom by EMBs to properly train and discipline or dismiss them from the electoral service.

The Governmental Model in the Member States of the African Union

It is perhaps a little surprising to see that there are only four EMBs of the governmental model in the Member States of the African Union, (see note 32 above,) since governmental interference is often cited by stakeholders and international election observers as rendering elections in the Union to be les than credible. The governmental model is characterized by the organization and conduct of elections by a branch of government, either by a ministry or by local authorities. Thus national elections are usually managed by public servants and controlled by the Cabinet through a minister. The electoral budget is of course managed by an appropriate ministry of government or local authority. The total control of the electoral machinery under the control of the ruling party and government of the day does not give comfort to many stakeholders in emerging democracies where the governmental model is not seen as facilitating a level playing field for the purpose of electoral organization. The governmental model often means that the election machinery is located within a ministry of government or in a local government authority, and policy formulations and implementation take place at the instance of the executive branch. Accountability for performance and results of electoral operations, as well as with respect to financial expenditures is overseen by the executive branch of government. The budget is often a component of a ministry's or local authority's budget, and the election officials are public servants or local authority's officers.

The Mixed Model of Electoral Management in the Member States of the African Union

The mixed model of electoral management consists of two components, not necessarily with standard features. One component may consist of policy-making powers, or monitoring or supervisory functions independent of the executive branch of government; and another which control the operations located in a ministry of government or local authority. The main task of organizing elections fall to the government component, while a measure of supervisory and oversight work fall to the independent component. In the African Union, the relative strength, powers and functions of the independent component relative to the governmental EMB, while not standardized, tilt in favour of the governmental EMB component, so much so that of the fourteen mixed model EMBs in the Union, note 33 above, perhaps no more than three, in the view of stakeholders, can be credited with organizing credible multiparty elections. The structure of the mixed model varies and in a few cases in the Member States of the African Union there are three entities rather than two, the third entity being a constitutional one.[42] These additional structures have the potential to strengthen the independent EMB component.

In the mixed electoral management scheme, the independent EMB components are vested with attributes not dissimilar to those of the independent electoral management type, except that the potential of the tasks to be undertaken is much more limited. For example, they are institutionally independent of the executive, and have autonomy to monitor or supervise or formulate policy. The component independent EMB does not report to the executive branch of government and is formally accountable to the legislature or head of state. It has power to supervise or monitor those who organize elections. Its members are outside of the executive branch and have security of tenure while in office. It budget is allocated separately from the ministry's.

---

[42]   In Chad it is known as the 'Constitutional Council' which deals with referendums only and in Mali the 'Constitutional Court'.

The component government EMB is located in a ministry or is under the direction of a department or local government authority. The implementation of policy regarding election organization is under the control of the government, and the implementation entity is accountable to the executive branch of government. The component government EMB has no members and is led by a minister and or public servants who are assisted by a secretariat. The budget is a component of the ministry or the local authority concerned.

The Strengths and Weaknesses of the Different Models of Electoral Management

The Independent Model in the Member States of the African Union

The independent model of EMBs have the potential for improved electoral administration free from the influence of outside entities, thus enhancing electoral legitimacy through greater perceived impartiality. They provide a sound environment for the development of professionalism of electoral staff and an institutional framework for fostering an electoral culture of fairness and non-partisanship. As a dedicated institution dealing with electoral matters, independent EMBs are able to offer better planning and more cohesive development and execution of electoral tasks. The independent model facilitates the creation of a wider pool of expertise than is available in a particular ministry or in local authorities, while also enabling the institution to control its own funding and implementation of its electoral activities.

Its main weaknesses consist in the higher expenses that are invariably involved in establishing new structures and offering improved incentives to members and staff. Unless special mechanisms are constructed, independent EMBs may experience adverse effects of being cut off from the decision-making arm of the state and may have difficulty securing budget approval and disbursement of funds on a timely basis. Small and even medium-sized EMBs may suffer membership and senior staff turnover which reduce institutional experience and memory. New independent EMBs may not have the experience and skills to deal effectively with bureaucratic environments.

Governmental Model of Electoral Management in the Member States of the African Union

The strengths of the governmental model of electoral management include the build up and sustainability of corporate archival memory; creation and maintenance of experienced staff; facilitation of cost-sharing arrangements with other government departments in electoral services; and are well-placed to requisition support services from other government departments in times of crises.

The weaknesses of the government model include, particularly in the context of emerging democracies of the African Union, the inevitable cloud of compromised credibility due to perceived seepage of influence of the government and ruling party of the day; funding allocations may suffer due to competing priorities for funding in the appropriate ministry or local authority; often staff with relevant experience and appropriate skills are lacking through transfer to higher positions elsewhere in the institutions concerned; often the bureaucratic management styles of ministries and local authorities are not suited to deal with the nuances of electoral organization with masses of details; and frequently the ministry or local authority dealing with elections also deals with a variety of other activities and that leads to fragmentation of the electoral administration.

The Mixed Model of Electoral Management in the Member States of the African Union

The strengths of the mixed model electoral management include the potential for the component independent EMB to have outstanding members who add credibility to the institution, while the component government EMB provides sustainable institutional memory; the two component EMBs have the potential to bring together bureaucratically experienced staff supported by independent expertise; the component government EMB is well-placed to facilitate cooperation with other government relevant departments in providing electoral services; and the combination of the two components EMBs have the potential to generate cost-effective measures through cost-sharing and tight internal supervisory activities.

The weaknesses of the mixed model in electoral management in the Member States of the African Union include the distrust that stakeholders in the Union have in the component government EMB and that distrust is not counterbalanced by the perceived weak component independent EMB; the component independent EMB may lack political influence to secure sufficient funding and the component government EMB may be prevented from improving the allocation to elections through internal policy in the ministry or local authority; and the component government EMB may be hampered by fragmented electoral administration in the executive branch each having different priorities.

Relations between the Executive and EMBs

Many EMBs of the independent model experienced difficulties in establishing regular channels of communication with the legislature and, even more important, with the executive branch of government during the first decade of the 21st Century. The problem persisted even in countries where some form of formal channels existed, as in Lesotho, Liberia and Nigeria, and the result was often that approval and disbursement of election budget were not done on a timely basis. Similar difficulties arose with respect to the staffing of EMBs with public servants. Inadequate consultation between the relevant ministry of government and the EMB concerned usually led to personnel unsuited for electoral work.

The problem may be solved through a dual approach, that is, by the electoral legislative scheme having suitable provisions for the budget consideration and approval directly by the National Assembly and timely disbursement by the Treasury; and by agreed procedures with the Treasury on the steps to facilitate timely disbursements in the case of the budget and in other cases with the relevant ministry or department, for example relating to staffing by public servants or amendments to the Electoral Law.

Some independent EMBs, like those of Lesotho and Liberia, tried to avoid delays in budget disbursements through personal contacts between the staff of the EMB and the Finance Department and the Treasury of the Finance Ministry. Perhaps that is a pragmatic way to solve the problem, but problems are likely to arise with this approach when the staffs of the EMB or the ministry change and relations have to be rebuilt. In appropriate situations, the practical steps to enhance smooth and regular communications between an EMB and executive branch might be set out in a memorandum of understanding so that incoming staff will be able to follow the procedures in place.

The concept of a constitutionally independent entity is not always well understood and often the executive either inadvertently or intentionally stray unlawfully into the domain of constitutionally autonomous entities. It may be that there is a case for greater efforts to be made to create improved awareness among the executive branches of government of the need to respect and support the status of constitutionally independent bodies, including EMBs. Sometimes it may be just lack of timely communication between the EMB and the department concerned as was the case in Malawi in 1996-7.[43]

The Path to Good Practice

Internal democracy

Given that the predominant number of EMBs in the Member States of the African Union are of the independent model and the component independent EMB of the mixed model, it is important that their internal structure be consistent with democratic practices. The electoral law would normally cover important procedural aspects such as the quorum of meetings of the body for the purposes of ordinary or special meetings, sometimes, though not often, the selection and role of the chairman and the nature and scope of any delegated powers.

---

[43]   In that instance the Malawi Electoral Commission had proposed certain amendments to the electoral law and for 18 months the Attorney General's Department never responded to the Electoral Commission's proposals. The matter came up for discussion at a problem-solving workshop convened by the Commission to discuss the relationship between the Electoral Commission and the Government. The Attorney-General's contention was simply that the right procedure in seeking the opinion of the Attorney-General was not followed.

However the details of the decision-making processes may be left to the EMB to be set out in standing orders or administrative procedures to be debated and agreed by the members of the commission. These issues will largely determine the nature and level of internal democracy achieved and the quality of governance that prevail in the institution. They include the role of the chair, if not fully dealt with in the electoral law; method of calling EMB meetings; the procedures for decision making; the responsibility for calling and the frequency of holding meetings; the quorum, (if not yet decided), of meetings; who may attend meetings; taking of minutes of meetings and their authentication; the role of the secretariat at meetings, the method of suspending or altering the standing orders; and the method of issuing policies and directions of the EMB.

The issue of whether or not meetings of an electoral commission are open to the public may be covered by the electoral legislative scheme, but, if not, it may be decided by the EMB. Open meetings do give an air of transparency in the conduct of the affairs of the EMBs concerned. Meetings of EMBs should be held frequently, particularly during election preparation. The decisions of meetings which are not confidential should be conveyed to staff, particularly affected field staffs, on a timely basis. Closed meetings can appear to be less transparent if a press release or conference is held immediately after the meeting of the EMB. Some closed EMB meetings may be opened to representatives of partners or donors, as was the case of Liberia in 2005.

EMBs' Independence in Member States of the African Union

An election management body regardless of the model needs to be independent of outside influence of any kind. It should at all times operate under the guiding principle of a culture of impartiality and non-partisanship with respect to all contestants in an election. The independent model of electoral management is probably best placed of the three discussed above to display independence not because of its label but rather due to its institutional structure and in many cases constitutionally recognized status. The ultimate test of ensuring that an EMB safeguards its independent decision making and, thus protecting its integrity, lies with its members and to a less extent its staff. The electoral environment during an election period or during the conduct of major electoral processes can be politically charged with pressures and complaints and so much care needs to be taken so as not to depart from the stipulated procedures in favour of any stakeholder. Electoral officials must be imbued with a keen sense of fairness and non-partisanship.

Although the preponderance of the independent model of electoral management in the African Union presents a good basis on which to build the 'independence' of EMBs, the complaint against most of the EMBs of the Union is precisely that their independence is often compromised through too close ties with the governments and ruling parties of the day. Deeper awareness of the importance of non-partisanship in electoral organization and better understanding of the role of an independent EMB in shaping the acceptable outcome of free and fair election might help in improving the behaviour of some EMBs. The political directorate of the day in the respective AU countries also has a responsibility to refrain from influencing the EMBs in any way.

EMBs' Impartiality in the Context of the African Union Member States

It is encouraging to note that despite the setback in Kenya (2007) and Zimbabwe (2008) where the impartiality of the EMBs was questioned and which had horrific consequences, a number of subsequent elections in the AU in 2008, for example, Angola, Rwanda, Zambia, Guinea–Bissau and Ghana, did not experience that complaint. The consequences of failure to act impartially by EMBs were seen in Kenya where the widespread perception that the Electoral Commission of Kenya did not conduct the 2007 general elections in an impartial manner led to catastrophic riots which left many dead, and serious destruction of property. A similar development in Zimbabwe towards the end of the March elections of 2008 ended calamitously and was compounded by a farcical run-off election in which the only contestant was the candidate of the ruling party. Impartiality and non-partisanship can best be conveyed to stakeholders generally through complete transparency at all levels and at all stages of election organization by the management and staff of EMBs. Perhaps the Ghana presidential run-off elections in 2008 illustrate the point that when partisanship is not imputed differences can be dealt with more easily. In that situation one constituency out of 230 was not polled on the date of the run-off election. That constituency had 54,000 voters on the register and the opposition candidate had a lead of 23,000 votes which could be overturned by polling in Tain Constituency. The EMB set Friday 2 January 2009 for polling in Tain Constituency and the candidate of the ruling party boycotted the polling on the grounds that the security in place was not conducive to the conduct of free and fair election. There was no accusation of partisanship by the EMB. Polling went ahead in the Tain Constituency; and the opposition candidate was declared the winner of the run-off election.[44]

Transparency in Electoral Organization in the Member States of the African Union

Transparency in electoral organization is not confined to observing good accounting practices, although that also is a vital aspect of sound electoral management. Operational transparency in electoral management encompasses openness with stakeholders and with the general public regarding significant developments in the electoral process. Transparency in electoral organization can be greatly facilitated by the timely publication of an Election Calendar and by the timely release of information on how the calendar's schedule of activities is being followed. Transparency in electoral organization means sharing information on important electoral developments in a timely manner and on a non-discriminatory basis with primary stakeholders such as political parties and candidates who are contestants in an election. Equally, regular releases to the media for publication, or press conferences do enhance the transparency mechanism of electoral management.

Most national elections during the decade of the 21st Century in the African Union were conducted under the gaze of domestic and international election observers. Transparency was rightly interpreted to mean access to observers to witness all phases of the polling, counting, tabulation, and tallying processes culminating in the announcement of the election results. Election observers were showing greater interest in forming three

---

[44] Polling was unable to take place in Tain Constituency on the run-off election date because of failure to deliver election materials.

categories of election observation, namely, short, medium and long term, in order to track the performance and totality of transparency exhibited by a given EMB during the preparatory process of electoral organization. In general, the EMBs of the Member States of the AU were expected to be under scrutiny for much longer periods during the preparation for election than ever and transparency will be one of the elements under the microscope.

The EMBs in the African Union Member States had a poor track record with respect to transparency in electoral organization. Some EMBs, notably Cape Verde, Botswana, Ghana, Liberia (2005), Mauritius, Namibia and South Africa, have managed to sustain a high level of transparency in election organization during the period under review. Countries that emerged from one-party regimes in the 1990s struggled to achieve a reasonable level of transparency in election organization largely due to the dominant role of the ruling party of the day coupled with the influence of the publicly owned media. Examples of this somewhat strange phenomenon were to be found in Kenya, Nigeria, Zanzibar (Tanzania), and Zambia, despite a change of the ruling party a couple of times since 1991. As Kenya in 2007 and Zimbabwe in 2008, the lack of transparency during the closing processes of the elections destroyed the confidence of stakeholders in the whole electoral process.

Efficiency of EMBs in Member States of the African Union

Constructing the organization of election conduct consists of undertaking a series of processes which encompass masses of details. The nature of periodic national elections requires working towards a strict timetable. Managing the holding of national elections may be seen as a series of separate election processes forming a part of one electoral process and contributing to the successful election of representatives and leaders of a community. Success in such endeavours depends on the managers and officials responsible for the electoral organization displaying the capacity to deal with procedural and administrative details. Efficiency in electoral organization also depends on thorough training of electoral officials at all levels of the EMB, particularly the field officers. Efficiency requires electoral officers to conduct themselves in a manner that protects the integrity of the EMB as an institution and that means that the officers should always behave in accordance with the culture of non-partisanship and impartiality.

Few of the EMBs of the Member States of the African Union can be happy with the level of efficiency achieved to date, but the future in this regard looks bright as a growing number of them are being exposed to systematic training courses and many partners are showing interest in offering cooperation in this area.

Professionalism in Electoral Management

There is great potential for the development of professionalism in electoral management in the Member States of the African Union. The number of democratic multiparty elections is on the increase.[45] At the same time international partners have been showing a growing willingness to assist with professional training for EMBs' staff, but there is an urgent need for national or regional tertiary and other institutions to offer professional training in electoral and related subjects.

The benefits from wider professional training in electoral management would quickly be seen in improved application of electoral procedures and electoral rules. It is submitted that greater professionalism in electoral organization would reduce the incidence of partisanship as well as irregularities in conducting election processes.

The small size of many AU EMBs in Member States may limit the scope for professionalism in so far as career prospects in those institutions may be limited. The reliance on co-opting electoral staff from the public service may also be an impediment to development of staff professionalism to its full potential in small EMBs of the AU. The great challenge for many EMBs will be training the field staff, particularly returning officers and presiding officers, to achieve professional level notwithstanding the fact that they are temporary officers. Mechanisms and incentives should be developed to enable such officers to remain in the system and be available for hiring during election periods.

---

[45] The AU election Calendar for 2009 listed 16 national elections.

The Secretariat of EMBs in the Member States of the African Union

The secretariat, by whatever name called,[46] plays a key role in the governance of African Union EMBs. The preponderance of the independent model followed by the mixed model in the Union means that the majority of EMBs in the Union potentially have significant control over the constitution of the respective secretariats. It is expected that the governmental model of EMBs have secretariats which are staffed by public servants and so have the component governmental EMBs in the cases of the mixed model. However, in the case of independent and the component independent of the mixed model, many of them also draw on the public service and mainly on the civil service for their staffing. Despite the fact that their constitutive instruments allow for freedom to appoint their staff as they see fit, for example in Lesotho and Liberia, the EMBs still found it convenient to rely on civil service transfers. This is due to a variety of factors, the chief of which is that despite what is in the electoral law the EMBs have not developed sufficient independence to implement that aspect of their mandate. Sometimes the hesitance of the EMBs to employ their own staff is due to the reluctance of the public service staff joining the EMB permanently and thereby losing the civil service perquisites and broader career prospects. The question of pensions also plays a part in EMBs having difficulties shedding their civil service staff. Moreover, some constitutive instruments establishing independent EMBs, as in the cases of Botswana and Nigeria, expressly reserve the right of appointing the head of the EMBs' secretariat to the Head of State. These cases should be corrected by amending the instruments concerned as they tend or appear to compromise the independence of the secretariat.

The relationship between the EMB and its secretariat should be clearly defined to avoid overlapping of tasks or lack of distinction of mandates. The board of commissioners should normally deal with policy matters and the secretariat should be in charge of implementing those policies. In other words, the secretariat should be concerned about operations. In practice the distinction is often blurred for a number of reasons, for example, where members of an EMB are given oversight duties administratively,

---

[46] Sometimes called the 'Directorate', as in Namibia.

such duties often allow individual Commissioners to meddle in operations in area of oversight,[47] in some cases difficulty arose over the competence to recruit the staff of the secretariat as between the head of the secretariat and the EMB's Chairman or members,[48] or the electoral law may have been badly drafted as to confer particular election tasks on a particular position in the secretariat, thus rendering it unclear whether the board of commissioners can deal with the issue in the absence of amendment of the provisions concerned.[49] There needs to be close coordination between the head of the secretariat and the chairman and members so that information released, particularly on technical operational matters, to the public is accurate, so as to avoid embarrassing correction of misleading statements on operations by the board of commissioners.

Financing Election Organization in the Member States of the African Union.

The financing of core electoral activities of EMBs as well as the staff and administration of the electoral machinery is generally funded by the respective Member States of the Union. However the big picture is rather deceptive as in practice funding of electoral institutions and activities on a timely basis in the Union has been one of the perennial problems in putting democratic elections on a sound footing. Many electoral institutions are inadequately housed and staffed and are not given sufficient recognition and respect that would contribute to the key role that such institutions play in the national democratic development. With few exceptions, the EMBs of the Member States of the African Union complain of shortage of funding to undertake preparatory work for elections, particularly the acquisition of new technology. As a consequence, there is extensive reliance on contribution by partners,

---

[47] That used to happen in Sierra Leone before the allocation of oversight duties was changed, and it happened in some instances in Liberia in 2005.

[48] This occurred in South Africa shortly after the first post-apartheid Electoral Commission was established. Sometimes the issues of patronage lurk behind the rivalry.

[49] The Electoral law of Lesotho confers certain powers on the Director of Elections with respect to certain electoral processes in such a manner as to make it difficult to discover the role of the Commission in those processes.

friendly governments and international non-governmental organizations. Two other issues that affect electoral funding in the Member States of the African Union are the lack of researching ways of reducing the cost of elections which many states find to be burdensome; and the seepage of funds through patronage in awarding electoral contracts without adequate tender procedures to allow for genuine competition with respect to price and quality.

The funding of EMBs the world over has been long in discussion in many emerging democracies and the African Union has had its fair share of the arguments. In addition to the issue of adequacy of the electoral budget, and bearing in mind that in normal circumstances election year budget has to be planned for, the frequent concern is how to ensure timely approval and disbursement of EMBs' budget. There are two aspects to the solution of the problem, namely institutional and administrative. In some states, multiple dimensions have been introduced to treat the problem. The Nigerian approach is to make the remuneration of the members of the EMB a charge on the national reserve or 'Consolidated Fund' as it is called in some jurisdictions. Stakeholders feel that the constitutional provisions did not go far enough and should be extended to the election budget in order to prevent the government of the day from delaying approval of the election budget. The further constitutional step was taken in Lesotho and Namibia where the National Assembly was given a role in approving the budget submitted by the EMB concerned. That approach helped in avoiding a particular ministry of government having power to deal with the matter. That institutional improvement did not necessarily lead to swift disbursement of the budget, as was experienced in Lesotho. The administrative mechanisms have been shown to work in many countries even without the constitutional support in linking electoral funding to direct charging to the consolidated fund. The key is for the EMB concerned to create the awareness of the political directorate that proper administrative mechanisms should be put in place to ensure timely approval and disbursement of electoral budget.

Usually the most expensive single electoral process to conduct during the preparatory phase for a national election is voter registration. In order to prevent electoral fraud a number of identity mechanisms may be introduced into the voter registration process thus adding significant costs. This could include photograph, finger or palm printing or other biometric features of each voter. The other heavy cost components of most voter registration processes are the scanning of data and the production and issuance of voters' cards. A growing number of EMBs are introducing continuous registration of voters. There have been mixed reports on the cost of continuous versus periodic registration of voters. Namibia which had used continuous registration for sometime announced that it was abandoning continuous and returning to periodic registration on account of cost considerations.

Donors' (partners') funding of electoral activities takes many forms in the African Union. The partners in this endeavour are at two levels, namely, bilateral agencies such as the European Union, United States International Development Agency, individual countries of the EU, Canada and Japan; and international non-governmental organizations (NGOs) and civil society organizations (CSOs), such as International Foundation for Electoral Systems (IFES), National Democratic Institute (NDI), the Carter Center, and the International Republican Institute (IRI), and others. The partners have contributed to specific processes such as voter registration, voter education, and management of electoral logistics. (See Annex 4 for types of EMBs in the AU).

National EMBs and the AU

The forging of a strong working relationship between the national EMBs and the AU during the first decade of the 21st Century made steady progress. Measurable progress was achieved through arranging a continental meeting with EMBs; arranging training for EMBs' staffs with partners, as BRIDGE courses with International IDEA; organization of training (orientation) courses for AU election observers with contribution from IFES, Carter Center and EISA; a programme of raising standards of election processes for EMBs; and the creation of an election database to which EMBs, will eventually have access will extend the influence of the AU on election activity in Member States.

There are officers in the AU Commission and some of the regional bodies who are watchful of the central of the role of the AU C in elections and particularly election observation, but so long the AU C, through the DPA and the DEAU plays a coordinating rather than a controlling one the cooperation between the AUC and the national EMBs and regional entities will be healthy and beneficial to the AU as a whole.

Chapter VII

Limitations of Political Parties in Democratic Elections in the Member States of the African Union

Introduction

Democratic elections cannot exist and flourish without the existence of strong political parties. The African Union was known for strong ruling parties and fragmented, weak and under-funded opposition parties. There are exceptions to the general picture, as seen with recent elections in Ghana 2008-09 and Sierra Leone in 2007, but the general perception was that ruling parties in the African Union's Member States benefited from their hold on public resources while the lack of access to any reliable forms of resources reduces the competitiveness of opposition political parties. The inability of many countries of the African Union to develop and sustain strong opposition political parties was in part attributed to small and weak private sectors which themselves depended on the government and ruling parties of the day for support. Small parties in countries as far a part as Liberia, Malawi, Namibia, and Sierra Leone, complained of the hardships they face to access funding if they were not a part of government, or did not have substantial representatives in the National Assembly concerned.

There were limits to what the AUC could do to strengthen opposition political parties in Member States, since it would be seen as political interference in the internal affairs of Member States. The other major consideration was the considerable financial resources that would be required to make any meaningful impact on the multitude of small struggling political parties in Member States of the AU. A few international CSOs and bi-lateral agencies of partners had offered limited assistance to political parties in specific periods of election cycles (usually during preparation for polling), but such unsustainable assistance proved to be largely ineffectual during the decade under consideration.

Despite the constraints on the ability of the AUC to influence the fortunes of political parties, particularly small opposition parties, in the Member States of the AU, the role of political parties in the direction of democratic elections merits some treatment in this book.

Influences on Political Parties—Ethnicity and Religion

There are many ethnic groups with different languages in the individual Member States of the Union, and this fact, coupled with the existence of multi-religious faiths, has had a profound impact on the formation and development of political parties. This general view had been confirmed by studies in selected countries by several scholars.[50] It was clear that the overwhelming dominance of a particular ethnic group in Namibia maintained the Southwest Africa Peoples Organization (SWAPO) in power since independence. Large ethnic groups contributed to strong parties in Kenya (the Kikuyu-supported the ruling party for a long period, and Lou constituted some form of opposition); in Mali (the Bambari, Fulani and Songhai supported the ruling Alliance for Democracy in Mali), Niger (Hausa and Djerma supported the ruling National Independent Union for Democratic Renewal), and Nigeria (Yuroba and Igbo form the ruling party and the Fulani and Hausa form the main opposition).

The religious diversity in many Member States of the Union played a part in the quest to gain political support. A survey of religions in the Union showed that 19 Member States were predominantly Christians, 15 were predominantly Muslims and 11 subscribed to traditional religions, while 12 had no majority religion.[51] The existence of many religious political parties did show the importance of the role of religion in the Union's

---

50   See for example, Mohamed Salih, M. A. (ed.) *African Political Parties: Evolution, Institutionalization and Governance (London: Pluto Press, 2003);* also Norris, Pippa, and Mattes, Robert, paper on *'Does Ethnicity Determine Support for the Governing Party?'* Afrobarometer paper no.26, 2003.

51   See World Religions, Infoplease.com/ipa/A0855613.html (visited 12/01/2009)

political landscape. Examples of religious political parties included the Islamic Salvation Front in Algeria, the Muslim Brotherhood in Egypt, the National Islamic Front in Sudan, the Islamic Resistance Party of Tanzania, the South African Islamic Party, and the African Muslim Party both of South Africa, and the Mauritian Islamic Political Party of Mauritius. The Islamic Party of Kenya had been banned. Some political parties had deep religious roots but preferred to operate under a secular banner for fear of breaking political party rules. These included the Justice and Development Movement of Morocco, the Democratic Gathering Party of Mauritania and the National Congress Party (the ruling party) of Sudan, as well as the opposition party of Sudan, the New National Congress of Sudan.[52]

Parties that were ethnically or religious based had not distinguished themselves in government. In government, they too thrived on public resources and took advantage of incumbency. Sudan was an example, where ethnic and religious mix served the ruling party well.

Types of Political Parties and their Impact on Democratic Elections

For over two and one-half decades the African political landscape was dominated by one-party, military or apartheid regimes until the early 1990s. Since then there had been an almost complete change of the political landscape, except for a hangover of the one-party system, whereby one-party regimes had been replaced by two or more parties vying for power in a more competitive manner. During the heyday of one-party system, the constitution of the states using the system allowed for only one political party and so to create more than one party the constitution of those states had to be amended. In the case of Eritrea, the People's Front for Democracy and Justice (PFDJ) operated as the only legal party, although the Transitional National Assembly in 2002 accepted political pluralism in principle. No party other than the ruling party was registered.

The mushrooming of several political parties in many Member States immediately after the one-party system was abolished, gradually gave

---

[52] See Political Parties in Africa: Challenges for Sustained Multiparty Democracy, International Institute for Democracy and Electoral Assistance 2007, p.33.

way to two-party systems, mainly on the basis that in a competitive field for supporters and resources only the strongest will survive. A number of countries in the Union showed signs of two-party systems emerging, for example, Benin, Ghana, Kenya, Seychelles, and Sierra Leone. The situation in Zimbabwe was unclear (at the time of writing) as to whether or not the political environment in that country would foster a two-party system.

The countries with dominant political parties were not all erstwhile one-party states, and indeed the characteristics of a dominant-party system were different from those of the one-party systems. Nevertheless, it spoke volumes about democratic multiparty elections in the AU that as many as 16 countries of the Union, namely, Angola, Botswana, Cameroon, Chad, Côte d'Ivoire, Djibouti, Equatorial Guinea, Ethiopia, Gambia, Mozambique, Namibia, Rwanda, South Africa, Tanzania, Uganda and Zimbabwe, were governed by dominant political parties during the first decade of the21st Century.[53] Where the dominance of these parties was due mainly to ethnicity, or religion, or linguistic cleavages, the party's dominance may linger until changes are brought about by internal upheavals as appeared to be the case in South Africa beginning in 2008.

Genuine multiparty democracies which offered strong and healthy electoral competition between two or more political parties were uncommon in the Union, but according to Mohamed Salih fourteen countries in the Union on their electoral record could be classified as multiparty democracies.[54] A special effort was made in the 1990s after the demise of the one-party regimes, which dominated the continent, to foster multiparty systems, but before too long multiparty systems developed into the dominant party systems which more closely resembled the one-party rather than genuine multiparty systems.

---

[53] See Mohamed Salih, *African Political Parties: Evolution, Institutionalization and Governance (London: Pluto Press, 2003).*

[54] Ibid., Algeria, Burkina Faso, Burundi, Central African Republic, Congo, Liberia, Malawi, Mali, Mauritius, Niger, Nigeria, São Tomé and Principe, Senegal, and Zambia.

Competitive Politics in the Member States of the African Union

Competitive democratic elections entail lawful political parties or qualified individuals freely canvassing for votes in order to contest elections. Elections should be held at regular intervals and the 'playing field' should be level for every contestant, that is to say, there should be equitable access to the media, and public resources, including personnel, should not be improperly used to the advantage of any contestant and at the exclusion of others. There should be complete freedom of movement for each contestant and their supporters to campaign, and unrestricted freedom of speech limited only by language deemed libelous, or slanderous, or obscene, as well as language calculated to stir up hatred in volatile ethnic situations.

The media, particularly the publicly owned media, should undertake objective reporting on the election campaign and grant fair access to parties and candidates contesting elections. Political parties and candidates, including independents, should commit themselves to a proper code of conduct governing the election campaign, and ensure that their supporters at political rallies and elsewhere also subscribe to it.

The EMBs concerned also have a role to play in ensuring that elections are competitive. They are to ensure that the law and rules relating to the election organization are observed, particularly rules dealing with the campaign such as campaign financing, access to the media, behaviour at rallies, and that the rules, if any, relating to incumbency are observed.

General Overview of Structure and Management of African Political Parties

To the extent that political parties of the Member States of the Union evolved from the community in which they operated, they reflected some aspects of the society, particularly the ethnicity, religion and the economic conditions of their members and supporters. For those political parties that aspire to gain power realistically, their supporters saw them as institutions that could facilitate their participation in power and accrue the benefits that went with that status. National political parties, as distinct from regional or provincial, were usually centrally managed with the party headquarters based in the capital city.[55] Some parties, ruling or opposition, developed a system based on the Westminster model of keeping Members of the National Assembly to tow the line. The whip system, as it came to be called in the United Kingdom, enabled a party to keep its parliamentary members informed about, among other things, voting on issues and on Bills. The governing party's chief whip was responsible to get the backbenchers out when important government measures were being voted on. Although most ruling parties were under the firm control of the leader as had been shown by President Mugabe over the ZANU-PF in 2008; there was the exception of the African National Congress (ANC) which dismissed the sitting President, Thabo Mbeki, in 2008 after he lost the leadership of the Party to Jacob Zuma.[56]

The ANC had a developed internal democratic system strong enough, not only to unseat the sitting State President as Leader of the party, but subsequently remove the incumbent State President from his post. However few other ruling parties were strong enough or as well organized as the ANC. Several political parties, including in Ghana, Kenya and Malawi, had been cited as having weak internal democracy in so far as accountability to the membership was concerned.[57]

Some general weaknesses in the internal democratic structure of many political parties in the Union included the following factors:

- Party leadership was either selected or elected on a purely formal basis, after the leadership question had been settled through patronage;

---

[55] Despite legal requirement to have the party headquarters in Monrovia, some political parties had no party headquarters there in 2005.

[56] President Mbeki was apparently wrongly cited by the Judge hearing a case of corruption against Jacob Zuma of instigating political interference in the case. The trial Judge then dismiss the charges against Mr. Zuma, but the case against Zuma was restored on appeal and the Court castigated the Judge of the lower Court for exceeding his powers in alluding to political interference in the case.

[57] See Mohamed Salih (note 45 above).

- Leadership may be fashioned by geopolitics and policy orientations prompted by global policy influences; and
- Grooming of party leadership may be done to ensure that old policies were continued, as was the case with some of the party-dominated systems during the past decade; examples of that approach could be seen in Nigeria (2007). Gabon and Botswana.

Financing Political Parties in the Member States of the African Union

Political parties in the Union were financed mainly by donations, public funding, membership fees, trust funds, and private sector businesses. Membership contribution to African political parties was not significant due to the socio-economic position in many of the States. Incumbent parties were often in the felicitous position to access public funds and other support, sometimes improperly. The public media and government vehicles were co-opted to support the incumbent parties. Opposition parties in such circumstances suffered double disadvantages in being unable to raise sufficient resources independently and having no realistic hope of competing fairly with their incumbent counterparts. This situation had persistently placed opposition political parties in a disadvantageous position when contesting election against incumbent parties. Many stakeholders realized the financial predicament of the African medium and small opposition political parties that their survival depended on either funding by the private sector, including corporations, which encouraged 'money politics', or public funding for political parties. Private funding of political parties in Africa had come in for criticisms on the grounds that it often resulted in parties serving the private rather than public interests, and that it encouraged a patronage syndrome which militated against the evolution of internal party democracy. Further, private funding in the circumstances of the Member States of the Union was believed to encourage autocratic party leadership and lead to corruption where the highest bidders won out in matters such as candidates' selection and top party posts.

In the light of the foregoing weaknesses of reliance mainly on private funding of political parties in Africa, a number of positive arguments had been advanced in support of public funding for political parties. Foremost among the arguments in favour of public funding of political parties in

Africa was the fact of the small base of private funding made it infeasible that opposition parties would secure sustainable party funding. Further, it is believed that public funding based on an equitable formula would make opposition parties and their members less prone to fragmentation and fewer opposition parliamentarians would be tempted to cross the floor or indulge in corrupt practices. Public funding could be organized in a manner as to encourage greater campaign accountability, improved representation of women, minorities and youth. Public financing of parties would roll back the influence of private and corporate interests on party policies. If the foregoing factors pointed to the strengths of public funding, there were weaknesses that opponents of public funding had raised. For example, that public funding had a tendency to de-emphasize the importance of contacts with and reliance on membership fees and contributions by supporters. Some opponents of public funding of political parties believed that parties became less accountable to supporters and ultimately to the voters and hence may indirectly lead to greater voter apathy.

Political party financing in the Member States of the Union was a major worry for the development of democratic elections. The low socio-economic base of party members in many Member States, encouraged sources of illicit party funding. There was a strong case for the introduction of party finance regulations (including emphasis on disclosure of sources of funds), and regular periodic auditing of party accounts by accountants of good standing.

Party Leadership Succession in the Member States of the African Union

The health of a political party is usually reflected in its ability to elect its leader and other senior officers in a democratic manner in accordance with its constitution. In the past decade, many ruling parties' leaders have tried not only to cling on to leadership of their party but to secure a change of their countries' constitution in order to lengthen their respective term in office as Head of State. Many conflicts on the continent had their roots in the ruling party leader's meddling with the constitution to secure further terms in office. Conflicts ascribed to attempts to increase terms of office included Sierra Leone, Rwanda, Burundi, Côte d'Ivoire, Liberia,

Togo, and Zimbabwe.[58] Through strong and swift action the 'third term' presidential syndrome did not succeed in Malawi, Nigeria, and Zambia. In a similar vein, there had been the practice in some countries in the Union whereby when the State President demits office he retains office of party leadership—for example, Julius Nyrere in Tanzania, Joachim Chissano in Mozambique, Sam Nujoma of Namibia, and Bakili Muluzi in Malawi. In 2008 President Thabo Mbeki (whose presidential term was due to end in 2009) contested the leadership of the ANC and lost to Jacob Zuma). This mindset of many party leaders in Member States of the Union to retain party control caused considerable instability in their parties. While there may be some positive aspects in particular circumstances, as perhaps when Nyrere stepped down from the presidency, the destabilizing factor for the parties in question outweighed the perceived advantages.

Women and Political Party Leadership in the Member States of the African Union

Despite having a female State President since 2005 in Liberia, very few Members States of the African Union had women in party leadership roles. Sometimes there was reluctance of women to participate in politics even when the environment was not unfavourable to such participation. For example, in Liberia in 2005 the election rules recommended that each political party should reserve 30% of their candidatures for women, but only a couple of parties achieved that goal, largely because women did not step forward. However, as Julie Ballington pointed out, where there was a quota system for women in parliament there was an average of 17% as against 9% where there was no quota in place.[59] She also pointed out that Rwanda, Mozambique and South Africa had the highest rate of female

---

[58] In Guinea (Conakry) upon the announcement of the death of the long-serving President Conte, the army took over and thus interrupt the constitutional designated path of succession.

[59] Julie Ballington, 'Electoral Systems, Electoral Processes and Gender Equality' in Electoral Reform in Commonwealth African Countries, p.193 ed. by Carl W. Dundas, Commonwealth Secretariat 2001.

representation in parliament on the continent.[60] The state of women's representation at the local government level was not well researched.

Party Protection Measures in the Member States of the African Union.

It is debatable as to whether a governing party should embark upon a path of self protection. The compatibility with democratic principles would be the key to the legitimacy of such measures. Memories of the recent past with one-party systems will present instant example of a failed system of self protection of incumbent parties. Moreover, the current development surrounding the dominant-party system, its resemblance to the one-party system and its impingements on true multi-party democracy did not found favour with stakeholders.

Measures which were seen as somewhat less devious than one-party systems were greeted with perhaps less skepticism, as had been the case with prevention of 'crossing the floor', that is to say, leaving the party on whose ticket a member was elected to parliament and joining another party. A number of countries of the continent however passed legislation to prevent a member of the National Assembly leaving one political party to join another without vacating his/her seat. In Namibia, Seychelles, Sierra Leone and Zimbabwe, crossing the floor would result in the seat of the member becoming vacant. The procedure may differ as to how and when the seat became vacant, but ultimately the result was the same. The rationale appeared to be attractive in that the party ticket on which the member was elected was the party that should benefit, but the longstanding Westminster concept was that a member of the Assembly was a representative of the constituency and not of the sponsoring political party. However, the Westminster concept may hold well for first past the post systems, it was hardly true of List PR systems.

---

[60] See Julie Ballington (ed.), *The Implementation of Quotas: African Experiences* (Stockholm: International IDEA, 2004)

Political Party Regulations in the Member States of the African Union

It is true to say that an overview of political parties' general operations in the Member States of the African Union leaves one with the impression that parties are not well regulated in critical aspects of contesting elections in the pursuit of gaining political power. A cursory look at how the major political parties conducted party primaries to select candidates for presidential and parliamentary elections in Kenya and Nigeria illustrated the problem of insufficient regulations and the inability of the parties to implement whatever party rules existed. Frequently, political party primaries were bedeviled by unhealthy rivalry, patronage and cheating. This often resulted in resort to the court to resolve issues that should be settled according to party procedures and rules. Internal party difficulties had been seen in several countries, in particular, Liberia (2005), Malawi, South Africa, Zambia, and Zimbabwe. While there was little doubt that more and better party regulations were needed in some areas of party operations, a more serious problem was the absence of proper mechanisms to implement and enforce the existing party rules. Some stakeholders took the view that the EMBs concerned should be given a prominent role in regulating parties and ensuring that regulations were complied with in a timely manner. However in countries, such as Liberia, Kenya and Nigeria, where the electoral law or rules vested certain powers in the respective EMBs to monitor party congresses the result had not been positive.

In discussing this broad issue of party regulations in the Member States in the African Union, one should be mindful of the scope of party regulations and the varying levels of democratic elections achieved in the Union. Some matters lend themselves more readily to regulation by the EMBs concerned: for example, the application of quotas for women or minorities, but perhaps less so in administering campaign finances.

Political Party Requirements for Contesting Elections in the Member States of the African Union

The formation and registration of political parties had been widely permitted in the Member States of the Union in the first decade in contrast to the early 1990s when the formation of new parties was forbidden to compete with the ruling party. The dominant-party system resembles the one-party system, but was not protected by legislation, rather by ethnicity and or religion. The no—party system survived in Uganda until 2005 and political parties were not allowed to form and develop in Eritrea and Swaziland. Ethnic and religious parties were not allowed in Ethiopia, Mauritius, South Africa and Sudan. In general, parties and candidates had to comply with the requirements laid down to contest national elections, the presidency or National Assembly. There were requirements to sign a registration form and or payment of a deposit as a pre-condition to contesting elections.

Financing Political Parties' Campaign in the Member States of the African Union

Funding electoral institutions in the Member States of the Union, be it national EMBs, or political parties or their election campaigns, was a difficult issue to treat as resources were so scarce. There was no coherent pattern or scheme to manage election campaigns by parties or candidates. The surest, or more accurately, constant pattern of campaign financing was found among ruling parties which unabashedly use public resources for campaign purposes. There was no common rule in the Union relating to foreign donations, although some countries, for example, Mali and Namibia, had rules relating to foreign donations. Many countries still looked favourably on foreign donations mindful of such assistance during the struggle for independence. Parties relied on support by members through fees and donations from supporters, party activists raised funds from private sector firms and wealthy individuals. Ruling parties had avenues which were seldom open to opposition parties though most of these avenues were not transparent and were probably improper, or even unlawful. Such avenues for fund raising included patronage, kickbacks, use of public resources; and in a few cases legitimate investments. Donations formed a significant part of the election campaign financing for both ruling and opposition parties. Citizens abroad were important contributors to election campaign funds for ruling as well as opposition parties in many countries of the AU.

Public Funding of Election Campaigns in the Member States of the African Union

Public funding of electoral campaign took the form of direct contribution to electoral campaigns or indirect public financial support through free access to the public media, or tax reductions on some party activities. A number of African countries introduced some form of public funding.[61] Direct public funding was often criticized because of the formula for distributing the funds to parties. Formulae which based the allocation of funds on the number of representatives in the 'last' or 'current' parliament usually produce unfair results in countries, like Namibia and South Africa, where there were consistent large majorities for the ruling party due to ethnic or religious considerations.[62] A reference to representation in parliament had the potential to prejudice assistance to new parties. The enforcement of financial rules varied according to the type of EMB that was in place. In the case of independent EMBs, the usual enforcement authority was the EMB concerned, but in some like Benin, the Ministry of Internal Affairs, Namibia, the Auditor General, and Seychelles, the Party Finance Regulatory Board, a body other than the EMB was responsible. In Liberia, tight campaign finance rules were introduced in 2005, including disclosure of assets by candidates. The enforcement mechanism was the EMB which sought earnestly to enforce the rules, and although the rules were perhaps too complex to start with, there was relatively high level of compliance. The major problem was with unsuccessful candidates and parties, who ignored the rules that required disclosure.

Reducing the Deficits of Political Parties Competitiveness in the Member States of the African Union

One of the impediments to healthy political party development in Africa was the practice of dominant parties setting up satellite opposition parties with little prospect of growth or achievement of national political power.

---

[61]   Including Benin, Burkina Faso, Cape Verde, Ghana (only free media), Malawi, Mauritius (only free media), Mali, Morocco, Mozambique, Namibia, Niger, São Tomé and Principe, Seychelles, South Africa, and Tanzania.

[62]   Such or similar formulae are to be found in Benin, Mozambique, Namibia, Niger, South Africa and Tanzania.

Several of those political parties were established in Liberia during the Taylor Administration in Liberia. The dominant-party system was believed to resort to that practice instead of encouraging genuine party alliances or coalitions. The unfair advantage gained by incumbent ruling parties prevents fair competition between parties contesting elections. Because of the unusual ethnic distribution of the electorate in some countries, as Namibia, public funding of parties benefited the incumbent most and opposition parties got little help.

The advent of detailed scrutiny of election organization and conduct by local and international election observation groups no doubt had a positive effect on election transparency, but the conduct of some of the crucial election processes such as compiling the register of voters and the delimitation of the boundaries of electoral districts were not often observed by international observers. Furthermore, too frequently sensitive computer processes with respect to collation, tallying and posting of final election results were hidden from open scrutiny of party agents and observers, domestic and international. Often such incidents were merely labeled as lack of transparency but the damage to the overall election was not assessed and quantified to see if such action rendered the election not credible. As time goes by and elections continue to undergo closer scrutiny, it should be possible to grade processes that were hidden from observation and to arrive at a credible conclusion that the lack of transparency rendered an election to be not credible. Perhaps, as some stakeholders opined from time to time, there was an urgent need for EMBs' field staff to be subjected to more rigorous training, before their electoral performance was put under the microscope. Nevertheless, there should be greater gains to be seen from the almost countless election observations that visited the continent each year during the period under review.[63] There needed to be a concerted effort by EMBs to review and implement recommendations made by observer missions, so that the same criticisms did not recur time and time again.[64]

---

[63]   The OAU-AU since1992 mounted approximately 150 observation missions and there have been many from the SADC and ECOWAS regions, as well as international and domestic observer teams to elections all over the continent.

[64]   The DEAU of the AU has a program of assistance to EMBs aimed at helping them to implement the recommendations made by African Union election observation reports.

Some stakeholders had singled out political party financing as an issue that would militate against democratization and particularly elections. The reasoning was that party financing had the potential to corrupt political institutions based on political appointments. Political patronage, flowing from 'money politics', had the potential to lead to poor governance. The other troublesome aspect of parties' impact on democratic development in the Union was the frequency of unstable leadership succession in the Union. As was seen in Kenya in 2007, Zimbabwe in 2008, South Africa in 2008 and Guinea in 2008, except perhaps for Guinea, these succession crises were largely party-driven. These succession issues had to be taken seriously as they frequently lead to open conflict.

There was a clear case for much greater education in political party governance, particularly the rules relating to leadership succession. The organization and management of political parties needed strengthening particularly to ensure improved transparency, accountability and effectiveness. Measures to drastically curb incumbency abuses should be urgently put in place. In this regard, either party regulations or codes of conduct along the lines of incumbency rules adopted by the Indian Elections Commission may provide a useful example.

Chapter VIII

Electoral Campaign in the African Union

Introduction

The quality of electoral campaigns in the African Union varies considerably, although most countries need to strengthen significant aspects of political parties' and candidates' campaign. In general, since the retreat of the one-party system from the1990s, the qualitative improvement of electoral campaign in the Union has been considerable. This can be seen from the statements of stakeholders, and election observers, domestic and international, as well as reports of EMBS. The deficits in this area of election organization during the period under review were frequently found in ill-defined campaign period, failure to follow codes of conduct for political parties, abuse of incumbency, violence and intimidation, inadequate campaign finance regulations, and uneven access to the publicly owned media.

Some of these deficits should have been tackled during the first decade of this century, but they were not. The abuse of incumbency with regard to improper uses of public resources for party political campaign purposes was a widely acknowledged practice throughout the Member States of the AU and made the issue a prime one for action from the centre through seminars and a special code of conduct for governments and ruling parties. Similarly, the AUC should have done more to advance the cause of fair access to the publicly owned media by opposition parties and candidates contesting elections in Member States during the decade, since this campaign deficit was widely complained of in Member States throughout the AU.

Campaign Period

The campaign period was not always clearly defined and this adversely affected the accurate declaration of campaign expenses where campaign expenses were required to be declared. It also had the potential to affect the sanctions regime for early campaigning by candidates or political parties, because of the lack of a definite time frame for opening of the campaign period. A number of Member States of the Union like Cameroon and Uganda did provide for a stipulated period for election campaign. In Cameroon the campaign period stipulated in the law was 15 days, but it was not strictly enforced and so election campaign usually began before the designated period. On the other hand, opposition parties in Cameroon usually complained that they were constrained to begin campaigning late in the period because of late disbursement of public funding for political parties. During the presidential campaign in Cameroon in 2004, for example, the ruling party, the Cameroon People's Democratic Movement (CPDM) began campaigning several weeks before the official campaign period, while other parties which had to depend on state funding did not receive such funding until the end of the campaign period. As a consequence of the lack of a level playing field in this regard, stakeholders called for the electoral law to be reformed to allow clear rules on when campaigning should be allowed.

When multiparty system was reintroduced into Uganda in 2005, the election campaign period was limited to 61 days. The Government had promised to enact all election related legislation six months before the elections were held. Instead political parties became legal on 21 November 2005[65] and elections were held 23 February 2006. The ruling party, the National Resistance Movement-Organization (NRM-O), relied on the existing structures of the Movement system which remained active throughout the campaign. The new parties were disadvantaged by the shortened campaign period. Moreover, the Electoral Commission issued a directive which restricted parties and candidates to campaigning between the hours of 7a.m. and 6 p.m. The restricted campaign hours were strictly enforced against opposition parties resulting in the use of teargas where

---

[65] The date when the Political Parties and Organisations Act was gazetted.

the opposition rallies did not disperse immediately at 6 p.m., but were not rigidly adhered to the same extent against rallies by the ruling party.

In Liberia in 2005, several parties were fined by the Electoral Commission for breach of the rules and code of conduct by campaigning before the commencement of the campaign period.

Nature of Political Campaigns in the Member States of the African Union

Political campaigns in the Member States of the Union differed in style and content in the various regions of the continent and although there may be varying degrees of restrictions on campaign rallies, stakeholders began reporting gradual improvement in quality of campaigns. In South Africa, for instance, election observers and political parties recorded the disappearance of 'no go areas' which featured prominently in the 1994 campaign. With the exception of Zimbabwe, the African Union election observer missions, and supported by international election observers, reported relatively peaceful electoral campaigns in some 8, including run-off, elections in 2008.[66] Frequently, the main issues surrounding election campaigns in the Union were with respect to conduct of political parties, including incumbency, and campaign financing, the media and intimidation and violence. The practice whereby parties published party manifestos in good time was growing, but was not done consistently, and in some cases, as in the Cameroon presidential campaign 2004, the party manifestos did not focus on party policies. The failure to issue party manifestos in a timely manner, or at all, led many election campaigns to deteriorate into personally attacks and 'hate' campaigns. In fact, however, most national election campaigns in the Union were characterized by colourful and lively campaign slogans, posters, motorcades, door-to-door canvasses for votes, and party-sponsored concerts. Public party rallies and meetings were usually the main visible feature of campaigns, but in a number of countries the requirement of police permits was abused by delaying, re-routing transportation to such meetings, or refusing permit applications, usually by opposition parties. The record of issuance of police

---

[66] Comoros (Anjouan, including run-off election), Angola, Rwanda, Swaziland, Guinea Bissau, Zambia, and Ghana, (including run-off election).

permits to opposition to hold election campaign rallies, for example, in Rwanda, Uganda, Zanzibar (Tanzania), Zimbabwe, did not do the Union proud. In contrast, the approach to permit for election rallies in Sierra Leone, where the EMB played a more prominent role in determining the outcome of a permit application, was a positive approach in the right direction. Also, despite the huge concern of stakeholders with election organizations in Cameroon, election observers to the 2004 presidential election noted some positive developments of the display of tolerance. It was recorded by one observer that supporters of the opposition, Social Democratic Front (SDF), visited rallies of the ruling Cameron People's Democratic Movement (CPDM) without incident. It was also observed that multiple booking of rally venues was resolved amicably by the parties.

Code of Conduct/Incumbency

There was a growing awareness among national EMBs that codes of conduct for political parties during election campaigns was useful in keeping parties, their candidates and supporters in line with good conduct at campaign rallies and elsewhere during the campaign. While South Africa had success in getting parties to adhere to the Code of Conduct, the same could not be said for some other countries. For example, the Electoral Commission of Uganda issued Campaign Guidelines for Presidential Elections 2006, but they were not respected by the candidates and parties who resorted to personal attacks and defamatory language. One observer group's report noted the Ugandan Police Force placed an advertisement on television in which words of the presidential candidate of the Forum for Democratic Change (FDC) were taken out of context and juxtaposed with images of burning cars . . . The view was that the advertisement could be construed by some as an incitement to violence. An example drawn from South Africa during the campaign for the 1999 elections demonstrated the willingness to abide by party Code of Conduct. The leader of the United Democratic Movement (UDM) Bantu Holomisa was prevented from campaigning at the University of Western Cape by African National Congress' (ANC's) supporters. The ANC subsequently apologized to the UDM for the behaviour of their supporters.

Some countries of the Union had codes of conduct for political parties that worked, for example, Lesotho, Liberia, Kenya (for the 2002 elections), and South Africa, among many others. On the other hand, Cameroon for the 2004 presidential elections had no party code of conduct.

Incumbency deals with the governing party and government of the day. Without regulations or binding code of conduct there is the likelihood that the advantages of incumbency would be abused. The indistinguishable line between party and government property was meant to be removed when the one-party system was abolished in many Member States of the Union in the 1990s. However, the rise of the dominant-party system and other ruling parties sought to revive the close link between the government and ruling party and put an end to the decoupling of the party and state that took place in the 1990s.

Incumbency abuse took many forms, such as the use of public resources for party campaign purposes, improper use of Treasury funds, government vehicles, government houses by party officials, civil servants, and public buildings as party offices. Frequently, it was the ruling party's control of the public media that created the uneven playing field syndrome for candidates and political parties. There were few exceptions, but in the main the publicly owned media leaned heavily in favour of the ruling party of the day.

Incumbency can and should be regulated either by law or codes of conduct in order to achieve a level playing field. There was an urgent need for the incidence of abuse of incumbency to be curbed with respect to election campaigning. The Elections Commission of India, for example, issued stiff rules governing incumbency whereby ruling parties and ministers were forbidden to make use of public resources and property for campaign purposes. The use of government guesthouses, for example, should be open to opposition candidates in appropriates circumstances, and government ministers were not allowed to make announcement of new projects within the campaign period, and combine public duties with campaign activities, thus avoiding the use of public vehicles for campaign purposes.

Curbs on the abuse of incumbency were not well established in the Member States of the African Union. For example, in Cameroon during the campaign for the 2004 presidential elections, election observers reported that many civil servants were seen campaigning for the ruling CPDM and using government vehicles to do so. The CPDM posters were seen in many public buildings, and civil servants were seen wearing the ruling party's T-shirts, dresses and scarves. In Uganda where there was an unclear stipulation in the Presidential Elections Act 2005,[67] there was widespread use of public resources by the presidential and other candidates of the ruling party. The evidence clearly showed that the incumbent would enjoy certain advantages by design. Indeed, the Deputy Prime Minister and Minister of the Public Service on 2 January 2006 laid before Parliament, pursuant to the Act, the entitlements of the President which were: 'The usual transport facilities provided to the President, the usual security detail facilities provided to the President, the usual personal staff and their facilities attached to the President, the usual information and communication facilities attached to the President'. Many stakeholders were confused by the vagueness of the language and the fact that few persons knew what the usual facilities of transport, security, personal staff, information or communication facilities of the President were, and so those things were incapable of being monitored in a credible manner. Much needed to be done to harmonize incumbency rules relating to ruling political parties and incumbent candidates for the presidency in Member States across the Union.

Campaign Financing

Campaign financing is a controversial issue in the Member States of the Union. A number of the Member States, including Cameroon,

---

[67] Presidential Elections Act, [16 of 2005] states that: (1) Except as authorized under this Act, or otherwise authorized by law, no candidate shall use Government resources for the purpose of campaigning for election, (2) Notwithstanding subsection (1), a candidate who holds the office of President, may continue to use government facilities during the campaign, but shall only use those Government facilities which are ordinarily attached to and utilized by the holder of that office. (3) For the purposes of subsection (2), the Minister responsible for public service shall lay before Parliament a statement of those Government facilities which are attached to and utilized by the President.

Mozambique, Namibia, Seychelles, and South Africa, have limited form of public financing of political campaigns. Some States like Botswana and Liberia do not offer public financing of election campaigns. In 2005, Liberia introduced a relatively tight regulatory system of campaign financing centred on reporting and disclosure of contributions. The requirements proved too much for some parties and candidates. Breaches of the requirements were not strictly enforced. In Botswana during the lead up to the 2004 general elections, stakeholders clamoured for the introduction of public financing, but the ruling party, the Botswana Democratic Party (BDP) would have none of it. Public financing has often been welcomed by stakeholders whenever introduced, but criticized on the grounds of its scope due to the formula followed, as in Mozambique, Namibia, and South Africa, or on grounds of poor implementation, as in Cameroon.

Despite the controversial nature of public financing of political parties and electoral campaigns on philosophical grounds, in the view of some critics, and on the principle that tax payers' money should not be used to fund political parties, in the view of others, there is a strong case put forward by small political parties in many Member States in the Union for campaign funding (as distinct from general funding of political parties). The case for campaign financing by tax payers can be made out on grounds of creating a level playing field for parties and candidates during election campaigns. It could create an incentive for incumbents to reduce their reliance on improper use of public resources, and could enhance the accountability and transparency in funding election campaigns. Moreover, in the context of the Union public funding of election campaigns of parties and candidates (including independent candidates, where permitted by the law) would assist the competitive nature of democratic elections.

Although some election researchers rightly assert that not much is known about the details of money in political parties or election campaigns,[68] certain situations were well known about ruling parties' tendency to use improperly public property and their ability to entice private funding through patronage to the exclusion of opposition parties. There had

---

[68]   See for example, *Money in Politics: A Study of Party Practices in 22 Countries* 2005 ed. Shari Bryan & Denis Baer. National Democratic Institute for International Affairs

been persistent complaints by small struggling opposition parties in countries as far separated geographically as Sierra Leone and Malawi, and Liberia and Namibia, about the inability to survive and to find the deposit to contest national elections. A large number of political parties, big and small suffered from weak party structures and lack of internal democracy which did not enable them to offer sound accountability and good transparency practices. It cannot be ruled out that the fuzziness of the records and accounts of some parties existed more by design with intent to hide illegal contributions or improper use of public resources. Unverified reports suggested that the proceeds of illegal drug trafficking had been finding influence and could infiltrate the electoral systems of small States in West Africa. Proper disclosure of contributions to parties and or candidates should arrest the spread of any such practice.

The potential for a preponderance of electoral campaigns that were free from 'money politics' was good, and would be enhanced through the spread of public financing, if done on an equitable basis. This would have a profoundly positive impact on the competitive quality of election campaigns. The EMBs should be given a large role in monitoring and ensuring compliance with campaign finance regulations.

The Media and Electoral Campaign in the Member States of the African Union

The media played a key role in the election campaigns of political parties and candidates. Media houses and journalists covering election campaigns were expected to conform to basic journalistic rules of objective and factual reporting. Many media houses and individual journalists managed to stay in line, but others usually from the public media found it difficult to tow a non-partisan line. In order to facilitate journalists and media houses in reporting on election developments and on the campaign of parties and individual candidates, they were usually invited to enter into voluntary codes of conduct. Often the EMBs and the relevant ministry or department of government get together and agree on the contents of a code of conduct for particular elections where the law did not make specific provisions for such contingencies. In some jurisdictions, journalists who worked with privately owned media would develop their own voluntary code on how to report on election campaigns. The media was multifaceted and elections in a given country may be covered by each arm of the media. There may be the customary electronic media, that is, television and radio, or more recently the Internet or text messaging using mobile phone. The print media, which may also be published in electronic form on the Internet, continued to play a prominent role in election campaigns. These various arms of the media, in terms of ownership and control, may be either privately or publicly owned.

Concern was often voiced about the inability of the publicly owned media to operate outside of the influence of the ruling party or government of the day. It was the practice for the EMBs concerned to seek to ensure that not only a level playing field be achieved and maintained throughout the campaign, but that candidates and parties kept within the code of conduct (if any) and avoid 'hate speeches' at rallies and meetings. The issue of 'hate speeches' had been discussed recently in Kenya and Zimbabwe in the context of post election violence in 2007 & 2008 respectively and the questions ask as to the extent to which, if at all, the media reporting contributed to the eruption of violence in those two situations.

One significant issue surrounding the public media was that of access for opposition parties and candidates. Some countries like South Africa and Malawi used formulae such as 'equitable', or 'equal' free time on the publicly owned electronic media, and an equivalent formula for free column of advertisement in the print media. Where the legislation was silent, the practice was for the EMBs to discuss the issue with the media houses and or the ministry concerned to achieve detailed programme of allocation of free broadcast, where that was allowed, and non-discriminatory charges for political advertisement, or broadcasts. Similarly, privately owned media houses which cover election campaigns, or carry election broadcasts should not be allowed to charge discriminatory rates, or to give less prominent print exposure for equal rates to contesting candidates.

Media Freedom

Media freedom cannot be taken for granted in the Member States of the Union. There have been reports of media houses that supported, or were believed to be sympathetic to the opposition parties being harassed and or closed down in Zimbabwe. In Cameroon private newspapers, radio and television stations were subject to licensing arrangements. Licensing by itself was not necessarily inconsistent with free media, but stakeholders in Cameroon reported that licensing arrangements in that country were used by the Government to inhibit the broadcast media. The privately owned radio and television were not awarded actual licence in the first instance; instead they were given approval to broadcast pending approval of their application. In such circumstance, they were obviously not free to broadcast as they would otherwise do. Thus when two independent television channels broadcast political debates criticizing the Government in the run up to 2004 presidential election, they were promptly closed down for a period. In a similar vein, an FM station was closed after it aired views that were critical of Government.

Criminal libel laws were used in some Union Member States, for example, Cameroon and Uganda, to muzzle the critics of the incumbent regime.

In Botswana, stakeholders complained strongly about the role played by the Minister of Telecommunications, Science and Technology, who was accused of restricting the public media from covering political news, particularly major opposition activities. The political parties generally were unimpressed with the manner in which the public media covered their campaigns.

Stakeholders in South Africa generally expressed satisfaction with the structures and their performance in election campaigns since apartheid was vanquished at the 1994 elections. In the 1999 elections parties generally followed the Code of Conduct for Political Parties, and the limited number of breaches of the Code of Conduct was promptly reported to the relevant Independent Electoral Commission's Party Liaison Committee or the Conflict Management Committee, as the case may be. There was a Broadcasting Media Act of 1999 which was aimed at establishing and developing a broadcasting policy in South Africa. An Independent Broadcasting Authority Act was passed in 1993 and it established the Independent Broadcasting Authority (IBA). The Authority was mandated to ensure that all political parties were treated equitably by the electronic media during the election period. The IBA was made accountable to the South African public. The IBA issued Regulations and Guidelines in 1999 which covered broadcasters in their coverage of elections. Party broadcasts on radio, as well as free political advertisement and editorial matters were covered by the Guidelines. Campaigning was not allowed 48 hours prior to the opening of the polls. Party election broadcasts were strictly regulated, and the allocation of time was largely controlled by each party's share of the votes in the previous election and its number of candidates nationally and in each province. The party broadcasts were restricted to two minutes and had to be consistent with the Independent Electoral Commission's Code of Conduct. The IBA aimed to achieve equitable treatment of political parties through:

- The monitoring and regulation of election coverage;
- Assessment and adjudication of complaints by the public and political parties of editorial coverage of the election campaign;
- Implementation of a procedure to allocate party election broadcasts equitably to political parties on public service radio stations throughout the country and on any other stations offering to run them; and
- Implementation and regulation of a system to ensure that all political parties had a fair opportunity to book political advertisement on the radio during the campaign period.

Although not all the Guidelines of the IBA were followed,[69] for the most part they were followed in the 1999 elections and it set a good example of clear and concise rules governing the allocation of equitable access to the media. That positive media treatment of contesting parties was built upon in the 2004 elections. The Independent Communications Authority of South Africa (ICASA) which oversees the enforcement of the Independent Broadcasting Authority Act of 1993 issued regulations in 2003 reaffirming the need for broadcasters to ensure the political parties had the opportunity to present their views and that all political parties should be treated equitably.

---

[69] There were credible reports of a number of party leaders, including the Democratic Party leader, transmitted appeals for votes during the period of 48 hours prior to the opening of the polls.

Intimidation and Violence during Electoral Campaigns in the Member States of the African Union

The African Union Members States in the main had a long and uncomfortable past with intimidation and violence touching election organization and conduct. There had been no single factor leading either to pre-election, polling, or post-election intimidation and violence. However, a combination of factors can be identified as the frequent causes of pre-polling intimidation and violence. One such factor had been the unsatisfactory manner in compiling the voters' register, or the issuance of voter's card to voters. Incomplete registration of voters through political consideration or incompetence of registration officials led to intimidation and violence, usually isolated incidents of violence, in many countries, for example, in Lesotho, Liberia, Nigeria, Kenya, and Zimbabwe. Occasionally, registration of candidates or parties to contest elections triggers considerable intimidation and violence, as occurred in Uganda in 1980 and Kenya in 1992. The majority of cases of intimidation and violence in pre-poll scenario occurs during this period and was carried out by party supporters, often in breach of party code of conduct.

The nature of polling day violence usually revolved around breach of polling station security by party activists, sometimes with the connivance of the security personnel at or in the vicinity of the station. An example of intimidation on polling was exhibited in Zanzibar, Tanzania, in 2000, when many polling stations were disrupted by shortage of ballot papers and activists, reportedly from the then ruling party.

Post-election violence can be triggered by failure to announce the polling results or through the failure of the losers to accept the results of the election, or fear that the rightful winners were cheated of victory. Whatever the reasons for not accepting national elections results, be it presidential or legislative, the consequences could be disastrous as was seen in Kenya in 2007-08. The violence was triggered when, in what was seen as a very close presidential race, the Kenyan Electoral Commission, handled the announcement of the election results poorly and without much transparency. The results were perceived as not credible by the opposition and the long simmering ethnic questions came into play. The upshot was national conflagration of looting, killings along ethnic lines, and widespread displacement of people. In a curious way the issue of whether or not the election was stolen soon receded into the background, and was replaced by issues which needed immediate resolution, as stopping the killing of innocent people and saving a nation on the brink from collapse.[70] International mediation involving a former United Nations Secretary General, Kofi Annan, intervened and succeeded in brokering agreement between the incumbent president who was declared the winner of the disputed election and the opposition, and a government of National Unity between the losers and the winners was formed.

As if the African Union had not had enough of disputed elections in 2007, the Zimbabwe experience came while the Kenyan disaster was still to be finally disposed of. In March 2008, Zimbabwe held general elections. The opposition presidential candidate claimed to have won absolute majority, that is, 50 % of the votes plus 1 vote, but that was not confirmed by the Zimbabwean Electoral Commission. The Commission however delayed the publication of the presidential election results and that put the veracity of the results in doubt. When the results were finally released, the incumbent president received fewer votes than the opposition candidate, but the opposition candidate did not achieve the absolute majority to win on the first round of voting. The Commission then announced that the run-off presidential election would be held in June 2008. After refusing to contest the run-off election initially, the opposition candidate, Morgan Tsvangirai, decided to contest the run-off election. Soon, the ruling party under the leadership of the incumbent President, Robert Mugabe, unleashed a murderous campaign of intimidation, beatings, detention (including of the opposition candidate and senior officers of his party), abductions (even of civil society officials), and killing of hundreds of opposition supporters. The opposition presidential candidate withdrew from the run-off election which went to the vote and the incumbent won without any opposition. The extraordinary spectacle of violence against the opposition was condemned by stakeholders locally and international

---

[70]   See Annex (Discourse on Kenya for a fuller account). A similar incident occurred in Guyana in 1997 when a disputed election provoked massive rioting and killings. The issue had to be settled by regional efforts which included auditing the election results and cutting short the term of the victorious party.

observers. The election was deemed to be farcical and not credible by local and international observers.[71]

The events in Kenya in 2007 and Zimbabwe in 2008 were not typical of elections in the Union. There were some seven elections in 2008 after Zimbabwe's, including Angola, Rwanda, Zambia and Ghana, which went off smoothly. On the other hand, there has been unacceptable harassment of opposition candidates in the presidential and parliamentary elections in Uganda in 2006 which limited their ability to campaign freely.

The South African experience since multiparty democratic elections were introduced in 1994 has been encouraging. The 1999 national elections in that country showed considerable improvement in the reduction compared to 1994, and the 2004 and 2009 elections showed further reduction in the number of complaints of intimidation and violence.[72]

The EMBs of the Member States of the African Union, along with political parties, should embark upon a drive to clean up election campaigns by strengthening mechanisms as inter-party liaison committees and codes of conduct, including the rules relating to incumbency. Subtle forms of intimidation of the kind reported in Cameroon during the 2004 presidential elections that, if certain groups did not produce a 'high score' in their areas for the ruling party, members of the group would be deported, should be avoided at campaign rallies.

---

[71] See Annex (Discourse on Zimbabwe) for more on Zimbabwe.
[72] See EISA observer mission report on the 2004 elections in South Africa. P.15-17.

Chapter IX

Civil Society Organizations' Potential to Contribute to Democratic Elections in the African Union

Introduction

There is growing recognition internationally of the potential of civil society organizations (CSOs) to contribute positively to free and fair multiparty democratic elections. There are lacunae to be filled in many new and emerging democracies where the election management bodies are either unable or unwilling to offer a comprehensive election service in certain areas, for example, civic and voter education or monitoring the registration of voters and polling processes. Such lacunae become more discernible when democratic elections are held in transitional circumstances such as post-conflict jurisdictions as in Liberia 2005, or in Nigeria after military rule in 1998/99 and 2003 at national level, in the African Union.

During the first decade of the 21st Century CSOs in Member States of the AU made measurable contributions to democratic elections overall. However, their contribution was not only unevenly spread among Member States, but also in the five regions of the AU where North Africa and many States in East Africa (Eritrea, Ethiopia, Somalia, Sudan, Uganda, Rwanda and Madagascar) had imposed restrictions on the activities of CSOs in election matters. While the North and East Africa Regions are singled out here, there were many other individual Member States from other Regions that were not welcoming to CSOs with respect to CSOs working in the field of elections in the first decade of 21st Century, for example, Gambia, Niger, Swaziland, and Zimbabwe.

Nature of Civil Society Organizations

The influence of civil society organizations (CSOs) was felt in multiparty elections across the world during the first decade of he 21st Century. The international emphasis on free and fair elections since the demise of the cold war in the 1990s triggered the need to scrutinize all aspects of election organization with a view to giving each general or presidential election 'a clean bill of health.' CSOs have the ability to operate and survive in unfavourable environment such as apartheid South Africa, war-torn Liberia or in the military regime in Nigeria during the 1990s. They thrive in Western Europe and North America, are emerging in Eastern Europe and other new democracies, and show signs of growth even in failed States. They may be community-based, nationally—regionally—or internationally based. Some CSOs are dedicated to a particular election or to elections generally, or may cover several fields of activities.

The nature and scope of CSOs have attracted the attention of researchers in several countries and regions of the world. Perhaps the most comprehensive attempt to study the structure and scope of CSOs to date has been undertaken by the Johns Hopkins Comparative Non-profit Sector Project,[73] but there are other studies that focus on a particular region or a particular country. These studies are useful in analyzing the nature, structure and scope of CSOs generally. They do not throw much light on the qualitative influence of CSOs on election organization.

The role of CSOs in poverty alleviation, health, particularly HIV/AIDS, and major natural disasters has been making internal headlines frequently; less frequent and even less prominent headlines are given to the role of CSOs in multiparty election organization. However, CSOs are known to be involved in many aspects of elections in many jurisdictions, especially in voter and civic education, election observation, conflict resolution and gender issues.

The diversity of CSOs is pronounced. They include faith-based organizations, environmental groups, professional bodies, self-help

---

[73] See Global Civil Society, An Overview: Lester M. Salamon, S. Wojciech Sokolowski and Regina List. The Johns Hopkins University, Institute for Policy Studies, Center for Civil Society Studies.

groups, co-operatives, sport clubs, social clubs, human rights bodies and community development entities. Sometimes many of these bodies, though of different interests, bond together in networks to further a particular goal, such as, for example, assisting the achievement of free and fair elections.

The distinguishing feature of CSOs is the fact that they form a sector locally, regionally or internationally, that is separate and a part from the institution of the family, the government or the market, that is to say, the commercial sector. It is arguable whether bodies which lay claim to CSOs status in centrally planned economies, for example China and Vietnam, or to an extent Russia, and which have the support of government, are truly CSOs. However CSOs in many jurisdictions have to operate within rules laid down by the legislature.

Another feature of CSOs is that they are voluntary, in that persons are free to join. Notwithstanding the freedom of action by individuals to join CSOs, the strong religious impulses that lie behind some religious organizations (sects) do raise questions about the true voluntary nature of a few CSOs.

The criterion of non-profit or charitable status enjoyed by CSOs distinguishes them from the commercial sector. This does not mean that the revenues earned by CSOs are insignificant and it should not mask the important employment opportunities created by CSOs.

The diversity of CSOs is so great that it almost defies proper functional classification, particularly the community-based ones. Several broad classifications have been attempted, none of which claims to be exhaustive. For example, in dealing with the issue of terminology and CSOs, Annette Zimmer, citing Sachbe's classification, sets out four types, namely, membership organizations, interest organizations, service organizations, and support organizations.[74] The Johns Hopkins Comparative Non-Profit Sector Project preferred to distinguish five general categories, namely,

---

[74]   Annette Zimmer, Civil Society Organisations in Central and Eastern European Countries: Introduction and Terminology in "Future of Civil Society", A. Zimmer & E. Priller (Eds.) VS Verlag 2004.

organizations with an institutional form and structure; private organizations separate from the state machinery; entities that do not distribute profits; independent self-governing entities; and that they are voluntary. While these characteristics are the general attributes of CSOs, single-purpose CSOs, like those created by small groups of individuals to monitor or observe a particular election would not exhibit all these features, as their whole existence is functional.

The term civil society organization (CSOs) is used to embrace a variety of entities such as non-governmental organizations (NGOs), non-profit organizations (NPOs), and community-based organizations (CBOs). The term CSO is commonly understood to be wider than NGOs and CBOs. Local groups who get together to defend their rights to land, or their environment may not necessarily be classified as NGOs or even as CBOs. In China, the term civil society attracts differences in interpretation rather than in the scope of the entities covered by use of the term. The term is sometimes used to mean civilized society, or civic society or mass society. If used to mean mass society, it may be quickly translated to have political overtures, that is, an association with grassroots (people's) power, which may be perceived as potential opposition to the state. The interpretation of civil society as civic society also carries a concept of mild emphasis on the value of political involvement by the citizens. The preferred interpretation of civil society in China is that it implies greater respect for individual and human rights and the rule of law.

Facilitation of the Growth of CSOs.

The goal of CSOs is to occupy the fourth sector, that is to say, outside of the family, government and the profit-making activities (the market). CSOs will therefore thrive best in circumstances that create the right environment for their establishment and growth. In general terms, the growth of CSOs in the last decade and a half is due to several factors including the ability of the non-profit sector to provide a measure of services. The persistent domination of emerging democratic societies by the state and state agencies and the need to achieve a fairer society than that fostered by the market system has encouraged the growth of CSOs. The challenge to improve governance, in part through the promotion of free and fair multiparty elections has also opened up space for CSOs to complement existing inadequate democratic institutions. In order for CSOs to thrive and sustain themselves, there must be a framework of rules (constitutional rules) which guarantees the rights of individuals to freely associate and allows any resultant associations to create relationships with the state, individuals and legal persons. In some jurisdictions, a status conferred by law on CSOs, through registration or otherwise, has worked positively, but this is not always so.

The ability of small single-purpose (particularly those that are community-based) CSOs to sustain themselves depends on good management and adequate human and financial resources. Many CSOs encountered, for example in Liberia and Nigeria, were formed to monitor and observe elections and lacked good management, and were inadequately resourced to achieve their stated goals. Moreover, as the number of CSOs operating in the field of elections increased in a given community, the incidence of conflicts of interests becomes greater. For instance, the cases of individuals who are political functionaries or staff members of election management bodies (EMBs) forming CSOs to undertake voter education and other election related activities are many. These developments are likely to have a negative effect on CSOs' influence in the area of election organization in a particular community.

Creating a framework for their registration and operation is sometimes met with negative response from CSOs, if proper and timely consultation does not take place before the implementation of such framework. This situation can become even more controversial where the motive for the new or amended framework for CSOs operation is either unclear or aimed at curbing the freedom of operations. Thus in late 2005, when a Bill called "Amendments to Several Laws of the Russian Federation" required all CSOs to be registered; there were protests and street demonstrations against the Bill. A link was made between the introduction of the Bill in the Russian Parliament and remarks made by then Russian President, Vladimir Putin, to human rights activists that he would not tolerate foreign money being used to finance the political activities of non-governmental organizations.[75] There were some reports in Moscow that the Ukraine's

---

[75]   See article by Anatoly Medetsky in Moscow Times, 9 November 2005.

Orange Revolution and Georgia's Rose Revolution were financed by Western countries through NGOs.

Whatever the real motives behind the Bill were, CSOs in Russia were in little doubt that it would have negative effects on their operations. The Bill would require all currently registered NGOs in Russia to reregister within one year with the Ministry of Justice.[76] The Bill would prevent international organizations from having representative or branch offices in Russia. These entities would have to register as local NGOs and be financially independent of their head offices. They would not be eligible for most sources of foreign funding. The Bill would prohibit anyone who is not a permanent resident of Russia from working with an NGO. It was believed that if the Bill were passed in its then current form many international human rights groups, including Human Rights Watch, think-tanks, foundations, social welfare and humanitarian aid organizations would be threatened with closure. One human rights official expressed the view that the Bill signified a new chapter in the government's crackdown on civil society institutions.[77]

In a similar vein, Human Rights Watch reported that on January 6 2009 Ethiopia's Parliament enacted new legislation on non-governmental organizations (NGOs) that criminalizes most human rights work in the country. The Charities and Societies Proclamation (NGO Law) according to the Ethiopian authorities is aimed at ensuring greater openness and financial probity on the party of nongovernmental organizations; but instead it, according to human rights and other NGO organizations, places severe restrictions on all human rights and governance-related work as to make most of such work impossible without running the risk of violating the Proclamation. The new law classified any civil society group that receives more than ten percent of its funding from abroad foreign, and is thus disqualified from doing any work that deals with human rights and governance and related subjects.

---

[76] There were 450,000 registered NGOs in Russia and many unregistered ones.

[77] Holly Cartner, Executive Director, Europe and Central Asia Human Rights Watch, Human Rights News, November 2005.

The facilitation environment for CSOs in China is evolving. As the founder of a CSO in China put it: 'In China you do things not because there is a legal channel to do them: you occupy the space before the government claims it, and the legal mechanisms all happen after the fact.'[78] However, another view of the Chinese CSOs' landscape was put forward by Professor Yu Hai. He suggested that if NGOs are unregistered, their status is precarious since they lack legitimacy and may face resource challenges. Where they are registered, according to Professor Hai, their activities are limited by government policy and they cannot advocate policy recommendations and organize their own activities.[79] Notwithstanding these differing points of view, Bentley pointed out that virtually all the organizations interviewed felt that their autonomy was adequate, in that they made their own decisions without outside influence.

Of particular relevance to this work were the views of the New Citizen Education and Research Center (NCERC) which promotes village democracy and autonomy, including election training and voter education. NCERC considered itself entirely autonomous, as it received no government funding and no direct affiliation with government. It is very important however to bear in mind that China has a great many CSOs with widely differing degrees of autonomy.[80] Hadi Soesastro expressed the view that civil society organizations in China had their own 'Chinese characteristics' in that they are half official and half non-official'. He concluded that state-led civil society was prevalent in China.[81]

The growing incidence of 'failed states' has added a new dimension to the creation and development of CSOs which have shown the ability to thrive in circumstances where government, the market, and even the family,

---

78 Xie Lihua, founder of Rural Women Knowing All, Interview in May 2002 cited in 'Survival Strategies for Civil Society Organizations in China' by Julia Bentley, in The International Journal of Not-for-Profit Law, January 2004.

79 Interview in May 2002 with Professor Hai cited in paper by Julia Bentley.

80 The Ministry of Civil Affairs put the registered organizations at 244,000, but unofficial estimates put the number as high as 870,000.

81 Hadi Soesastro was the Executive Director of the Centre for Strategic and International Studies in Jakarta, Indonesia, in a paper entitled *Civil Society and Development: The Missing Link.* 1999.

disintegrate. This was the situation in Liberia in 2004 after 14 years of civil wars. As Nathan Van Dusen pointed out, a system of governance that was accountable and elicited meaningful participation by citizens eluded Liberia for decades. He noted that civil society organizations had re-emerged from the trauma of the war years and got voter education messages out to constituents on a national scale, despite the lack of basic transportation and communications infrastructure throughout the country.[82] The civil society organizations, including faith-based ones, played a significant role in educating the voters with respect to the registration of voters and preparation for and the conduct of polling in 2005 in Liberia. This demonstrated that CSOs can survive and perform successfully in unfavourable environment, even in competitive politics involving former warlords and ex-combatants.

Regional Approach in Fostering CSOs.

Many regions and sub-regions of the world have embarked on a quest to foster an enhanced role for civil society organizations in the affairs of their respective regions or sub-regions as the case may be. The emphasis may vary, as some regions may highlight human rights, governance, development or resolution of conflicts, but the net result is renewed effort to create the atmosphere regionally in which CSOs can be established and thrive.

In the Southern African Development Community (SADC) considerable emphasis was placed on governance and specifically on free and fair elections. This had been a region of emerging democracies where the majority of the states had either an apartheid, a one-party or military regime where the influence of CSOs was limited. As Michael Davies[83] pointed out, democratization in the region was moving from a phase of transition to one of consolidation with some countries (Botswana, Malawi, Namibia, Mozambique and South Africa) of the region having

---

[82]   Nathan Van Dusen is a former programme manager for West Africa at IFES. His comments were contained in article entitled: "Liberian Elections Commission, Civil Society Rise to the challenge", September 2005

[83]   "The Role of the Media and Other Civil Society Organizations in Elections in SADC" *SADC Barometer Issue 4 2004 South African Institute of International Affairs.*

held at least three general elections since 1990. He noted that CSOs had an important role to play in the region, but that Zimbabwe was in political turmoil and that Swaziland was ruled by an absolute monarch. He opined that political space must be opened to allow civil society to make a contribution. According to Davies, the potential constraints to the growth of CSOs in SADC were: government regulations, such as the Private Voluntary Organization Act of Zimbabwe which gave the Government tight control over CSOs; government action in co-opting civil society leaders; and lack of funding.

In the Americas, the Inter-American Civil Society Partnership Initiative (the Initiative) was launched in 2005 designed to secure greater participation of CSOs in the activities of the Organization of American States (OAS). The aim of the Initiative was to:

- Build and improve the quality of channels of communication and exchange of information among the CSOs and the specialized OAS organs and agencies within the General Secretariat;
- Facilitate the formal interaction of CSOs with the political bodies of OAS, through organizing forums with CSOs on specific issues; and
- Strengthen civil society participation in the Summits of the Americas Process and engaging CSOs to monitor and implement Summit initiatives.

The Initiative served to institutionalize cooperation between the CSOs and the OAS and thereby expand and strengthen the network of civil society organizations throughout the Hemisphere.

In collaboration with the Open Society Institute, the Summits of the Americas Secretariat created a fund to promote and encourage civil society to make inputs in the agendas of Summits and contribute to policy-making within the Inter-American agenda. The fund initially amounted to US$140,000.00 to support projects that would be implemented by civil society organizations. A Selection Committee was set up to determine the dollar amount, not to exceed US$20,000.00, for each selected project. The fund would be used to support projects that civil societies developed in their respective specific fields which helped to monitor and implement Summit mandates.

In addition to the fund created under the Initiative, there were three other areas of action, namely:

- Production and dissemination of an updated manual for civil society participation;
- Support for ministerial meetings and civil society forums; and
- Maintaining and further developing the CSO Website.[84]

The facilitation and growth of CSOs in the Central and Eastern European region is enhanced by the expansion of the European Union to incorporate the countries in that region. The European Union places much emphasis on the role of CSOs in good governance in the development of democracy.[85] Organized civil society allows for civic engagement and enhanced participation of individuals in the development of the democratic process. Organized civil society is better able to occupy the space between government and the market and meet the growing needs and demands of citizens that government and the market cannot meet.

CSOs are being keenly observed in Central and Eastern Europe because of the late arrival of democracy to the countries of that region. The countries and societies of Central and Eastern Europe have been going through a period of rapid political and economic change, and CSOs are playing a role in the transformation process and proving to be important partners of the state and the market.

---

[84] Inter-American Civil Society Partnership Initiative, Summits of the Americas Secretariat, Organization of American States, 1889 F Street, N.W. Washington, DC 2006.

[85] See, for example, the European Commission's White Paper on 'European Governance' 2001.

The Africa Union's Initiative—Economic, Social and Cultural Council (ECOSOCC)

The ECOSOCC was established under the provisions of Articles 5 and 22 of the African Union's Constitutive Act. The Statute of ECOSOCC was adopted by the African Union in 2004. The ECOSOCC was designed to be an advisory organ of the African Union and composed of African social groups, professional groups, non-governmental organizations (NGOs) and cultural organizations. It is mandated to:

- Promote dialogue between all segments of African people on issues concerning the Continent and its future;
- Forge strong partnerships between governments and all segments of civil society, in particular, women, youth, children, the Diaspora, organized labour, the private sector, and professional groups;
- Promote the participation of African civil society in the implementation of the policies and programmes of the Union;
- Support policies and programmes that promote peace, security and stability and foster Continental development and integration;
- Promote and defend a culture of good governance, democratic principles and institutions, popular participation, human rights and social justice;
- Promote, advocate and defend gender equality; and
- Promote and strengthen the institutional, human and operational capacities of the African civil society.

The functions of the ECOSOCC are to:

- Contribute, through advice, to the effective translation of the objectives and policies of the Union into concrete programmes, as well as the evaluation of these programmes;
- Undertake studies that are recommended or deemed necessary by any other organ of the Union and submit recommendations accordingly;
- Carry out other studies as it deems necessary and submit recommendations as appropriate;

- Contribute to the promotion of popularization, popular participation, sharing of best practices and expertise, and to the realization of the vision and objectives of the Union;
- Contribute to the promotion of human rights, the rule of law, good governance, democratic principles, gender equality and child rights;
- Promote and support efforts of institutions engaged in review of the future of Africa and forge Pan-African values in order to enhance an African social model and way of life;
- Foster and consolidate partnership between the Union and CSOs through effective public enlightenment, mobilization and feedback on the activities of the Union; and
- Assume such other functions as may be assigned to it.

The composition of ECOSOCC—

The ECOSOCC's membership consisted of 150 CSOs each with a mandate for 4 years and may be elected once. The members were elected as follows:

- Two CSOs from each AU Member State following appropriate national consultations;
- Ten CSOs operating at regional level and 8 at continental level following an appropriate consultative process to determine modalities;
- Twenty CSOs elected from the African Diaspora as defined by the Executive Council, covering the various continents of the world following an appropriate process for determining modalities; and
- Six CSOs in ex-officio capacity, nominated by the Commission based on special considerations and appropriate criteria, in consultation with Member States.

Except for the CSOs nominated by the Commission, representation must ensure fifty percent gender equality and fifty percent of the representatives must be between the ages of 18 to 35.

The requirements of membership of ECOSOCC are the following:

- Be national, regional, continental or African Diaspora CSO, without restriction to undertake regional or international activities;
- Have objectives and principles that are consistent with the principles and objectives of the Union as set out in Articles 3 and 4 of the Constitutive Act;
- Be registered in a Member State of the Union and/or meet the conditions set out in Part I of the Criteria for Granting Observer Status to the AU applicable to non-governmental organizations;
- Show a minimum of three years proof of registration as either an African Diaspora CSO prior to the date of submission of application, including proof of operations for those years;
- Provide annual audit statements by an independent auditing company;
- Show proof that the ownership and management of the CSO is made of not less than fifty (50%) of Africans or peoples of African origin;
- Provide information on funding sources in the preceding three years;
- For regional and continental CSOs, show proof of activities that engage or are operative in at least three Member States of the Union;
- CSOs that discriminate on the basis of religion, gender, tribe, ethnic, racial or political basis shall be barred from representation to ECOSOCC; and
- Adherence to a Code of Ethics and Conduct for civil society organizations affiliated to or working with the Union.

The Structure of ECOSOCC—

The ECOSOCC consists of a General Assembly, a Standing Committee, Ten Sectoral Committees, a Credential Committee, and the Secretariat.

The ECOSOCC General Assembly is the highest decision and policy-making body and consists of all members of the Council. It meets once every two years in general session and could meet in extraordinary session when necessary. The main tasks of the General Assembly are the following, to:

- Elect the 18 members of the Standing Committee for a term of two years and oversee its work;
- Elect a Bureau composed of a Presiding Officer and five Presiding Officers for a term of office of two years on the basis of equitable geographical distribution and rotation, including one from the Diaspora;
- Prepare and submit advisory opinions and reports as appropriate;
- Submit proposals on the budget and activities of ECOSOCC;
- Approve and amend the Code of Ethics and Conduct for CSOs affiliated to or working with the Union; and
- Review the activities of ECOSOCC and propose appropriate actions and recommendations.

The Standing Committee of ECOSOCC runs the organization between sessions of the General Assembly and consists of the Presiding Officer and the other members of the Bureau, the Chairpersons of the ten Sectoral Cluster Committees and two representatives of the AU Commission. The main tasks of the Standing Committee are to:

- Coordinate the work of ECOSOCC;
- Prepare the meetings of the General Assembly;
- Follow-up on the implementation of the Code of Ethics and Conduct developed for civil society organizations affiliated to or working with the Union;
- Prepare and submit annual reports of ECOSOCC to the Assembly of the Union; and
- Determine the criteria and modalities for granting observer status to ECOSOCC in consultation with the AU Commission.

The ten Sectoral Cluster Committees are important to the operational mechanisms of the ECOSOCC in making inputs into the policies and programmes of the AU. The ten committees are:

- The Peace and Security which dealt with conflict anticipation, prevention, management and resolution, post-conflict reconstruction and peace building, prevention and combating of terrorism, use of child soldiers, drug trafficking, illicit proliferation of small arms and light weapons, and security reforms.

- Political Affairs—human rights, rule of law, democratic and constitutional rule, good governance, power sharing, electoral institutions, and humanitarian affairs and assistance;
- Infrastructure and energy;
- Social affairs and health;
- Trade and industry;
- Rural economy and agriculture;
- Economic affairs;
- Women and gender; and
- Cross-cutting programmes.

The other two important organs are the Credential Committee and the Secretariat which was provided by the African Citizens Directorate Organization (CIDO) within the office of the Chairperson of the African Union.

The first permanent General Assembly of ECOSOCC was held in Dar es Salaam in Tanzania. It was not an auspicious start as only 25 Member States were fully represented. One problem appeared to be the requirement that CSOs had to be funded by no more than 50 percent foreign funding, if they wished to be qualified for membership of the ECOSOCC. The inaugural three-day meeting was reported to be bogged down with bureaucratic chores, but some CSOs saw the development of the convening of the ECOSOCC as affording an opportunity to civil society to directly address the African Heads of State and Government without the diplomatic shackles of formalities that often were seen in regional bodies. The ECOSOCC was expected to have directed input into the policies and programming of the African Union. In launching the ECOSOCC in Tanzania in September 2008, the then Chairman of the AU, President Jakaya Kikwete, said that Africa had gone beyond the mere process of consultation to which other institutions adhered.

An Electoral Dimension

In many jurisdictions, CSOs which are involved in electoral activities are subjected to greater oversight by the government authorities and by political parties. Such CSOs are expected to contribute to election organization in a non-partisan manner. However, in some new and emerging democracies, neutrality and non-partisan operation is often construed as unsympathetic to the ruling authorities. In jurisdictions such as Russia's, there is suspicion of CSOs whose election activities are financed in part or wholly by funds from abroad. That perception gained ground as a result of the change of regimes in Georgia and Ukraine which was believed to have been influenced by NGOs funded by Western donors. There have been many examples however of CSOs being affiliated to a particular political party and therefore having a political agenda. Such CSOs must be carefully monitored to ensure that they do not prejudice the work of particular election management bodies and jeopardize the delivery of free and fair election.

The emergence of networking of CSOs delivering election services nationally, regionally and internationally, is aimed not only at strengthening the non-partisan qualities of CSOs in the governance and electoral fields, but at exchanging information on good practices in delivering election services.

Election administration is being strengthened by the creation of networks of professional administrators. In the United Kingdom, for example, there is the Association of Election Administrators (AEA) to which all senior electoral administrators belong. The AEA is concerned with the training and education of electoral administrators and provides a network of resources and expertise for its members. It organizes professional qualification courses for appointment to electoral-related position in local authorities in the United Kingdom. In the United States, the National Association of State Election Directors and the National Association of Secretaries of State provide forums for election managers to exchange information and views. The International Association of Clerks, Recorders, Election Officials and Treasurers (IACREOT) conducts regular electoral development courses for its members and organize annual trade fairs with respect to electoral-related equipment and supplies. The Electoral Council of Australia, a consultative forum which comprises the national and state electoral commissioners and chief electoral officers, and whose objective is to improve electoral administration in Australia, meets at regular intervals.

At the regional level, a growing number of electoral associations have been formed over the last decade to foster and sustain cooperation. In 1991 the Inter-American Union of Electoral Organizations (UNIORE) was established to promote cooperation between the electoral organizations and associations of the countries of Latin America and the Caribbean. The initial goal of promoting broad cooperation quickly deepened into the promotion of specific goals such as the promotion of free and fair elections, independent and non-partisan election administration, and transparent election procedures. Other election-related areas that attracted cooperation included the review and improvement of electoral laws and practices, promotion of citizens' participation in the electoral process, and establishing research centres. The region associations devoted much attention to the development of professional electoral officials, with a strong commitment to democratic elections.

The CSOs which sprung up in the form of regional associations devoted to furthering the cause of democratic elections included the Association of Central and Eastern European Electoral Officials (ACEEEO), established 1991; the Association of African Election Authorities (AAEA), established in 1997; the Association of Asian Election Authorities (AAEA), established in 1997; and the Association of the Caribbean Electoral Organizations (ACEO), established in 1998. Other bodies with the similar goals and were created around that time in Southern Africa, SADC Electoral Commissions' Forum, in Latin America, the Center for Electoral Promotion and Assistance, (CAPEL), and in the Pacific, the Pacific Islands, Australia, New Zealand Electoral Association network (PIANZEA). These CSOs are primarily interested in improving the quality of election administration through assistance to the respective national election management bodies. They provide an important channel for newly created EMBs within the region to receive support, ranging from capacity building to the borrowing or exchanging of election materials.

Global Election Network

The representatives of several regional electoral associations met at a conference in Ottawa in 1999 to launch the Global Electoral Organization (GEO) Network. The representatives were essentially election officers and the objectives of the conference were to:

- Create a link between the different association of election officials in a global network;
- Facilitate organizational collaboration between associations;
- Provide a forum in which to identify areas of need in electoral governance; and
- Identify a common agenda for all election management bodies worldwide.

A global network of regional election associations has considerable potential to facilitate the publication and dissemination of election materials and to promote the exchange of expertise and secondment of specialists in technical fields. Similarly, certain electoral issues, such as the principles of good practices in election management, the effectiveness of new technologies in election administration, legislative regimes for elections, and mechanisms for election dispute settlement, can be treated effectively at the global level.

Legal Status

Many CSOs in Member States of the AU did not realize their full potential during the first decade of the 21st Century to contribute to democratic elections because they had not met the legal requirement to operate properly as a civil society body. Civil society bodies may be clothed with a formal legal structure such as incorporation and or registration, or allowed to operate as informal voluntary groups of individuals. Where incorporation is required or is preferred, a flexible, comprehensive legal framework, which permits of a full democratic internal process consistent with the rule of law and the fulfillment of the objectives of the organization, should be developed.

The legal framework should embody the principal attributes of CSOs, namely, among other things, that they are voluntary autonomous bodies. They should enjoy freedom of expression and same capacities generally conferred on other legal persons within a particular jurisdiction, subject to the same obligations and sanctions arising under the administrative, civil and criminal law. The objectives of a CSO should be formulated to be pursued within the law, even if the main objective is to achieve a change in the law. A CSO should have the ability to engage in lawful business activities to support its non-profit-making goals. CSOs should be able to form networks and be members of federations in the pursuit of their objectives.

A general legal regime seeking to grapple with the issue of the creation of CSOs, should allow for the establishment of such bodies by any person natural or legal. Groups of persons or foreigners should not be excluded. The minimum number of persons required for setting up a membership-based CSO, or one with a legal personality, could be as low as two. A CSO should be capable of being created through a fund, trust of bequest.

The instrument which creates a CSO with legal personality should specify its name, objectives, powers, organs and stipulates the basic internal democratic procedures, such as quorum for meetings, frequency of meetings, and the manner in which decisions in general are taken, as well as particular decisions dealing with amendments, mergers or dissolution.

The procedure for a CSO to achieve legal personality should be clearly set out and objectively formulated. It should avoid conferring any discretionary or subjective judgments by the granting authority. This should not preclude relevant consideration, such as criminal conviction or bankruptcy, if sanctioned by the local law. There should be transparency and openness in the procedure which should be widely publicized. The administrative fees and charges for applying for and acquiring legal personality should have regard to local circumstances, and not be at such a level as to discourage applications. A CSO's application for legal personality should be considered objectively by an independent body within a stipulated time frame. The procedure should be such that an application can be refused only because of the applicant's failure to comply with the requirement of the law. A refusal of a CSO's application for legal personality should be given, and communicated to the applicant, within the stipulated period set out in the law and be accompanied by the reasons for the refusal. There should be an appeals procedure whereby aggrieved applicants can challenge the decision of the granting authority. Where legal personality is granted, provided that it continues to meet the requirements of the law, it should not be required to renew its legal personality. There should be a register of CSOs which are granted legal personality, and such register should be open to the public.[86] The effect of legal personality status is to create a separate legal persona distinct from the founders or members of the organization, so that liabilities and obligations of the CSO are not those of such founders or members. An organization should lose its legal persona only by a voluntary act by its members or management, or through unusual circumstances of prolonged inactivity, misconduct or bankruptcy.

In Russia, in late 2005 and early 2006, a Bill, called "Amendments to Several Laws of the Russian Federation" which was later signed into law by President Putin, caused quite a stir among civil society groups, largely because it was feared that the effect of the new law would require all non-governmental organizations to reregister and thus give more government control over such bodies. Supporters of the new law felt that it would prevent foreign money from aiding political activities of NGOs, but opponents feared that the new law would be used against NGOs that criticized the government's policy. Many commentators expressed fears that the new law would affect NGOs adversely in many ways, such as preventing foreign NGOs from setting up branches in Russia, pay increased taxes, subjected to tighter financial oversight, and generally subjected to greater administrative burden.[87]

The legal landscape of CSOs in China has also experienced changes recently in 2004. The Regulations on the Management of Foundations

---

[86] For information on the position in Europe, see Fundamental Principles on the Status of Non-governmental Organizations in Europe Strasburg, 13 November 2002.

[87] See, for example Human Rights News—Human Rights Watch, 22/11/05, and Anatoly Medetsky in Moscow Times, 9/11/05.

were adopted by the State Council of the People's Republic of China in 2004. These Regulations improved the legal environment for CSOs in so far as the restrictions on the registration of more than one organization addressing the same issue in a particular administrative region were removed. Also the 2004 Regulations allowed the representative offices of foreign foundations to register and given the same treatment as Chinese foundations. However these regulations continued to ensure that the Chinese Government authorities retained considerable oversight and control over CSOs through the requirement of sponsor organization for each one. The role of the sponsor organization is to support the registration of the foundation and any changes to its constitutive instrument. The sponsor organization also assists with the annual review of the foundation and ensures that its activities are consistent with the law and regulation. The sponsor organizations are approved by the State Council and the respective provincial tier of government. The Ministry of Civil Affairs (MOCA) is the authority responsible for the registration of foreign representative offices of foreign foundations, and often remains as the sponsor organization those foundations.[88]

Structure of Civil Society Organizations

The structure of CSOs which operated in the Member States of the AU during the period under review was diverse, and many of the informal bodies which fell within the category had only embryonic operational institutional organs. At the bottom end of the scale, there are CSOs that were created and operated by a single individual or members of one family, often with a loose governance structure. At a more formal level where CSOs were required to register or incorporate to achieve legal personality, a structure with certain minimum attributes was desirable or even necessary.

---

[88]   See report of the Congressional-Executive Commission on China 2004—civil society. Also see article on New Chinese Regulations on Foundations by Carl Minzner.

Governance

In general, small informal CSOs encountered in election activities in some Member States of AU, such as Liberia and Nigeria, did not have proper governance mechanisms. The governance structure of a CSO should include a management board (by whatever name called) with a stipulated number of directors who are appointed to serve for a specific period, but reappointment may be allowed. Members of the management board should be eligible to receive payment for their services, but there could be a limit on the number of directors who may be allowed to be compensated for their services. The legal framework within a given jurisdiction may require CSOs to include in their statute or constitutive instrument certain procedural rules to ensure minimum internal democracy in order to ensure good governance. In this regard, CSOs might be required to state in their statute that the management board should meet a stipulated number of times each year and that the quorum for meetings should be a specified number of members of the board. Certain decisions of the board might be identified for qualified majority, either 2/3 or ¾ of the members, because of their importance. Such decisions might include changes to the statute of the CSO, mergers or divisions, investments or fund-raising activities of the type so specified in the statute of the CSO, and the removal of the senior officials of the board—such as the chair, vice chair or general secretary. The statute of CSOs should contain provisions that ensure accountability and transparency. With respect to accountability, CSOs should be required to establish an audit committee, the members of which should have a specified term of office. The audit committee should serve as a financial oversight body in respect of all financial related matters. In addition to the internal democratic regimes of CSOs, transparency should take the form of reporting by the board of management on important issues within the CSO to its members or to the registration authorities, and by publishing an annual report.

Management

In order to realize their full potential as a CSO that can contribute to meaningful electoral development in Member States of the AU, there should be a functional management structure in place and that was often lacking in small CSOs operating in electoral activities. The management of a CSO should be established in accordance with its statute. The procedure for taking decisions should be consistent with the law and the statute of the CSO. The content of decisions should be in line with the objectives of the CSO and not influenced or directed by outside entities. In other words, the autonomy and integrity of the decisions taken must be that of the management. The issue of autonomy is a key attribute in the determination of a CSO's freedom from outside influences. Restrictions on a CSO's autonomy may come about by the relevant local law or through concealed influences of governmental authorities. The autonomy of a CSO may be impinged upon by outside influences whether or not it is incorporated or otherwise. The lack of autonomy may adversely affect a CSO by inhibiting its ability to freely advocate its policy and make recommendations to potential beneficiaries. Its ability to organize its activities may also be inhibited. For some CSOs, adequate autonomy may be measured in terms of their management's ability to freely take decisions with respect to staffing, programme and project activities, and administration and governance. Where there is funding of a CSO from a government agency it may be difficult to shed the perception that outside influence will filter through.[89]

Good managerial practices should foster transparency and accountability. This is especially important with respect to CSOs, as they invariably depend for their funding on donations from their members, the public or wealthy benefactors. CSOs should submit an annual report to their members or directors on their accounts and activities. Where any donor requests a report with respect to his/her donation, the CSO should make an appropriately detailed report regarding that donation demonstrating the fulfillment of any conditions attached to it. Where required by the supervising authority, a CSO should make available relevant books, records and accounts for inspection, subject to the protection of the legitimate privacy of business confidentiality, and of the privacy of donors, staff and beneficiaries. The accounts should be audited by an independent auditor. In the case of foreign CSOs, the reporting requirements should be limited to their activities in the local jurisdiction.

---

[89] See for example the position of some CSOs in China mentioned in *Survival Strategies for Civil Society Organizations in China* by Julia Bentley in the International Journal of Not-for-Profit Law, Vol. 6 Issue 2 January 2004.

Staff and Workforce

One of the problems encountered frequently during the first decade of the 21st Century with small CSOs undertaking election activities in the Member States of the AU was the uncertainty with staff recruitment. The reason was that many such bodies actually depended on the approval of the project being proposed in project document submitted to fund staff and so their involvement would be conditional to the successful outcome of the their project bid to donor agencies of international CSOs. The CSOs should conform to all the applicable standards governing employment, including pensions and insurance obligations within the local jurisdiction. Subject to the legal requirements, the management of a CSO should be free to recruit, discipline or dismiss any member of its staff or workforce. In some countries, the workforce of CSOs is significant and contributes much to the local economy.[90] The workforce may be divided into two broad categories, namely, voluntary and paid, but both categories may be further broken down into full-time and part-time workers. The non-profit, and in many cases charitable, nature of CSOs' work enables them to mobilize large numbers of volunteers.

Policy-Making

The management organ of a CSO should be responsible for making its policies, which should aim at achieving the objectives set out in the statute. Where the objectives are in line with government policy and are pursued within the law, their pursuit may not attract much attention. However, if the policy objective is to influence the nature and shape of global and or national public policy, the policy-making role of the CSO becomes rather more high profile and may even be controversial. The involvement in policy making in its self need not be controversial, but often it is the extent and the nature of the involvement that causes adverse reaction from government authorities. Although this problem is not unknown to Western Democracies, where the advantages of good governance and transparency is appreciated, the advent of CSOs into the shaping of

---

[90] See the findings of the *Johns Hopkins Comparative Non-profit Sector Project* by Lester Salamon, S. Wojciech Sokolowski & Regina List, and the Johns Hopkins University Institute for Policy Studies.

national and global public policy is under much greater challenge in the emerging democracies of the African Union, Russia and Eastern Europe, and even more so in China. In the older democracies, CSOs are often asked to furnish information and policy advice to opinion leaders, such as parliamentarians and the media. In less tolerant and non-democratic environments the decision-making organ of CSOs may need to proceed more carefully when considering approaches to participate in initiatives to influence national policy in particular, notwithstanding whether or not it enjoys full autonomy.

Notwithstanding the normal practice that CSOs should be responsible for their own policy-making, when operating in the electoral field they should be guided by the policies of the EMB in question in the areas of election preparation in which they work.

Election environment

Most CSOs, local, national and international, were aware of the particular need for those working in election activities to be scrupulously non-partisan. However, occasionally representative of CSOs were expelled on the grounds of bias or partisanship, for example in Ethiopia in 2005 and Zimbabwe 2008. Often CSOs representatives like some stakeholders get caught up in the competitive campaign environment where suspicions and rumours flourish.

A general or presidential election environment is usually one of the largest activities in a country. Where such an election is contested by multiple candidates from different political parties, competition is often fierce. This charged competitive atmosphere sometimes triggers partisanship on the part of those who manage the organization and conduct of such elections. Moreover, since elections at the national level determine the political party and or individuals who take charge of the governance of the country concerned, there is great temptation for the contestants to bend the election rules to their advantage. In this atmosphere, basic criteria have evolved which are designed to assist those responsible for organizing national elections. The accepted goal of all national elections is that they should be free and fair and be seen to be such by independent bystanders. Given the competitive atmosphere in which national elections are usually organized, the attributes of free and fair elections need to be clearly articulated in a manner readily understood by all stakeholders in the elections concerned.

Elections requirements for CSOs

Unlike many areas in which CSOs work, elections do have some particular demands on those which offer assistance in election organization. Perhaps the primary requirement of CSOs working in election activities is that they operate in a non-partisan manner with respect to political parties and candidates contesting an election, especially during an election campaign period. To do otherwise means that the CSOs involved forfeit credibility in the eyes of the stakeholders and run the risk of attracting hostile behaviour from the supporters of political parties and candidates who feel that their campaign might be adversely affected by such partisanship conduct. The close scrutiny of CSOs in election organization stems from the competitiveness of multi-party democratic elections and the widely held view that the contestants should have a level playing field, in other words, no unfair advantage or disadvantage, in which to put their message across to the voters. By way of examples, a CSO should not endorse or use the symbol or motto or colour of a political party or candidate, and should not in any way seek to engage prospective voters on behalf of a party or candidate. In other words, a CSO which undertakes to offer neutral assistance to the election organization under the auspices of the EMB concerned must not operate in a manner which compromises the impartiality of that EMB.

CSOs which operate in the sphere of election organization should display competence and reliability. In the field of voter/civic education, CSOs should work in a coordinated manner with the EMB involved. The programme should be done according to agreed format and content, and in accordance with the stipulated schedule. Posters, flyers, billboards, buntings, stickers and the text of messages need to be delivered on time and in the geographic areas agreed, in order to avoid delays and wasteful duplications (as often happens). Similar requirements apply to jingles on the electronic media, and announcements in the print media. The timing agreed with the EMB for the release of such messages and announcements, and the quality control measures established must be met in time for the scheduled commencement of the publicity programme. The informal CSOs often play a significant role in delivering voter and civic education materials and messages to outreach areas which are remote and not easily accessible. In the nature of election organization, it may not always be possible to have in place good supervisory mechanisms in remote rustic areas in which these CSOs operate and so they need to possess a high level of reliability.

High level of collaboration is needed between CSOs in local areas, regions and nationally. Such collaboration facilitates the widest possible coverage of the target areas geographically and makes it more likely that minority groups even in the remotest of areas are brought into the net. Besides aiding harmonious geographic coverage, collaboration between CSOs enables them to keep on the messages, thus ensuring consistency and minimizing distortion of text and delivery. It may even be cost-effective in so far as greater competition to reduce costs can lead to suppliers of materials and services charging prices which are below the normal commercial rates, if bulk purchasing methods are used.

Training of staff and workforce in voter/civic education good practices is the key to successful delivery of voter and civic education programmes. The training for internal staff should cover the basic routine attributes of running an office—punctuality, reliability, good record keeping and continuous up-dating of schedule of daily and weekly tasks to be performed. Equally important is the preparation of training materials relating to the substantive subject matter in question. The workforce may be operating almost exclusively in the field conveying the message of the EMB by distributing materials or performing drama to persuade qualified persons register to vote or to go out and vote, as the case may be. The content of training materials must be consistent with the election law, rules and regulations, and relevant directives from the EMB. Members of any workforce operating in voter and civic education relating to voter registration and polling should strictly adhere to the practice of non-partisanship.

Observing elections requirements for informal CSOs are usually flexible and revolve around a few core rules which must be followed. The observers should be well trained and be clear on their role which is merely to observe the proceedings of the election process, be it registration of voters, nominations of candidates, polling or the counting of the votes. Each observer should understand the procedures and rules governing the election process which is being observed, so as to be able to note or record accurately what was done. The observer's role does not allow for any intervention in the conduct of the process. In this respect, the role of an observer differs from that of a monitor whose task may entail intervention in the proceedings of the process to secure remedial measures to correct irregular procedures. Observers usually have to receive some form of accreditation and identification, sometimes these may be provided through the EMB concerned to the CSO. Observers must comply with any applicable code of conduct prepared by the EMB, and the election law, rules and regulations. Failure to comply with any stipulations of any of these instruments can lead to the withdrawal of accreditation to observe and in the case of the legal provisions failure to comply may constitute an offence. The observers should conduct themselves in a manner which does not allow them to get in the way of the election process, that is to say, they should not cause any disruption or delay, and should not interfere with voters. The CSO in charge of the observers and the observers themselves should act in a non-partisan manner and refrain from pursuing any goal inconsistent with that of the EMB's, which is to conduct free and fair election.

Informal CSOs frequently have difficulty getting training materials in good time. The surest way to ensure early access to training materials is to liaise with the EMB concerned, but often the materials prepared by the EMB are late and so CSOs might be forced to construct their own training instructions based on the law, rules and regulations, and directives on the subject matter issued by the EMB.

Report and evaluation

Good practice requires informal CSOs to prepare a report on any election activities undertaken, whether in connection with voter and civic education or observation. Such report may be required by any donor which offered assistance to the CSO, or by the EMB. It will also form the basis of a good recording system of the CSO's performance in the particular area of election activities. There is no stipulated format for report by CSOs, but it should be written in clear and simple language that can be understood by the members and workforce of other CSOs. The final report on the undertaking should state the time and place of the commencement of the activities, as well as the geographic scope thereof. A careful summary of the main difficulties encountered in delivering the services and the solutions applied to those problems should form part of the report. The lessons learnt from the development and implementation of the project should be carefully noted and form part of the report. The CSO's own verdict on the outcome of the project should be recorded and recommendations made, where appropriate, and form part of the report.

Where the election activities of an informal CSO are considered extensive in geographic terms, it is advisable that an evaluation of the overall development and execution of the project be undertaken. With respect to small informal CSOs, funding for post-election evaluation may be had from donors or the EMB concerned. A CSO's contribution to post-election evaluation may consist of inputs into a wider and comprehensive election audit of an election organization and conduct, which may be commissioned by the EMB concerned. A good election report by a CSO would form a sound basis for its contribution to an evaluation exercise. The trend is to encourage EMBs to commission a post-election audit to enable a comprehensive assessment of all tenets of the planning, organization and conduct of a national election. The inputs of stakeholders, individually or through stakeholders' forums, are important to develop a complete picture of the overall contribution to the holding of the election concerned. The real import of an election audit is to assist the EMB concerned to identify strengths and weaknesses in the organization and conduct in the election and to make recommendations for remedial measures to be taken.

Choice of areas of operation

Some areas of election organization are suited to the nature and type of assistance that informal CSOs offer. In remote rustic parts of some countries, CSOs that are locally based may be best placed to reach prospective voters and to communicate freely with them in their local dialect or language. These factors make CSOs that are locally based especially suited to assist with civic and voter education programmes in such areas.

Civic and voter education programmes

Civic and voter education programmes are sometimes taken together when the civic education is essentially about voters' registration and polling, but in fact the two areas can be treated separately, as has been done in some countries.[91] For the purposes of the appreciation of informal CSOs, programmes of civic and voter education are treated similarly here, but the differences in programme contents will be noted. Civic education, with which CSOs operating in election assistance are concerned, is related to election organization, and does not embrace the wider related fields of political education which may include political ideology. Civic education content in the context of election may include the democratic and electoral landscape in the country concerned, the nature of free and fair elections, the nature of free choice, the secrecy of the ballot and the importance of participating in the elections process by all qualified persons in the country concerned. Voter education is sometimes used to embrace those aspects of civic education that relate to election organization, as well as election procedures on polling day. The election procedures are usually formulated by the election laws, regulations, rules, and manuals and instructions prepared by the EMB concerned. Voter education should ensure that all changes (if any) recently made to the laws and other instruments are taken into account, and that any information on the procedures that is imparted to the electorate is accurate.

A civic and voter education programme should begin with planning the nature, scope and cost of the particular projects to be undertaken. The nature of particular projects that may be pursued could include the use of electronic and print media, posters, fliers, stickers, and live drama performances. However some of these channels may not be appropriate for use in some circumstances and remote geographic areas. For example, in some countries the radio dominates the geographic news reach of the entire territory, while in other countries the print media distribution may be significant even if they do not command the largest demographic penetration. Perhaps it is still the case that television

---

91 For example, in Nigeria an agency of government, the National Orientation Agency (NOA) deals with civic education, and in Ghana, a commission deals with the subject.

coverage in many new and emerging democracies is limited to mostly urban areas. Notwithstanding the level of coverage by the electronic and print media, EMBs and CSOs always resorted to complementary methods of disseminating civic and voter education messages, using one or more of the following physical means of dissemination, posters, fliers, stickers, buntings, banners, consultative and interactive sessions with community members and traditional leaders where appropriate, and drama performances which may be mobile or otherwise. Informal CSOs may use any or all of the foregoing methods of dissemination of the civic and voter education messages. The use of the number of methods chosen may be influenced by the particular CSO's budget. Basic research would quickly demonstrate that the cost of jingles on radio cost more during peak hours than at other times, but the largest audiences can be reached during these times. Similarly, the CSO would find that television jingles slots are usually much more expensive than those on radio. In the print media, it is generally the case that columns or advertisements on certain pages—front and editorial—are more expensive than on other pages.

Many informal CSOs have experienced difficulties in formulating credible estimates for civic and voter education projects, because of inflated cost estimates which do not reflect the true cost per unit of the items, which can be easily checked. Attempts are often made to obscure the simple straightforward method of calculating total cost of items by the listing of the actual cost per unit. This is not good practice and is not transparent. One approach to preparing credible estimates for a civic and voter education project is to secure tariffs of rates for radio and television broadcasting, where appropriate and use those quotations as a basis for costing. Of course, commercial discounts are often available for prolonged projects and such discounts can reduce the actual expenditure substantially. A similar approach is possible with respect to the use of the print media where advertisement rates and column rates can be had from the media houses concerned. Competitive bidding in order to ensure transparency as well as the best price for the design and production of posters, fliers, banners, buntings, stickers, and related civic and voter education materials is a good procedure to follow. New and emerging technologies in election organization like the use of the Internet and Websites in particular would be of growing interest to some informal CSOs, but for the most part would be open to very limited access to the electorate in remote rustic regions of many emerging democracies in the foreseeable future. Project budget estimates that are realistic and credible are likely to attract support from potential donors.

The geographic area to be covered by a CSO civic and voter education project will determine the amount of rresources that will be required to deliver the services planned. Thus the project estimates should take account of production and dissemination of civic and voter education materials that would be adequate for the geographic area contemplated. Other factors, such as the topography and the road conditions, may be relevant.

Collaborative measures may assist CSOs which are operating in particular regions to avoid wasteful duplications in the design, production and dissemination of civic and voter education messages and materials. It may also help to save CSOs from flooding prospective donors with multiple requests for funding with respect to the same project in a particular area. Collaboration between CSOs may be achieved through regular contacts at stakeholders' forums or otherwise.

CSOs and election observation

Election observation attracts the involvement of many local and foreign observers. Foreign (or international) observers need to be accredited either by or through the foreign ministry or the EMB concerned. Local CSOs are also usually required to be accredited by the EMB. The basic requirements that any CSO is called upon to follow are non-partisan behaviour, accurate recording of events, thorough familiarization of the procedures which are being observed, and general refrain from getting involved in the process. Informal CSOs which are new to election observation may need guidance as to how to follow a smooth path to a successful outcome of its observation exercise. A CSO may choose to observe any or all of several election processes in particular cases. For example, delimitation of electoral districts of constituencies, registration of voters, nomination (registration) of political parties and or candidates to contest an election, conduct of polling, the counting of the votes, and the announcement of election results. The preparatory requirements for each of these processes are different and the procedures for implementation are also different.

Observing delimitation of electoral districts and constituencies in a federal state such as Nigeria with hundreds of electoral districts and constituencies may best be done through collaborative effort by CSOs with relatively small numbers of observers. In many circumstances, voter registration, nomination (registration) of political parties and or candidates to contest an election, or the conduct of polling would require more intensive and closer observation than delimitation of electoral districts. With an ever increasing use of computerization in the voting, counting of votes and the announcement of election results, CSOs should ensure that their observers are trained to be able to meaningfully observe such procedures. A similar situation obtains in some countries where the registration of voters' exercise is carried out with the aid of technology—biometric identification systems and scanning of data, not all aspects of which may appear completely transparent to an observer. The training of observers should ensure that they fully understand how these processes work so that informed critical comments may be made in appropriate cases.

Monitoring/Observing voter registration

Some CSOs prefer to play a proactive role during voters' registration in order to achieve an accurate voters' register. If such an undertaking is carried out in a non-partisan manner and irregularities are brought to the attention of the proper authorities in a timely manner, it may be difficult for stakeholders, particularly the EMB concerned and political parties, to complain. Proactive behaviour by CSOs in this manner may raise their level of operation from that of merely observing the process to that of monitoring it with a view to identifying irregularities and seeking remedial measures. CSOs which set out to perform this role would be well advised to seek the prior endorsement of the EMB concerned.

Voters' registration may take one or a combination of many forms. The voters' register may be compiled using the national civil registry (where appropriate)[92], or a combination of list of names from public records and other means of enumeration, whether by house-to-house counting or otherwise[93], or qualified persons may be asked to attend at centres to

---

[92]   As in the Scandinavian countries.

[93]   For example, as in Malta and Singapore.

register.[94] Registration of voters may be done periodically and updated through annual revision, or may be undertaken through continuous or rolling registration whereby a qualified person can apply for registration at any time. Registration for the purposes of voting may be compulsory or voluntary. Compulsory registration renders close scrutiny by CSOs less important as it would be an election offence for a qualified person not to register. Voluntary voters' registration requires a high level of civic and voter education in which CSOs may be involved. It also benefits from the presence of local observers who are able to witness the process in remote areas. Whatever the method of registration, there is scope for CSOs to observe the process of compiling the voters' register and pronounce upon its accuracy or otherwise.

Observing nomination (registration) of candidates or political parties to contest an election has attracted the attention of some CSOs, although in many cases the process is straightforward. In some countries, for example, Liberia in the 2005 elections, the nomination process was complex and required a prospective independent presidential candidate to be supported by several thousand registered voters drawn from a stipulated number of counties. Each prospective candidate for the Senate and the House of Representatives respectively had to be supported by several hundreds of registered voters from their respective electoral district.[95] That rather complicated procedure offered plenty of opportunities for irregularities to take place and CSOs, particularly local ones, are well placed to assist in calling attention to such breaches. In cases where prospective candidates are required to declare their assets when submitting their nomination papers, observation by CSOs can ensure that each applicant properly complies with the requirement of the law.

---

[94] In many countries, registration centres are also used as polling places to facilitate ease of identification.

[95] An independent candidate applicant for the Senate election is required to demonstrate the support of 500 registered voters, and an independent candidate for the House needed the support of 300 registered voters.

Observing preparation for and conduct of national polling

For many informal CSOs, the observation of national polling preparation and conduct is their primary interest. The activities related to preparation and polling have the potential to generate local and national interest and so various community-based groups, regional or national CSOs have an interest in observing and reporting on how well or otherwise the preparation for and the conduct of polling was carried out. Perhaps the main benefit of election observation at this level is to ensure that the process is executed in accordance with the election law, rules and procedures in a transparent manner. Election observation may also bring to bear a calming influence on the proceedings in disturbed circumstances, as troublemakers are likely to keep away from the eyes of observers who may be able to identify them and their connections.

Most observer groups, whether formal or informal CSOs, local or international, carry out election observation with a view to forming an opinion as to whether or not the election was conducted in a free and fair manner. However because of the complexity of forming a clear cut opinion on the freeness and fairness of the election, many observer groups shy away from making any such pronouncement and use phrases such as 'the electorate expressed their will freely and fairly', or 'voters were given an opportunity to express their will', or that 'the election was substantially free and fair, despite the occurrence of irregularities'. One difficulty for election observers who seek to pronounce of the freeness and fairness of national elections is that the conduct of polling is only one of many processes in election organization and while polling itself might be properly conducted, other processes in the chain of preparation, such as voters' registration, might have been flawed. Thus unless election observers witnessed each of the main election processes, it may be unwise to give general endorsement that a particular national election was free and fair.

What constitutes free and fair elections?

There are many interesting aspects of identifying the attributes of free and fair elections from the point of view of an observer group. Members of that group have to compile their report on what they witnessed in the area or areas where the proceedings were carried out. Although the practice is not uniform, many observer groups would discuss their findings before a conclusion is reached on whether or not the execution of the election process concerned was done in a free and fair manner and in accordance with the election procedures. In perhaps what is a minority of cases, individual observers are mandated to form their own judgment as to whether of not the election proceedings witnessed were free and fair.[96] There may of course be different levels of performance by election personnel in the areas observed and these differing levels have to be averaged out where appropriate. Some times the election process in given areas may be so poorly carried out that the election may not take place, or if it does, it may properly be considered to be invalid. Observers, whatever their approach, should be in a position to report on the situation witnessed accurately and objectively.

A big problem for observers generally, and informal CSOs are no exception, is to form a judgment on whether an election was free and fair. In the competitive atmosphere of the immediate aftermath of a national election, it often happens that the losers draw upon every alleged election irregularity, whether substantial or otherwise, in order not to concede defeat. Although most election results are contested on the grounds of flawed organization of the preparation for and conduct of polling, in forming judgment on the freeness and fairness of an election, each major process observed should be brought into focus. One difficulty in grappling with the question of freeness and fairness of an election is to identify the test to be applied. One could start from the truth—that no election organization will be entirely without some errors, hiccups or irregularities, by whatever name called. The question is, at what point then do the errors, hiccups or irregularities become so discernible that an election is not free and fair and is invalid or unacceptable? Some election laws give an indication by stating that if the election law, rules, regulations and procedures were not substantially followed the election is invalid. However, there could be considerable election irregularities in a particular election organization and yet it could be shown that the procedures, laws, rules and regulations were all substantially complied with. Where situations of natural disasters, civil disturbances or sudden outbreak of

---

[96] This approach is followed by Commonwealth observers.

health epidemics occur, election managers are mandated under many election legislative schemes to postpone elections in the areas concerned. If there is a complete breakdown in the election organization in an area on Election Day, so that the majority of voters could not exercise their franchise, the election would be unfair and most likely invalid. If there were widespread fraudulent election activities particularly with respect to voters' registration, polling or counting of the votes, the election would not only be not free and fair, but invalid.

Counting votes and announcing results

The counting of votes and the announcement of election results represent a high point in election organization. Although electronic voting and counting will have a positive impact on these two election processes, this election technology, at the time of writing, is only used by a few countries. The use of electronic voting and counting, in any event, would not diminish the need for election observers, since accuracy and transparency with respect to these processes would still need to be verified. The counting of votes marks a very vulnerable point in the cycle of processes in election organization. Vulnerability comes about because of the nature of the judgment which the counting officers may have to make in borderline cases as to whether or not a particular ballot is valid and should be counted or invalid and should not be counted. In addition, the counting process often attracts election irregularities through tampering with the ballots and or the tallying of the ballot count. Some times CSOs and other stakeholders support the counting of votes at the polling station in order to minimize the opportunity for improperly interfering with the ballots by ensuring that the agents of candidates and political parties, as well as observers are given copies of the statement of the count at the end of polling. This procedure is useful in case attempts are made to interfere with the ballot box while it is being transported to the counting centre. If this happens, the authenticated copy of the statement of the count issued by the counting officer at the polling station can serve as evidence of correct outcome of the voting. Ironically, security is often the reason why ballot counting cannot take place at the polling station in some areas of a country or even in the country as a whole. There may be inadequate election infrastructure, for example, an absence of buildings or proper lighting facilities, to carry out the count immediately after the close of polling and so the process may become susceptible to irregularities. Counting at centres away from the polling station poses challenges for EMBs and for election observers. The ballot boxes and other election materials have to be transported to the counting centres safely and without interference with the ballots. The transportation of the ballot boxes must be done in a transparent manner, accompanied by election officials, agents of political parties and candidates, as well as by observers. An obvious issue is the meaning of 'accompanying' the ballot box in this context. If the vehicle conveying the ballot box and other materials to the counting centre is large enough to take a representatives of agents and observers, that would settle the matter. It often happens that the means of conveyance and the accommodation available does not allow for large numbers of agents of political parties and observers to hold in the transportation.[97] In given situations, it may be possible for agents of political parties and candidates, and observers to select from among themselves representatives to travel in the vehicle transporting the ballot box, while others follow behind the vehicle. The procedure at counting centres should not be dissimilar to that followed at counting the ballot at the polling station. The role of observers at the counting of the votes is to witness the conduct of the process noting the accuracy and the transparency and particularly the ruling on invalid ballots.

Announcing election results marks another vulnerable phase in the counting of the votes. The announcement of election results necessarily follows the counting of the ballots, but often there is an intervening step, that is, tallying the number of votes obtained at each polling station in each electoral district. If the tallying process goes wrong, as it sometimes does,[98] the efficacy of the election organization will be questioned. The presence of election observers and the agents of candidates and parties at the tallying centres help to strengthen the perception of transparency

---

[97] For example, in remote areas small planes or small motor boats may be used as to collect ballot boxes and materials, but the real concern is when vehicles are used which are incapable of carrying few if any agents or observers and which tend to hideaway the boxes and materials from outside view.

[98] See for example, in Zanzibar (Tanzania) 1995 and Guyana in 1997, where, in each case, irregularities and lack of transparency in the tallying process drew negative responses from stakeholders.

of the process. The tallying process needs to be conducted accurately and without undue delay so that the results are announced regularly to the stakeholders. The practice is emerging whereby election results are announced at press conferences which are opened to accredited press representatives and observers and which are done at a prearranged place (usually at the press centre of the EMB concerned) and time daily, where appropriate.

Conflict resolution

Many informal CSOs try to equip themselves to contribute to conflict resolution in election-related matters at the local or community levels. There are usually two levels of potential involvement by CSOs in this regard. The one level may entail civic and voter education programmes which target the causes of local conflicts which may arise through differences of views with respect to religious, ethnic, land rights, or political activities. The other level may relate to observing the conduct of proceedings to determine complaints and disputes being heard by election tribunals or by the EMB concerned. In Nigeria, for example, there are many small informal CSOs which carry out valuable work in the field to prevent or reduce tension locally often caused by religious, ethnic or land disputes. A large part of the effort goes into tackling small local disturbances before they become large and unmanageable and promoting better understanding between the ethnic and religious groups. With respect to observing the proceeding of complaints, observers' presence is aimed at enhancing the transparency of the process, as well as ensuring that the procedures are followed the tribunal or hearing officer. It is an important feature of good practice in election organization that there are sound procedures for dealing with complaints by stakeholders in a timely and transparent manner.

Bidding for election projects

Competitive bidding for projects

Informal CSOs may from time to time face competition from other bodies in seeking to undertake election activities. This approach is aimed at pricing project costs competitively, while providing adequate transparency in each transaction in accordance with good practice. The process of attracting interested CSOs in bidding for projects is through advertisement of the project to be undertaken and stipulating the key aspects that the bid should address, for example the cost, timeframe for completion, staff/workforce requirement, programme content (where appropriate) and work supervision and reports.

Informal bids may be handled with little formality, but that approach is always open to suspicion of favouring a particular bid which may not be the best or most advantageous from the point of view of the project. Informal bidding procedure should at least deal with the basic elements of how the applicant CSOs plan to tackle the project, quoting details of cost elements, highlighting goods and services required, stating the geographic covering envisaged, and indicating the time frame involved. These basic bits of information would form a good way of comparing the proposals submitted from the interested CSOs within the stipulated time frame for considering the bids.

Consideration of informal bids should be done transparently and through careful consideration. Each proposal should be assessed against the background which the project is designed to achieve and the ability of each applicant CSO to execute it in a cost-effective and timely manner. Where the proposals are assessed by a panel, the procedure for taking decisions should be clear, that is to say, by consensus or majority agreement. The successful applicant CSO should be informed promptly of the decision. If the proposal of the successful applicant was approved with modification, the applicant should be given an opportunity to consider the modifications and indicate its agreement, or otherwise.

Formal bids require much more formality and some informal CSOs find it difficult to meet the formalities needed to comply with tendering procedures. Formal bidding is likely to become the normal method of securing goods and services contracts of 50,000.00 US$ or more, and some jurisdictions might even opt for the lower amount of US$25,000.00 and over. The rationale for having clear procedures governing the granting of contracts to supply goods and services is to ensure transparency and avoid corruption in the operations of CSOs and EMBs and other entities. In the quest to introduce comprehensive legislative schemes setting out detailed procedures to deal with public expenditures with respect to goods, services, works and concessions. These procedures are usually contained in a public procurement and concessions law which applies to all publicly funded entities, including EMBs, whether constitutionally autonomous or otherwise. This development will affect CSOs which seek contracts with EMBs in areas such as civic and voter education, as well as training and election monitoring. Most international donors have rules and procedures that are similar to those contained in a typical public procurement and concessions law.

Current Approach to Public Procurement

The current approach to procurement in the public sector is to achieve maximum economy and efficiency, and obtain the best value for public expenditures. The wider aim includes building capacity of officials and institutions, including EMBs, in procurement. The procedures will facilitate competition and encourage participation in procurement proceedings by qualified suppliers, contractors and consultants, as well as ensure fair access free from discrimination to all eligible providers of goods, works and services and equitable treatment to all bidders. The current approach to public procurement is also aimed at strengthening the integrity, fairness and accountability in the procurement process. It has the potential to enable the achievement of transparency in the procedures, processes and decisions with respect to procurement agreements. The structures governing the procurement procedures can be designed in a manner that facilitate decentralization of public procurement to procuring entities such as EMBs, thus avoiding an erosion of their autonomy. Equally important, is the potential for the new approach to mitigate the incidence of monopolies and patronage, particularly in respect of the supply of election equipment, goods and services.

Procurement Structures

The preferred approach in designing structures to deal with public procurement is to establish a central statutory body, a commission, with the general powers to regulate procurement using public funds as well as powers of oversight with respect to any subordinate entity undertaking procurement using public funds. The statutory framework would include 'procurement or concessions entities' which are entities using public funds to which the statute in question applies. The head of every entity would be responsible and accountable for any action taken in pursuit of his/her responsibilities. Every procurement entity created within the meaning of the governing statute would be required to establish a procurement committee consisting of five or more members, and a procurement unit consisting of two or more members. The procurement unit would operate under the supervision of the procurement committee.

The functions of a procurement unit would include the following:

- Planning of procurement.
- Preparation of invitations to bid and of bidding documents.
- Publication and distribution of invitations to bid.
- Receiving and safeguarding bids.
- Conducting bid opening procedures in accordance with the rules set out in the governing statute.
- Administering the implementation and monitoring of contracts.
- Assessment of the quality of the procured goods works and services.
- Sourcing and profiling of all suppliers, contractors and consultants, and the maintenance of a database for that purpose.

Bid Evaluation Panel

Each procurement committee would be required to constitute a bid evaluation panel with the required expertise as and when required. An evaluation bid panel would be responsible for the evaluation of bids in accordance with the predetermined and published evaluation criteria as would have been outlined to bidders in the bid documents and would prepare and submit an evaluation report for the consideration of the procurement committee.

Who may bid?

A person who wishes to bid for goods, services or works contract pursuant to a statutory regime like the one being considered would need to qualify by meeting the criteria stipulated by the particular procurement entity concerned and those criteria may include the following:

- Professional and technical qualifications.
- Equipment availability, if applicable.
- Past performance.
- After sales service, where applicable.
- Spare parts availability.
- Legal capacity.
- Financial resources and condition.

A procuring entity must disqualify a bidder if it finds at any time that the information submitted concerning the qualification of the bidder was materially inaccurate or materially incomplete.

Procedures

Prequalification—Where prequalification for bidding is required the details of that requirement should be set out in prequalification documents as well as in the bidding documents. Where the requirements for prequalification apply, they should be applied to all bidders without discrimination and should be applicable only to the extent stated in the prequalification documents. At prequalification proceedings, the procurement entity should ensure that the following tasks are performed:

Supply all prospective bidders who responded to the invitation to pre-qualify with the relevant documents which would assist the bidders to prepare and submit their applications for prequalification.

Allow bidders adequate time to acquire, prepare and submit prequalification documents.

Inform each applicant of the results of the assessment of the prequalification and all the applicants that meet the minimum requirements for prequalification shall be invited to bid.

Clarification and Modification of Bidding Documents

A bidder may seek clarification from the procuring entity concerned of a prequalification or bidding document within the stipulated time frame . . . The procuring entity would be required to respond within three working days to any request for clarification. The responses to requests for clarification or modification of bidding documents or prequalification documents should be communicated to all the bidders participating in the procurement proceedings so that they may take the clarifications or modifications into account in preparing their submissions. Where required, the procuring entity may have to extend the deadline for submission of bids or applications to pre-qualify for bidding.

Invitation to Bid

An invitation to bid or pre-qualify should be publicized through the media. Whenever feasible, and if the relevant regulations allow, invitations to bid or to apply for pre-qualification could be published on the Internet. The bidding documents should contain information with respect to the nature and time frame of the procurement, including the terms of reference, contractual terms of the procurement and the manner of entry into force of the contract. The bidder's qualification requirements, if a prequalification procedure was not followed, should be submitted. Information should be provided concerning site visits and pre-bid conferences, if any. The bidding documents should contain instructions for preparation and submission of bids, including the deadline for submission of bids, time and place of bid opening. The documents should contain information with respect to the components to be reflected in the price, the currency or currencies in which the bid should be stated, and the currency and related exchange rate to be used for comparison of bids. The criteria and methodology for the evaluation of bids and the selection of the successful bidder should be stated. If suppliers are allowed to bid for only a portion of the goods, works or services to be procured, a description of the portion or portions for which bids may be submitted should be indicated. Matters such as the validity period of bids, the amount and acceptable forms of any required bid, and the conditions of the contract which would be entered into by the successful bidder should be set out in the bidding documents. Further, notice of conflict–of–interest restrictions and anti-fraud and corruption rules should also be stated in the documents. So too should be the manner in which bidders may be able to request a review of actions, omissions and decisions of the procuring entity.

Deadline for Bids

The procuring entity should set a deadline for the submission of bids and applications for prequalification so as to allow sufficient time for their preparation and submission.

Submission of Bids

Usually, unless otherwise stated in the bidding documents, a bid should be submitted in writing, signed and in a sealed envelope by hand or mail or by courier at the option of the bidder. The bidding documents may stipulate the method of submission of bids which may include electronic mail. Bids remain valid for the period of time indicated in the bidding documents, but modification or withdrawal of a bid during the bid validity period may lead to forfeiture of the bid security. Bids received after the deadline for submission of bids would be returned unopened.

Bid Security

The bidding documents may require bidders to submit a bid security which should apply to all bidders. The bid security may be forfeited in certain stipulated circumstances, including:

- Modification or withdrawal of a bid after the deadline.
- Refusal of a bidder to accept a correction of an arithmetical error appearing on the face of the bid.
- Failure of the successful bidder to sign a contract in accordance with the terms set forth in the bidding documents; or
- Failure by the successful bidder to provide a security for the performance of the contract if required to do so by the bidding documents.

Opening Bids

Bids should be opened as soon as practicable after the deadline for the submission thereof and at the place and time stated in the bidding documents. Bidders or their representatives may attend the bid opening. The procedure usually requires the name of each bidder to be called out when the turn comes up. The amount of each bid, any discounts or alternatives offered and the presence or absence of any bid security, along with essential supporting documents, is announced. The documents should be recorded and a copy made available to any bidder upon his/her request. Documents with financial implications should be signed by the chairman and two other members of the bid opening committee. During the opening session, no decision relating to the disqualification or rejection of any bid should be announced. No bidder should seek to influence the procuring entity's evaluation of the bids in any way.

Examination and Evaluation of Bids

Upon the opening of the bids, the procuring entity should first examine the bids in order to see whether the bids are complete, signed and if the documents meet the requirements, including the technical specifications, if any, and the contract conditions, stated in the bidding documents. Bids, which are not complete, should be rejected and excluded from further evaluation. If a prequalification procedure was used, a bid received from any one who was not pre-qualified to bid should be rejected and excluded. Bids that were not rejected should be evaluated pursuant to the criteria and methodology set out in the bidding documents. The procuring entity may seek clarification from any bidder to facilitate the evaluation, but should not permit any change to the bid. If a bidder amends the bid such a bid should be rejected and any bid security paid forfeited. Where there is an arithmetical error, such error may be rectified and the bidder notified and if the bidder refuses to accept the correction, the bid should be rejected and the bid security forfeited. Where during an evaluation of a bid, minor discrepancies which did not merit rejection were found, the cost of any variations caused by the discrepancies may be taken into account when comparing other bids in order to determine the lowest evaluated bid. If a prequalification procedure was applied, the qualifications of the lowest evaluated bidder should be verified to take account of any changes since the original prequalification. Where there was no prequalification procedure, the qualifications of the lowest evaluated bidder should be checked against the criteria set out in the bidding documents; and if that bid fails, a similar check should be carried out to the next ranked bid. The procuring entity should prepare an evaluation report setting out the details of the examination and evaluation of the bids and stating the recommendation for the award of the contract in accordance with the evaluation criteria specified in the bidding documents.

Award of Procurement Contract

The successful bidder would be the one who submitted the lowest evaluated and most responsive bid which met the evaluation criteria which were specified in the bidding documents. Within the period of bid validity, the procuring entity should notify the successful bidder of the proposed award and indicate the time when the contract would be ready for signing. If the value of the contract exceeds the levels set by the regulations, notice should be given to the other bidders and the national governing body stating the particulars of the proposed successful bidder and the price of the contract. In such a case, the contract should not be signed before the expiration of the period stipulated in the regulations. Where a successful bidder fails to sign a written contract as required, or fails to provide any performance security in respect of the contract within the stipulated period, the procuring entity is required to accept the next ranked bidder from among the remaining bids that are in force.

Acceptance of Bid

In general, a successful bidder may be required to sign a written procurement contract within 30 days after being notified of the award. The procurement contract then enters into force when it is signed by the bidder and by the procuring entity and the notice is dispatched to the bidder to that effect. The procurement contract should normally be signed by the head of the procuring entity, but he or she may delegate that power with respect to small contracts to the head of the procurement unit or to a senior official of the entity concerned.

Codes of Conduct

In order to facilitate ease of implementation and to foster a user-friendly application environment, a procurement legislative scheme may contain specimen codes of conduct for procuring entities and bidders respectively.

A *Code of Conduct* for procuring entities may contain the following stipulations namely, that any public officer involved in any aspect of procurement or implementation of contracts shall:

- Discharge his or her duties impartially.
- At all times act in the public interest.
- Avoid conflict of interest in discharging his/her duties.
- Immediately disclose any conflict of interest and excuse him or her from any further involvement in that matter.
- Avoid committing or aiding corrupt or fraudulent practices, coercion, solicitation or acceptance of any inducements.
- Observe confidentiality in respect of the information that comes into his or her possession relating to procurement proceedings and to bids.
- Be prohibited for a period of three years after departure from a procuring entity from taking up a position of authority in any private concern with which he or she undertook procurement activities.
- Not participate or allow any close relative to participate as a bidder in procurement proceedings of the procuring entity to which he or she belongs.

Further, a procuring entity shall reject a bid if the bidder offers, gives or agrees to give an inducement and immediately notify the rejection to the bidder concerned and to the relevant law enforcement authorities.

In general, a procuring entity should not award a contract to a bidder who prepared the specifications or bidding documents for the contract or supervising the execution of a contract, or any affiliate of such a bidder.

A public officer involved in a procuring entity should excuse himself or herself from participation in a procurement proceeding where a bid has been submitted by a bidder who is a close relative of the public officer, or by a bidder by whom the public officer or a close relative is employed in a management capacity, or as an agent or in which he or she is member of the board of directors, or has a financial interest.

Public officers and other persons involved in public procurement shall cooperate and disclose their interest in any matter being considered by any authority, including the Auditor General of the jurisdiction concerned, exercising monitoring and supervisory jurisdiction over public funds.

Public officers involved in public procurement should be required to make a declaration of their assets and liabilities within 60 days after assuming responsibility and 30 days after leaving office. The declaration should be in a form consistent with any form approved by the national authority charged with procurement responsibilities. The declaration should be updated annually, as well as when there is a substantial change in assets and liabilities.

Conduct of Bidders.

A bidder shall comply with the relevant laws and the conditions governing the contract. A bidder shall not engage in corrupt or fraudulent practices. He/she should refrain from offering or giving any inducement or making any misrepresentation of facts in order to influence a procurement process. A bidder should not interfere in any way with the ability of competing bidders to participate in procurement proceedings. Bidders should avoid engaging in any activity that might reasonably be construed as aimed at influencing, or depriving the procuring entity of the advantages of free and open competition. In particular, bidders should not indulge in coercive, corrupt or fraudulent practices or enter into any collusive or price-fixing acts. Bidders who indulge in these practices run the risk of prosecution.

Impact of Competitive Bidding on CSOs.

The formalities of public procurement procedures might not readily commend themselves to many CSOs, particularly the small informal ones. However the trend in new and emerging democracies is to strengthen governance by introducing sound procurement procedures to govern acquisition of goods, services and works, as well as concessions from public funds. The threshold applicable to competitive bidding might be as low as US$25, 000.00. In the field of elections, civic and voter education projects, as well as training and election monitoring and observation might be caught in so far as CSOs are relying on public funding for participation in such programmes. The only way to get on top of the seemingly complex procedure is to organize rigorous training with EMBs and other stakeholders.

Public Sector Support

Many CSOs derive a significant portion of their revenue from public sector funding through grants or contracts or reimbursement payments by governmental agencies.

Private Philanthropy

CSOs revenue through private philanthropy embraces funding from sources such as individuals, foundations, and corporations or companies.

Volunteers' Contribution

The contribution by volunteers is often considered to be revenue derived through private philanthropy. The size of volunteers' component varies from country to country, as well as with CSOs in a given country. There is also significant variation between the dependence on volunteer services by formal and informal CSOs. The latter, often due to the lack of sound antecedents, is forced to rely on voluntary services. CSOs, including informal ones, usually have a high degree of dependence on voluntary services in post-conflict situations, particularly in election organization, as was seen in Nigeria in 1998-99, Lesotho in 2001-2003, Liberia 2004-05 and Aceh in 2005-2006.

One of the extraordinary developments which began in the early 1990s is the ability of CSOs and community-based organizations (CBOs), both formal and informal, to attract large numbers of volunteers as domestic observers to observe election processes, particularly the registration of voters and polling. The CSOs and CBOs sometimes consist of large networks nationally and they have the ability to harness many thousands of volunteers to help with election observation. Increasingly, faith-based CSOs are being co-opted to broaden the base of the local and national activity in this field. Volunteer services are not the only source of assistance in these endeavours, as often grants from public agencies and private contributions also play a role.

In its endeavour to engage civil society organizations in conflict-affected and fragile states, the World Bank carried out case studies in three African countries, namely, Angola, Guinea Bissau and Togo in 2005. The studies revealed that when public services have broken down due to conflict or a weak public sector, NGOs, religious groups and other CSOs, become more important providers of basic social services. However they also showed that donors', and other development partners', engagement with CSOs was fragmented and short-term, and had not promoted institutional development. Moreover, the studies found that donor preferences for financing CSOs on a project-by-project basis gave those organizations limited opportunities for developing capacity, specialization, strategic planning, and long-term investments in beneficiary communities. The executive summary of the report on the studies pointed out that the basic message of the report was for donors to move away from a project-by-project approach to supporting CSOs, toward more sustained engagement focused on institution building among CSOs and networks. Such an approach, according to the report, would entail a strategic shift from ad hoc project funding and one-off training events to more systematic cooperation and commitment, including partnering and funding long-term development of CSOs.

Although these case studies addressed post-conflict or weak States scenarios, the recommendations or some of them are relevant to the situation of many CSOs in more stable environments and so for ease of reference they are repeated here thus:

- More rigorous and systematic analysis of CSOs could help inform more effective engagement.
- Longer-term financial support to CSOs would create better incentives for capacity and institutional development, strategic planning and specialization.
- Long-term partnerships between international and national CSOs could ensure transfer of capacities and improve sustainability.

- Financial support to networks and umbrella organizations could promote more effective use of resources, cross-learning, and accountability.
- Strengthened forums for CSO-government communication may contribute to better coordination and effectiveness, and underpin more systematic government engagement with CSOs in policy formulation, as well as more clear rules of engagement.

The foregoing arguments in favour of enhancing the prospects of sustainability of CSOs, apply mainly to revenue sources of public sector support and earnings from fees.

Philanthropy and CSOs Support

Philanthropy, along with volunteer labour, is the third main source of funding for CSOs. While funding from this source may be difficult to forecast on a longer-term basis, nevertheless the prospects for individual as well as corporate philanthropy look good. There is a trend in some countries, for example China and some countries in the south-east Asia, which are actively encouraging not only state agencies, but also individuals and corporate entities to contribute to philanthropic endeavours locally and nationally. In a similar vein, there are encouraging movements towards greater philanthropic endeavours among women in countries like Canada and among Afro-Americans in the USA. Equally interesting is the resurgence of wealthy entrepreneurs, particularly in North America, donating vast sums of money to foundations for humanitarian and environmental causes.

Relations with Governments

The diversity of CSOs makes it difficult to identify the convergence of purpose and to structure a harmonious relationship between them and governments. The complexity of the issue multiplies when informal CSOs (unregistered), CBOs and faith-based organizations (FBOs) are added to the equation. In new and emerging democracies the CSOs field seems so unbridled and seemingly out of any control operationally that it may take a long time to design appropriate mechanisms to harness the potential of CSOs to impact on the improvement of their respective communities.

However, a promising start has been made in establishing functioning mechanisms to foster good and harmonious relationship between CSOs and government. The concept is not a new one. For some time certain Western Governments have worked closely with and funded non-governmental organizations (NGOs) through their overseas aid agencies, but the movement towards the creation of an umbrella mechanism nationally under which the public sector and CSOs can interact in a systematic and principled manner, began in earnest little more than a decade ago.

CSOs Compacts Arrangements—Can they Work in The AU?

Compacts are instruments in the nature of formal agreements between government and CSOs, that is to say, the voluntary and community sector. Agreements belonging to the compact family are known by different names in different jurisdictions, for example, *compact* is used in the United Kingdom, separate ones in England, Scotland, Wales and Northern Ireland, *accord* in Canada, *concept* in Estonia, and *cooperation framework* in Croatia. Can compacts take root in the African Union? Can the quest for the promotion of democratic elections and the on-going African Peer Review process in the African Union create the environment for CSOs compacts to flourish? (Please Discourse within for further discussion).

Faith-Based Organizations

Faith-based Organizations (FBOs) Faith-based organizations (FBOs) have a long history of offering services to local communities in a variety of fields, particularly in education, homelessness, health, development, governance and elections. FBOs have many dimensions, indeed so many as to almost defy classification. They may be formal CSOs, informal CSOs, or CBOs; they may be national, regional or international in scope. Some FBOs are well funded, while others starved of resources. Some are internally or centrally organized, others are decentralized or even fragmented, and yet others are supported and organized internationally. FBOs are diverse and may be formed by established locally-based, nationally-based or internationally-based religious bodies. In many communities, many FBOs are informal, revolving around particular congregations, but often several congregations forming a loose network for delivering specific services to needy members.

In recent years, there is a trend internationally for FBOs to expand their work from the traditional areas of mainly social services and education to include health issues, such as HIV/AIDS, conflict resolution and election organization. FBOs have been proving their almost unique position in some post-conflict jurisdictions in conflict resolution and election organization. Examples of the role of FBOs in post-conflict scenarios, national and local, were witnessed in Liberia in the 2005 elections and in Nigeria in the 1998-99 and the 2003 elections. Multi-faith organizations are especially useful in countries that are sharply divided between two or more of the major religions today. When in 2003 prior to the elections in that year in Nigeria, the Supreme Council of Islam for the first time assisted in the voter education programme, it was considered to be a positive development. FBOs' ability to positively influence election preparation in Nigeria has not been lost on the stakeholders in elections in that country as was shown by the fact that the National Pact for Free and Fair Election which was agreed in 2005 in Abuja, assign a role to FBOs as follows, that they should:

> . . . "Live up to their responsibility to educate and enlighten their members on the sacrosanct nature of the franchise and the mandate and commit themselves to playing the role of democracy stakeholders.

> . . . Ensure that the principles of honesty and peaceful relations they preach are extended to the political terrain. Specifically, by sanctioning their members who engage in corrupt or violent practices, they can play a major role in promoting the culture of free and fair elections.

> . . . Commit them to devoting their time, energy and resources to the monitoring of all stages of the electoral process."[99]

---

[99] The 'Pact' was formulated at a conference sponsored by Global Rights: Partners for Justice and the UK Department for International Development (DFID), August 2005.

FBOs have shown that they can assemble large groups to participate in and or observe voter/civic education programmes and to observe polling and counting of votes. In emerging and new democracies in the Third World, FBOs have shown that they can mobilize large numbers of young people/volunteers to monitor and observe election preparation and conduct.

FBOs and Other Partners

In particular areas of operating, FBOs may be required to work with many partners. An example of this may be seen in the National Pact for Free and Fair Elections of Nigeria agreed in August 2005. The Pact was subscribed to by stakeholders in elections in Nigeria and assigned tasks to the various partners which were listed as the Federal Government and subordinate bodies as the States' governments and local governments, the Independent National Electoral Commission (INEC), the Judiciary, political parties, law enforcement authorities, CSOs, FBOs, media and the public. Although in general terms, FBOs work in harmony when the occasion warrants it, the partnership between government and FBOs sometimes stirs constitutional questions, political and even issues relating to interference by government authorities in religious affairs.

An examination of the faith-based initiatives taken by President Bush of the United States in December 2002 throws up some valuable insights into the nature of partnerships between governments and FBOs.[100] The Executive Order of December 2002 was directed to selected federal agencies to development charitable choice policies. The President made his faith-based initiative a priority of his domestic policy. An analysis of the President's faith-based initiative, suggested that FBOs could effectively deliver federally funded services in a wide range of programme areas. It pointed out however that the initiative raised institutional issues about the potential FBO effectiveness, accountability, and the working relationship of FBOs and state and local governments. The analysis lists effectiveness issues as including: range of services; lack of evaluation data; qualification of FBO personnel; inclusion of religious content; and availability of secular

---

[100] Executive Order 13279, December 2002.

alternatives. Accountability issues were seen as including: FBO ability to report results; and separation of government funds.[101]

The Executive Order instructed agencies to develop policies that ensured equal treatment and protection for faith-based and community organizations. The order aimed at increasing FBOs' access to federal funds in programme areas, such as children's services, job training, counseling and mentoring, literacy, housing, and substance abuse.

The President established an Office of Faith-Based and Community Initiatives in the White House to coordinate the initiative. A further order established two additional faith-based offices in the Department of Agriculture and the US Agency of International Development.

CSOs and Political Parties

Civil society organizations and political parties are sometimes partners in the quest to advance the quality of democracy in a particular country. This partnership is evidenced in a strong form in post-conflict situations, and also in local communities between informal CSOs and local branches of political parties. These general observations of factual situations do exist, but may properly be regarded as an over simplification of an often diverse and crowded field of CSOs and political parties in pursuit of different short and long-term goals. Furthermore, there are the odd cases of the merging of the goals of particular political parties and particular CSOs in fields such as labour, environment and even politics.

The quality of partnership between CSOs and political parties may be shaped by the strength of a particular party and the desire of a particular CSO to forge good working relationship with that party. Sometimes relationships between political parties and CSOs, even informal CSOs, are recognized impliedly in conflict situations and their immediate

---

[101] See Report for Congress, (updated January 2003) on Faith-based Organizations and Their Relationship with State and Local Governments: Analysis of Recent Initiatives.

aftermath.[102] But CSOs are becoming increasingly engaged in advocacy roles, especially with respect to the environment, governance, law reform, and election organization. In these and in other fields, a minority of CSOs have become so committed as to launch off-shoot political movements which eventually became political parties. Conversely, many political parties ally themselves with CSOs to gain renewal in credibility in local communities.

The nature and diversity of CSOs and political parties is so great that general propositions do not offer much clarity in the relationship between the operations of the two entities. The general scenario in new and emerging democracies differ significantly from that in the old and mature ones. In the former group, training of political parties at all levels and in all relevant fields by international CSOs constitutes the basis of a good partnership between the two entities. In both groups of countries, political parties are increasingly relying on CSOs for conducting opinion polls and the direction of popular preferences rather than on in-house research.

The view[103] has been put forward that weak political parties may be giving rise to CSOs transforming themselves into political parties as is the case of Thailand and the Philippines, but it should be pointed out that it is not a new phenomenon to have CSOs spawning political parties or vice versa. The Labour Party of the United Kingdom was created by labour associations more than a hundred years ago. Many of the political parties of today in the Caribbean islands, including the two main parties in Jamaica, were formed by trade unions. Certain trade unions in South

---

[102]   In Liberia at the time of the signing of the Comprehensive Peace Agreement (CPA) in 2003, civil society and special interest groups, and political parties were among the six entities given seats in the National Transitional Legislative Assembly (NTLA). Similarly, the Memorandum of Understanding between the Government of Indonesia and the Free Aceh Movement (GAM) signed in August 2005 made provisions for local (provincial) political parties to be formed. CSOs, local and international, were working with GAM even before it established its political party arm.

[103]   See paper "Civil Society Groups and Parties: Supporting Constructive Relationships" by G.G. Bevis, for The Bureau for Democracy, Conflict, and Humanitarian Assistance, USAID, 2003.

Africa kept the flame of freedom of association alight in that country when the African National Congress (ANC) and other political parties run by people of colour were banned. Sometimes CSOs officials also hold office as political party officials. Perhaps this type of relationship should be frowned upon when it occurs in respect of CSOs sponsoring domestic election observers or monitors, because of the obvious partisanship nature such partnership creates.

CSOs and Free and Fair Election in Member States of the AU

Civil society organizations have contributed much to the observation of elections throughout the world, including in the African Union during first decade of the 21st Century. While their activities have been felt most earnestly in the new and emerging democracies, election observers are considered a stabilizing force in established democracies as the United Sates of America since the botched presidential elections in Florida in 2000. International CSOs play a significant role in observation of elections in many scenarios, particularly in post-conflict situations, but it is the rise of domestic observers that has been truly phenomenal in the past decade and a half. These observers in their thousands often are recruited, trained and mobilized by CSOs of diverse nature, joined together for the particular purpose of election observation.

Domestic Observers

Domestic observers are drawn from local people usually members of national and local CSOs, FBOs and CBOs.[104] Many of these entities are formal, that is to say, registered or incorporated associations,[105] but in

---

[104] Some Member States of the AU appeared to be less than enthusiastic about domestic observers as showed in the 1997 elections in Cameroon when the Government cancelled the programme for training more than 2000 domestic monitors with notice.

[105] In Belarus, four civil society activists from an election observation group (Partnerstva) which observed the 2004 parliamentary elections but were denied registration to observe the presidential elections set for 19 March 2006 were detained on 21 February 2006. They were convicted under Article 193 of the Criminal Code of Belarus which makes it a crime for a member of

jurisdictions where informal associations are allowed, the majority of local observers are usually from ad hoc groups which are formed for the sole purpose of observing elections in which the observers are stakeholders and a part of the electorate. It is sometimes said that domestic observers have their own agenda and are prone to partisan practices. Experience has shown that the incidence of partisanship among domestic observers is surprisingly rare. Perhaps this is in part due to proper screening of individual observers and further screening of CSOs themselves when they apply for accreditation by the EMB or other authorized entities.

Another reason for the relatively low display of partisanship by election observers is good training in election procedures and adherence to codes of conduct for observers, which have become common practice. Domestic observers are often credited with having knowledge of local customs and habits, dialects and language, as well as the local geography.

The diversity of domestic observers is often a positive factor in election observation as often the presence of faith-based groups from different religions creates a soothing atmosphere in sensitive areas at election time.

In order to be able to send election observers to observe any election process whether registration of voters, preparation for polling, polling or counting of votes or any other election process, a CSO should seek accreditation from the proper authority, usually the EMB in question. The accredited CSO then makes arrangements for its observers to be accredited and properly identified while observing. Some EMBs accredited CSOs from time to time to engage in election work, whether advocacy work, or voter education or training, but further accreditation may be necessary to send out election observers.[106]

---

an unregistered public association to observe elections, and sentenced on 4 August 2006 to jail terms (Nikola Astreiko to 2 years, Timofei Dranchuk to 1 year, and Aleksandr Shalaiko and Enira Bronitskaya to 6 months each.)

[106] An example of this may be seen in Liberia when in 2005 a list of 159 CSOs was accredited by the National Elections Commission, not all of which pursued active interest in election activities or in observation. Those which sponsored observers were accredited to do and had to secure accreditation for their observers.

International CSOs

International CSOs have blazed the trail for domestic CSOs in many emerging democracies in the field of election observation. They have often trained and provided guidance to domestic CSOs. In addition international CSOs are a source of funding for domestic CSOs. International CSOs often have better access to resources than domestic ones, but may encounter constraints in operating in foreign countries. Their access to local funding may be restricted as in China and Russia, or may have to secure sponsors before commencing operations, as in China. Like domestic election observers, international observers are required to seek accreditation before commencing observation. They are usually required to give information on the size of the observation group and their general plan for deployment. Notwithstanding these basic requirements, most international CSOs would object to any undue restrictions on their freedom of movement and operation in carrying out their tasks.

General Principles of Operation

The basic principles of election observation apply to domestic and international observers alike. They are both expected to abide by the laws of the host country and by the rules and guidelines laid down by the EMB concerned. A common code of conduct applies to both; most importantly all election observers are expected to carry out their tasks in a neutral and non-partisan manner. Although their methodologies may differ, both domestic and international election observers are expected to report their findings objectively and accurately.

CSOs' Influence on Free and Fair Elections

The impact of CSOs participation in multi-party elections has been profound. Perhaps the influence of these organizations is more pronounced in transitional situations, such as post-conflict, post military or post one-party regimes. In such circumstances, the presence of CSOs, particularly domestic observers who can be and are often mobilized in great numbers, lends a calming and at the same time a prying dimension to the preparation and conduct of all election processes observed. EMBs are aware that the presence of election observers, especially international observers, has a positive effect on election officers in the field. They are aware that election observers are familiar with the election rules and procedures that are to be applied to the election process which is being observed and so they improve on their performance, avoid errors and irregularities. Positive endorsement of an election as being free and fair by CSOs does have the potential to contribute to the acceptance of the election results by the defeated candidates/parties, thus enhancing the legitimacy of the incoming political administration.

There are limitations on the extent to which CSOs can impact free and fair elections because their presence is usually effective at a minority of the critical election processes, mainly due to the lack of resources and some times lack of interest in the less high-profile election processes. This observation is true of domestic and international observers. Few show a high degree of interest in registration of voters, delimitation of electoral districts or nomination (registration of candidates to contest elections). Most election observer groups are busiest a few weeks leading up to polling and the subsequent counting of the votes. Few observers bother to attend hearings of complaints before the EMB concerned or of election disputes before the courts or election tribunals.

Increasingly, CSOs, both domestic and international, are playing important roles in training election officers and civic and voter education officers. Their participation as partners of EMBs in the production and dissemination of voter/civic education materials is important, particularly in outreach programmes.

Challenges for CSOs in Election Organization in the Member States of the African Union

The rapid growth of democratization, globalization, and that of the third sector (CSOs) in the Member States of the AU happened during the first decade of the 21st Century and is continuing. The simultaneous occurrence of these events had an influence on each other. But it was the impact of democratization—governance and particularly elections that concerns us here. The potential of CSOs in the expanding field of election organization, its modernization and growing privatization of election processes offers challenges in the African Union for creative CSOs.

Training—The field of training election officers, political parties, CSOs' staff and workers, candidates and party agencies continues attracting funding from important donors like the USAID and the European Union, as well as other traditional donors. Much of these funds are passed on through international CSOs which make them available to national CSOs through regional and national agencies. This is a welcome development which should assist CSOs, CBOs and FBOs, formal and informal, to secure funding for training in order to draw down on more funding through better project preparation and improved budget presentation. New training techniques such as those embodied in Building Resources in Democracy, Governance and Elections (BRIDGE) should be developed and disseminated through CSOs.

Project design—CSOs should ensure that they are equipped to deal effectively with election project design, particularly in the areas of voter/civic education, training and procurement, in order to assist or monitor a given EMB in these areas.

Electoral districts etc.,—As the 'fairness' element of free and fair elections becomes more to the fore, a growing number of CSOs which favour an advocacy role are displaying interest in areas of election organization still hidden from popular concern and inputs. Included in these 'hidden' areas is the management structure of an EMB, the choice of electoral systems, delimitation of electoral districts'/constituencies' boundaries, use of advanced election technologies and improved election implementation techniques.

Cost-effectiveness—There is need for CSOs, domestic and international, to play a more positive advocacy role with respect to the cause of identifying improved cost-effective ways of organizing free and fair multi-party elections in African Union Member States. There is evidence to suggest that some CSOs enjoy the patronage flowing from the acquisition of election supplies. The introduction of good practices in procurement procedures and competitive bidding will undoubtedly mitigate the incidence of dubious patronage in this area.

Transparency—The presence of observers and their observing or monitoring activities with respect to election organization encourage

EMBs to develop greater transparency in election administration. CSOs potential to influence this aspect of EMBs' behaviour is considerable and should be encouraged.

Anti-corruption measures in elections—Various levels of corruption have been alleged in election organization and conduct with dramatic effects in Eastern European countries-Georgia, Serbia and Ukraine in recent years. Of equal concern, even if somewhat less dramatically managed, has been the conviction of many election officials after the 2004 elections in Indonesia, and the reported admitted interference with election officials by the leading presidential candidate in recent elections in the Philippines. CSOs are well placed to detect and expose incidence of election corruption through observation or monitoring of the processes of polling and counting of votes, as well as preparatory processes of elections.

Chapter X

Analysis of the Influence (if any) of Regional Economic Communities (RECs) on Regional Democracy

Introduction

There are eight Regional Economic Communities (RECs) in the African Union. Their primary role is to stimulate economic development within the respective regions that they serve, but the Union appreciated their useful and facilitating role in the fostering of democracy and democratic elections in their respective areas during the decade under review. In this chapter an attempt will be made to analyze each Regional Economic Community and see the extent, if at all, it contributed to the development of democratic elections during the first decade of the 21st Century and to see if each is structurally equipped to play a part in future development, and promotion of democratic elections. With respect to the contribution of the RECs to democratic elections, it should be remembered that each REC has competence to deal only with its member states and so its influence would always be limited geographically. Indeed, the majority of the RECs showed little interest in contributing to democratic elections during the period under review and further most of the RECs were not equipped structurally to expand into the field of elections. However for the sake of completeness each REC, as well as a few other relevant continental and regional bodies, is examined in this chapter.

The Community of Sahel-Saharan States (CEN-SAD)

The Community of Sahel-Saharan States (CEN-SAD) consists of 28 Member States[107]. It was established in 1998 and was recognized as a regional economic body in 2000 by the OAU at its ordinary session of the Conference of Leaders and Heads of State and Government in Lomé, Togo. The CEN-SAD obtained observer status in the General Assembly in 1992.

The objectives of CEN-SAD were listed as:

- Establishment of a comprehensive economic union based on a strategy implemented in accordance with the development plan that would be integrated in the national development plans of the member states. It includes investment in the agricultural, industrial, social, cultural and energy fields.
- Elimination of all obstacles impeding the unity of its member states through adopting measures to guarantee the following—

    (i) Facilitating the free movement of individuals, capital and meeting the interest of states.
    (ii) Freedom of residence, work, ownership and economic activity.
    (iii) Freedom of movement of national goods, merchandise and services.
    (iv) Encouragement of foreign trade through drawing up and implementing an investment policy in the member states.
    (v) Enhancement and improvement of land, air and sea transportation and telecommunications in member states through implementation of joint projects.

---

[107] Benin, Burkina Faso, Central African Republic, Union of the Comoros, Côte d'Ivoire, Djibouti, Egypt, Eritrea, The Gambia, Guinea, Guinea Bissau, Ghana, Great Socialist People's Libyan Arab Jamahiriya, Liberia, Kenya, Mali, Mauritania, Morocco, Niger, Nigeria, Senegal, Sierra Leone, Somali Republic, Sao Tome and Principe, Sudan, Chad, Togo and Tunisia.

> (vi) Consent of the community member states to give the citizens of member states the same privileges provided for in the constitution of member states.
>
> (vii) Coordination of pedagogical and educational systems at the various educational levels, and in scientific and technical fields.

The organs of the Community consist of the Conference of Heads of State which is responsible for policy and decision making of the Community. It meets once a year in ordinary session on a rotation basis in the capitals of the member states. It may meet in extraordinary session at the request of one member country. There is an Executive Council which is responsible for the preparation of programs of integration for the consideration by the Conference of Heads of States. The Council is composed of the Ministers responsible for external relations and cooperation; economy, finance and planning; and interior, and public security.

There is a General Secretariat which serves as the administrative and executive organ of the Community and which is responsible for the management of the daily work and the monitoring of the regular functioning of the institutions and the implementation of the objectives and policies defined by the Conference.

The Sahel-Saharan Investment and Trade Bank were established in 1999 under the auspices of the Community. The objective of the Bank is to exercise banking, financial and commercial activities including with respect to financing development projects and external trade.

There is an advisory body called the Economic, Social and Cultural Council (ESCC) composed of ten (10) members designated by each member state to assist the organs of CEN-SAD with design and preparation of programs of economic, social and cultural nature. The ESCC meets once a year in ordinary session and its headquarters are in Bamako, Mali.

This Regional Economic Community (REC) does not have a structure or mandate to deal with democratic elections and made no significant contribution to democratic elections during first decade of the 21st Century.

The Common Market for Eastern and Southern Africa (COMESA)

The Common Market for Eastern and Southern Africa (COMESA) was established in 1994 to replace the Preferential Trade Area which went back to 1981. COMESA has 21 member states[108]. Some of the objectives of COMESA are on target to be met. For example, the creation of a free trade area and the promotion of trade targets including trade liberation and customs co-operation.

The objectives of are to:

- Attain sustainable growth of the member states by promoting a more balanced and harmonious development of its production and marketing structures;
- Promote joint development in all fields of economic activity and the joint adoption of macro-economic policies and programmes to raise the standard of living of its peoples and to foster closer relations among its member states;
- Cooperate in the creation of an enabling environment for foreign, cross border and domestic investment and in joint promotion of research and adaptation of science and technology for development;
- Cooperate in the promotion of peace, security, and stability among member states in order to enhance the economic development in the region;
- Cooperate in strengthening the relations between the common market and the rest of the world and in the adoption of common positions in international fora; and
- Contribute towards the establishment, progress, and the realization of the objectives of the African Economic Community.

---

[108] Including Burundi, Comoros, DR Congo, Djibouti, Egypt, Eritrea, Ethiopia, Kenya, Libya, Madagascar, Malawi, Mauritius, Rwanda, Seychelles, Sudan, Swaziland, Uganda, Zambia and Zimbabwe. (Angola, Namibia and Swaziland had not ratified the COMESA Treaty). Lesotho suspended membership on the grounds the Treaty was incompatible with SADC membership. Tanzania announced its withdrawal from COMESA in July 1999.

COMESA established several institutions to promote sub-regional cooperation and development, including a Trade and Development Bank in Nairobi, Kenya, a Clearing House in Harare, Zimbabwe, an Association of Commercial Banks in Harare, a Leather Institute in Ethiopia, and Re-Insurance Company in Nairobi, Kenya. COMESA has also established a Court of Justice in 1994 with its seat in Khartoum since 2003.

Unlike some of the other Regional Economic Communities (RECs) of the African Union, COMESA was intended to be dedicated to trade and investment organization. However, it has established a Committee on Peace and Security which meets twice a year. COMESA's structure gives no hint that it wants to be involved in promoting democracy or democratic elections directly.

The organs of the Community are a Conference of Heads of States and Governments and a Council of Ministers which is responsible for policy making. There is a Court of Justice which became operational in 1998. The Court has seven judges and is concerned with the interpretation and application of the Treaty. A Committee of Governors of Central Banks advises the Authority of Heads of State and Government and the Council of Ministers on monetary and financial matters. An Intergovernmental Committee consisting of Permanent or Principal Secretaries designated each member state has responsibility for developing programmes and action plans in all fields of cooperation, except with respect to finance and monetary co-operation. There are 12 technical committees which are responsible for preparing and monitoring the implementation programmes and making recommendations to the Intergovernmental Committee. The Technical Committees are as follows: Administrative and Budgetary Matters; Agriculture; Comprehensive Information Systems; Energy; Finance and Monetary Affairs; Industry; Labour, Human Resources and Social Affairs; Legal Affairs; Natural Resources and Environment; Tourism and Wildlife; Trade and Customs; and Transport and Communications.

There is a Secretariat located in Zambia, which is the principal administrative organ of the Common Market.

COMESA and Democratic Elections

Although COMESA is not directly involved with elections, it did sign an agreement with the United States Agency for International Development (USAID) in areas of democracy, conflict management and regional economic integration. In 2001, COMESA Foreign Ministers moved in the direction of working with the private sector, NGOs and civil society in the promotion of peace and security. Further the Foreign Ministers agreed in 2002 that the Parliaments of the COMESA regional level had responsibilities in the promotion of a culture of peace and security. The Ministers took note of a proposal of the Parliamentarians to establish a 'COMESA Association of National Assemblies'. The Ministers expressed the view that the COMESA Secretariat could assist the National Assemblies to establish links with each other in areas including enhancing an interface with good governance and corporate governance (accountability and transparency), human rights, the rule of law, and constitutionalism; enhancing networking on electoral processes; networking on the role of political parties in enhancing 'checks and balances' and 'separation of powers' and culture of political tolerance. The Ministers also noted the proposals of the Parliamentarians that training programmes in conflict management be put in place for parliamentary candidates before an election takes place so that they are aware of the responsibilities of a parliamentarian; and that training programmes in electoral processes could be arranged on a continuous basis to equip parliamentarians with greater knowledge and information on peace and security and on the events in other member states.

COMESA's structure and its activities during the decade under review had not indicated that there was much potential for directly furthering the cause of democratic elections in the African Union. As is indicated in its terms of reference, its focus is more on greater industrial productivity, and competitiveness, increased agricultural productivity and food security, more rational exploitation of natural resources, more harmonized monetary, banking and financial policies, and more reliable transport and communications infrastructure.

East African Community (EAC)

The present East African Community was formed in July 2000 and in 2001 replaced the interim structures that followed the demise of the first East African integration movement in 1977. The Treaty provides for a customs union and a monetary union. The ultimate goal is a political federation. The current membership with the joining of Burundi and Rwanda in 2007 is five.[109] The objectives of the Community are to improve and strengthen co-operation between the member states and in particular in the fields of transport and communication, trade and industry, security, immigration and promotion of investment in the region. The regional organization aims to achieve its goals through the following:

- Promotion of a sustainable growth and equitable development of the region, including rational development of the region's natural resources and protection of the environment;
- Strengthening and consolidation of the longstanding political, economic, social, cultural and traditional customs and associations between the peoples of the region in promoting a people-centred mutual development;
- Enhancement and strengthening of participation of the private sector and civil society;
- Mainstreaming of gender in all its programmes and enhancement of the role of women in development;
- Promotion of good governance, including adherence to the principles of democracy, rule of law, accountability, transparency, social justice, equal opportunities and gender equality; and
- Promotion of peace, security and stability within the region.

The East African Community operates on a five-year development cycle. Its strategy places emphasis on economic co-operation and development with a strong focus on the role of the private sector and civil society in partnership with the public sector.

The main organs of the EAC are the Summit of Heads of State and Government, the Council of Ministers, the Coordination Committee, the

---

[109] Burundi, Kenya, Rwanda, Uganda, and Tanzania.

Sectoral Committees, the East African Court of Justice, the East African Legislature, and the Secretariat.

The Summit consists of the Heads of State and Government of the Partner States. It meets once a year and receives an annual progress report and other reports submitted by the Council of Ministers. It may meet in extraordinary meetings where necessary.

The Council of Ministers is the policy-making organ of the Community. It consists of the Ministers responsible for the operation of each Partner State and such other Ministers of the Partner States as each Partner State nominates. The functions of the Council are to promote, monitor, and keep under constant review the implementation of programmes of the Community and ensure the proper functioning of the organization. The Council meets in regular session twice a year. It may establish Sectoral Councils whose decisions have the same effect as decision as the Council of Ministers.

The Co-ordination Committee consists of the Permanent Secretaries responsible for regional co-operation between Partner States and such other Permanent Secretaries of the Partner States as each Partner State may determine. It reports to the Council of Ministers and coordinates the activities of the Sectoral Committees.

The Sectoral Committees report to the Co-ordination Committee. They are established by the Council on recommendation of the Co-ordination Committee which sets out their composition and functions.

The East Africa Court of Justice has jurisdiction over the interpretation and application of the Common Market matters. The Court's appellate, human rights and other jurisdiction are to be determined by the Council of Ministers in a Protocol at a later date.

The Treaty which established the EAC provided for an East African Legislative Assembly (EALA) The EALA may be described as the independent legislative arm of the Community. It was formally inaugurated in November 2001, and the Second East African Legislative Assembly held it first sitting on 5th June in 2007 in Arusha.

Membership & Functions of EALA

Under the old allocation, there were 27 elected Members of the EALA, 9 from each partner state and 5 ex-officio Members. Members are indirectly elected by their respective National Assemblies. The Treaty formula requires that the Members elected do represent a diversity of views in their National Assembly and have a gender component as well. The EALA has the following major legislative functions to:

Liaise with National Assemblies of Partner States on matters relating to the Community;

Debate and approve the budget of the Community;

Consider annual reports on activities of the Community, annual audit reports of the Audit Commission and any other reports referred to it by the Council of Ministers; and

Discuss all matters pertaining to the Community and make recommendations to the Council as it may deem necessary for the implementation of the Treaty

The Assembly has a wide remit being the legislative arm of the Community with oversight mandate on all matters that fall within the Community's work. The Assembly members have visited many parts of East Africa to familiarize themselves with the conditions, resources and challenges of the region and to publicize the work of the Community. The EALA is empowered to make its own rules of procedure and to set up committees. The EALA has constituted seven Standing Committees—Accounts; Agriculture, Tourism and Natural Resources; General Purpose; House Business; Legal, Rules, and Privileges; Regional Affairs and Conflict Resolution; and Trade Communication and Investment.

The terms of reference of the EALA do not directly deal with democracy development and democratic elections, but the existence of an Assembly created a measure of awareness about the need for the member states to be active in the furtherance of democratic elections. Indeed, when the East Africa Region was selected to host the first orientation course for AU election observers in Nairobi, Kenya, in September 2009, the member states of the EAC sent representatives to the orientation course.

Economic Community of Central African States (ECCAS)

The Economic Community of Central African States (ECCAS) emerged from the Central African Customs and Economic Union (UDEAC) in 1981. The ECCAS was formally established in 1983 by the UDEAC members and the members of the Economic Community of the Great Lakes States (CEPGL) (Burundi, Rwanda, and the then Zaire) and Sao Tomé and Principe. Angola was an observer until it joined in 1999. Due to conflict in the area, for many years the ECCAS was not fully functional (Angola and Rwanda fought on opposite sides. There was a measure of revival of the ECCAS as a functioning Community in 1999, the year that Angola joined as a full member. The 10th Ordinary Session of Heads of State and Government were held in Malabo in June 2002. The Summit adopted a protocol on the establishment of a Network of Parliamentarians of Central Africa (REPAC) and the standing orders of the Council for Peace and Security in Central Africa (COPAX), including the Defence and Security Commission (CDC), Multinational Force of Central Africa (FOMAC) and the Early Warning Mechanism of Central Africa (MARAC). Rwanda rejoined ECCAS as a full member at that Summit. The membership of ECCAS stood at eleven at the time of writing.[110] At the 11th Ordinary Session of the Heads of State and Government held in Brazzaville in 2004, it was announced that the Protocol on Mutual Security Pact in Central Africa (COPAX) had entered into force. That Summit adopted a declaration on gender equality.

Objectives of ECCAS

ECCAS seeks to achieve collective autonomy, raise the living standard of its population and maintain economic stability through harmonious cooperation. The ultimate aim is to establish a Central African Common

---

[110] Angola, Burundi, Cameroon, Central African Republic, Chad, Congo (Brazzaville), Democratic Republic of Congo, Equatorial Guinea, Gabon, Rwanda, and Sao Tomé and Principe.

Market. At its Summit in Malabo in 2002, four priority areas were identified, namely, to:

- Develop capacities to maintain peace, security and stability, which are essential prerequisites for economic and social development;
- Develop physical, economic and monetary integration;
- Develop a culture of human integration; and
- Establish an autonomous financing mechanism for ECCAS.

The Structure of ECCAS

The formal structure of ECCAS consists of the Conference of Heads of State and Government; Council of Ministers; the General Secretariat; Court of Justice; and a Consultative Commission.

ECCAS and Democratic Elections

The ECCAS does not directly have any objective devoted to promote democracy or democratic elections. However it does have a protocol establishing a Network of Parliamentarians of ECCAS which can foster democratic procedures. The first meeting of the Network of Central African Parliamentarians was held in Luanda, Angola, in November 2000, and in September 2001, the Human Rights and Democracy Centre held its first meeting in Libreville, Gabon. However during the first decade of the 21st Century, the contribution of ECCAS to democratic elections in its member states was imperceptible.

Economic Community of West African States (ECOWAS)

The concept of a West African community was first put forward in 1964 by President William Tubman of Liberia. Four States, Côte d'Ivoire, Guinea, Liberia and Sierra Leone, responded positively and signed an agreement in February 1965, but the idea and the agreement withered away. The idea was re-launched by General Gowon of Nigeria and General Eyadema of Togo in 1972 and eventually led to the signing of the treaty for an Economic Community of West African States in Lagos in May 1975. Further protocols launching ECOWAS were signed in Lomé, Togo, in November 1976. A revised ECOWAS Treaty aimed at accelerating economic integration and increasing political co-operation was signed in 1993. The membership of ECOWAS is 15.[111]

Objectives

ECOWAS seeks to promote cooperation and integration in economic, social and cultural activity, ultimately leading to the establishment of an economic and monetary union through the total integration of the national economies of member states. It aims to raise the living standards of its peoples, maintain and enhance economic stability, foster relations among member states and contribute to the progress and development of the African Continent. The revised treaty of 1993 was designed to extend economic and political cooperation among member states and designate the achievement of a common market and a single currency as economic objectives. With respect to political objectives, a West African parliament, an economic and social council and an ECOWAS court of justice was proposed to replace the existing Tribunal and enforce Community decisions. The Community was charged with the responsibility of preventing and settling regional conflicts.

Structure of ECOWAS

The Community of the Authority of Heads of State and Government, the Council of Ministers, the Community Tribunal, the ECOWAS Parliament, the Executive Secretariat and six Specialized Commissions.

The Authority of Heads of State and Government of Member States is the supreme organ of the Community and are composed of the Heads of States or Government of Member States. It is responsible for the general direction and control of the Community and takes all measures to ensure its progressive development and realization of its objectives. The general role of the Authority includes the following, to:

---

[111] Benin, Burkina Faso, Cape Verde, Côte d'Ivoire, The Gambia, Ghana, Guinea, Guinea Bissau, Liberia Mali, Niger, Nigeria, Senegal, Sierra Leone, and Togo. Mauritania withdrew from the organization in 1999.

- Determine the general policy and major guidelines of the Community and give directive there to;
- Harmonize and coordinate the economic, scientific, technical, cultural and social policies of Member States;
- Oversee the functioning of Community institutions and follow up implementation of Community objectives;
- Prepare and adopt its Rules of Procedure;
- Appoint the Executive Secretary in accordance with the provisions of the Treaty;
- Appoint on the recommendations of the Council, the External Auditors;
- Delegate to the Council, where necessary, the authority to take such decisions as stipulated in the Treaty;
- Refer where it deems necessary any matter to the Community Court of Justice when it confirms, that a Member State or institution of the Community has failed to honor any of its obligations, or an institution of the Community has acted beyond the limits of its authority or has abused the powers conferred on it by the provisions of the Treaty, by a decision of the Authority or a regulation of the Council;
- Request the Community Court of Justice as, and when necessary, to give advisory opinion on any legal questions; and
- Exercise any other powers conferred on it under the Treaty.

The Authority meets annually in ordinary session. It may meet in extra-ordinary session if convened by the Chairman of the Authority or at the request of a Member State if that request is supported by a simple majority of the Member States. The Chairman of the Authority is a Member State elected annually by the Authority.

Council of Ministers

The Council comprises the Minister responsible for ECOWAS Affairs and any other Minister of each Member State. Except as otherwise provided in the Treaty, the Council is mandated to:

- Make recommendations to the Authority on any action aimed at attaining the objectives of the Community;

- Appoint all statutory appointees other than the Executive Secretary;
- Through the powers delegated by the Authority, issue directives on matters concerning coordination and harmonization of economic integration policies;
- Make recommendations to the Authority on the appointment of External Auditors;
- Prepare and adopt rules of procedure;
- Adopt the Staff Regulations and approve the organizational structure of the institutions of the Community;
- Approve the work programmes and budgets of the Community and its institutions;
- Request the Community Court of Justice, where necessary, to give advisory opinion on any legal questions; and
- Carry out all other functions assigned to it under this Treaty and exercise all powers delegated to it by the Authority.

Tribunal

The Treaty provides for a Community Tribunal, the competence of which is determined by the Conference of Heads of State and Government. The Tribunal interprets the provisions of the Treaty and disposes of disputes between member states.

Executive Secretariat

There is an Executive Secretary who is elected for four years, but may be re-elected once only.

Community Court of Justice

ECOWAS established a Court of Justice in 1999. It deals with complaints from member states and institutions of ECOWAS, as well as issues relating to defaulting states. The Court is a permanent body with seven judges, a president and a chief registrar.

ECOWAS Parliament

The ECOWAS Parliament was convened in 2002. It has 120 seats with MPs representatives. Each of the 15 Member States had a guaranteed minimum of five seats. The remaining 40 seats were shared on the basis of population. The over all allocation of seats in the Parliament was as follows—Nigeria 35 seats, Ghana 8 seats, Côte d'Ivoire seven seats, Burkina Faso, Guinea, Mali, Niger, and Senegal had six seats each. Benin, Cape Verde, the Gambia, Guinea Bissau, Liberia Sierra Leone and Togo, had five seats each. The allocation of seats would be reviewed periodically. The members of the Parliament are drawn from the membership of the national parliaments of each member state. The Parliament is mandated to consider issues concerning human rights and fundamental freedoms of citizens; interconnection of energy networks; interconnection of telecommunications systems; increased cooperation in the area of radio, television and other intra—and inter-community media link; as well as development of national communication system. The Parliament may be consulted on matters dealing with public health policies for the community; common educational policy through harmonization of existing systems and specialization of existing universities; adjustment of education within the Community to international standards; youth and sports, scientific and technological research; and community policy on environment. The Parliament may review any issues affecting the Community, including the ECOWAS Treaty, Community citizenship and social integration. The Parliament may make recommendations on these issues to the appropriate institutions and or organs of the Community.

Network of National Electoral Management Bodies of ECOWAS Member States

In its endeavour to strengthen its democratic credentials and particularly democratic elections, the National Electoral Management Bodies (NEMBs) of ECOWAS Member States in 2008 established a Network of National Electoral Management Bodies. The broad aim of the Network was to underpin the democratization process in the ECOWAS region. The specific objectives of the Network aim to:

- Promote transparent and credible elections in West Africa;
- Promote independent and impartial electoral management bodies;

- Promote public confidence in election processes through transparent and credible electoral procedures;
- Develop professional capacity of electoral officials with integrity, probity and a strong sense of public service;
- Commit to the deepening of a democratic culture and creating a favourable environment in which elections can be held peacefully;
- Exchange experiences, information, technology and literature pertaining to elections among election management bodies and other relevant organizations;
- Cooperate in the improvement of electoral laws and practices;
- Pool and share electoral resources to reduce cost and harmonize electoral processes, and
- Promote the welfare of its members in the pursuit of their professional duties.

ECOWAS and Civil Society Organizations (CSOs)

ECOWAS has worked closely on various issues in its region. An example of this was the active role that CSOs played at the ECOWAS conference on the International Criminal Court (ICC) in Abidjan in 2002. The mainly legal and human rights related CSOs adopted common strategies of support to urge those Member States of ECOWAS which had not done so to speed up their ratification process, and those that had ratified to accelerate implementation of the ICC instruments. Similarly, ECOWAS had shown an interest in collaborating with CSOs that were involved in conflict resolution in the region. Even in the late 1990s there was concern that the civil society groups in the ECOWAS region were scattered throughout the region and focused individually on conflict prevention. Gradual improvement with the assistance of partners began to take place and with the participation of women. CSO groups formed a coalition for conflict management in Mali, and women also formed the African Women's Anti-War Coalition with membership in several Member States of ECOWAS.

Contribution to democratic Elections

The ECOWAS region had been a troubled one throughout the period of the first decade of the 21st Century when conflict was seen in many member states of the region including Côte d'Ivoire, Guinea, Guinea Bissau, Liberia, Mauritania, Niger and Sierra Leone. The ECOWAS played a commendable role in bringing most of these conflicts to an end within the decade and with respect to the restoration of democratic elections. ECOWAS was also active in the field of regional election observation and many of its member states sent representatives to the AU's second orientation course for election observers held in Dakar, Senegal in March 2010. The ECOWAS has certain structures which facilitates contribution to the development of democratic elections in its region and hence also in the AU as a whole, namely, a Parliament and Network facility among the EMBs of ECOWAS. The contribution to democracy and democratic elections by ECOWAS during the first decade of the 21st Century in its region and hence to the AU as a whole was considerable.

The Intergovernmental Authority for Development (IGAD)

The Intergovernmental Authority for Development had its origins in the disastrous droughts that struck the region in 1973 and 1984. With the support of the international community the Intergovernmental Authority on Drought and Development (IGADD) was launched in 1986 and was superseded in 1996 by the Intergovernmental Authority on Development (IGAD). The IGADD is headquartered in Djibouti and until Eritrea joined shortly after its independence in 1993,[112] there were six members, namely, Djibouti, Ethiopia, Kenya, Somalia, Sudan and Uganda.

The IGADD was revitalized in 1996 when it re-emerged with the new name of IGAD. It adopted a Vision Statement, 'IGAD will be the premier regional organization for achieving peace, prosperity and regional integration in the IGAD region.' It also adopted a Mission Statement:

---

[112] Eritrea suspended its membership in 2007.

'The IGAD Mission is to assist and complement the efforts of the Member States to achieve, through increased cooperation:

- Food and security and environmental protection
- Promotion and maintenance of peace and security and humanitarian affairs, and
- Economic cooperation and integration.
- Objectives of IGAD
- The objectives of IGAD are to:
- Promote joint development strategies and gradually harmonize macro-economic policies and programmes in the social, technological and scientific fields;
- Harmonize policies with regard to trade, customs, transport, communications, agriculture, and natural resources and promote free movement of goods, services, and people within the region;
- Create an enabling environment for foreign, cross-border and domestic trade and investment;
- Achieve regional food security and encourage and assist efforts of Member States to collectively combat drought and other natural and man-made disasters and their natural consequences;
- Initiate and promote programmes and projects to achieve regional food security and sustainable development of natural resources and environmental protection, and encourage and assist efforts of Member States to collectively combat drought and other natural and man-made disasters and their consequences;
- Develop and improve a coordinated and complementary infrastructure, in areas of transport, telecommunications and energy in the region;
- Promote peace and stability in the region and create mechanisms within the region for the prevention, management and resolution of inter-State and intra-State conflicts through dialogue;
- Mobilize resources for the implementation of emergency, short-term, medium-term and long-term programmes within the framework of regional cooperation;
- Promote and realize the objectives of the Common Market for Eastern and Southern Africa (COMESA) and the African Economic Community; and

- Facilitate, promote and strengthen cooperation in research development and application in science and technology.

The Structure of IGAD

The Assembly of Heads of State and Government

This is the supreme policy-making organ of the Authority. It determines the objectives, guidelines and programmes of IGAD. It meets once a year. The Chairman is elected from among the Member States in rotation.

The Council of Ministers

The Council of Ministers is composed of the Minister of Foreign Affairs and any other Minister designated by each member state. The Council formulates policy, and approves the work programme and annual budget of the Secretariat at it biannual sessions.

The Committee of Ambassadors

The Committee of Ambassadors comprises IGAD Member States' Ambassadors accredited to the country of IGAD Headquarters. It meets as often as the need arises to advise the Executive Secretary.

The Secretariat

The Secretariat is headed by an Executive Secretary appointed by the Heads of State and Government for a term of four years and renewable once.

Contribution to Democratic Elections

IGAD showed no particular interest in expanding into areas of democratic elections. It was not equipped with any relevant structures to deal with elections and its objectives did not include elections.

Southern African Development Community (SADC)

The Southern African Development Community (SADC) was the successor organization to the Southern African Development Co-ordination Conference (SADCC) which was transformed into the new Community in 1992.

Objectives

The objectives of SADC are to:

- Achieve development and economic growth, alleviate poverty, enhance the standard and quality of life of the people of Southern Africa and support the socially disadvantaged through regional integration;
- Evolve common political values, system and institutions;
- Promote and defend peace and security;
- Promote self-sustaining development on the basis of collective self-reliance, and the interdependence of Member States;
- Achieve complementarity between national regional strategies and programmes;
- Promote and maximize productive employment and utilization of resources of the region;
- Achieve sustainable utilization of natural resources and effective protection of the environment;
- Strengthen and consolidate the long standing historical, social and cultural affinities and links among the people of the Region.

The Main Organs

The policy-making organ of SADC is the Summit which comprises Heads of State and Governments. The Summit meets once a year and is responsible for the overall policy direction and control of the Community.

The Troika system which consist of the Chair, Incoming Chair and the Outgoing Chair, has become a formal feature of the SADC structure. Other members may be co-opted to the Troika, if needed. The Troika system has been credited with facilitating expeditious execution and implementation of decisions. The Troika system operates at the level of the Summit, the Organ on Politics, Defence and Security, Council and Standing Committee of Senior Officials.

The Organ on Politics and Security is coordinated at the level of the Summit on a Troika basis and reports to the Chairperson of SADC. The Chairperson of the Organ is selected annually on a rotation basis. The Member State holding the Chairperson of the Organ provides the secretariat services. The Chairperson of the Summit cannot simultaneously hold the Chair of the Organ.

The Council of Ministers consists of Ministers from each Member State, usually from the Ministries of Foreign Affairs and Economic Planning or Finance. The Council is responsible for overseeing the functioning and development of SADC and ensuring that policies are properly implemented.

The Integrated Committee of Ministers was designed to give policy guidance, coordination and harmonization of cross-sectoral activities. It oversees the activities relating to trade, industry, finance and investment; infrastructure services; food, agriculture and natural resources; social and human development and special programmes, including the implementation of the Strategic Plan in their areas of competence. It is constituted by at least two Ministers from each Member State. It provides policy guideline to the Secretariat and makes decisions on matters relating to the Directorates as well as monitor and evaluate their work.

Tribunal-the Treaty makes provision for the establishment of a Tribunal to deal with the interpretation of the Treaty, and adjudicate upon disputes referred to it.

The SADC National Committees are composed of key stakeholders from government, private sector and civil society in Member States. Their main functions are to provide inputs at the national level in the formulation of regional policies and strategies, and co-ordinate and oversee the implementation of such programmes at the national level.

The Secretariat is the principal executive body of SADC. It is responsible for strategic planning, coordination and management of SADC programmes. It is located in Gaborone, Botswana.

SADC Parliamentary Forum

The Southern African Development Community Parliamentary Forum (SADC PF) was established in 1997 as an autonomous institution of SADC. It is a regional inter-parliamentary body comprising thirteen parliaments with more than 3500 parliamentarians in the SADC region.[113]

The main aims of the Forum are to:

- Promote human rights, gender equality, good governance, democracy and transparency;
- Promote peace, security and stability;
- Hasten the pace of economic cooperation, development and integration on the basis of equality and mutual benefits;
- Facilitate networking with other inter-parliamentary organizations;
- Promote the participation of non-governmental organizations, business and intellectual communities in SADC activities;
- Familiarize the peoples of SADC with the aims and objectives of SADC; and
- Inform SADC of the popular views on development and issues affecting the region.

The Forum has shown interest in election observation in the SADC Member States and has carried out election observation in several Members States, including Mauritius, Mozambique, Namibia, Tanzania and Zimbabwe. Drawing on its practical experience, the Forum developed and adopted electoral norms and standards for the SADC region which serve as bench marks for assessing the management and conduct of elections in the region.

---

[113] The member parliaments are Angola, Botswana, Democratic Republic of Congo, Lesotho, Malawi, Mauritius, Mozambique, Namibia, South Africa, Swaziland, Tanzania, Zambia and Zimbabwe.

The Forum developed a strategic plan for the period 2006-10 which included a review of regional trends and challenges, and the Forum's strengths and weaknesses.

The SADC Electoral Commission's Forum

This Forum was launched in July 1998 and comprised 12 electoral commissions of the SADC region. The Forum seeks to foster cooperation between members in order to promote a culture of democracy and free and fair elections.

The objectives of the Forum are to:

- Strengthen cooperation amongst electoral commissions in SADC countries;
- Promote conditions conducive to free, fair and transparent elections in SADC countries;
- Confirm a commitment and dedication to the development of democracy in SADC countries;
- Promote democracy as a political system of responsible and accountable government through the conduct of regular elections;
- Encourage the utilization of systems and processes that will encourage the full participation of the electorate in the election process;
- Ensure the development of a democratic culture and a dynamic electoral process in SADC countries through close cooperation, fellowship and consultation.

SADC and Civil Society Organizations

The SADC has had a long experience in working with civil society organizations (CSOs). Indeed, the SADC National Committees provision listed CSOs as among the key stakeholders that should provide inputs at the national level in the formulation of regional policies and strategies. However, some CSOs have expressed dissatisfaction with SADC's relations with CSOs. For example, the Communiqué of the Civil Society Forum on 'Democratic Governance and Regional Economic Integration' held in Lesotho in August 2006 stated that while the SADC Treaty commit relevant SADC structures to involve civil society in the region in their deliberations and processes, civil society remained excluded and marginalized from key SADC processes. It went on to state that that trend ran against the spirit and commitment contained in the SADC Treaty in chapter seven.

In a similar vein, the Civil Society Organizations meeting at the SADC Civil Society forum in Lusaka, Zambia, in August 2007, called upon the SADC Heads of State and Governments to, among other things:

- Institute immediate measures to transform and create concrete interface among all the SADC structures in order to allow effective participation of civil society;
- Undertake progressive dialogue between civil society and governments in advancing the development agenda of the region;
- Take immediate measures to institutionalize civil society involvement in key decision-making processes aimed at national and regional development;

Further, at the NGO roundtables to strengthen capacity building on advocacy activism at the SADC summit at Houghton in Johannesburg, South Africa in August 2008, it was noted that the SADC Treaty expressly recognized the role that NGOs can and should play in the activities of SADC, but that there was no express provision in the treaty stipulating the manner and mechanism in which NGOs can participate in the SADC processes. They went on to recommend that the SADC Treaty should be amended to enable an NGO/Civil Society Institution or mechanism to be expressly included as one of the SADC institutions.

Despite the several expressions of dissatisfaction by the civil society organizations themselves, it is encouraging to note that the Executive Secretary of SADC, Dr. Prego Ramsamy, in his address entitled 'Role of Civil Society Promoting Regional Integration' in March 2004 noted that SADC had accorded top priority and given full recognition to the key role and significant contribution of civil society and non-governmental organizations.

Contribution to Democratic Elections

The SADC region had limited success during the first decade of the 21st Century in promoting democratic elections as a REC. Within the ambit of SADC many member states of the REC consolidated their ability to organize credible elections including Angola, Botswana, Lesotho, Malawi, Mozambique, Namibia, South Africa and Zambia. Swaziland and Zimbabwe were the two exceptions which did not have proper democratic elections during the decade and SADC was unsuccessful in influencing both countries to join the path to democratic elections. SADC had credible structures in the SADC Parliamentary Forum and the SADC Electoral Commissions' Forum, both of which were discussed above and both of which have the potential to make contributions to democratic elections the EMBs in member states through technical assistance and creation of greater awareness about the democratic electoral process. In turn, the AU as whole will benefit from improved quality of election organization in a substantial number of AU Member States.

Union du Maghreb Arabe (UMA)

The Union du Maghreb Arabe has been recognized as one of the eight regional economic communities within the African Union. It consists of five members, namely, Algeria, Libya, Mauritania, Morocco and Tunisia. The Treaty to establish the Arab Maghreb Union (AMU) was signed on February 17 1989 in Marrakech. There are a number of multilateral agreements covering economic, social and cultural areas, but the Union has not been active. Although it has been designated a pillar of the African Economic Community (AEC) it has not yet signed up to the Protocol on relations with the AEC.

Objectives

The main objectives of the AMU Treaty are aimed at strengthening ties among the Member States and to introduce free circulation of goods and services. The Treaty covers common defense and non-interference in the domestic affairs of partners. It also charts the broad economic strategy to be followed by its members.

Structure

The Council of Heads of State is the supreme institutional organ. It meets annually. The Council of Foreign Affairs Ministers meets regularly and prepares for the annual Heads of State Meetings. There is a Consultative Assembly made up of 30 representatives from each Member State the can advise the Council of Heads of State. A Court of Justice, composed of two judges from each Member State has been set up. There is a Secretariat established in Rabat and the budget is contributed equally by the Member States. The organization is served by a number of specialized committees in areas such as food security, economic and financial affairs, basic infrastructure, and human resources.

Contribution to Democratic Elections

The UMA was not equipped structurally to contribute to democratic elections and had not sought during the period under review to expand into the promotion of democratic elections.

The RECs as Pillars of the Economic Community of Africa

The African Economic Community (AEC) was launched in 1994 when the Abuja Treaty, which was signed in 1991, came into force. The broad goals of the AEC were to create free trade areas, custom unions, a single market, a central bank, and a common currency, all leading to the formation of an economic and monetary union. The Regional Economic Communities (RECs) which are primarily trade blocs that in some cases have developed cooperative mechanisms in military, political, peace and security, as well as the promotion of democracy. The RECs, or most of them, constitute the pillars on which the AEC envisaged building its various economic and monetary institutions. One slight complication that the AEC has to deal with in using the RECs as its pillars is the fact that a number of the RECs have overlapping membership. Further, some of the 'pillars' contain subgroups which have their own customs and or monetary unions. The pillars are *Community of Sahel-Saharan States* (CEN-SAD), *Common Market for Eastern and Southern Africa* (COMESA), *East African Community (EAC), Economic Community of*

Central African States (ECCAS/CEEAC), *Economic Community of West African States* (ECOWAS), *Intergovernmental Authority on Development* (IGAD*), Southern African Development Community(SADC), and the Arab Maghreb Union* (AMU/UMA). The subgroups include the Economic and Monetary Community of Central Africa (CEMAC) subgroup of ECCAS, West African Economic and Monetary Union (UEMOA) and West African Monetary Zone (WAMZ) both of which are subgroups of ECOWAS, and the South African Customs Union (SACU) a subgroup of SADC. There are several trade blocs in the African Union which are not 'pillars' of the AEC.[114] The AEC's creation was scheduled to take place in six phases, namely, phase 1 creation of regional blocs in regions where such did not exist, to be completed by 1999;[115] phase 2, consisted of strengthening intra-REC integration and inter-REC harmonization, to be completed by 2007;[116] phase 3 entail establishing a free trade area and customs union in each regional bloc, to be completed by 2017[117]; phase 4 aimed at establishing a continental-wide customs union to be completed by 2019; phase 5 aimed to establishing a continental-wide African Common Market, to be completed by2023; and phase 6 aimed to establishing a continental-wide economic and monetary union and parliament to be completed by 2028. The end of the transition period was set for 2034 at the latest.

Africa Free Trade Zone

Phase 3 of the AEC was given a significant boost when the African Free Trade Zone (AFTZ) was announced at the EAC-SADC-COMESA Summit in October 2008. Analysts believe that the AFTZ may in time serve to eliminate duplicative membership in other regional economic

---

[114] These include Greater Arab Free Trade Area (GAFTA) (which also extend to many Middle Eastern States); Economic Community of the Great Lakes (CEPGL), Indian Ocean Commission (COI), Liptako-Gourma Authority (LGA) and Mano River Union (MRU).

[115] Phase 1 completed, although the Arab Maghreb Union members and Sahrawi Republic were not participating. The way was left open for Somalia to participate when the conflict situation was resolved.

[116] Believed to be met generally, but difficult to assess factually.

[117] Work in progress.

cooperation schemes, and enhance intra-regional trade and increase growth. The membership of the AFTZ stands at 26 countries.[118]

The New Partnership for Africa's Development (NEPAD)

Like most of the Regional Economic Communities, the New Partnership for Africa's Development (NEPAD) had a brief but multi-dimensional history before assuming its current form and nomenclature. In its early stages, NEPAD emerged from two schools of thought, the Millennium Partnership for African Recovery Programme promoted by Former President Thabo Mbeki of South Africa, Former President Olusegun Obassanjo of Nigeria, and President Abdelaziz Bouteflika of Algeria, and the OMEGA plan for Africa attributed to President Abdoulaye Wade of Senegal. The two plans were merged with the help of the UN Economic Commission for Africa (UNECA) and submitted to the Conference of African Ministers of Finance and Ministers of Development and Planning in Algiers, May 2001. The OAU Assembly of Heads of State and Government adopted the merged plans in Lusaka, Zambia, in July 2001 under the name of the New African Initiative (NAI). The plan was subsequently endorsed by partners of the AU, namely, the leaders of the G8 countries, European Union, China and Japan. In October 2001 the Heads of State and Government Implementation Committee (HSGIG) for the Project named it the New Partnership for Africa's Development, and NEPAD became a programme of the AU, (which had replaced the OAU in 2002). NEPAD set up its Secretariat in South Africa to coordinate and implement its programmes.

NEPAD's objectives are to:

- Eradicate poverty;
- Promote sustainable growth and development;

---

[118] These countries are: Angola, Botswana, Burundi, Comoros, Djibouti, Democratic Republic of the Congo, Egypt, Eritrea, Ethiopia, Kenya, Lesotho, Libya, Madagascar, Malawi, Mauritius, Mozambique, Namibia, Rwanda, Seychelles, Swaziland, South Africa, Sudan, Tanzania, Uganda, Zambia and Zimbabwe.

- Integrate Africa in the world economy; and
- Accelerate the empowerment of women.

It is based on the principles of good governance, democracy, human rights and conflict resolution. NEPAD aims to attract increased investment, capital flows and funding.

The July 2002 African Union Summit committed the members of NEPAD to a Declaration on Democracy, Political, Economic and Corporate Governance, (Annex 5 herein) and in accordance to which the participating states of NEPAD agreed to adhere to just, honest, transparent, accountable and participatory government and probity in public life. They also agreed to subscribe to the rule of law; equality of all citizens before the law; individual and collective freedoms; the right to participate in free, credible and democratic political processes; and adherence to the separation of powers, including protection of the independence of the judiciary and the effectiveness of parliaments. The Declaration on Democracy, Political, Economic and Corporate Governance committed the states to establish an African Peer Review Mechanism (ARRM) to promote the compliance of the states with their obligation pursuant to the Declaration.

Status of NEPAD

From the outset NEPAD posed certain challenges as it was set up outside of the framework of the African Union programmes. The perception of some AU Member States was that NEPAD was seeking to rival the AU, although NEPAD was conceived as a programme of activities and not an organization. The closer integration of NEPAD into AU's structures and processes has been the object of several AU Summits and efforts by the HSGIG, the latest of which was in 2008 when five Heads of State, Presidents Mbeki of South Africa, Wade of Senegal, Bouteflika of Algeria, Mubarak of Egypt and Yar'Adua of Nigeria, met in Senegal under a mandate to consider progress in implementing NEPAD.

The Structure of NEPAD

The Heads of State and Government Implementing Committee (HSGIC) is the principal 'organ' to which the NEPAD Secretariat reports. It comprises three states for each region of the AU and meets several times a year, and reports to the AU Assembly of Heads of State and Government.

There is a steering committee, which comprises of 20 AU Member States and which oversees projects and program development.

The NEPAD Secretariat is based in Midrand, South Africa. Its role is to coordinate programmes and mobilize resources.

Programmes of NEPAD

There are eight priority programmes of NEPAD, namely, political, economic and corporate governance; agriculture; infrastructure; education; health; science and technology; market access and tourism; and environment.

Criticisms of NEPAD

The NEPAD model was not liked by a great cross section of CSOs and NGOs and indeed many rejected it, and later they were joined by African scholars and intellectuals in a Declaration in 2002 in Accra on Africa's

Development challenges. Many of those who did not favour NEPAD were disappointed by the lack of wide consultation before it was launched. Other critics, notably President Wade of Senegal, have become disenchanted with NEPAD because of its poor output to date, slow decision-making and weak implementation record.

The African Peer Review Mechanism

Peer review of the kind set out in the African Peer Review Mechanism refers to a methodical examination and evaluation of a participating State by other participating States in the Mechanism with

A view to offering assistance to the reviewed State to improve its policy making and adopt improved practices in order to comply with agreed standards and principles.

The African Peer Review Mechanism (APRM) was conceived as an element of the NEPAD at the 38th Ordinary Session of the Assembly of Heads of State and Government of the OAU in July 2002 in Durban, South Africa. The APRM was created as a voluntary instrument aimed at an African self-monitoring mechanism. As set out in the voluntary constitutive instrument, the primary purpose of the APRM is to foster the adoption of policies, standards and practices that lead to political stability, high economic growth, sustainable development and accelerated sub-regional and continental economic integration through sharing of experiences and reinforcement of successful and best practice, including identifying deficiencies and assessing the needs for capacity building.

The key operating principles of the APRM are technical competence and freedom from political or other manipulation. Membership of the APRM is open to Member States of the African Union.

The structure of the APRM consists of a Panel of 5-7 Eminent Persons from Africa appointed by the Heads of State and Government of the participating countries, and who will serve for a period of up to 4 years and retire by rotation. The Chairman of the Panel is appointed by the Heads of State and Government of the participating countries for a period of 5 years. The Panel exercises oversight over the review process to ensure the integrity of the process. The Panel is supported by a Secretariat with technical competence to do the technical work to support the peer review process.

The stipulated types of reviews set out in the APRM Instrument are:

- The first country review is the base review that is carried out within eighteen months of a country becoming a member of the APRM process;
- Then there ia a periodic review that takes place every two to four years;
- In addition to these, a member country can, for its own reasons, ask for a review that is not part of the periodically mandated reviews; and
- Early signs of impending political or economic crisis in a member country would also be sufficient cause for instituting a review.

Such a review can be called for by participating Heads of State and Government in a spirit of helpfulness to the Government concerned.

The APRM process involves periodic reviews of policies and practices of participating states with a view to ascertaining the progress being made toward achieving mutually agreed goals and compliance with agreed political, economic and corporate governance values, codes and standards as outlined in the Declaration on Democracy, Political, Economic and Corporate Governance.

The Peer Review Process encompasses four stages, the first of which consists of a study of the political, economic and corporate governance and development environment in the country to be reviewed. Stage two involves the Review Team visiting the country concerned to carry out wide-ranging consultations with the Government and other stakeholders, and stage three is the preparation of the Review Team's report which is first discussed with the Government which will be allowed to append its views to the report. The fourth stage commences when the Team's report is formally submitted to the participating Heads of State and Government through the ARM Secretariat. The consideration and adoption of the final report by the Heads of State and Government brings the fourth stage to an end. However, the review process continues and if the reviewed country accepts the findings in the Review Team's report and agrees to rectify the identified shortcomings, participating Governments should provide whatever assistance they can and should encourage donor governments also to assist. Where the necessary political will is not forthcoming from the reviewed Government, a series of constructive dialogue engagement are proposed in the Instrument.

Six months after the report has been considered by the Heads of State and Government of the participating member countries, it should be publicized in regional and sub-regional bodies such as the Pan-African Parliament and the African Commission on Human and Peoples' Rights. This marks the Fifth and final stage of the process.

At the time of writing the membership of the APRM stood at 30[119]

Some commentators have expressed the view that the APRM's mandate is too wide to be implemented competently.[120]

In 2003 the Heads of State and Government of the Member States of the African Union participating in the African Peer Review Mechanism enter into a Memorandum of Understanding (MOU) in which they re-affirmed their acceptance of the principles of the APRM and commit themselves to their implementation, through the provisions of all necessary resources involved at the national level and to guarantee all the appropriate privileges and immunities to the Country Review Team. The MOU also provided for, inter alia:

- Development and implementation of a national programme of action to improve performance in governance and socio-economic development;
- Ensuring the participation of all stakeholders in the development of the national program of action;
- Implementation of the recommendations adopted at the completion of the review process within a specified time frame;
- Cooperate and assist each other by sharing best practices and strengthening capacity to rectify identified short-comings including requesting cooperation of external development partners; and

---

[119] Algeria, Burkina Faso, Congo, Ethiopia, Ghana and Kenya joined in March 2003, Cameroon, Gabon and Mali joined in April and May 2003;, Benin, Egypt, Mauritius, Mozambique, Nigeria, Rwanda, Senegal, Uganda, and South Africa in March 2004; Angola, Lesotho, Malawi, Sierra Leone, Tanzania in July 2004; Sudan and Zambia in January 2006; Sao Tome and Principe in January 2007; Djibouti in July 2007 and Mauritania in January 2008,Togo in July 2008 and Cape Verde in July 2009,

[120] See paper by Ravi Kanbur, www.people. Cornell.edu/pages/sk145, who usefully drew comparisons of the APRM with OECD Country Review, and rather inappropriately with the IMF Article IV Consultations and with Academic Peer Review, entitled, "The African Peer Review Mechanism (APRM):An Assessment of Concept and Design".

- Acceptance that constructive peer dialogue and persuasion would be exercised, where necessary, in order to encourage improvements in country practices and polices in compliance with agreed African and international best practices where recommended.

The base document of the APRM is attached hereto as **Annex 6**.

The APRM and Elections

Although the focus of the APRM had been on governance and open governments in the NEPAD, some election experts (including this writer) believe that many of its features could be transplanted to democratic elections. Thus it was no surprise when the theme was taken up at the African Conference on Elections, Democracy and Governance held in Pretoria, South Africa, in April 2003. Under the caption 'Peer Review', the conference Statement at paragraph 13 (2) and (3) called on EMBs of the AU to establish an African peer review mechanism amongst themselves along the lines of the NEPAD's APRM.[121] The short case studies towards the end of the book are aimed at taking a closer look at the potential for an APRM-type facility to aide election organization within the AU Member States.

Five short APRM case studies at the end of the book look at the nature and content of Country Reviews pursuant to the NEPAD APRM.

The RECs Potential to Promote Democratic Elections

A growing number of the RECs are equipping themselves with institutions and mechanisms to play a role in the promotion of democracy and good governance. The several examples of democratic structures are:

- The Protocol for an ECOWAS Parliament (ECOWAS-P) was signed in 1994 and entered into force in March 2000. Its first

---

[121] Paragraph 13 (2) read as follows: '(2) Election management bodies should establish a peer review mechanism to appraise one another of their capabilities of managing elections'; and (3) 'Election management bodies' peer review mechanisms should be harmonized with NEPAD's APRM'.

session was held in January 2001. Also the ECOWAS Protocol on Democracy and Good Governance was signed in 2001.

- The East African Legislative Assembly (EALA) was inaugurated in 2001 subsequent to the new EAC Treaty being signed in 1999.
- The SADC Parliamentary Forum was launched in 1996;
- The SADC Electoral Commission's Forum was launched in July 1998 and aimed to foster cooperation between members as a way of promoting a culture of democracy and free and fair elections.
- The Inter—Parliamentary Union of IGAD Member States (IPU-IGAD) was launched in February 2004.
- The Network of Parliamentarians of the Economic Community of Central African States which was launched in 2002.
- The Parliament of West African Economic and Monetary Union (UEMOA) was launched in 2003; and
- The Network of National Electoral Management Bodies of ECOWAS Member States which was launched in February 2008.

The foregoing list of instruments and mechanisms associated with the RECs aimed in one way or another to further the cause of democratic elections and practices in the African Union. However, many of these institutions or mechanisms were in an embryonic stage of development during the first decade of the 21st Century and had only limited influence on individual member states, or, indeed, within the region covered by their respective institutions. For example, close examination of the competence of the ECOWAS Parliament reveals that it has very limited mandate to deal with democratic elections and related issues. The SADC Parliamentary Forum is in a stronger position than its ECOWAS counterpart in that its objectives include 'promotion of human rights, gender equality, good governance, democracy and transparency'. The Forum has taken part in election observations in many countries of the Community.

On the whole, the regional parliaments and parliamentary assemblies have limited competences to make recommendations to their respective RECs, their investigative powers are weak and need to be strengthened, for example, the RECs' parliamentary assemblies should have the right to set up special investigation committees. The SADC-PF and the EALA have substantial powers to scrutinize and discuss the budget of the Community, but such powers do not include revising the budget. The EALA has limited powers to put forward and vote on motions and bills if they have no cost implications on any fund of the Community. The ECOWAS-P had power to review the Revised ECOWAS Treaty so as to enable it to carry out legislative function. At this stage of their evolution, the Regional Assemblies are ill-equipped with adequate sanction machinery to enforce their decisions, or effective regional judiciaries to properly determine disputes.[122]

The ECOWAS Protocol on Democracy and Good Governance contained two sections devoted to elections and election observations respectively. Section II of the Protocol contained some brief but essential provisions which if implemented would undoubtedly contribute to improved election organization within ECOWAS. The substance of the main stipulations in the Protocol relating to elections is as follows:

- Election laws should not be substantially modified within the last six months before an election, except with the consent of the majority of the political actors;
- Election dates should be in accordance with the periods fixed by the Constitution or electoral laws;
- Member States shall ensure that women have equal rights with men to vote and be voted for in elections;
- EMBs should be independent or neutral and have the confidence of all political actors;
- Each ECOWAS Member State should establish a reliable registry of births and deaths;
- Each Member State should cooperate in exchanging experiences and in assisting each other where possible in the production of reliable voters' lists;
- Voters' lists should be prepared in a transparent and reliable manner and with the collaboration of the political parties and voters;

---

[122] See also paper by Ulf Terlinden, on 'African Regional Parliaments/ Parliamentary Bodies as Engines of Integration: Current State and Challenges' at roundtable on 'The Interface between Regional Parliamentary Bodies and Pan-African Parliament' August 2005.

- The preparation, conduct and announcement of elections should be done in a transparent manner;
- There should be appropriate mechanisms for the hearing and disposal of election petitions;
- Member States should the services of CSOs involved in elections to educate the public in the need for peaceful elections;
- The losing party or candidate should accept the election results and concede defeat within the deadline set by the law; and
- The winners should refrain from intimidation and harassment against the losers and their supporters.

The ECOWAS Protocol provides a mechanism for Member States of the Organization to request electoral assistance through the Executive Secretary of ECOWAS. The Protocol also contains provisions regulating the organization and dispatch of election observation missions to Member States.

The Pan-African Parliament

The Pan-African Parliament (PAP) was inaugurated in March 2004. The geographical scope includes that of the other sub-regional parliaments. Some commentators would like to see the PAP as the legislative arm of the African Union, but given its objectives and status it has not yet achieved that distinction. The objectives of the PAP are to provide (for the first five years at least) oversight, as well as advisory and consultative facilities at Union level, and provide a continental-wide deliberative forum for the representatives of African peoples. In time, the competence of PAP will expand to decision-making with respect to matters of concern to the Union as a whole.

The headquarters of the PAP is in Midrand, South Africa. The PAP has 265 Parliamentary representatives, elected by the legislatures of the 53 Member States of the Union and not directly elected. The PAP has been undertaking election observation within the Union and has been forthright in drawing attention to weaknesses in election organization and conduct in its missions' reports.

The PAP came under close scrutiny at the African Union Summit in January 2009. The Executive Council of the AU drew attention to certain acts of departure of the PAP from the provisions of the Protocol relating to the PAP and requested remedial measures. The Summit's Assembly authorized the AU Commission to initiate a review of the Protocol to the Treaty establishing the African Economic Community relating to the PAP. The Assembly also requested the PAP to amend its rules of procedure to conform to the legal instruments of the AU, and to fix a term limit for its Bureau and to immediately hold new elections to renew the mandate of the current Bureau or elect a new one.

From the foregoing decisions of the AU Summit, it can be deduced that the PAP was not acting in accordance with its Protocol in important aspects of proper governance and so stern remedial measures were instituted.

In 2010, the PAP reached an accommodation with the AUC to merge their electoral observation capabilities and send a single observation mission under the umbrella of the AUC represented by the DEAU. As a compromise, the PAP sought up to 40% share of the members of observation missions which was probably too high if they were to fill those slots with legislators only. Nevertheless, this type of rationalization of activities within the AU and some of its attendant bodies was long over due and could also be cost-effective. It also strengthened the move towards the central control over a very fragmented collection of election observation groups with limited international credibility in election observation within the AU.

The African Charter on Democracy, Elections and Governance

The African Charter on Democracy, Election and Governance was born out of the determination of the African Union to promote and strengthen good governance through the institutionalization of transparency, accountability and participatory democracy. The Charter was adopted at the Eighth Ordinary Session of the Assembly of the AU in Addis Ababa in January 2007. At the time of writing it was not in force having been ratified by no more than two counties, Mauritania and Ethiopia,—it needed 15 ratifications to bring it into force.[123] So far as elections and democratic institutions were concerned, the Charter is emphatic and clear. Regarding democratic elections the Charter stipulates that the Member States should commit to the following, namely:

- To hold regular transparent, free and fair elections in accordance with the Union's Declaration on Principles Governing Democratic Elections in Africa;
- To establish and strengthen independent and impartial national electoral bodies responsible for the management of elections;
- To establish and strengthen national mechanisms that redress election-related disputes in a timely manner;
- To ensure fair and equitable access by contesting parties and candidates to state-controlled media during elections;
- To ensure that there is a binding code of conduct governing political stakeholders prior, during and after elections; the code should include acceptance of the results by the contestants or challenge them through exclusively legal channels;
- State Parties may seek assistance through the Commission from the DEAU;
- Each State Party was required to invite the Commission to observe elections;
- That observer missions should be afforded security, free access to information, non-interference, freedom of movement and full cooperation by the host country;
- The Chairman of the Commission should first send an exploratory mission prior to elections;

The Charter, in its Article 21, sets out certain conditions which AU election observer missions should comply with and these conditions are not dissimilar to the standard set by the AU's Guidelines for Election Observers and Monitors.

In its Chapter 8, the Charter deals with sanctions with respect to unconstitutional changes of government. Illegal means of accessing or

---

[123] See Article 48.

maintaining power in the Union would evoke sanctions by the AU. Such illegal means of acquiring or maintaining power include the following:

- Any putsch or coup d'état against a democratically elected government;
- Any intervention by mercenaries to replace a democratically elected government;
- Any replacement of a democratically elected government by armed dissidents or rebels;
- Any refusal by an incumbent government to relinquish power to the winning party or candidate after fee and fair and regular elections; or
- Any amendment or revision of the constitution or legal instruments, which is an infringement on the principles of democratic change of government.

The Charter stipulated that if diplomatic initiatives failed to restore constitutional government, the Peace and Security Council shall suspend the State Party immediately from the exercise of its right to participate in the activities of the Union. Notwithstanding its suspension, the State Party concerned is required to fulfill its obligations to the Union, particularly with regard to those relating to respect of human rights. At the same time, the Union was required to maintain diplomatic contacts and take any initiatives to restore democracy in that State Party. The persons involved in unconstitutional change of government should not be allowed to participate in elections held to restore the democratic order or hold any position of responsibility in political institutions of their State. The Charter further stipulated that perpetrators of unconstitutional change of government may be tried before the competent court of the Union. It stated that the AU Assembly could impose sanctions on any Member State that was proved to have instigated or supported unconstitutional change of government in another state, and may decide to apply other forms of sanctions on the perpetrators of unconstitutional change of government including punitive economic measures. The Charter provided that the perpetrators of unconstitutional change of government must not be given sanctuary by any State Parties, and that State Parties should bring to justice perpetrators of unconstitutional changes of government or take necessary steps to effect their extradition. The Charter exhorted State Parties to enter into bilateral extradition agreements and the adoption of mutual legal assistance instruments.

The African Charter on Democracy, Elections and Governance was considered little more than a codification of democratic principles that existed in various instruments centrally or regionally on the continent. Thus the meeting of Experts on the draft Charter on Democracy, Elections and Governance in Addis Ababa in 2004 saw the Charter as based largely on existing commitments by African states. As approved the Charter was merely an affirmation of commitments already entered into Member States of the Union. The objectives of the African Charter on Democracy, Elections and Governance aimed at reinforcing commitments to democracy, development, peace and security. It aimed to ensure the supremacy of the constitution and foster the culture of constitutionalism in the Union. The success of these objectives will not be capable of assessment until the Charter enters into force.

Despite the noble intentions of the Charter, certain of its provisions, for example, Article 14(3)[124] may give rise to bullying of weaker Member States by stronger neighbour. That eventuality may be possible, but the spirit of the Charter should militate against such occurrences. The provisions of the Articles 18 and 19 of the Charter were sometimes criticized as being too weak, particularly because, in line with the AU Guidelines for Observers and Monitors, the AU needed an invitation from the host State to observe elections. Further, one commentator[125] argued that the Charter's provision dealing with the submission of observation missions' reports within a reasonable time (Article 21(4)) is weaker than equivalent provisions (Article 17(1) of the ECOWAS

---

[124] Article 14(3) states that, 'State Parties shall cooperate with each other to ensure that those who attempt to remove an elected government through unconstitutional means are dealt with in accordance with the law'.

[125] See Solomon T. Ebobrah in 'The African Charter on Democracy, Elections and Governance: A New Dawn for the Enthronement of Legitimate Governance in Africa?' Open Society Institute, Africa Governance Monitoring & Advocacy Project.

Protocol on Democracy and Good Governance, which stipulated a specified time frame of 15 days.

The African Charter on Democracy, Elections and Governance may be criticized for not providing stronger provisions to curb excesses by incumbents and their supporters. The view has been put forward that the Charter should have required constitutional change to be subject to referendums (as in Liberia). Some commentators express fear that the civilian control of the armed and security forces[126] could lead to intimidation or repression.[127] The Charter was said to be weak on the role of women in the development of African democracy.

Shared Values in the African Union

The concept of shared values has been a fitting framework within which the African Union aimed to promote democratic practices throughout the continent. Senior officers of the African Union Commission had been spelling out the nature and scope of shared values as seen by the AU Commission. In a statement delivered to the Tenth Ordinary Session of the Pan-African Parliament in October 2008, His Excellency Erastus Mwencha, Deputy Chairperson of the African Union Commission, indicated that many instruments had been adopted by the African Union, including the Charter of the OAU; the AU Constitutive Act; the Declaration on Unconstitutional Change of Government; the Charter on Democracy, Elections and Governance; the Human Rights Instruments; and several others including those that relate to Gender & Youth, that demonstrated shared values in the Union. The Deputy Chairperson singled out the African Peer Review Mechanism as having a special role to play in promoting shared values.

Another senior officer of the AU Commission, Commissioner Her Excellency Mrs. Julia Dolly Joiner, of the Political Affairs Department,

---

[126] See Article 14 of the Charter.

[127] For example, see comments by Ajong Mbapdah L, 'African Charter on Democracy, Elections and Good Governance: Changing Times or another Mirage? The Seriousness of a Challenge.' Pro-Democracy Activist, Cameroon.

in a statement at a conference African Constitution Building in November 2008, had much to say of shared values in the African Union. Commissioner Joiner said that the conference on constitution building in Africa was a landmark event in furtherance of the African Union's agenda of promoting 'shared values' on democracy and governance. She indicated that the conference on African Constitution Building was located in the large mandate of the Commission on the promotion of 'shared values' within and among Member States of the African Union. The Commissioner acknowledged that in reality in many instances African countries were trying to establish shared values in a context where there had been limited time to build such values from the bottom-up, through effective and sustained people-to-people engagements, across cultures and strongly rooted traditions. Commissioner Joiner contended that it was important that the Conference on constitution building in Africa reflected on the processes and manners in which 'shared values' were constructed across societies. She intimated that some values such as the separation of powers, independent judiciary, good governance through institutionalized transparency, accountability and participatory democracy, and regular periodic democratic elections, were on the way to being recognized as values shared throughout the African Union.

The Quest to Rationalize the Regional Groupings in the AU

The quest to rationalize the various integration groupings in the AU started in the 1980s and to date very little progress has been made. In order to understand the evolution of regional integration groupings and their rapid growth within the AU, a step back in time is necessary. In 1976, the OAU created five regions, namely, Northern, Western, Central, Eastern and Southern.[128]

The Main Five Regions of Africa

The five Regions of the African Union were stipulated in resolution CM/Res.464 (XXVI) at the Twenty-sixth Ordinary Session in Addis Ababa, Ethiopia, in February-March 1976, naming the regions as Northern,

---

[128] Resolution CM/Res. 464 (XXVI) 27th Ordinary Session of the Council of Ministers 1976.

Western, Central, Eastern, and Southern. The geographical distribution of the five regions was as follows:

1.   West Africa, sixteen Member States Benin, Burkina Faso, Cape Verde, Côte d'Ivoire, Gambia, Ghana, Guinea, Guinea Bissau, Liberia, Mali, Mauritania, Niger, Nigeria, Senegal, Sierra Leone, and Togo.
2.   East Africa, thirteen Member States:Comoros, Djibouti, Eritrea, Ethiopia, Kenya, Madagascar, Mauritius, Rwanda, Seychelles, Somalia, Sudan, Tanzania, and Uganda.
3.   Southern Africa, ten Member States:Angola, Botswana, Lesotho, Malawi, Mozambique, Namibia, South Africa, Swaziland, Zambia and Zimbabwe.
4.   Central Africa, nine Member States:Burundi, Cameroon, Central Africa Republic, Chad, Congo, Democratic Republic of Congo, Equatorial Guinea, Gabon, and Sao Tome & Principe.
5.   Northern Africa, five Member States:Algeria, Egypt, Libya, Tunisia and the Saharawi Arab Democratic Republic.

The Final Act of Lagos in 1980 called for the strengthening of existing economic communities and the establishment of others where none exists in order to cover the entire Continent. The Council of Ministers in 1986 requested the OAU Secretary General to examine the practical and operational modalities for coordinating and harmonizing the activities and programmes of existing sub-regional economic groupings.[129] In 1987 the Heads of State and Government requested the Secretary General of OAU, the Executive Secretary of the ECA, and the authorities of sub-regional economic groupings, particularly ECOWAS, PTA, SADCC and ECCAS to take the necessary steps to ensure coordination, harmonization and rationalization of activities, projects and programmes of all the African inter-governmental cooperation and integration organizations in their respective regions in order avert overlaps, power conflicts and wastage of efforts and resources.[130]

---

[129]   See Resolution CM/Res.1043 (XLIV) of the 44th Ordinary Session of the Council of Ministers 1986.
[130]   See Resolution AHG/Res. 161 (XXIII) adopted at the 23rd Ordinary Session.

The Abuja Treaty of 1991 recognized the five regions into which the African Union was divided for the purposes of the African Economic Community which was established by that Treaty. However, at the time of writing, instead of five regional integration groupings, there were fourteen.[131] The overlapping of membership by AU Member States has become so complicated that their unraveling has defied all attempts by the AU assisted by the UNECA and other partners so far. There have been many notable attempts to solve the problem through various schemes of rationalization, but in practice they have failed to impress the Member States with membership in multiple regional integration groupings.

The arguments in favour of rationalization, though strong and rational in theory, so far have failed to persuade, or perhaps even to impress, Member States that the adherence to the Abuja Treaty's objective of one economic community per each of the five regions would be best for the Union and for Union's Economic Community, as a whole. The UNECA has set out a number of benefits that would flow from rationalization of the regional integration groupings of the AU, including the following, namely, facilitate:

- Larger trading blocs would provide more trading opportunities;
- Economy of scale with respect to small countries by pooling resources and combining markets;
- Improved international negotiating positions;

---

[131] These are: *In West Africa*-Economic Community of West African States (ECOWAS); the West African Economic and Monetary Union (UEMOA); the Mano River Union (MRU); and the Community of Sahel-Saharan States (CEN-SAD). *In Central Africa*—there are the Community of Central African States ((ECCAS); the Central African Economic and Monetary Community (CEMAC) and Economic Community of the Great Lakes Countries (CEPGL). *In Southern Africa*-the Southern African Development Community (SADC); the Southern African Customs Union (SACU); the Indian Ocean Commission (IOC); and the Common Market for Eastern and Southern Africa (COMESA). *In Eastern Africa-there are* COMESA; the East African Community (EAC); and the Intergovernmental Authority on Development (IGAD). *In North Africa*-there is the Arab Maghreb Union (UMA).

- Improved productivity, as well as increased wages for workers.
- Significant improvement in quality and quantity of public goods provided regionally, particularly infrastructure; and
- Greater opportunities for the peaceful resolution of conflicts.

Pilot Schemes for Rationalization of AU Regional Groupings

In their report on Assessing Regional Integration in Africa II, the Economic Commission for Africa and AU Study list some of the early attempts at rationalization of regional groupings in the African Union.[132] Over the years of 1983, '86 and '87, the UNECA conducted several studies which would have made ECOWAS the sole regional community for West Africa and transforming all other institutions into specialized institutions. In 1994, a programme and timetable for merging and absorbing the different organizations in the institutional framework of ECOWAS was proposed. The proposed programme failed as any of the West African institutions did not accept it. The concept of the sole regional community in West Africa being ECOWAS with the others being absorbed by that institution, although in line with the Abuja Treaty did not commend itself to the West African States.

In an attempt to rationalize the groupings in Central Africa, an approach similar to the one tried in the ECOWAS region met with no greater success. ECCAS as the primary regional institution was no more attractive to the Central African States than ECOWAS was to the West African States. The inability of the AU to solve the practical difficulties associated with rationalization has not dampened the need for searching for a solution and several new approaches have been put forward. However even as new approaches are being formulated, the appetite for multiple membership in regional groupings by Member States continues to grow and as the UNECA/AU Study pointed out, since the Abuja Treaty was signed in 1991, some of the countries that had already belonged to eight regional economic communities that pre-dated the Treaty signed up with the six regional economic communities established after the Treaty.

---

[132] See ECA /AU Study on Rationalizing Regional Economic Communities, p. 47.

Later, in 1995 UNECA formulated a 'softer' strategy for rationalization based on priorities, guiding principles for efficiency, and less rigid approaches for dealing with intergovernmental organizations. In formulating the second approach, the best option gave way to the second best option that was rationalization of the market rules in each region. Again those proposals were not implemented. The UNECA-AU Report on Rationalizing Regional Economic Communities perceived the overlapping pattern of the membership in regional groupings as so interwoven that it was dubbed 'the spaghetti bowl', which is illustrated below.

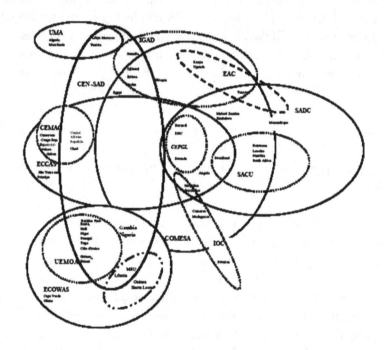

The 'spaghetti bowl' illustrates the complex nature of trying to rationalize the regional groupings of the AU. Actually, had there been a supranational body within the AU structure, the implementation of the Abuja Treaty would be quite 'doable' legally. The core requirement is reducing the 8 recognized RECs[133] and the 6 non-recognized RECs[134] to five recognized

---

[133] These are UMA, CEN-SAD, COMESA, EAC, ECOWAS, ECCAS, IGAD, and SADC.

[134] These are CEMAC, CEPGL, IOC, MRU, SACU and UEMOA.

RECs according to Abuja Treaty.[135] If sole objective of each Member State of each of the five regions was economic integration, the mandatory rule to join one economic community in the geographic region designated by Abuja Treaty would be easy enough, but when individual States factors in political and strategic advantages in joining multiple groupings, the exercise of State sovereignty points mainly in extension rather than contraction of the number of groupings to be embraced.

The spaghetti bowl syndrome of the AU's regional groupings' membership which connotes a perception of impossibility of practical solution reminds election commentators of Arrow's impossibility theorem, or Arrow's paradox, which demonstrates that no voting system can convert ranked preferences of individuals into a community ranking while meeting a stipulated set of reasonable criteria with three or more separate options from which to choose. Perhaps the essence of Arrow's theorem is that no voting system can ever possess all of the properties that may be deemed desirable. The difference between Arrow's paradox and the spaghetti bowl situation is that in theory the latter is solvable, but in practice the solution is nowhere in sight. Many scholars have offered proof of Arrow's impossibility theorem.[136]

---

[135] Those would be North Africa Economic Community (NAEC), the West African Economic Community (WAEC), Central African Economic Community (CAEC), East African Economic Community (EAEC), and Southern African Economic Community (SAEC).

[136] Kenneth Arrow developed and demonstrated his theorem in his Ph. D thesis in 1950 and elaborated on it in his 1951 book *on Social Choice and Individual Values,* but the original paper on the theorem was entitled *A Difficulty in the Concept of Social Welfare.* Arrow was co-recipient of the 1972 Nobel Prize in Economics. A recent paper by John Geanakoplos offered three proofs of Arrow's Impossibility Theorem, Cowles Foundation Paper No.1116, Yale University, 2005. See also Alexander Tabarrok *Arrow's Impossibility Theorem* Department of Economics, Ball State University, Muncie, IN 47306, 2005.

Chapter XI

Election Education in the Member States of the African Union

Introduction

There had been insufficient election education programmes in most of the AU Member States. The need was always unevenly spread throughout the continent, but at best there had been a continuing need for more extensive election education at the national levels. Election education was necessary primarily to enable voters to cast their ballot in accordance with the rules and to encourage voters to go out and cast their votes. The discussion of educating primary stakeholders will here in be centred on election education which should be extended to political parties, candidates, representatives, agents, as well as the electorate. However, in the wider context voter education may be seen as a three-dimensional issue encompassing civic information relating to elections; information targeting politicians, parties, candidates, party officials, representatives, agents and the media; and information directed at the voters. At a meeting of EMBs from all over the continent held in Accra, Ghana, in December 2009, there was a strong call for on-going election education across the continent. This issue was put forward with considerable emphasis by the representative of the Zambian EMB. The concept of continuous voter (election) education was not new. It had been recommended, for example, by the COG to Antigua/Barbuda in 1999.[137]

---

[137] See Report of the Commonwealth Observation Group of 9 March 1999 p.25.

Information designed to promote civic responsibility can be important in providing training in avoiding election conflict, violence and intimidation, corruption and election fraud. Election education designed to target politicians, that is to say, political parties, candidates, party officials, representatives, agents and the media should include the election laws, rules, regulations and procedures, the role of the parties, candidates, agents, and behaviour on election campaign trail. Election information and training should also focus on the tasks of parties' agents and representatives during voters' registration, as well as during preparation for polling, during polling, and counting of the votes. Information aimed at the media houses and journalists should include glossary of election terms, relevant provisions of the election laws and procedures, as well as major events on the Election Calendar. The information aimed at the voters should focus primarily on the voting rules and procedures, particularly on new amendments to voting procedures. Other relevant information such as location of polling places, date and time of polling, and the protection of the secrecy of the ballot.

There is an urgent need to re-examine the scope of the 'traditional' voter education to emphasize the compelling African need for election education targeting voters as well as other primary stakeholders as political parties, candidates and their representatives and supporters. Election education should encompass, but not entirely subsume, civic education relating to elections. It should focus on the attributes of democratic elections such as tolerance towards other contestants, willingness to be prepared to win or lose and to accept the results of the election. Election education should target election campaigns to ensure that any code of conduct that may be in place is observed and that 'hate' speeches, intimidation and violence cease to be a feature of any African election. The renewed approach to election education should highlight the acceptable behavioural conduct during election campaign, and conduct which ought to be unacceptable.. The term 'voter education' connotes too narrow an approach in the African context and should be broadened to embrace the candidates and political parties contesting an election.

Regardless of the scope, target groups or contents of election education, the real purpose of educating the stakeholders in democratic elections is to urge each voter to vote and demonstrate the power of each vote. As the

American Association of University Women (AAUW) demonstrated one vote can make a difference in an election.[138]

The Architects of Election Education

The principal architect of election education ought to be the national EMB which should approve and coordinate all election education programmes in order to ensure that objectives are achieved and that partisanship is avoided. However, the legislative schemes of several countries of the African Union do not vest primary responsibility for election education in the national EMB. Mauritius, for example, did not provide for civic and voter education in the electoral legislation and political parties and NGOs pay scant attention to educating the voters and other stakeholders as normally happens in most other African countries. The explanation that had often been given for the unusual situation was that Mauritius was an established democracy and most of its citizens were familiar with the electoral system. The situation in Cameroon had not been as extreme as in Mauritius, but only limited civic and voter education had been dispensed to stakeholders in the past by the EMBs, namely, the Ministry of Territorial Administration and Decentralization (MINATD) and the National Elections Observatory (NEO) on the grounds that key responsibility for civic and voter education rested with the political parties. In Nigeria, the National Orientation Agency (NOA), a Government-run agency, which was set up during military rule, had primary responsibility for civic and voter education. The Independent National Electoral

---

[138] In 1645, one vote gave Oliver Cromwell control of England. In 1649, one vote caused Charles I of England to be executed. In 1776, one vote gave America the English language instead of German. In 1845, one vote brought Texas into the Union. In 1868, one vote saved President Andrew Johnson from impeachment. In 1876, one vote gave Rutherford B. Haves the presidency of the United States. In 1923, one vote gave Adolph Hitler leadership of the Nazi Party. In 1960, a one-vote change in each precinct of Illinois would have denied John F. Kennedy the presidency. In 1968, Hubert Humphrey lost and Richard Nixon won the presidential election by a margin of fewer than three votes per precinct. In 2000, one vote in the US Supreme Court lost the presidential election for AL Gore and won it for George W. Bush. (AAUW's Action Alert. Sept. 2004).

Commission (INEC) did a good job in co-existence with NOA in mounting programmes in educating voters concerning voting procedures and location of voting places. There were a number of other countries in the Union whose national EMBs were not mandated to deal with civic and voter education, including Botswana, Namibia and Seychelles. In the SADC region the majority of the countries' EMBs had a mandate to deal with voter education including Angola, Democratic Republic of Congo, Lesotho, Madagascar, Malawi, Mozambique, South Africa, Swaziland, Tanzania, Zambia and Zimbabwe.

Election Education Targeted Groups

In the context of the Member States of the African Union, certain groups needed to be targeted in order to optimize the impact of election education (encompassing both civic and voter education) throughout the territorial jurisdiction of the Member States concerned. In large multi-ethnic, multi-religious and multi-lingual States such as Democratic Republic of Congo, Nigeria, South Africa and Sudan, all entities must be catered for in planning, preparing, and disseminating election education materials. People in remote rural districts should be included in the programmes. So should nomadic peoples where appropriate. Gender may be singled out for special treatment where tradition, custom or religion warrants it. Faith-based groups may also attract particular treatment in appropriate circumstance. In conflict or post-conflict areas there may be the need to develop special programmes for refugees in neighbouring countries with the permission of those host countries.[139] Internally displaced persons (IDPs) may need special election education focusing on where to register as a voter (if qualified to vote), and where and how to vote. Other groups of people such as the sick in hospitals, the old and infirm in hostels, prisoners serving time in prisons and persons in detention and not yet tried, all these groups may require election education

---

[139] It is important for the country planning elections to ensure that neighbouring countries give permission in good time for election processes including election education to be carried out on their territory. It ought not to be taken for granted. In 2005, some of Liberia' neighbours indicated that election processes should not be conducted on their territory.

The Role of the Media in Elections Education in the Member States of the African Union

The general impression one got of the media in the Member States of the Union, during elections in the period under consideration, was that the information environment had always been dominated by the media, despite the fact that the landscape was always filled with messages from parties and candidates on billboards, posters on vehicles, buildings, trees, and balloons in the sky. The media had many dimensions so far as elections and election education were concerned. The electronic media, that is, television, radio, the Internet and mobile phone (text messaging) were assuming increasing importance on the continent. Perhaps the radio had been the medium with the greatest outreach in most countries of the Union and so for the purposes of election education, perhaps the most valuable medium. Nevertheless, the print media remained popular in some countries with the literate electorate. For the purposes of election education the print media, national as well as regional and local newspapers were important for disseminating election education messages.

Publicly Owned Media

The publicly owned media was the most controversial so far as elections were concerned. The contention centred on the near monopolization of access to the publicly owned media by the governing party and government. With few exceptions, the general perception had been the failure of the publicly owned media to remain non-partisan and report in a balanced manner during election campaigns. There were many countries in the Union in which the public media, both electronic and print, were moderating their partisanship and move to a more balanced reporting and even access for opposition parties. The steady progress in the move to balanced publicly owned media performance achieved in Member States such as Benin, Cape Verde, and Botswana, Ghana, Mauritius, and South Africa, points to the future direction. In some countries, like South Africa, there are structures which provided the framework for equitable, and Malawi where the law required equal free time on the publicly owned electronic media for political parties, the electorate was assured of a balanced party election education. Other countries, like Kenya and

Zimbabwe, preferred to issue regulations dealing with access to publicly owned media during the campaign period.

Privately Owned Media

The privately owned media had shown no less partisanship than the publicly owned media, but was usually under less scrutiny than the publicly owned which benefited from taxpayers funds. Some private media sometimes opted to forego broadcasting of election campaign materials and so was not bound morally or voluntarily by a legal code of conduct to report in a particular way. Most media codes of conduct had not been directed at the privately owned media, but it was always opened to the private media to enter into a voluntary code of conduct with respect to elections.

Election education may be promoted by both public and private media through political parties airing their manifestos, and CSOs promoting civic and voter education programmes.

The Role of Civil Society Organizations (CSOs) in Election Education in the Member States of the African Union

Civil society organizations provided invaluable assistance to national EMBs and particularly in the area of civic, voter and election education. Support to civic, voter and election education often took the form of granting funding to local NGOs' and national EMBs' efforts in producing education materials and providing trainers. CSOs had been instrumental in designing their own voter education programmes or jointly with the EMBs concerned. Experience had shown that for the partnership between CSOs and EMBs to be successfully executed, there must be close collaboration between the two sides. Issues such as the budget, programme design, and texts of messages for advertisements should be in line with the broad approval of the EMBs concerned. A minority of EMBs often displayed non-cooperation or even hostility towards CSOs engaged in election education. However, with a growing trend in the direction of democratic elections in the Member States of the Union more EMBs were showing a willingness to work with CSOs in election education.

The work of CSOs has come under the spotlight from time to time. Their work in many countries has won high marks, for example, in Zambia in 1991, in Kenya in 1992, South Africa in 1994, Malawi in 1994, and more recently in Liberia in 2005, Angola in 2008 and Rwanda in 2008. However, occasionally CSOs encounter difficulty in operating in some countries, for example, many CSOs and NGOs were expelled from Ethiopia in 2005, and the activities of local and foreign CSOs were severely restricted in Zimbabwe during the 2008 elections.

The NGOs and CSOs, taking account of the political situation and the social and cultural traditions of a given country, use a range of election education techniques including non-partisan posters, pamphlets, voter awareness kits, radio and television announcements and dramatizations, voting simulations and candidate forums.

The Content of Election, Civic and Voter Education in the Member States of the African Union

The content of election education in the African Union was always fascinating and had shown great adaptation to local needs. The diversity in tradition and local customs had also revealed itself in a variety of ways through local song and dance and indigenous plays. However, in designing election education programmes, the traditional contents should not be ignored although local modifications should be taken into account. Election education (voter and civic education) programmes should be designed to educate primary stakeholders, particularly voters and political parties and candidates, to participate properly in the electoral process. The primary thrust of election education was to enable the main stakeholders to understand and appreciate the user-friendly campaign and polling procedures. In some Member States, like Ghana, the Constitution pointed to the nature of voter education which should be provided by the Electoral Commission, that is, to educate the people on the electoral process and its purpose.[140] Similarly, Electoral Commission of Malawi was mandated to promote through the media and appropriate and effective means the civic education of the citizens concerning the election.[141]

---

[140] See article 45 of the Constitution of Ghana, 1992.

[141] See section 5 of the Parliamentary and Presidential Elections Act.

The Nigerian structures were framed to cater for a broader need than voter education, although designed for purposes less worthy than the promotion of democratic elections. The INEC (Independent National Electoral Commission) shared the mandate with the NOA (National Orientation Agency) to educate the electorate. However, the NOA was established back in 1993 as an agent of Government (during the Military Administration) to ensure, among other things, discipline, patriotism, integrity and accountability. The main rationale of the agency was the need for orientation, sensitization and mobilization of the populace. The methodology used included, workshops, lectures, seminars, rallies, drama sketches, community theatre and interactive sessions. The NOA mounted election education programmes jointly with agencies of foreign governments, as it did for the 2003 elections, (although NGOs and other foreign partners were reluctant to work with NOA on the ground that it was partisan in favour of the Government and ruling party).[142]

In designing an election education project for a large African country as Nigeria, there were many factors to be taken into account. Nigeria had the largest electorate by far in the Union-over 60 million. The ethnic and religious diversity was very pronounced. The territory was relatively large with minority ethnic groups interspersed within larger ethnic groups. Radio had for some time been the medium with the greatest geographical reach. If the election education budget was limited (and that was always the case), the radio with its greatest reach across the territory of the country offered the most cost-effective medium for the purposes of reaching the largest number of voters. The television had substantial reach in the urban areas, and the lively press had considerable reach, particularly regional papers. The production of materials for election education in a large African country as Nigeria encompassed a range of materials such as messages in the form of jingles for television and radio, plays relating to elections for radio and television, interactive sessions at town halls and in villages. Visual materials such as posters, sketches, fliers, billboards, and advertisements in newspapers had always been used throughout Nigeria.

---

[142] In 2003 the author worked closely with NOA as a Consultant with the Department for International Department (DfID) to design a civic and voter education programme for the then pending elections in Nigeria.

In some AU Member States the election education programmes had been tailored to meet the local needs, for example, in Democratic Republic of the Congo, the Independent Electoral Commission along with the UN and NGOs like the International Foundation for Electoral System (IFES) introduced the boîte á images or picture box. The picture box contained some 27 pictures that illustrated important concepts of democracy, free elections and civic responsibility. The target was primarily illiterate voters. In the Gambia where the voters used marbles to cast their ballot, the voting procedures were different and hence the content and requirements of election education were different from the rest of the continent.

Cost of Election Education in the Member States of the African Union

The cost of mounting an effective election education programme designed to cover the entire territory of the State often proved to be beyond the resources of the EMB or other entities responsible for educating the electorate and other stakeholders. Election education was a high-cost activity in many countries in the Union. That was due to the topography, conflict or post-conflict situations, for example, the Democratic Republic of the Congo where the election budget as a whole was $432 million of which some $46 million was pledged for the election education in 2006. At the time of writing, the post-conflict elections were being organized in Angola (presidential), Côte d'Ivoire, Guinea Bissau, Guinea (Conakry), and Mauritania. Though there had never been enough resources to undertake a complete and effective national programme, international partners played a prominent role in funding and training election education officers in the countries of most regions of the African Union. Election education usually generated considerable local expenditure, engaging artists who produced plays, jingles and posters. In the process, patronage developed; and sometimes gave way to petty corruption.

The majority of the expenditure on election education usually went on television slots for jingles or advertisements in many countries, including mature democracies. Radio always had a wider reach in most African countries and so it was the main medium for election advertisements.

Election education should be applied to many electoral processes and should not be seen as confined to the polling process. Substantial election education was required to support registration of voters, as well as the delimitation of electoral districts (where delimitation was required). The costs of these programmes of election education should be factored into the overall costs of election organization. Hence election education should embrace all these processes and target stakeholders other than the voters, such as the political parties, candidates, their representatives and agents. An appropriate wider definition, or perhaps more apt description, of election education might be a process by which qualified citizens were educated on how to register and vote, develop adequate knowledge of the electoral process, as well as the civic duty to participate in the electoral process and the commitment to abide by the result of legitimate elections.

Way Forward for Election Education Programmes in the African Union

Election education will continue to be designed to clothe qualified citizens with the knowledge and appreciation of the values which will strengthen participation in the political process. It has been primarily concerned with programmes addressing the voters' ability to take part in the electoral process with confidence. Addressing the key role of primary stakeholders as the political parties, candidates, their representatives and agents, and voters, election education sought to make these persons targets of not only of registration and polling, but also to emphasize the importance of the vote and enhance the sense of civic duty and knowledge of democratic principles, as well as commitment to accept electoral outcomes. The growing working relationship between EMBs and CSOs and NGOs will continue to generate confidence of stakeholders in the electoral process. Conflict and post-conflict situations, of which there are many in the Union at the time of writing, will continue to pose a threat to comprehensive territorial coverage through degraded infrastructure and poor security.

Measuring the Impact of Election Education

Election education did not perform well in many Member States of the AU during the first decade of the 21st Century due to inadequate resources; too narrow a focus in content and target and insufficient training of election education officers. During the second decade of the 21ˢᵗ Century, the African Union countries need to take a number of measures to ensure that election education throughout the continent continues to develop steadily and improve in quality. The national EMBs need to intensify their involvement with election education programmes in partnership with NGOs and CSOs. In general, election education will need more resources and commence earlier during voter registration exercises and prior to polling day.

Election education programmes should be designed with verifiable or measurable indicators which aide post-election peer reviews and facilitate lessons learned. Each activity of such programmes should be justified for the approval of the EMB, NGOs or CSOs concerned. There could be verifiable interim indicators in appropriate cases to measure how well the activity or programme as a whole was performing in order to effect remedial actions. Indicators of election education will vary according to the election process being addressed, for example, in a voter registration exercise an indicator would be the number of qualified persons registered. With respect to the preparation for the poll, appropriate indicators would be voter turn out on polling day, and the number of spoiled ballots at the polls.

Selected Examples of Election Education

Election education in the Member States of the African Union during the decade of the 2000s can be seen through a random selection of countries, namely, Botswana, Liberia and Nigeria. These were typical approaches to election education in Member States.

Botswana

Botswana was highly criticized by stakeholders who met a group of experts assembled by the Independent Electoral Commission (IEC) to evaluate the organization operations of the 1999 national elections. The report of the experts indicated that 'the record of the IEC in respect of Voter Education was attacked by all parties as poor. Voter Education was claimed by one party to be "woefully inadequate, so bad as to lead to suspicions of Government sabotage". It was argued that the Commission should have involved the NGOs and Churches, particularly in an effort to reach young people. Newspaper and radio publicity were inappropriate to reach people in the rural areas of Botswana, and a poster-based strategy was suggested as more effective, particularly having regard to the need to ensure that voters understood the new system to be used for voting (ballot papers replacing tokens). Fears were expressed that this perceived inadequacy could result in substantial numbers of rejected votes when the ballots were counted'.[143]

Taking account of the shortcomings of the election education in the 1999 elections, the IEC sought to rectify the situation in the 2004 general elections. A programme of election education was mounted with respect to registration of voters. Voter apathy in 1999 and delay in voting were attributed to inadequate education, and so the IEC took care to remedy those shortcomings. The IEC mounted a rigorous multi-faceted registration educated programme during 2003-04 to encourage more people to register for the 2004 elections.

Election Education Activities—Advertisements

The IEC placed advertisements in the media, including public and private news papers, and the local television. Posters were widely used on buses and electronic boards were used to flash election messages. Various businesses were co-opted to advertise election messages.

Dealing with Voter Apathy Head-on

The IEC targeted young voters with entertainment, particularly music. The Information and Education Unit of the IEC produced a Setswana song, *Ditlhopo di tsile*, which carried election messages aimed at encourage people to register and vote. It also adapted the song in a manner that it could be played at weddings and entertainment centres. The song was very successful and even became commercialized against the wishes of the IEC.

---

[143] Report of the team of experts which evaluated the 1999 general elections of Botswana, p.24.

Election Education Drama

The IEC sponsored a drama, *Tlhopho seabe sa Borena,* which became popular throughout the country. The IEC acquired an outdoor audio-visual system which provided mobile services. In order to improve its efficiency in disseminating its messages through drama and song, the IEC enlisted the assistance advisers from the tourism sector, the Telecommunications Authority, Botswana television, Botswana Youth Council and Department of Culture.

Faith Sector Participation

The IEC organized an election education workshop for the faith sector which was attended by religious leaders from all over the country. Some 100 faith leaders attended the workshop and shared views with representatives of local groups like the Youth Council and the Botswana University. The faith leaders pledged their support and cooperation with the IEC to conduct election education among their followers. Some of the faith leaders appeared in television advertisements carrying electoral messages about the election process.

Liberia

Liberia in 2004-05 was in a post-conflict mode. There was a newly reformed EMB which was ably assisted by a number of partners including the UN, European Commission, and IFES-USAID in the organization of the 2005 general elections. Election education was generously assisted by the main partners, as well as others. Several million dollars were made available towards election education programmes for the registration of voters and polling.

In post-conflict Liberia, election education was particularly important as many hundreds of qualified persons were dispersed either as refugees abroad or displaced internally. Furthermore, fourteen years of conflict had degraded or completely destroyed the infrastructure in many parts of the country.

Unlike the case of Botswana in 2004 where the IEC spearheaded the election education programmes, in Liberia the CSOs and NGOs played a prominent role, although the programmes were coordinated by the National Elections Commission (NEC).

Activities-Advertisements

Radio had the greatest reach in Liberia and so the bulk of the election education messages were presented through advertisements on the radio. There were several radio stations and so the stations which were most popular were selected to broadcast election messages and jingles. There were experienced local entities in designing and producing election messages and jingles. The costs were modest and the programmes were effective with respect to polling, but less effective during the registration of voters because the programmes were mounted late and not effectively monitored. It was also due to unfriendly and damaged physical infrastructure and insufficient knowledge of how to deal with such obstacles.

The press in Liberia was limited in reach serving mainly urban areas, but it performed well and was mainly non-partisan.

Visual Forms of Advertisements

Visual advertisements such as posters, fliers and billboards played an important role in the rural parts. However such was the of the state of the roads and the difficulty in organizing transportation that it took several weeks to get the billboards out to the designated locations. Vehicles, trucks and buses were also used to carry election messages from the NEC to the countryside.

Drama

There were several experienced drama groups of which probably the best known was *Talking Drums* which were able to produce plays and other presentations to audiences around the countryside. Those groups were employed by the NGOs and CSOs to take their shows on the road.

Oversight

The NEC approved the election education programmes proposed by NGOs and CSOs and kept a monitoring vigil in order to move in complement programmes where necessary.

Evaluation

The election education programmes performed below requirements and expectations of the stakeholders. Stakeholders quickly complained about the inadequacies of the election education programmes during the registration of voters and the complaints were acknowledged by the NEC and the partners. There were improvements with respect to timing and quality of messages that were broadcast during polling preparation and in particular with respect to the election logistics. There was significant improvement in the quality and the coverage afforded during polling preparation compared to what was available during the registration of voters. The joint efforts between the NEC and NGOs/CSOs were successful and could point the way forward with election education in the African Union.

Nigeria

Nigeria has the largest electorate in the AU and occupied relatively large territory geographically. The Nigerian authorities had for sometime even before democratic government was restored in 1999 sought to extend election education beyond mere voters to wide sectors of the community. The NOA which had responsibility for election education was also mandated to deal with a range of civic and nationalistic education. The NOA and INEC worked closely with NGOs and CSOs to mount education programmes for the 2003 and 2007 elections.

Activities

Election education in Nigeria has had the potential to be very expensive because the need was always great and the country is large with many languages and ethnic customs. There were many television stations and radio stations, as well as a multitude of daily newspapers. NOA always had limited budgets to mount advertisements of television and radio. NGOs and CSOs also of necessity had been able to mount limited programmes because of the lack of resources. Nevertheless, television and radio election education messages, together with jingles and plays were broadcast to stakeholders. While like many other African countries, television had a wide reach in the urban areas radio had greater reach among the electorate in rural parts. The press also had a relatively wide reach in Nigeria and was used by the NOA, INEC as well as NGOs and CSOs to disseminate the election education jingles and other messages.

Interactive Sessions

Interactive sessions are used to get across messages to the rural population. It was a popular method of NOA to get across its messages through participation at meetings in town halls or elsewhere in rural areas. A typical interactive session in the rural areas may be announced by the equivalent of the village crier. The session would be accompanied by entertainment and refreshment for the participants. Those popular gatherings were designed for impartation of messages to the rustic masses.

The Stakeholders Election Forum Committees

The stakeholders' election forum committees at the national level consisted of representatives of the political parties; NGOs and CSOs; INEC; agents of the government with direct relevance to the electoral process; security agencies such as the police and state security service; professional associations such as the Nigerian Bar Association, Nigeria Union of Journalists; representatives of the Legislature; the National Orientation Agency; the media; and international organization. The forum was designed to meet periodically.

Public Enlightenment Tours

The enlightenment tours were proposed mainly for the Federal Capital Territory and were designed for the election 2007 as a kind of pilot project to develop informal ways of stimulating voter interests. It intended to encompass live drama performances, meetings with community-based organizations and other stakeholders, courtesy visits to traditional rulers, and seminars for political editors and correspondents.

The Nigerian authorities had shown significant creativity in designing election education programmes. The NOA organized interactive sessions in rural areas as well as stakeholders forums that sought to cast a wider participatory net than even civic and voter education. While the NOA role and history might have been rightly frowned upon, the election education that NOA and the stakeholders forums represented pointed to wider scope that election education might take in the future.

Chapter XII

Election Disputes Resolution within the Member States of the African Union

Introduction

Peaceful resolution of electoral disputes is indispensable for the establishment and fostering of democratic elections in the Member States of the African Union. In general, the mechanisms and procedures for resolving electoral disputes are not strong and need strengthening. It may be useful and timely for the Union to strive for a measure of harmonization of disputes settlement procedures. Sound disputes resolution in election organization facilitates the acceptance of election results and may reduce the number of defeated candidates resorting to extra-legal or extra-constitutional measures.

Although examples of weak or even the absence of electoral dispute resolution mechanisms abounded in Member States of the AU, an example of what it was like operating an electoral apparatus without any proper dispute resolution mechanism in place was illustrated by an example drawn from the fledgling village elections system in China.

Toward the end of the decade under review, the AUC, the DEAU, launched a programme of raising standards in electoral processes conducted by national EMBs of Member States of the AU, starting with a study of the electoral disputes resolution mechanisms of the SADC region. The aim of the programme was to have a consultant or two study the dispute resolution mechanisms in each region of the AU and make recommendations for implementation by the respective EMBs and Member States in each region. This programme was work in progress which will have to go far into the second decade of this century and beyond.

Origins and Nature of Electoral Disputes

Election disputes relate to the management and the organization and conduct of election processes, or relationship between stakeholders touching election organization and conduct. Many election disputes start out as complaints about differences between eligible individuals or organizations over rights or obligations with respect to their participation in the organization or conduct of elections. Most election complaints, if properly handled, that is, promptly and pursuant to clear rules, will advance no further and not transform into disputes. The main players in election disputes are often eligible persons (for registration and voters); election management bodies (EMBs), political parties/candidates/ supporters, the government of the day or any of its administrative branches, and occasionally other stakeholders such as the media, and civil society organizations. The distinguishing feature is that their origins lay in matters relating to election planning, preparation or conduct. This narrow definition might exclude legal action for or against an EMB with respect to motor vehicle accidents or with respect to its office premises.

Election disputes may arise out of the interpretation or application of the provisions (including the constitutional clauses relating to elections) of the legislative framework governing particular activities or tasks. There may be differences of approaches in applying election rules to particular issues, or failure to abide by election procedures. Intentional or inadvertent departure from stipulated criteria governing participation in an election process, for example, failure to register a political party may give rise to election dispute.

Types of Election Disputes

Most election complaints that arise in the heat of political campaign are disposed of before they become disputes. Some election disputes arise out of partisanship on the part of an EMB and or government of the day. An example of this may be seen in the Kenya case of *Odinga et al vs. the Electoral Commission*. In that case, the Attorney General issued a Legal

Notice on 23rd October 1992 purporting to rectify Section 13 (3)(b)(1) of the National Assembly and Presidential Act. The Legal Notice was issued in exercise of the powers conferred on the Attorney General by Section 13 of the Revision of the Laws Act. The Attorney General's amendment had changed the word 'less' to 'more' in the following passage;

The day or days upon which each political party shall nominate candidates to contest parliamentary elections in accordance with its constitution or rules which shall not be less twenty-one days after the date of publication of such notice.

The action of the Attorney General was challenged by the leader of one of the opposition parties. The Court found that the amendment by the Attorney General was null and void and of no effect. The Court further found that the notice by the Electoral Commission issued pursuant to the amendment of the Attorney General giving the political parties eight days to nominate their candidates was also null and void and of no effect.

Justice Mbaluto, in her judgment described the Attorney General's action as a misuse, if not an abuse, of the powers conferred upon his office. [144]

Election disputes may arise where a law or regulations are believed to have been inconsistent with the provisions of the constitution of the Member State concerned. An example of this scenario may be found in the Nigerian case of *Independent National Electoral Commission and Another v. Balarabe Musa & Ors.* In that case, the Constitution laid down the conditions which a society or organization should meet in order to be registered as a political party in Nigeria. The Electoral Law passed by the Legislature and Election Rules promulgated by the Independent National Electoral Commission (INEC) seemed to unlawfully extend the conditions laid down by the Constitution and some associations which applied for registration as political parties were refused. They took the matter to Court and the Court found that the provisions of the legislation and the

---

[144] Civil case no.5936 of 1992. (See also Compendium of Election Laws, Practices and Cases of Selected Commonwealth Countries Volume 2 Part 1 p. 65 ed. Carl W. Dundas, (1998), Commonwealth Secretariat.)

Rules complained against were indeed inconsistent with the Constitution and could not stand.[145]

Disputes may arise during the conduct of major electoral processes, such as delimitation of electoral boundaries, registration of voters, registration of political parties, registration of candidates or political parties for elections (nomination process), election campaign period, polling and counting of votes . . . Disputes may arise between stakeholders and EMB and its staff. Sometimes the *locus standi* of a stakeholder to mount a challenge to the Chairperson of an EMB may be denied, as in *Odinga et al v. Zachariah Chesoni et al.* In that case, the leader of an opposition party brought a motion complaining that the Chairperson of the Electoral Commission was unfit to serve and sought to stop the voter registration exercise on the grounds of irregularities by the Electoral Commission. The Court held that the applicants had no *locus standi* to bring the motion.[146] Disputes may also arise with the respect to alleged deprivation of individuals' right to exercise their franchise.[147] Disputes may arise from the return of the winning candidate, or deprivation of the right to sit in Parliament on grounds of breach of nomination rules or campaign finance rules.

Mechanisms and Procedures to Deal with Election Complaints

Mechanisms and procedures to resolve electoral disputes should be user-friendly, clear and swift in order to produce transparent and prompt determination. Most electoral legislative schemes of Member States of the Union do not have such mechanisms or procedures to satisfactorily deal with election complaints. For example, the team that audited the 2004 Botswana elections found that although the court system in Botswana had a high degree of confidence of the community generally, the slowness

---

[145] See *Independent National Electoral Commission and Another v. Balarabe Musa & Ors.2FR (2003) PP.145-216.*

[146] Civil Application no. 602 of 1992

[147] In Mauritius in 1995 two voters challenged a new law which gave each voter multiple votes in certain circumstances, but the Court threw out the challenge, *Valayden et al v. President of Mauritius and Electoral Commissioner et al,* record no.52619 1995.

and high cost of using that system made it unsuitable to deal with many election complaints and disputes, and so alternative procedures had to be devised to rectify the concerns of stakeholders. Countries like Ghana, Liberia, Namibia and South Africa, which have a functioning political party liaison committee (by whatever name called), are assisted in disposing of some election complaints expeditiously and transparently. In Liberia, for the 2005 elections, in addition to having an Inter-Party Committee to help settle certain types of complaints administratively, the Electoral Commission was mandated by the law to have the first shot at determining election complaints, with lines of appeal to the court by aggrieved persons.

Electoral complaints' mechanisms should have the following characteristics, namely, clear, simple but comprehensive, and user-friendly. Such mechanisms should facilitate the application of natural justice so that complainants be allowed a full hearing, and contain clear time frames for the hearing and clear procedures for the aggrieved parties to appeal to a higher tribunal or court. In practice, complaints' mechanisms and procedures require experienced, non-partisan, dedicated staff to administer the timely implementation of the procedures. An efficient complaints procedure has the potential to dispose of many complaints that would otherwise develop into full-fledged disputes.

Categorization of Electoral Disputes

For the purposes of convenience, electoral disputes may be broken down into four broad categories, namely, issues that can be raised at any time, pre-polling, polling day, and post-polling day disputes. However, the categories are not clearly defined as many potential disputes that originate before polling day are sometimes by law deferred to be dealt with only by way of election petition after polling day. For example, in countries such as Botswana, Kenya, (and India & Malaysia,) an aggrieved person may seek redress by way of an election petition in cases of failure to win registration to contest parliamentary elections.

Issues that can be raised at any time

This category of issues would mainly relate to constitutional interpretation and application, and may touch the status of the electoral law or actions by an EMB.[148]

Pre-Polling Disputes

It is possible that any electoral process conducted prior to polling day could trigger a complaint that would travel up the dispute ladder to the court or election tribunal, as the case may be. Such issues could arise from review of electoral systems,[149] delimitation of electoral districts, registration of voters, and registration of candidates and parties[150] in many countries. Malawi's electoral law allows an aggrieved prospective candidate to appeal to the court prior to polling day, while other countries like Botswana and Nigeria do not. Disputes often arise as a result of political parties splitting into two parts with each claiming to use the original party name and or logo. Although this type of dispute can arise at any time, whenever it occurs prior to registration to contest an election, the EMB concerned may have to make a ruling as to which of the two wings of the party should inherit the original name or logo. The aggrieved party should

---

[148] See Notes 130 & 131 above as examples. See also writ petition no. 805 of 1993 in the Indian Supreme Court, Seshan, Chief Election Commissioner of India v. Union of India & Ors.

[149] See for example, the Liberian case of Coalition Transformation of Liberia (COTOL) v. The National Elections Commission (NEC) where transitional electoral districts which were created for Senators and each voter were to have one vote in districts that had two Senators. The law was challenged in Court prior to polling and the Court held in favour that each voter should have two votes. [Unreported Supreme Court September 2005].

[150] In the Liberian case of Jones et al vs. The National Elections Commission (NEC) 2005 in the Supreme Court, September, (Unreported), the Court ruled in favour of aggrieved prospective independent candidates on ground that they were not given a fair opportunity to complete their registration process to contest the elections.

have the right of appeal[151]. Another category of pre-poll dispute that is frequently met with in the African Union arises out of the incidence of political alliances. Sometimes party alliances triggered disputes because the attempt to operate as an alliance was not formally constituted. That happened in Malawi and Nigeria during the late nineties. Such disputes can be avoided by having proper legal frameworks for political party alliances or coalitions.

The treatment of aggrieved qualified persons who have had their efforts to register as a voter thwarted should be given much greater opportunity to seek redress through administrative means or through the court system. Deprivation of the franchise of a qualified person must be taken seriously and be open to thorough administrative or legal consideration.

Disputes Arising out of Polling Day Process

Most election complaints on polling day surround deficits in the management of election logistics. In particular, complaint about failure to open polling stations on time, poor location of the station, inadequate equipment of the station, insufficient space to accommodate polling staff, party agents and election observers. There may be shortage of vital election materials such as ballot papers or seals, or even ballot boxes However, often these complaints are settled when remedial measures are taken by polling staff. Where these complaints are serious and persistent so as to affect substantially the outcome of the elections in a particular district or constituency, the results may be challenged after polling day by way of election petition.[152] The nature of most polling day election complaints means that they are either disposed of quickly, or, if they rise to the level

---

[151]   There have been many instances of political parties splitting in Lesotho, Liberia, South Africa, and Zimbabwe.

[152]   An example of polling day irregularities which led to the invalidation of an election can be seen in the Caribbean-Antigua & Barbuda case of *Halstead vs. Simon et al* 1989. The High Court held that the election was invalid because of widespread election irregularities, including late opening of polls, shortages of ballot papers and illegal extension of polling beyond the prescribed hours.

of a serious election dispute, they are deferred to be resolved by election petition.

Post-Polling Day Disputes

Post-polling day complaints and disputes may originate because stakeholders are dissatisfied with the accuracy of the counting of the votes or the tally process, or delay in announcing the election results. Also not infrequently there is deliberate tampering with the counting, tallying or announcement of results which give rise to challenges by the losing side to the election results as announced. Election dispute may arise with respect to seat allocation in Parliament or National Assembly, as the case may be, as happened in Lesotho when the mixed member proportional (MMP) electoral system was introduced into that country. The events which led to the appalling post-election violence in Kenya in 2007 was due largely to polling and counting irregularities which were so widespread and serious that the Chairman of the Electoral Commission stated that he did not know which candidate won the presidential election, although the incumbent was declared the winner. The March 2008 elections in Zimbabwe gave rise to serious complaints when the Electoral Commission failed to release the results of the presidential vote in a timely manner.

The situation in Kenya post-election 2007 and Zimbabwe after the March 2008 elections was attributed to partisanship on the part of the respective EMBs, as well as lack of professionalism. The situations in Kenya and Zimbabwe in December 2007 and March 2008 respectively may be contrasted with that which developed in Ghana in December 2008 when, during the presidential run-off election which was very competitive and closely fought, election was not held in one constituency on 28 December 2008. The Electoral Commission showed itself to be in full control of the situation and although the candidate of the then ruling party did not contest the election in that constituency on the 2 January 2009, the election went off smoothly and a presidential winner was declared. The Commission was not accused of partisanship, as in the cases of Kenya and Zimbabwe.

Election Dispute Settlement Mechanisms

The frequent outbreaks of conflicts between groups or political factions within States, or inter-State conflicts within the African Union have thrown up many mechanisms to resolve disputes. There have been accords between warring groups, comprehensive peace agreements, and brokered arrangements between political parties, but the outcomes which these forms of agreements represent were often preceded by various methods such as fact-finding, inquiries, conciliation and mediation. These methods have been tried and succeeded many times over, though with many failures along the way. Recent experiences in the African Union have shown that disputes resolution, whether originated in botched election organization or otherwise, can be achieved by similar methods. Many years of conflict were brought under control and resolved in many countries of the Union including in Angola, Democratic Republic of Congo, Lesotho, Liberia, Mozambique, Sierra Leone, and South Africa by different forms of negotiated arrangements. Some of those conflicts resulted directly as a result of the electoral process and these include Lesotho, Kenya and Zimbabwe. The mechanism adopted in Kenya and Zimbabwe was a holding one under which a power-sharing regime was set up in each case in lieu of resolving the electoral outcome in favour of one or other side. That approach could only lead to an interim solution until new elections are held.

Appropriate Mechanisms for Dispute Resolution in the Member States of the African Union

Some electoral disputes are more suited for resolution by the court, for example, where constitution requirements are involved. In most other cases, the choice available to legislative designers is wide, and most mechanisms to resolve election disputes elsewhere in the world are available to African systems. However as Liberia, Namibia and South Africa had shown that where the existing court system was considered unreliable additional measure may need to be considered. In Namibia at the time of the pre-independence elections in 1989, the existing apartheid court system in the territory was considered unsuitable for dealing with election disputes and so the court system was bypassed. A similar situation obtained in South Africa in 1994 post-apartheid elections when a number of new structures were established to ensure that the election was not obstructed by the apartheid court system. In Liberia in 2005 there was sharp division between the stakeholders about the reliability of the court to dispense fair and impartial justice with respect to the elections. Drafts to set up election tribunals independent of the court system were prepared, but those who argued for confidence to be shown in the national court system won the argument. The commitment to succeed with free and fair elections allowed the parties to resolve differences within the Inter-Party Committee and put the many years of conflict behind them. In South Africa during the 1994 elections parties' rivalries and the desire to circumvent the apartheid system led to frequent resort to negotiation, facilitation and mediation. The African Union Commission, assisted by the Democracy and Electoral Assistance Unit (DEAU), had been helping to smooth the path of political parties which were having problems such as in Malawi in 2009, or countries which had been suspended because they had changed governments by unconstitutional means as Guinea (Conakry) in 2008, Madagascar in 2009, and Mauritania in 2008.

Requirements of Credible Elections Disputes Resolution Mechanism in the Member States of the African Union

The attributes of a credible elections disputes resolution mechanism in the AU are not unlike those of other regions, but recent history of election disputes settlement in Africa had not been good. The apartheid regime of Southern Africa, one-party regimes of the 1970s, 80s and 90s, and the current dominant-party regimes of many of the Union's members have not laid a sound foundation on which to build reliable and credible election resolution mechanisms. The key factors in promoting credible election dispute resolution mechanisms are independence and impartiality on the part of such mechanisms. These are the factors around which stakeholders would invest their confidence and around which credibility could be fostered. In this context, independence means that the elections disputes resolution mechanisms must be able to operate free from the influence of government and ruling party, or any other outside influences. Impartiality connotes that the persons appointed to adjudicate disputes should be seen to be persons of integrity, be competent and be imbued with the culture of fairness. It follows that the method of appointment of persons to dispute resolution mechanisms should be free from political or other influences, and their tenure of office should be protected, removal from office should only be on grounds of misconduct or ill health, and only after following a stipulated procedure.

Treatment of Election Disputes in the African Union

With probably few exceptions, election disputes in Member States of the African Union, particularly those disputes that are to be settled by way of election petition, are often subject to very long delays. In some cases, an election cycle ends without the list of election petitions being disposed of before the next set of national elections are due, and whenever that happened the outstanding petitions merely fell away. Another problem with election petitions in many countries of the Union has been a longstanding weakness of the inability of the legal team attached to the national EMBs to conduct petition hearings with equal vigour as the other side (petitioner) due to lack of training.[153]

The officers and staff of elections disputes resolution mechanisms should be well trained, efficient and achieve a high level of professionalism. Training, supported by periodic refresher courses, is a necessary prerequisite for such officers to offer the best possible service.

There should always be an appellate channel for aggrieved persons to take their case. Where the mechanism is an electoral tribunal, there should be a second tier to hear appeals, if the court system was barred from use at that stage.

Mechanisms for Settling Election Disputes

Facilitation

Facilitation is a process which involves a person (facilitator) who is of standing and respected by all sides to the conflict and is used to assist the communication between the parties with the aim of clarifying or

---

[153] This assertion is without prejudice, but is based on personal knowledge as well as request for training of legal staff of EMBs in prosecution of election petitions.

bridging the gap in the differences. The method of facilitation is usually to bring the parties together in a meeting. If that goal is achieved, the facilitator may chair or manage the meeting between the parties or their representatives.[154] This mechanism is not confined to election disputes, and consists of all sides agreeing to appoint one or more persons to make proposals to either side for a settlement.[155]

Memorandum of Understanding (MOU)

The memorandum of understanding is a commonly used method of dealing with administrative differences, and has been used to smooth out election hitches between the EMB and government in respect of election budget disbursement and election staff recruitment, in some countries.

Brokered agreement

This is an arrangement brought about by the good offices of an influential individual or organization to settle a specific dispute or impasse, usually between two factions of a political party, or between two or more political parties, or sometimes with the EMB concerned. Examples of brokered agreed may seen in Kenya in 2008 led by former United Nations Secretary-General, Kofi Annan, and Zimbabwe also in 2008 under the auspices of the SADC initiative and led by the former President of South Africa, Thabo Mbeki.

Conciliation

Conciliation is a well-known procedure to induce entities, which have disagreements to settle their differences amicably. This approach has been used in election disputes in southern Africa, particularly in South Africa and Lesotho.

---

[154] The author served on a facilitation effort between the ruling and opposition parties of Guyana, organized by the Commonwealth Secretariat in the late 1990s.

[155] For example, the author was a member of a facilitation team on a boundary dispute between Belize, Guatemala and Honduras.

Mediation

Mediation process is some times used interchangeably with conciliation. It is a method of resolving election disputes, mainly when political parties are involved. It can provide a measure of secrecy in appropriate cases, but transparency should not be overlooked. It may involve the services of a person of standing acceptable to all sides because of impartiality. The mediator provides a neutral third party who can assist the parties in dealing with their dispute and lead the way to agreement. The mediator derives his/her authority from the parties to the disputes and has no independent mandate to render a decision. The decision-making authority remains with the parties to the dispute. The mediation process is a voluntary one and continues to be so as long as the process continues. The process can be terminated by either side at any time. The success of the process depends on the will of the parties to find common ground and settle the dispute by this 'negotiated' process. Mediation played a role in bringing about the IFP political party's participation in the South African election of 1994.

Negotiation

Negotiation is a process by which two or more parties might come to an agreement on the issue under consideration. Often negotiation is conducted in an agreeable environment and the outcome may be considered to be a 'win'—'win' for the parties concerned. In a competitive or political atmosphere the negotiating process may become acrimonious to the point of a breakdown in the talks and leaving room for other methods of resolving the differences to be applied. The value of the negotiating process is that it provides a forum where the parties involved may explain their interests to each other. Thereafter the nature and scope of their relationship can be fashioned and managed. The negotiating process has proved to be useful in electoral terms in forging understanding between political parties, particularly in conflict or post-conflict environment. Also in building political party alliances or coalitions, negotiations often play a pivotal role. Examples abound of the negotiating process playing a useful role in forging political and electoral links from South Africa in 1994, and Lesotho and Sierra Leone in the late 1990s. The negotiating process is also frequently used to reach agreement between electoral stakeholders such as the EMB, political parties and the media on codes of conduct issues and media access during election campaign periods in a given country.

Arbitration

Arbitration, like facilitation and mediation, offers a form of third party settlement, but unlike the latter two processes the impartial third party in arbitration decides the case after reviewing evidence and hearing argument from the parties. The force of the arbitral award will depend on the terms of reference of the arbitration, hence an award may be binding on the parties, or it may be advisory, or non-binding. Although there are circumstances where arbitration is compulsory, as when it is required by law, or prior agreement, in the case of elections, it is always likely to be voluntary in the African Union. Arbitration may arise between an EMB and government or between stakeholders and an EMB. This method has the potential to engender a swift outcome in a cost-effective manner. Arbitration procedures were embedded in the electoral law of South Africa, and even prior to the current laws were used with positive results in South Africa in the 1994 elections. Arbitration procedures had been applied in Australia and Canada with respect to the role of the media in elections. Advisory arbitral award may be used by an EMB against the conduct of political parties or candidates, as had been done in Bosnia-Herzegovina with great effect.

EMBs and other administrative mechanisms

Perhaps the majority of election disputes are settled at the administrative level of the EMB or its senior staff. These differences may range from certain levels of disagreement with political parties or candidates, to eligible persons for registration who have not been able to register to vote. Usually there is an appeal process open to persons or organizations, which are aggrieved with the decision of the EMB. An example of this approach may found in Liberia where the Electoral Commission was vested with wide powers over all types of election disputes with an appeal from the Commission to the Supreme Court.

Commission of Enquiry

In some jurisdictions, commissions of enquiry relating to electoral matters are viewed with suspicion as they are perceived as a procedure for delaying action. However in proper cases, commissions of enquiries may be used by the parties to a complaint or dispute to ascertain the facts of the circumstances giving rise to the complaint. The aim of a commission of enquiry is often no more than to investigate and identify the facts surrounding the circumstance in question and make recommendations to the parties. The terms of reference of a commission of enquiry may require the commission to make policy recommendations to the parties. A commission of enquiry which is constituted to investigate an electoral matter should be given a time frame within which to submit a report, unless the enquiry is being done pursuant to a statute in which case its parameter probably would be defined by the statute.

Fact-finding Procedure

Fact-finding procedure is appropriate where there is need to establish certain facts of a technical nature and where the parties to a complaint would be assisted by having those facts established and evaluated. The person or persons selected to undertake the fact-finding exercise should be a person or persons with technical expertise in the subject matter of the complaint. The fact-finder's/s' findings should indicate the relevant facts in the report, which should not deal with the resolution of policy issues.

Electoral Audit

Ordinarily, an election audit may have a wide embrace which empowers the auditor/s to examine the structure, management and activities of a national EMB in organizing general elections. Although an electoral audit may stand on its own, frequently it is resorted to as a part of a wider process of dispute resolution arising from the counting of votes and declaring of election results.[156] An election audit may be undertaken by an

---

[156] An example of this occurred in Guyana post the 1997 general elections when an election audit was agreed as a part of the resolution of the dispute surrounding the counting of votes and announcement of results.

EMB after a general election in order to evaluate how well or otherwise the entire electoral process performed.[157] An election audit may not be considered helpful where irregularities were suspected to be widespread and the damage in terms of violence and mass murder so alarming that priority had to be given to stopping the violence. That apparently was the nature of the post-election environment in Kenya in 2008.[158]

Election tribunals

Election tribunals are provided for in the place of the normal courts in some jurisdictions to expedite election matters and to create a dedicated body to deal with election matters. Election tribunals are used in countries such as Pakistan, and Nigeria, where their role is enshrined in the country's Constitution. (These election tribunals should be distinguished from election tribunals in some Latin American countries, such as Costa Rica, where the term embraces the entire EMB structure).

Election court

An election Court exits in some jurisdictions to allow for speedy trials of election matters, but this goal is not often met; in Kenya, for example, the election court is no more than an arm of the High Court which on its past record had proved quite inadequate in disposing of election petitions in a timely manner.

Constitutional court

Some countries, like South Africa, use the constitutional court to hear and dispose of election disputes. The South African experience has been encouraging.

---

[157] For some years the EMB of Botswana commissioned a comprehensive election audit post its general election-the author led the team that undertook the Botswana 2004 post-election audit.

[158] See Discourse 1 within.

High Court

In some jurisdictions, like Australia[159], the UK, the High Court, and in Canada, the Supreme Court, hears election disputes. In Australia and Canada, when election cases raise serious constitutional issues, the High Court and Supreme Court Bench respectively is strengthened, in what is called a 'Full Bench', to hear the particular case.[160]

Use of Combination of Methods

There can be a combination of the methods or procedures set out above for resolving election disputes. Facilitation measures may precede mediation which may precede arbitration and so on. Understandably, the choice of procedure or procedures may depend on the time element or cost factor entailed. South Africa in the 1994 elections utilized many of the foregoing procedures successfully because there was almost consensus on the part of the black opposition parties that the local court system was unreliable. Similarly, in Liberia in the lead up to the 2005 elections, it was found that even after use of the court system, the results in some cases were so impracticable in that the consequences of implementing the court's decision would delay the election and so negotiation had to kick in to save the day.[161]

---

[159] The Court is actually called the Court of Disputed Returns, which is a branch of the High Court.

[160] McGinty et al vs. The State of Western Australia (1996) in Compendium of Election Laws, Practices and Cases of Selected Commonwealth Countries, Vol. 2, Part 1 p.97 ed. Carl W. Dundas, (1998) Commonwealth Secretariat

[161] See Marcus Jones et al v. National Elections Commission et al in the Supreme Court of Liberia, Sept. 2005-(The Court ruled that the independent candidate Jones should be given enough time to file his nomination papers. That meant the October election date would have to be deferred which in the post-conflict environment would be de-stabilizing. The successful action could not be implemented in the circumstances and complainant stood down after negotiation.)

The Court System and Electoral Disputes in the African Union

The court system in electoral disputes resolution is alive and well in many countries in the African Union, but not unlike many other regions of emerging democracies it has often failed to produce swift outcomes in electoral disputes in the view of stakeholders. The complaints against the court system are many, namely that:

- It is slow and unresponsive to the current needs for speedy electoral disputes resolution;
- Examples abound of situations where electoral petitions remained unresolved between one general election and the next, thus frustrating the efforts of the aggrieved stakeholders;
- Often the judiciary is not perceived to be impartial or non-partisan, and at times is indeed partisan;
- The ordinary courts are usually overburdened with cases and cannot find time to deal with electoral complaints on a timely basis;
- Some countries of the Union, such as South Africa and others, have sought to tackle the problem by establishing constitutional courts, with reasonable success;
- Other countries, like Nigeria, have tried the use of electoral tribunals with limited success;
- The overall perception of stakeholders and others of the resolution of electoral disputes is that there is significant deficit with respect to most of the systems in place due dilatoriness, lack of confidence in the independence of judicial bodies, and lack of transparency of complaints procedures.

The case has been mooted by some stakeholders and commentators that there should be an African-wide judicial system to deal with electoral disputes resolution, but even in circumstances where the central court would be dealing with appellate jurisdiction only, the cost and volume might make it impracticable in the near future. In any event, the newly created African Court of Justice and Human Rights has not been vested with the competence to adjudicate electoral disputes. For the time being, national courts will continue to be the primary mechanisms to deal with electoral disputes and every effort should be made to improve their ability to deal with electoral disputes swiftly and effectively to the satisfaction of all stakeholders.

China-Village Election Disputes

The absence of a proper electoral dispute resolution mechanism can expose an electoral process to ridicule and render the election results not credible because they cannot be tested in an impartial judicial forum. That was what happened to the Chinese independent village elections in the period of the first decade of the 21ˢᵗ Century. Embryonic though the village democracy was, it demonstrated that without a credible electoral dispute resolution mechanism in place, the democratic experiment was going nowhere.[162]

A glance at the problems that China has been having with election disputes with respect to village elections expose the hazards of organizing any type of elections without having put in place proper structures to resolve disputes. The development of village democracy revolves around the introduction of the villager self-government system in which the election of the village committees forms an important component of the system. The villagers' right to vote is a legal right, which is governed by the Constitution, the Organic Law on the Village Committee and regional laws and regulations. The villagers' right to vote is seen as a democratic way for villagers to express their will. The right to vote is both a legal as well as a political right. The content of the right encompassed the villagers' right to nominate, the right to be elected, the right to vote, the right to confirm, the right to relief, the right to recall and the right to know.

Where a villager's right to vote is encroached upon, the villager is entitled to legal relief which means that the dispute must be resolved in a manner which allows the realization of the voting rights. In theory, the villager has a number of channels for relief when his/her right is infringed. There is self-governing relief, administrative relief and judicial relief. These various

---

[162] The author participated at the invitation of the Chinese Village Election authorities in an international seminar on electoral dispute resolution mechanisms in Beijing in November 2004.

tiers of relief were seldom enforced and so infringement of villagers' voting rights often went un-redressed.

The main categories of encroachment against the villagers' right to vote included the following:

(a)   Failure to elect village committees according to law—by the township organizations designating the members to the village committees; or the village Party organizations directly or indirectly selecting members of the village committees; former village committees designate members or appoint their own members to village committees; a few villagers organize selection of members for village committees without the approval of the villagers' conference; too few people were involved in selecting the members of the village committees; and improperly reducing the members of the village electoral committees without the approval of villagers.

(b)   Failure to conduct voter registration according to law—by wrong registration deliberately done; incomplete registration deliberately done; repeated registration deliberately carried out; and refusal to register, particularly those who switched from agricultural to non-agricultural occupation, or those peasants who married non-agricultural workers.

(c)   Failure to nominate and select candidates according to law—by township authorities designating candidates; village organizations failed to nominate and select candidates according to law; disregard the wish of those nominated and fail to select candidates according to the number of votes cast; and restriction on villagers' right to nominate candidates in a variety of ways.

(d)   Restrict villagers' rights to be elected—Those who violated the birth control policy cannot be nominated as candidates; those who complained to higher authorities about grievances were not allowed to put themselves forward to be nominated as candidates; those who were considered old were not allowed to be nominated as candidates; those who were punished for criminal offences were unable to be nominated as candidates; and those who owed taxes and fees were barred from nomination as candidates.

(e)   Failure to vote according to law—in case of election bribery; ballot dealing; failure to set up secret ballot-marking booths; threat of violence; destroying ballots, smashing ballot boxes, causing disorder at voting stations and interfering with ballot marking; fill in ballots illegally; marking ballots for other people contrary to their wishes; illegal proxy voting; illegal use of mobile ballot boxes; closing time for voting not being uniform; ballot counting was not done timely, open or legal; being elected illegally through fraudulent counting of votes, or through bribery, ballot dealing, ballot tampering, or coercion; election results were not published as scheduled; refusal to accept election results; and altering results without approval.

In addition to the numerous irregularities recorded above, there was often illegal selection of villager representatives. Villager representatives were selected through drawing of lots or bidding, or even through designation as natural representatives. Often the Party (Communist) branch committees were behind the encroachments on the villagers' rights, other players who often impinged on the villagers' right to vote included regional political powers and the township political powers. There were also impingements on villagers' right to vote by township officials, village officials, native villagers, or even by persons who were mere residents (non-native villagers).

There was no doubt that encroachment on villagers' rights particularly the right to vote undermined the very notion of democratic self-government organization in the villages. The encroachment often resulted in violent confrontation. The basic relief offered to aggrieved villagers was often less than adequate, and seldom available in a timely manner. Formal relief channel was available in the legal framework which was provided by the Constitution and the Organic Law on the Village Committee. The regulation and rules flowing from the law were worked out by 31 provincial administrative divisions and contained some relief methods after a villager's right to vote was encroached upon. Diverse relief models were developed in practice to offer relief to villagers' right to vote. Administrative relief proved to be among the most useful because it could be administered under supervision of higher administrative authorities.

In practice, the relief procedures revealed weaknesses including:

(a)   The Organic Law on Village Committee and the regional regulations failed to specify what acts constituted encroachments and must be corrected and punished.

(b)   The existing laws did not contain explicit provisions on how villagers could complain and what institutions should deal with their complaints when specific encroachments occurred or on the procedures for seeking relief to specific encroachments.

(c)   The existing laws failed to make explicit provisions on the relief function and responsibilities of the villagers' self-government organizations such as the village electoral committee, the village assembly or the village congress.

(d)   The existing laws did not contain explicit and specific standards for classifying the punishments to be handed out with respect to the different encroachments.

The judicial institutions were criticized for not showing sufficient motivation to deal with encroachments on villagers' rights. It was believed that one reason was because the judicial bodies could not offer effective relief.

Although the state of village democracy in China cannot be meaningfully compared with emerging democracies in the African Union, there are lessons to be learned from the devastating adverse impact of weak legal environment on the democratic electoral institutions. The China experience is young and fragmented but will grow stronger over a rather long period; nevertheless, the long catalogue of encroachments listed above showed that the culture of fair play and unwillingness to apply the governing electoral laws and rules makes the prognosis for democratic village elections in the near future seems at best foggy.[163]

---

[163]   The comment on the villagers' democratic self-government elections was based on a study report on Relief Mechanisms for Villagers' Rights to Democratic Election presented at an International Seminar in 2004 in Beijing, China, at which the author was a participant.

An African Union Election Court

The election debacle in Kenya in December 2007 and Zimbabwe in June 2008 prompted commentators to support the establishment of an AU-wide election court. Such a court would no doubt have continental authority with the legal ability to create a kind of legal and procedural precedent which would point the way to a limited measure of harmonization of election organization procedures. The court could be endowed with powers to issue directives to a particular EMB as to how identified flaws could be rectified and avoided. There would be no guarantee that situations like Kenya's and Zimbabwe's could not happen again elsewhere in the Union, but a central election court system in the AU could assist in strengthening electoral processes and procedures.

The emphasis here is on an electoral court system in the AU as distinct from the several regional court systems which serve to deal with the interpretation and application, as well as matters arising out of the implementation of respective constitutive instruments establishing the Regional Economic Communities and related bodies. In this context, it is appropriate to refer to the various court or tribunal systems that exist currently in the African Union:

African Court of Justice—Provided for by the Constitutive Act of the Union and was designed to rule on disputes concerning the interpretation of AU treaties. The protocol to set up the Court of Justice was adopted in 2003, but it has not yet entered into force.

The African Court on Human and Peoples' Rights—Was established in 2006 to aide the work of the African Commission on Human and Peoples' Rights. In July 2008 at the African Union Summit, the Justice Ministers formally adopted a single instrument to create an **African Court of Justice and Human Rights.** The resultant Protocol (the Single Protocol) on the Statute of the **African Court of Justice and Human Rights** had the effect of merging the African Court on Human and Peoples' Rights and the Court of Justice of the African Union. The decision to merge the two courts was based on efficacy and limited resources to fund two courts. The Single Protocol will come into force thirty days after the deposit of the instruments of ratification by fifteen Member States. The single Protocol superseded the Protocol to the African Charter on Human and Peoples' Rights on the Establishment of an African Court on Human and Peoples' Rights adopted on June 10 1998 in Ouagadougou, Burkina Faso, and which entered into force 25 January 2004, and the Protocol of the Court of Justice of the African Union, adopted on II July 2003 in Maputo, Mozambique. Individuals and NGOs can only access the Court against a Member State if that State had made a declaration accepting the competence of the Court to do so under Article 30(f) of the Single Protocol. This restriction on individuals and organizations to access the Court is seen as unsatisfactory, particularly when compared to the regional courts in the Union. The competence of the Court does not without more extend to the resolution of electoral disputes.

Regional Courts of Justice and Regional Tribunals—These include the following:

COMESA Court of Justice—Established under the COMESA Treaty and became operational in September 1998. It is composed of seven judges and has competence to deal with the interpretation and application of the Treaty.

The East African Court of Justice—

The East African Court of Justice was established as one of the main organs of the EAC and had jurisdiction with respect to Common Market matters, and there was to be an appellate human rights jurisdiction to be determined at a later date.

The Court of Justice of the Economic Community of Central African States-

The Economic Community of West African States (ECOWAS) was launched in November 1976 with a Community Tribunal as a part of its structure. The composition and competence of the Community Tribunal were to be determined by the Conference of Heads of State and Government. Its general terms of reference were to interpret the provisions of the treaty and settle disputes between member states. In 1999, ECOWAS decided to establish a Court of Justice to address complaints from member states and institutions of ECOWAS, as well as issues relating to defaulting members.

The Southern African Development Community (SADC) Tribunal-

The Treaty establishing SADC provided for the establishment of a Tribunal. A protocol to establish the Tribunal was signed in Windhoek, Namibia in 2000. The Tribunal would have upon entry into force competence to deal with the interpretation of the SADC Treaty and subsidiary instruments, and to adjudicate upon disputes referred to it.

The Arab Maghreb Union (UMA) Court of Justice had two judges from each Member State on UMA and had its seat of justice in Nouakchott.

Chapter XIII

Electoral Training in the Member States of the African Union for the 21ˢᵗ Century

Introduction

Electoral training in the Member States of the African Union during the first decade of the 21ˢᵗ Century was in the development mode, work in progress. National stakeholders and others often blamed flawed election preparation on insufficient training of registration and polling and counting officers. Lack of rigorous training of electoral officers often lead, not only to election irregularities occurring, but also gave the appearance of incompetence or partisanship with respect to the officers concerned. There was an urgent need for the upgrading of training of electoral officers, particularly the temporary field staff who were mainly responsible for the polling day activities. Upgrading or modernizing election administration in the African Union needed well-trained and confident staff that could respond to change. There was no infrastructure or strategy in most Member States of the African Union to plan for electoral training throughout the early years of the twenty-first century, although the Democracy and Electoral Assistance Unit (DEAU) had that goal within its contemplation.

Nature of Electoral Training

Electoral training can be categorized in different ways, but a straight forward way is training for permanent full-time and part-time staff and temporary polling and counting staff. The basic goal of electoral training is to ensure those who are involved in electoral administration are trained to carry out their tasks to a high standard. So far as the AU is concerned, electoral training can be used to spearhead the dissemination of knowledge and move the experience and qualification gained towards enhancing the status of electoral administration as a profession.

In order to really drive up standards in electoral training in the Member States of the AU, there needs to be a determined effort on the part of national EMBs to cultivate the commitment and secure the funding to develop and implement meaningful programmes. Care should be taken to ensure that electoral training programmes are properly designed so as to achieve good quality, attract wide participation and provide effective training. Electoral training in the context of the Member States of the African Union must always be tailored to meet the special needs of the particular Member State.

The Challenge and Meeting the Needs

The challenge posed by the electoral training needs of the fifty-three countries of the AU was great. The EMBs of some of the Member States involved had been at best a patchy history of sound electoral training programmes. Others had inadequate strategy to develop good training programmes which could turn out enough well-trained officers to ensure that elections were properly organized and conducted. There was an urgent need for EMBs of Member States to develop and deliver a high standard of customer care in electoral processes. It may be particularly foolhardy in the context of recent (2007-9) developments with post-electoral conflict in Kenya and Zimbabwe, coups d'état in Mauritania, Guinea and Madagascar, and assassination of a President in Guinea Bissau, as well as electoral experienced in Côte d'Ivoire and Sudan, to be advocating effective and efficient electoral services to twenty-first century standards, but the fact is that many national EMBs were striving hard to fulfill their true potential in this regard. The expectation was that with the necessary commitment and the use of appropriate strategy and electoral training methodologies, many EMBs of the Union will be able to deliver significantly improved electoral customer services, especially on polling day.

Overview of the State of Electoral Training in the AU

Electoral training standards in Member States throughout the AU were not very high, although there were some EMBs, including Botswana, Cape Verde, Ghana, Lesotho, Mauritius, Namibia, Rwanda, Seychelles and South Africa, which had achieved relatively high stands to satisfy domestic stakeholders. The lag in quality of electoral training by national EMBs was due to a variety of factors, including lack of adequate resources, poor commitment to high standards of electoral services that ought to be delivered to voters, and insufficient awareness of the adverse effects that poor electoral training could have on electoral organization.

There was no doubt that the AU needed to promote a framework of standards in electoral training which would include funding the development and delivery of training and training materials to EMBs that were in need. The DEAU was the best placed entity within the AU to get this going. Much useful work was being done in some regions of the Union, for example, in the SADC and ECOWAS regions, and such achievements should be coordinated and built upon.

In the context of the Member States of the AU as a whole, it may be important to identify electoral training for permanent fulltime and part-time staff, and temporary field staff. In other words, the administrative staff should be more accessible than the operational ones in the field. Already, relatively improved and sophisticated professional electoral training methodologies like BRIDGE (Building Resources in Democracy, Governance and Elections) and before it BEAT (Basic Election Administrative Training) had been employed by some EMBs to improve training standards, but the impact of these new methods had not yet been fully evaluated.

In some situations, the need was for comprehensive training of all staff and field officers, permanent, part-time and temporary staff, in order to foster and inculcate the culture of fairness, neutrality and non-partisanship in election organization and conduct. This approach required the designing of different types of training modules to fit the category of staff involved. Some categories of staff, for example, those with IT skills or who dealt with financial management, require training providers who concentrated mainly on operational issues, while others would benefit more from administrative or managerial techniques.

Developing Key Competences in National EMBs

The national EMBs of the Member States of the AU needed to identify and develop competences in key areas. Two such areas would be registration of voters, that is, training of registration officers, and matters relating to polling preparation and polling, that is, training of returning and presiding officers. Training of persons in other core competencies should include financial management and IT skills. The persons in charge of the management of recruitment and supervision of casual staff and data protection matters should be singled out for training in the key competence category.

The supply of experienced electoral administrators available to national EMBs in the Union was limited and needed to be increased significantly. Electoral training should include induction and formal training for those wishing to pursue that approach, and continuous professional development. Training providers should offer attendees course accreditation, which would enable employers to assess the progress and development of the attendees. African electoral associations representing electoral administrators should consider setting up their own electoral institute.

Good Practice in Electoral Training

Electoral training should be geared towards utilizing good practice. Such training should be done in a timely manner, particularly when dealing with registration and polling officers. Training formats, including modules, should be capable of meeting diverse needs, and in the context of the Member States of the AU be flexible to allow training products to local needs rather than being fashioned in the traditional manner to be delivered by traditional standard techniques. In proper cases, electoral training techniques should be employed to fit individual needs so that training can be accessed when and where needed. This approach may involve new methods of delivery such as 'teach-yourself manuals', interactive-IT based learning aids and learning sets. For the purposes of the national EMBs of the Member States of the AU, it is possible to develop a harmonized and structured approach to setting common standards of training delivery. There was an urgent need to promote training providers in the various regions, if not in each Member State, so that a competitive commercial environment can emerge and which can foster minimum acceptable standards. The AU training strategy should include quality standards for both the design and production of training materials and the delivery of training. A rigorous evaluation process should accompany any electoral training programme, and indeed should be a part of the training strategy. The evaluation should aim at verifying that the objectives and targets of the programme had been achieved and the expenditure was justified. Further, the evaluation should state the lessons learnt from the implementation of the training strategy at specified stages and be independent of the designer and implementer of the training strategy.

Electoral Training Audit Needed

The AUC's DEAU is best placed to commission a pilot electoral audit study of a random selection of EMBs in order to assess the state of electoral training that exists within the EMBs of the Union. An electoral training audit in selected EMBs of the Union would throw some light on the number of authorities that provide regular periodic training; those authorities that provide for a dedicated budget for training; those authorities that have no training programme; and those which desired more electoral training programmes. The audit could address other related issues such as cost of training services. EMBs should be encouraged to provide for dedicated budgets for training and identify incentives to attract individuals to participate.

Training Delivery in the Member States of the African Union

Electoral training courses should include induction and introductory modules which deal with the legal framework (including relevant constitutional provisions relating to elections) in the given country; the nature of electoral districts (where appropriate); the compilation of the voters' register; an overview of electoral administration by the EMB concerned; and the nature and benefits of the training available.

A comprehensive approach to electoral training in key competencies in electoral organization may involve two or more modules.[164] One set of modules may contain: *framework of the electoral legislation the country concerned; electoral registration—compilation, production, publication, and supply and sale; maintenance of the voters' register; postal and proxy voting (if allowed), data protection regarding human rights with respect to the register; IT and software use for data processing.* A second set of training modules may deal with core elements of elections administration: *outline of the main elements of the primary and secondary legislative scheme; nomination of candidates; announcement of election dates; selection of polling stations; polling agents; polling and counting staff recruitment and appointments; treatment of postal and foreign ballot papers (if any); and use of relevant IT and software.*

The foregoing would represent a simple but comprehensive approach for the average national EMB of the Member States of the African Union. The modules could be delivered in flexible formats and persons who complete each module should be so certified by the provider. The content of each set of modules should be designed to meet the level of staff targeted. The higher level staff may also need specialized competences in specific operational areas such as delimitation of electoral districts (including the use of up-to-date technology), and election finance.

Diversified Training Modules and Formats.

The African Union has 53 Member States with different levels of achievement in electoral training standards. It is therefore important that training providers have the capability to respond to the specific needs of a particular EMB whether by customizing an existing product or through the development of new products. For example, it is believed that some EMBs might be interested in meeting their training needs through distance learning, or e-materials, or mentoring or learning sets. However, conventional means of imparting training courses will continue to be the standard method for a long time in the Union. A growing number of EMBs in the Union have the capacity to dedicate training site electronically

---

[164] The BRIDGE electoral training course package contains twenty-three modules in its version 2.

to matters such as good practice guidelines; training needs analyses and training plans; training events, such as seminars and conferences; and access to remote learning materials.

A Real Twenty-first Century Challenge for the Member States of the African Union

Electoral training in the Union was at a low level during the first decade of the 21ˢᵗ Century. It was patchy at best in most countries, and largely supported by friendly foreign partners. There had been little serious attempt to raise standards on a national, regional or continental-wide. There was also no serious attempt to audit the performance of EMBs on an individual, regional or continental-wide basis in the area of electoral training. There was no thought given to harmonizing a basic strategy for raising the electoral training standard throughout the Member States of the AU, but it was becoming clear that the AUC needed to initiate such a strategy. The AUC should encourage electoral training providers to register with their national EMB or with the DEAU and a system of accreditation be introduced with respect to training providers and training courses. This approach would guarantee improved standards of electoral training by ensuring that:

- *Electoral training providers within the AU were accredited;*
- *Electoral training courses delivered by providers were also accredited;*
- *Training materials should be of high quality;*
- *Quality standard would apply to course providers and to the courses themselves;*
- *An assessment process should be designed to determine the high quality standard necessary; and*
- *The AUC should cause a handbook on the guidance of electoral training by EMB.*

Implementation of Training Strategy

An EMB wishing to implement the AUC training plan might wish to agree the terms of reference with the training manager, or if there is none, recruit an experienced person with the following terms of reference, to:

- Coordinate electoral training;
- Provide information of professional training;
- Develop and maintain an elections training website;
- Develop training and education standards;
- Accredit training courses and training providers;
- Ensure that there was sufficient number of training providers; and
- Liaise with academic institutions and relevant professional bodies.

Performance Target for National EMBs

The approach suggested above would require that the national EMBs should work towards a modest target of say 60% (including Commissioners) of new staff should receive quality induction within six months of appointment; 50% of permanent electoral services staff should receive core competence training according to their category at least once every 18 months, while training of temporary polling and counting should be concluded no later than a week prior to polling day.

There should be quality audit of training delivery by electoral training providers periodically.

Existing Electoral Training Pattern in the Member States of the African Union

Although a measure of professional electoral training, particularly the BRIDGE training modules, had been subscribed to, most national EMBs relied on well-known training methodologies to train officers to conduct electoral processes. The traditional methods are not uniform, seldom well delivered and invariably implemented without a strategy or clear goals. Moreover, evaluations or audits were rare and lessons learnt were not followed through.

Electoral training in many AU national EMBs was organized on the basis of a loose operational plan which defined the production and distribution of training materials, the time of training, location, the trainers, and the relevant category of officers to be trained. The delivery was done mainly by in-house trainers of the EMB concerned, but often complemented by a few outside consultants. Professional outside training providers with approved training materials was not routinely used and independent evaluators of the training materials or the provider were not usually used.

Electoral Training Methodologies in the Member States of the African Union

Electoral training in EMBs in the African Union took account of many factors, including: the time frame; availability of resources; cultural environment; and cost-effectiveness. The training structure was influenced by factors such as the size of the training groups, the number of trainers required, and the number of trainers of the trainers. An early determination would be made whether all the training would be carried out on the basis of face-to-face interactive training. Three face-to-face models frequently used are the cascade model, the mobile team model and the simultaneous training model.

The cascade model

The cascade model entailed small groups of trainers who trained small groups in training techniques and operational skills who subsequently trained small groups in training techniques and operational skills usually at different levels so that the functional skill were passed down the hierarchical tiers. Thus in a typical EMB, the training specialists and technical specialists would train headquarters management staff who in turn would train regional administrators, who in turn would train returning officers who would in turn train polling staff. This hierarchical pattern would vary according to the size and structure of the EMB concerned. The cascade model had considerable flexibility to deal with limited timeframes, geographic and topographic factors, as well as logistic and group sizes.

The strengths of the cascade model in the African context included the following:

- Its flexibility in delivering training to large groups of people in different geographical locations through mobile means;

- It had considerable cost-effective potential and hence was potentially sustainable;
- The methodology of relying on the use of small numbers of trainers and participants encouraged full and active interactive training sessions;
- Training could easily be dispersed locally thereby reducing costs;
- Its reliance on decentralization reduced the involvement of central resources;
- It could facilitate the training of large numbers of people in a relatively short period of time; and
- Facilitated the enhancement of local accountability through decentralization.

The weaknesses of the cascade model could be summarized as follows:

- It relied on a large number of non-professional trainers who were trained in a short period of time;
- Non-professional trainers were often unable to tap into the groups' attention and concentration as experienced professional trainers would;
- It required the preparation of detailed training manuals and presentational skills;
- Sometimes it presented difficulty in modifying sessions and presentations as required by interim evaluations;
- It often required central oversight to ensure that sessions and presentations were carried as per schedule;
- A frequent criticism of cascade training had been that staff selected for other skills might not make effective trainers;
- There had often been concern that training contents and tips could get distorted or lose emphasis during the process of imparting down the pyramid chain to the several tiers of staff; and
- The fear that any lack of attention on the part of a trainee up the ladder could cause wrong information to be passed uncorrected down the chain.

Cascade training method could be combined with other models discussed below to form an effective training combination.

The mobile training team model—mobile training through small training teams of two or more persons was commonly met with in areas circumscribed by topography, or hospital or detention. It played a role at the upper end of the cascade model. The mobile training team model invariably used professional trainers who were skilled in presenting training materials. It could be the most cost-effective way in imparting electoral training in certain cases, but was impractical for extensive training in large geographical areas.

The strengths of the mobile team training model could be summarized as follows:

- It used professional trainers to train staff at local levels;
- The use of small team of professional trainers brought along with it quality control;
- It could impart its presentations with competency and effectiveness;
- It was cost-effective;
- It allowed for flexibility in presentations to fit local conditions; and
- It utilized few organizational resources from the centre and facilitated sharing resources with local levels.

The weaknesses of the mobile training team were mainly the following:

- Its sustainability was doubtful;
- It did not facilitate building of training capacity;
- It required training professionals for long periods;
- Allowances had to be made in planning schedules for bad weather;
- Care needed to be taken that there was sufficient time to finish the training programme in good time;
- Special arrangements needed to be made for the availability of the trainers' manuals to be circulated to election staff for future reference;
- It was short on skills transfer to EMBs' field staff in particular; and
- In AU conditions, the time required to train all operational election staff would render extensive use of this model too expensive; and

the alternative of employing a very large contingent of professional trainers in order to cut time, rather impractical.

The mobile training team model worked best in areas of the Member States of the AU where it could be combined with the cascade to ensure that selected senior operational staff was trained by mobile training teams and the registration and polling staff were trained under the cascade model.

Simultaneous training model

The type of training was usually conducted over a period of a few days which were scheduled exclusively for the training of electoral officers of different tiers. With elections in the Member States of the AU coming more and more under international spotlight and the level of training being evaluated, the simultaneous training model had been fading from favour.

The strengths of the simultaneous training are few and could be summarized thus:

- It had the potential to create a high profile training event which could impact positively on the turn out of qualified persons for registration, and on voter turn out on polling day;
- It could be conducted over a short period of time;
- Where trainers were trained for this event, it had the potential to assist with an EMB's capacity building.

The weaknesses of the simultaneous training model could be summarized as follows:

- It required large numbers of trainers to be available at the same time;
- Because of the concentrated period of training, little or no evaluation could be undertaken during the training period;
- It required significant central planning and logistical management;

- The production of training materials required considerable effort, particularly in the case of small EMBs; and
- Much care was needed to get the trainers of trainers to complete their work in time for the training period.

Other forms of electoral training

Basic Election Administration Training (BEAT)

There had been cases in the AU where even an elementary electoral training course would fill a gap because there was nothing else available. For example in Nigeria post the series of elections in 1998-99. The International Foundation for Electoral Systems (IFES) detected the lacuna that existed in electoral training then in Nigeria and tried to provide a remedy for mainly the training of officials operating at the local levels. The training course was called Basic Electoral Administration Training (BEAT) and as the title suggested was aimed at achieving only modest goals. It was a two-week long course which was designed to assist with the improvement of basic skills in election administration in a relatively cost-effective manner. The contents of the course were sparse, covering in an introductory manner election administration and election planning and organization standards. The nature of free and fair elections and the attributes there of was also covered, as well as the management of election logistics and resolution of election conflict. The method of delivery of the BEAT course was intentionally short on formal lectures and instead focused on a participatory hands-on approach. The goal of standardizing BEAT as a course that could be customized for use in other African countries and elsewhere did not materialize partly because it did not develop beyond its basic phase when it was overtaken by the evolving training course which was designed to build resources in democracy, governance and elections (BRIDGE).

Building Resources in Democracy, Governance and Elections (BRIDGE)

In the context of the Member States of the AU, BRIDGE was first and foremost a professional development program. Its primary relevance to the DEAU during the period under review was its focus on the training of electoral administrators. The emphasis on capacity building had a good potential to assist many levels of electoral officials and other stakeholders in the Member States of the AU. As a professional developmental tool, BRIDGE had the potential to fill the void identified at the local levels among electoral officers in the States of Nigeria when BEAT was introduced there, and to play a wider role in assisting the training needs of EMBs throughout the Member States of the Union. As the title suggested, BRIDGE aimed at covering three broad areas, namely, democracy, governance and elections, but in this work the comments are focused only on elections and on the potential (if any) to impact positively on election organization in the Member States of the African Union.

The objectives of BRIDGE were to:

- Enhance the skills and confidence in the electoral process;
- Increase the awareness of the tools and resources available or necessary to build and maintain a sustainable electoral culture;
- Develop a support network for stakeholders in electoral processes and encourage a culture of sharing information and experiences; and
- Promote internationally accepted principles of democracy and good electoral practice.

These objectives were no doubt achievable in many Member States of the African Union. However, in the cases of many EMBs in the Union, developments had shown that they were not free of the influences of the government of the day or the ruling party and fell foul of the first objective of BRIDGE. Similarly, with the growth of the 'dominant party' phenomenon in many Member States with characteristics not dissimilar to those of the one-party regimes of the past, many States of the Union fell far short of meeting the fourth goal of BRIDGE.

The BRIDGE Curriculum

The BRIDGE curriculum (version 2) is expansive and has the potential to serve many EMBs of the Union well. With 23 modules—two foundation[165] and 21 thematic[166]—there will be plenty scope for individual EMBs to customize the curriculum to fit their needs. The curriculum was designed to focus on the principles underpinning properly organized elections and contained a mixture of modules aimed at skills development and promotion of good working relations with stakeholders. The topics covered under electoral architecture, namely, legal framework, boundary delimitation, electoral systems, electoral management design and electoral technology, were clearly not meant to confer competences in those areas, as some of those areas are highly specialized professional fields that could not be imparted or acquired within a few weeks. Electoral operations, particularly the modules dealing with *voter registration, pre-election activities, electoral training and polling, counting & results,* as covered in the BRIDGE Course has the potential to achieve much in the African context if it can assist EMBs to produce improved voters' registers and better management of election logistics. During the period under consideration, the evidence with respect to the achievement of BRIDGE in lifting the quality of election organization in AU Member States is scant, but BRIDGE has not been taught for a long time in the African Union.[167] The ability of BRIDGE

---

[165] These are *Introduction to Electoral Administration* and *Strategic and Financial Planning.*

[166] Electoral Architecture which contains *Legal Framework, Boundary Delimitation, Electoral Systems, Electoral Management Design and Electoral Technology;* Electoral Operations—*Voter Registration, Pre-election Activities, Electoral Training, Polling, Counting and Results, Post-election Activities, External Voting and Electoral security;* Working with Electoral Stakeholders—*Access to Electoral Processes, Gender & Elections, Electoral Contestants, Electoral Observation, Media & Elections, Electoral Assistance, Electoral Dispute Resolution, Voter Information and civic education.*

[167] At the time of writing BRIDGE Courses on elections had been held in many African countries, namely, Angola, Burkina Faso, Egypt, Ethiopia, Ghana, Lesotho, Liberia, Mozambique, Senegal, Sierra Leone and South Africa. In some of these cases, the staffs of other EMBs join in at courses hosted by a particular EMB; also on a few occasions civil society organizations (CSOs)

to address the huge deficits existing in the compiling of acceptable voters' registers and proper management of electoral logistics in many countries of the Union remains to be seen.

BRIDGE has considerable flexibility in that the modules can be used to fit the need identified by a given EMB or by a BRIDGE assessment team. BRIDGE may be combined with other types of operational training by mixing its modules and methodology to meet the needs of the client organization. BRIDGE can be used to promote openness by bringing different stakeholders together or different parts of an organization together. Furthermore, BRIDGE has the ability to operate at a regional level which, in the context of the AU, which has a number of regional groupings, including the Regional Economic Communities (RECs), makes it suitable to mount regional courses. In this regard, BRIDGE can be used in a manner which strengthens regional networks and partnerships within the AU structure. The wider structure within the AU with its various regional and sub-regional groupings and multi-cultural and multi-ethnic entities would benefit from regionalism which offered more effective use of human and financial resources. BRIDGE's ability to offer electoral training courses to regional groupings in the AU could facilitate the sharing of comparative experiences emanating from different cultural backgrounds. It could foster joint programming encompassing the members of a particular grouping and build regional cooperation between stakeholders. It could promote the sharing of training materials by the EMBs throughout the group of States involved and create synergies and partnerships between regional organizations and associations.

External Training-

Where it is possible to be had, external training of EMBs' staff should be utilized. This may be done through external consultants, specialists, or with the assistance of external organizations. This form of external training may include information exchange through networks with other national

---

and representatives of political parties. In February 2009, twenty-two senior election administrators from EMBs in Botswana, Madagascar, Malawi, Namibia, Seychelles, Swaziland, Zambia and Zimbabwe, participated in a five-day course.

or international election managers; through the secondment of staff to another EMB or to an organization; training by electoral specialists or consultants off site; sending electoral staff to external training; attending meetings and seminars on specific electoral issues; and training derived through membership in external organizations and associations.

Particular Areas of Concern in Electoral Training in the Member States of the AU

Training of Trainers; Training of Registration Officers; Training of Electoral Logistics Officers; and Training of Polling & Counting Officers.

The four areas singled out above have particular significance in election in AU Member States as too often election organization, during the period under review, were pronounced by stakeholders to be farcical because of the failure of one or more of these areas. Some training methodologies were not suitable for highly operational tasks. They involved large numbers of officers operating throughout rugged territorial expanse. The evaluation of BRIDGE has not yet thrown up its effectiveness in these operations in rugged African rural areas.

Training of Trainers

The training of trainers to train registration officers, logistics officers and polling and counting officers merits particular treatment as these were persistently failing areas in elections in many Member States of the Union. The majority of training sessions for electoral officers was done in-house within EMBs of the Member States of the Union. Electoral service providers were not widely used throughout the AU. International partners, including NGOs often provided a good measure of assistance to many EMBs in this regard. Training materials for training of trainers should be designed in a manner which helps the trainers to acquire sufficient knowledge of the subject matter involved so that they could respond to questions satisfactorily. Training courses for trainers should focus on the presentational skills as well as on the substance of the electoral issues involved. A comprehensive trainers' training course would vary according to the subject area being covered, that is, for example, registration of voter, or electoral logistics management, or polling procedures. Perhaps the simplest of illustrations might be taken from a course of training for the trainers of registration officers in a house-to-house enumeration of voters' scenario. The basic background approach would cover training issues such as:

- Adult learning and skills acquisition processes;
- Friendly learning environment;
- The dynamics of group learning ;
- Emphasis on the importance of competence and skills development;
- Selection of working-friendly venue;
- Length of sessions to take account of retention of concentration; and
- Fair attention to individual trainee's concerns.

The subject matter of registration of voters can be somewhat involved with the use of photograph and or thumb print, and or other bio-metric features of each voter. The trainer may need the assistance of an expert, depending on the complexity of the registration process. However, the training sessions should have a timeframe and the training programme should cover the following additional issues:

- The framework of information provided;
- Quality standards to be met;
- Group exercises to be undertaken and practical skill demonstration;
- Question and answer sessions;
- Practical methods of assessing each trainee's competency in carrying out set tasks; and
- Self-assessment of the trainer's performance.

Training Voters' Registration Staff in the AU

The training of registration of voters' staff had been singled out for highlighting mainly because this area of electoral organization had for a long time received either too little electoral training, or no training at all prior to the commencement of registration exercise. Imperfect voters' registers are a common feature of the African Union Member States' electoral environment. Overdue registration exercises, shoddy compilation of voters' registers and inaccurate and out of date registers were frequent complaints by stakeholders and election observers alike, which were reflected in reports over and over again. One of the main reasons for this persistent deficit, though not the only reason, was the failure to offer proper and timely training to registration officers.

Most voters' registers were compiled on a voluntary basis and so qualified persons were not obliged to register. This procedure, coupled with partisan registration officers, sometimes lead to the intentional omission of names from the register. In some countries, registration was conditional on the production of the national identification card (to prove nationality) which was usually issued by a government ministry and subject to manipulation or incompetence so the national ID cards were not issued in a timely manner, or at all. The actual registration of some categories of persons, for example, the young qualified persons, often proved to be difficult because birth certificates were not available. These factors make registration of voters in many AU Member States difficult and place a strong burden on the registration officers to find the right solution with respect to the particular individuals of the aforementioned categories.

The training of registration officers entailed special training for sub-categories of specialized officers such as photographers and officers who were responsible for taking bio-metric features, such as finger or palm printing, or other biological features such as eyelids or eyes, for the purposes of identifying voters. These additional requirements were not widely met with throughout the AU during the period under review, but the trend was likely to grow as the quest for improved voters' registers and better organized elections take hold within the Union.

Training Electoral Logistics Officers in the AU

The absence of proper electoral logistics management in the Member States of the AU was a major concern to electoral stakeholders in many countries. Much too often on polling day the sight of very long queues of voters in the main cities and towns of important countries of the AU were due to late opening of the polls, or shortage of election materials, or late delivery of election supplies, or even late turnout of polling officers.

One Chairman of an EMB in a Member State of the AU once gave an example of the lack of experience and insufficient training that visited his logistics officers. He explained that his staff in ordering ballot papers took the number of the electorate and divided that number by the number of polling stations. The ballot papers were then ordered in batches of 100 each. However, there were many stations with fractions of one hundred electors to which batches of 100 ballot papers had to be dispatched. The result was a significant shortage of ballot papers at many polling stations on polling day!

The shortage of materials was only one of the frequent occurrences in this field; another had been the inability to transport electoral supplies to polling stations on time. In most cases this was due to poor planning leading to insufficient vehicles, or lack of petrol, or late start.

The selection of registration (where registration is done at a central location) or polling site needed to be done according to specification and in consultation with stakeholders in appropriate circumstances. Due regard should be had to ease of access for people with disability, and reasonable health facilities.

Electoral training for logistics officers should focus on these issues which would have a significant impact on the quality of electoral services provided to the electorate on polling day.

Training of Polling and Counting Officers

Polling officers were key functionaries in the whole electoral process. They interacted with the voters and other primary stakeholders in the electoral process. Their tasks required the ability to deal with detail procedures in the polling process correctly. The training of these officers must be thorough and the main objective of which must be competence to apply the procedures correctly during the polling process. Training for polling officers should be held close to polling day, and if that does not happen, a refresher course should be held. Polling day had always been a tense period for polling officers, even when they had previous experience. Indeed, the first two hours of polling day had often appeared in mild confusion even in a well organized electoral environment in emerging democracies. Each training course for polling officers should seek to address the issue of tenseness and the merits of keeping calm.

The training of polling and counting officers should be compulsory and a pre-condition to employment for those tasks. Suitable inducements should be held out to trainees for these electoral tasks. Where it is possible, previously employed staff should be preferred. Where the voting and counting procedures had undergone changes, the changes should be emphasized and reflected clearly in manuals and instructions sheets, as the case may be. It is important that the election managers ensure that changes to procedures with respect to polling and counting of votes be done timely so that all field staff become familiar with those changes well before polling day.

The timeframe and importance of training for polling and counting staff make it necessary for carefully planned programmes to be undertaken. These programmes would address preparation of training materials, the target groups and the training activities. Proper planning will ensure that the training takes place in a smooth manner and render it more effective. If the training takes place too early, not only that the trainees may forget the contents, but late changes to the procedures may be missed. In such cases (which happen not infrequently in the AU Member States) a refresher course may become necessary, funds permitting.

There had been persistent complaints by stakeholders in Member States of the Union about the apparent incompetence of some polling and counting staff. Sometimes the complaints were directed at poor training and other times they were blamed on partisanship. Whichever factor was at play, poor performance by polling and or counting staff reflect adversely on the trainers and on those who recruited the staff members.

The record of polling and counting staff in Member States of the AU during the decade under review, with a few exceptions, was not particularly good and needed much improvement. The number of staff to be trained was relatively large and the resources available were often limited. The cascade model or a mixture of methodologies was often used to train polling staff. The effect of current electoral training methodologies, particularly to train large numbers of staff was rather uneven. Some countries of the Union, like Botswana, Lesotho, Benin, Ghana, Mauritius, Seychelles, and South Africa, provide positive examples of consistent positive outcomes with respect to the performance of polling and counting staff, while many other countries have been accused of lacking in confidence in their polling and counting staff.

The compelling nature of the capacity to handle details made it necessary for the trainers of these categories of electoral officers to have significant practical knowledge of voting and counting procedures and the ability to impart the knowledge to the trainees. Where appropriate, incentives should be held out to these categories of staff to stimulate competency development.

Election Case Studies I

Kenya

Elections 2007 and Subsequent Events

Kenyan Electoral Environment

The roots of Kenyan multiparty democracy were shallow. Indeed the foundation on which restored multiparty democracy was laid in 1991 was less than solid, as the then President Moi was known to be against multiparty elections and considered opposition party campaigns in his strongholds as provocation. The former President's disdain for multiparty election campaign did not help during the 1992 election campaign when violence became widespread in parts of the Rift Valley and many lives were lost and hundreds of homes were burnt out. The incumbent President Moi won the presidential election in 1992 and made some modest improvements to the electoral legislative environment in time for the 1997 presidential election. An Inter Party Parliamentary Group (IPPG) was created to facilitate greater communication between the ruling party and Government, and the opposition. The IPPG instigated an enlarged electoral commission from 12 members in 1993 to 22 members, an additional 10 members, all appointed by the President.

The improved collaboration at the parliamentary level between the ruling and opposition parties achieved some movement with respect to freedom of speech and assembly, and contributed to more credible national elections in December of 1997 which nevertheless the incumbent President Moi again won.

The elections of 1997 did not seem to stop the budding reform to the constitutional and electoral process. The Constitution of Kenya Review

Commission Act which was passed in 1997 provided a framework for discussion of constitutional change. In 1998 following negotiations between civil society groups and the political parties, a proposed general amending law was agreed. By the time the elections of 2002 were held the electoral environment had improved considerably to the point where international election observers declared those elections to be free and fair.

The elections of 2002 were seen as a turning point in Kenyan electoral history, or so it was thought. Election commentators were not agreed on what factors distinguished those elections from others but some attributed the difference to the somewhat limited reforms to the electoral legislative scheme ; others to the virtual landslide by the National Rainbow Coalition (NARC) which allowed irregularities to be overlooked; and yet others contended that with incumbent President Moi no longer contesting, the Kenyan African National Union (KANU), the ruling party, tried to shed its old image and electoral tricks with it.

The seemingly steady progress in tidying up the electoral environment up to the 2002 elections did not convey the full story as was evidenced in sporadic violence at election campaigns throughout the period for the re-introduction of multiparty elections. Moreover, there was significant 'carry over' from the days of one-party rule of partisan practice by election officials, running through from Election Commissioners down to district commissioners, as well as abuse of incumbency in the use of public resources for party political purposes.

But Why Did It Go So Badly Wrong In 2007?

Many election observers, stakeholders and commentators were puzzled at the sudden fatal twist in the immediate aftermath of the post-polling results. Indeed, several independent and credible international election observation missions had expressed satisfaction with the organization of the elections up to the point of the closing of the polls. In order to search for the answers of what went wrong, when, where and how, a closer examination of the electoral management, the election preparation and conduct needs to be undertaken.

The Kenyan Electoral Management in 2007

The Kenyan Electoral Commission (ECK) consisted of 22 members, including the Chairman, the maximum allowed under the Constitution. They were appointed by the President in his sole discretion, that is to say, he did not have to consult with any individual or authority. The term of appointment was five years which awkwardly coincided with election year, and which raised the possibly of new Commissioners taking office shortly before an election. In 2007, ten new Commissioners were appointed by the President in January. That was an ugly omen, as the new Commissioners were described as not knowledgeable about electoral matters and were not particularly agreeable with the Chairman and many of the then existing Commissioners. The Commissioners were not required to have any particular qualifications and the President had no legal criteria to guide him in making the appointments.

Although the ECK was clothed with apparent independence, in practice however it felt that it lacked sufficient financial independence and its independence was not always respected by the political directorate.

These were two of the main weaknesses of the institutional structure of the electoral management of Kenya and they contributed to the failure of the ECK ultimately. Notwithstanding that the President appointed each Commissioner, the picture that emerged from the ECK was one of dissention among the Commissioners with traces of partisanship.

The ECK Attitude to Performance of its Functions

The scheme for reviewing and creating new electoral districts in Kenya was flawed as the Parliament could object to proposals put forward by the ECK. That happened in 2006, the year before the 2007 elections, despite that fact that there was widespread departure from the principle of equality of the vote. That approach by the Parliament and the ECK led to the retention of unfair electoral districts/constituencies and contributed to stealing the elections by stealth.

Although the ECK had no doubt tried hard to get the registration of voter's right, it failed. The qualification to register was somewhat complex and required a national to reside for a period of at least five months in the preceding twelve months, carrying on business or being employed in a constituency for similar periods, or possessing land or residential buildings there. The ECK had a long experience in conducting national registration stretching back to 1992.[168] In 1997 the ECK computerized the register using optical mark recognition (OMR) forms. The 2002 elections were conducted on the register which was updated in 2000, 2001 and 2002. In 2002, continuous registration of voters was introduced in conjunction with yearly updates and in 2007 an update to the register was undertaken. The 2007 registration update brought the total size of the register to 14,296,180 voters or 71% of the estimated 19.8 million qualified persons.

The evaluation of the Kriegler Report (Independent Review Commission (IREC)) found that the continuous registration as conducted by the ECK was not cost-effective and had not worked. The productivity of the system was very low. A break down of the registration data revealed that women and young persons between the ages of 18 and 30 were under-registered. The ECK failed to ensure that the voters' register was purged of deceased persons estimated to be about 1.2 million persons. The ECK had a poor system of control over the registration process in which, for example, residence of voters was not systematically verified.

Nominations (Registration) of Candidates—Kenya did not allow independent candidates to contest elections. Contesting candidates had to be sponsored by political parties. The procedure in Kenya required that each nomination be conducted in accordance with the internal constitutional rules of the political party and was certified by a person whose specimen signature had been deposited with the Commission. Party primaries were always controversial[169] and 2007 was more of the

---

[168] The author observed the 1992 registration exercise.

[169] Going back to the first multiparty election in 1992 when the parties were given an unusually short period (November 3 to 9) to select their candidates. The opposition parties protested to the ECK, as in their understanding of the law a period of not less than 21 days should have been allowed. In response, the ECK referred them to a gazetted notice stating that the words *not less* than 21 days had been changed to *not more* than 21 days in section of

same in that regard. Media reports suggested that the primaries were characterized by chaos accompanied by claims of vote-buying which gave way to winners becoming losers and violence followed protests and nomination certificates were with held from some prospective candidates. A number of complaints were filed with the ECK and some were taken to court. The ECK's response was to set up a nine-member committee to listen to complaints, but complainants soon realized that the ECK had no competence to deal effectively with such matters. The provisions of the electoral law dealing with party primaries and the role of the ECK in that regard were in need of review and reform.

Electoral preparations—The main weaknesses identifies in the preparations for the elections were the following:

- Voters were not properly informed of the stream to which they were allocated;
- Some streams were empty, while others were overflowing;
- Ballot papers were printed overseas (in England) and that occasion was used by the ECK to send nine Commissioners, two senior officers and a Government Printer representative on a mission to the UK for several weeks to oversee the ballot printing and packing;
- The name of the candidates were not pre-printed on the counting forms as is normally done in accordance with good practice;
- Although staff recruitment was said by stakeholders to be reasonably transparent, they cited instances of selection being influenced by tribalism, and last-minute replacements of some returning officers by Area Commissioners;

---

the National Assembly and Presidential Election Act. In fact, the provision of the Act enabled the Attorney General to correct only clerical or printing errors in editions of revised laws. An opposition party, FORD-Kenya, filed a suit for a declaration that the purported amendment under the Revision of Laws Act by the gazetted notice was null and void. The Court granted the declaration and said that there was no error in the law to be rectified and that the notice had effected a substantial change which had been 'sneaked in mischievously'.

- Some returning officers showed evidence of being improperly trained;
- Polling kits did not include calculators which would have helped polling and counting staff;
- The staff of tallying centres also appeared to be inadequately trained;
- There was evidence of ballot stuffing in some areas;
- The voter education programmes were limited and inadequate;
- There were no disclosure rules, no ban on foreign donation, no campaign spending limits, no disclosure of individual donors and no contribution limits;
- The political environment was said to be saturated with money with little or no regulation and with the ECK powerless to step in;
- The Electoral Code of Conduct was not followed;
- Although the ECK was aware that materials aired by media houses were unacceptable, it took no action against such media houses;
- The ECK failed to develop a harmonious relationship with the media as an indispensable dimension of good election administration;
- The use of the 'black book' was abused and should be discontinued;
- The agents of some political parties were not allowed in areas of strongholds of other parties; and
- There were abuses in assisting voters who needed assistance to vote.

Measures to Address Some of the Shortcomings

With respect to improving preparations for elections, the ECK would be well advised to implement the following measures:

- Review and provide closer scrutiny of the job description of temporary field officers;
- Election field workers, especially returning officers and presiding officers should be exposed to longer periods of more intensive training;

- Thorough and adequate training should be extended to all categories of field personnel, based, where appropriate, on the cascade methods whereby personnel trained one level below;
- Training out-sourcing should be considered, where appropriate;
- Holding practice sessions of moot electoral activities for field personnel who should be required to attend as pre-condition to employment; and
- Operational instructions and manuals relating to training of election personnel should be reviewed to ensure that they are kept up to date.

The Kriegler Report made extensive and detailed recommendations to correct practices which were inconsistent with good practices in election organization and in particular that:

- Steps should be taken to construct fair constituencies' and electoral districts' boundaries;
- Significant improvements in the quality and delivery of election education programmes should be implemented;
- Measures to produce a much calmer political environment in which a level playing field prevailed during election campaigns should be promoted;
- Creation of enhanced access to the media and greater facilitation of freedom of expression should be developed; and
- Measures to reduce election bribery surrounding polling day operations, improving the quality of election services, particularly with respect to voters with disability should be undertaken urgently.

Vote Counting and Tallying—The fading of credibility among stakeholders in the 2007 Kenyan elections began with the vote counting and tallying. Among the significant weaknesses reported by stakeholders were:

- The notion of 'zoning' whereby opponents were prevented from campaigning in 'strongholds' of a particular party;
- Party agents of opponents were thrown out of polling stations during the counting of the votes;

- Party agents of opponents were often not allowed to accompany the ballot boxes to the tally centre by supporters of the dominant party in that area;
- In some areas, supporters of the dominant party were allowed to enter the polling stations without proper identification;
- Although there was strong suspicion that the tallying process at the constituency level was not thoroughly executed, there was little hard factual evidence adduced in support of that suspicion;
- Confusion in transmitting results, presidential and parliamentary, from some constituencies was caused by some returning officers departing from the rule that partial results should not be transmitted until the partial results were verified;
- The occurrence of discrepancies between parliamentary and presidential election turn out in several constituencies reflected in the ECK official results triggered concern among stakeholders, and even more so because, curiously, most of the discrepancies occurred in areas where support was strong for the incumbent President;
- The Chairman of the ECK in his evidence to the IREC stated that the presidential results in the computer database for 32 constituencies differed from what was recorded on those constituencies' form 16;
- The ECK's IT Department failed to provide reliable figures as to the sum of valid votes and contributed to the incorrect figures which came from the ECK;
- There were many accusations that tally forms were tampered with, but few concrete evidence adduced in support of that allegation;
- The lack of openness and transparency in the conduct of the tallying process gave rise to fear of tampering;
- Some aggrieved stakeholders alleged electoral fraud and pointed to the circumstances of the announcement of the final presidential results and the unusual low-key swearing—in ceremony at State House as supportive of the fraudulent conduct of the elections;
- The IREC Report concluded that the 'conduct of the 2007 elections in Kenya was so materially defective that it has been, and will remain, impossible for IREC to establish true and reliable results for the presidential and parliamentary elections.'

- A close audit of counting and tallying process through forms 16A (polling station counting results) and form 17A (constituency tallying centre) concluded that the transfer of results from polling stations to constituencies, the tallying in constituencies, the transfer of constituency of constituency-level presidential election results and the tallying at national level was of incredibly low quality.

The counting and tallying procedures employed in the 2007 Kenya elections were flawed and executed in such an incompetent manner that the result of the elections was rendered questionable and no doubt contributed to the nasty post-election developments.

Apportioning Blame?

The overall analysis of the 2007 elections in Kenya revealed a string of weaknesses in electoral framework touching the legislative scheme, conduct of the main processes, and linked through an unwieldy and divided election management body. The Commissioners and the election officials, including the crucial field officers, such as returning officers and presiding officers, were not sufficiently schooled in the culture of non-partisanship and impartiality. Moreover, many electoral officers displayed a lack of proper training and a low level of competence, as well as poor grasp of the capacity for details necessary for polling and counting processes.

The fundamental failure of the overall organization of the elections must be placed on the ECK. The members failed to observe the rules relating to transparency, competence and provision of adequate instructions to returning officers and counting officers. The ECK was found wanting in failing to enforce campaign rules and the Code of Conduct for Parties and Candidates. In a similar vein, there were inadequate rules dealing with 'hate' campaign speeches which were believed to have contributed to the post-election violence.

Additional Steps

Following on the Agreement on the Principles of Partnership of the Coalition Government signed by President Mwai Kibaki and Prime Minister Raila

Odinga on February 2008, a Statement of Principles on Long-term issues and solutions was signed by representatives of the PNU and the ODM, respectively, on 23rd May 2008. The Statement of Principles contained a framework for implementation of six issues which were considered central to the underlying causes of the post-election national crisis. The six issues identified were constitutional, institutional and legal reform; land reform; poverty, inequity and regional imbalance; unemployment, particularly among youth; consolidation of national cohesion and unity; and transparency, accountability, impunity. The Statement of Principles had annexed to it an agenda for implementation of the various elements such as specific actions, timeframe and focal points.

Notwithstanding the detailed agenda for implementation of the agreement on the Kenyan national dialogue and reconciliation, some aspects of the arrangement proved to be fragile and even contentious, for example, in April 2009 an impasse developed over whether the President or the Prime Minister had the right to appoint the Leader of Government Business in the Assembly. The Prime Minister was reported to be calling for elections as the Power-Sharing arrangements were not working smoothly.

Case Study II

Zimbabwe

Elections of 2008 and their Aftermath

Introduction

Ever since the birth of Zimbabwe as an independent State, multiparty democracy sat ill at ease with the dominant political party, Zimbabwe African National Union-Patriotic Front (ZANU-PF). But that was perhaps because independence was won more by conflict rather than by democratic means. The ZANU-PF, being the victorious at the pre-independence poll nurtured the paternal instinct of the nation and found it hard to let go, even when it was obvious that after almost thirty years in power, the leader, President Mugabe, was ill equipped to govern the nation in the twenty-first century. He steadily lost the confidence of the majority of the electorate, and after losing a constitutional referendum in 2000, national elections became less and less democratic.

Constitutional and Electoral Environment

ZANU-PF won the 1980 pre-independence democratic elections. Almost immediately the 'winner-takes-all' approach was adopted and former comrades-in-arms minority parties were not welcomed to share in the recently acquired power to govern the new State of Zimbabwe. That approach triggered conflicts which were particularly severe in Matabeleland. The 'colonial' independence Constitution of 18 April 1980 was subjected to several amendments during the 1980s and saw off the transitional provision reserving 20 House of Assembly and 10 Senate seats for the white population. The second Chamber of the Legislature (Senate) was also abolished in the 1980s constitutional amendments.

The 1980s constitutional amendments consolidated ZANU-PF's leader, Mr. Mugabe's, hold on power by providing for an executive presidency and by creating a total of 30 non-constituency members of the Assembly appointed by the President.

The end of the electoral dominance of ZANU-PF began with the loss of the government-sponsored referendum on constitution amendments in 2000. That electoral defeat ushered in widespread political violence and farm invasions. Thereafter, elections in Zimbabwe were marred or perhaps more accurately were characterized by unbridled and reckless violence perpetrated by supporters of the ruling party, ZANU-PF against political opponents and even against civilians, including white farmers. The perpetrators of the violence were headed by the war veterans and the youth militia which were associated with the ruling ZANU-PF party. The parliamentary elections of June 24-25 2000 and presidential elections of 9-10 March 2002, witnessed the unleashing of the full force of the ZANU-PF and government forces of open violence and intimidation against opposition candidates and supporters. Many stakeholders felt that the opposition would have won both elections had it not been for the wanton violence, threats, beatings and use of public resources by the ruling ZANU-PF. However, the ZANU-PF election tactics and the uneven playing field weakened the opposition and the ruling party, ZANU-PF did better in the 2005 parliamentary elections than previously in 2000.

In addition to objectionable and foul election campaign practices, government and the ruling party regularly employed despicable measures, such as retribution against persons who were believed to support the opposition—for example, exclusion from food distribution, against opposition supporters.

Electoral Management in Zimbabwe

The election management body of Zimbabwe was always multilayered consisting of four entities, namely, the Delimitation Commission, the Electoral Supervisory Commission, the Directorate of Elections, and the Registrar-General of Voters. That rather complex management structure led to unclear competences among the several bodies. Moreover, the Directorate of Elections comprised a number of government ministries contributing to logistics, transport and communication. Although some reform was undertaken with respect to the Zimbabwe EMB, complication with the lack of clear competences remained. Also the main negative perception of the EMB remained with the Zimbabwe Electoral Commission (ZEC), namely, that it remained under the influence of the ruling party and the government ministries, particularly, Foreign Affairs and Home Affairs. That was vividly demonstrated by the new power conferred on the ZEC to establish committees in which it could vest powers as it deemed fit. Using that power vested in it, the ZEC established a National Logistics Committee and sub-committees to assist it in mobilizing resources for the 2008 elections. The members of the Committee were drawn from several government ministries, the security forces and 'parastatal' sector.

Equally compromising for the ZEC was the perception that its members were persons who were friends of the President or ZANU-PF, or persons who were under the influence of both. There was no clear distinction between government powers and the writ of the ZEC as was demonstrated by the overlapping powers of the Ministry of Justice which invited and accredited domestic observers and the Ministry of Foreign Affairs which had the right to invite international observers and the ZEC acquiesced in the respective invitations. The Ministry of Justice often practised selective accreditation of domestic observers.

The main functions of the ZEC included the delimitation of constituency boundaries, prepare for and conduct elections, conduct registration of voters, and conduct voter education programmes. In exercising its functions during the March 2008 and the run-off election in June of that year, stakeholders accused the ZEC of acting under the influence of the ruling party and the government. Although the ZEC had power to employ its own staff, the legislative scheme allowed recruitment from the Public Service Commission, local authorities, statutory bodies and health services.

The Judicial Environment as Related to Elections

The general perception internationally was that President Mugabe's regime had compromised the independence of the judiciary in Zimbabwe. Some pointed to the fact that many Judges who had decided against ZANU-PF and the government were dismissed by President Mugabe. Others raised the slowness of the Court in disposing of contested cases from 2005.

2008 Election Environment

Many stakeholders and particularly the main opposition party contended that the president and ruling party prematurely cut short SADC sponsored negotiation process, led by Thabo Mbeki of South Africa, which would lead to constitutional amendments. However, somewhat unexpectedly, violence against the opposition mitigated in the lead up to the March 2008 elections. The increased level of political tolerance did not prevent the ruling party from seeking to carve maximum advantage, at times even by forcibly placing party posters on houses and buses. The utterances of President Mugabe and senior members of the security forces to the effect that there would never be regime change in Zimbabwe did not auger well for democratic elections in that country.

The election preparatory process for the elections was not always conducted in line with acceptable practice. For example, the delimitation of constituency boundaries was carried out shrouded in secrecy with little or no consultation with stakeholders, and the final delimitation report was published just a few days after the nomination date had been set. The opposition complained that the entire process was not transparent and did not afford the opposition sufficient time to properly organize their selection of candidates. They also complained of the gerrymandering of constituency boundaries in favour of the ruling party.

The voters register had mixed reception by opposition parties and other stakeholders. There were 5, 934,768 voters on the register, stakeholders felt that the final figure was inflated and the true size was nearer to 3 million. There were other criticisms of the register, for example, that the process was not transparent, and some complained that the time given for inspection of the preliminary roll was insufficient. The cost of the register was considered too high and was not always available to civil society organizations. The ZEC was alleged to be reluctant to supply electronic copies in a form that facilitated search.

The campaign period leading up to the March elections was marked by tolerance and accommodating to the campaigning by the opposition, although permission of the police was required to hold rallies. The apparent lull in the tension during the election campaign was interrupted by the frequent bellicose utterances by President Mugabe and the security chiefs that an opposition victory at the polls would not be recognized, and that put a cloud over the conduct of the elections.

The media landscape in Zimbabwe in 2008 was dominated by the influence of the ZANU-PF over the public media. The Media Monitoring Project of Zimbabwe (MMPZ) and the ZEC both monitored the performance of the media and had different findings. The MMPZ found that the opposition was almost always portrayed in a negative light in reports and editorials, while the ZEC found that the state media displayed matured coverage of the campaign.

The use of state resources by the President and the ruling party for party campaign purposes was widespread. The President was alleged to have made several donations, including buses, motor vehicles, generators, television sets, food aid and agricultural equipment to communities and organizations throughout the country under a programme funded by the Reserve Bank of Zimbabwe. The handouts were usually extensively covered by the media.

Ballot papers

The management of the election logistics was obviously not up to international standards in so far as the allocation of ballot papers to polling stations and postal voting was concerned. The size of the voters' register was put at 5.9 million voters. The election management ordered 9 million ballot papers for each of the four categories of elections that were being organized. That amounted to almost 50% excess ballot papers, which does not accord with acceptable international practice. Stakeholders complained that the process was not transparent, as timely information was not available. A similar complaint was made about the postal ballots the requirements of which was put at 10,000 voters, but for whom some 600,000 ballot papers were acquired.

Electoral Irregularities

Although many international election observer missions found that the March 29 2008 elections organization was credible up to the time of polling, there were many election irregularities which should be noted and corrected for future elections. One such preparatory process was the delimitation of constituencies' boundaries. The delimitation process was described as lacking transparency and participation by the stakeholders. The delimitation exercise was relatively extensive and involved 1,958 wards, and 210 House of Assembly constituencies and 60 Senate constituencies. The final report of the ZEC on the delimitation was published late; coming just a few days after the date for the nomination of candidates had been set. Stakeholders complained that there was evidence of gerrymandering through the merging of some urban constituencies with sub-urban and rural ones, while at the same time more rural constituencies than urban ones were created.

The register of voters did not escape a measure of shortcomings. The registration of voters in Zimbabwe was voluntary and was carried out in a continuous manner. Stakeholders complained that the continuous registration process was allowed to continue beyond the stipulated period. Some stakeholders felt that the 5.9 million voters on the voters' register represented an inflated register and the opposition parties complained that the roll was not user-friendly. Electronic copies were not always available, even to purchase. There was a perception that the roll did not have the general confidence of stakeholders.

The election campaign

The March 2008 electoral campaign was marred by hostile comments by officials of the ruling party and by threats by senior officers in the security services that they would not recognize an opposition election victory. Police permits to hold election rallies were not always granted on a timely basis or at all to opposition candidates. 'Hate speeches' directed at the opposition were often heard at rallies of the ruling party. Phrases, such as 'sell outs', 'political witches', 'political prostitutes' and 'traitors', were attributed to President Mugabe in describing his political opponents.

The publicly owned media dominated the electoral campaign environment and were under the control of the ruling party. The privately owned media largely supported the opposition, and a few of the print media, notably The Standard and The Independent gave balanced coverage of the campaign.

The use of state resources for election campaign purposes gave the government and ruling party unfair advantage over the opposition. The President of the country and leader of the ruling party made numerous donations, such as buses, motor vehicles, generators, television sets, food aid and agricultural equipment to communities and organizations across the country, which were funded by the Reserve Bank of Zimbabwe.

Counting the votes

Despite considerable preparation for the counting of the March elections' votes, the process did not proceed without difficulty. The process employed encompassed two stages, namely, a preliminary count immediately after the close of the polls and a re-count. In the case of the March elections, the recount did not take place until two weeks after the preliminary count as a result of late appeals in 23 constituencies by the ruling party, ZANU-PF.

Although the preliminary count at the polling stations was transparent, that was not the case with the Command Centres where the collation took place; it was suspected that the lack of transparency at those Centres aided political interference. The results from the Command Centres were not released by the ZEC in a timely manner. The requirement to post up the polling station count results was not followed with respect to the presidential results. Stakeholders, including the opposition MDC, were not allowed to witness the counting of the V-11 forms for the presidential vote. Independent observers were also barred from the counting of those forms.

The recount in the 23 constituencies which the ZANU-PF requested took place in seven provinces commenced on April 19 2008 and ended on 30 April 2008. The original winners of the House of Assembly and Senate constituencies were confirmed.

The official results of the March 29th election were released on 2nd May 2008 and the date for the run-off presidential election was announced for 27 June 2008. The opposition MDC had won 47.7% of the presidential votes to ZANU-PF 43.4% of the votes. That result was not accepted by the MDC initially, but was later acquiesced in when the MDC presidential candidate agreed to contest the run-off election. The 29 March 2008 House of Assembly results were the following: 99 seats for MDC-T (47.83% of the votes), and 97 seats (46.86 % of the votes) to ZANU-PF. Three by-elections were held on the same day as the run-off election and MDC-T won one and ZANU-PF won two making the final tally of 100 seats for MDC-T and 99 seats for ZANU-PF. The MDC-M held the balance of power with 10 Assembly seats, and one independent seat completed the complement of the House of Assembly.

In the elections to the Senate, ZANU-PF won 30 seats, while MDC-T won 24 seats and MDC-M won 6 seats. However, the balance of power in the Senate was determined by the 33 appointed Senate members who were indirectly elected or appointed under the influence of the President.

Run-off Presidential Election—The Environment

The origins of the run-off election were controversial as the opposition candidate, Mr. Morgan Tsvangirai, claimed to have gained more than the 50 % plus 1 to win the presidency at the first round election. His claim was not supported by the ZEC and was disputed by the ruling party. Eventually, Mr. Tsvangirai, backed down and decided to contest the run-off election. However, some distance into the contest, Mr. Tsvangirai withdrew on the ground of relentless violence against his supporters and obstruction to hold political rallies.

Ever since the date of the run-off election was announced on May 2nd 2008, the electoral atmosphere became charged with a high degree of political tension and the open hostility between the two main contesting parties increased in intensity. There was loss of life, intense intimidation, and displacement of people, abductions, rape, torture and beatings. The reports from stakeholders catalogued further outrages against innocent people who were suspected of supporting the opposition by the Youth Militia of the ruling party. Very serious atrocities were attributes to them, including invasion of villages, burning of houses and operation of torture camps in rural as well as in urban areas. The ruling party itself was said to have established over 3,000 militia bases throughout the country. Stakeholders reported that road blocks were set up in some areas and ID cards, without which one could not vote, were confiscated. The MDC opposition party reported more than 100 of its supporters were killed, more than 10,000 injured or maimed, in excess 2000 were detained and more than 20,000 homes were destroyed. The perpetrators of the violence against opposition supporters were carried by the youth militia, war veterans, the police force and the armed forces. There were widespread calls for postponement of the run-off election, including by the United Nations Secretary-General, Ban Ki-Moon, and the Chairman of the African Union, Jean Ping, but to no avail.

To compound matters, the ZEC at best was far from neutral in the alarming situation and was still clinging to the view that free and fair election could be held. Worse still, the ZEC dismissed 120 employees who had participated in the March 29 elections and filled their positions with persons who were thought to be sympathetic to the ruling party.

Changes for the Worse

There was a drastic scaling down of the numbers of domestic observers accredited to observe the run-off elections. Some domestic observer groups like the Zimbabwe Election Support Network (ZESN) thought that the number of observers they were allowed would not allow them to operate properly and withdraw.

The pressure on the opposition became intense, their offices were frequently raided by the security forces, their meetings were disrupted and Tsvangirai and Biti of the MDC-T were frequently detained so that they could not campaign on a sustained basis. The situation could be summed up by concluding that freedom of speech, movement and assembly was no longer available to the opposition during the campaign for the run-off election.

The state owned media was closed to the opposition candidate, Morgan Tsvangirai, and refused to carry his campaign advertisement. The state owned media carried a programme aimed at discrediting the opposition.

Unacceptable Aspects of the Run-off Election

The unbridled violence perpetrated or supported by the officialdom of the government or the ruling party was undemocratic. Many other aspects of the elections were also unacceptable in the context of multiparty elections. The conduct of postal voting was not transparent as the process was not open to observers.

The security forces were so politicized that they were openly partisan and lacked the confidence of most stakeholders. The leadership of the security forces openly pledged their support for the ruling party. The security forces acted discriminatory in granting permits to the opposition to hold rallies which were often denied or not granted in a timely manner. Perhaps worse of all the security forces were reluctant to arrest the supporters of the ruling party who perpetrated violence against the opposition.

Run-off Election Day

Despite the persistent violence during the campaign that forced opposition candidate, Morgan Tsvangirai, to drop out of the presidential race, polling day was relatively peaceful. The turnout was low, although the figures published were inflated to improve the picture. Stakeholders reported that some voters were forced to go to the polls and persons without the voting ink on their finger were threatened or even beaten up. There were a high percentage of spoilt ballots, some with obscene comments about the elections. The incumbent President, being the sole candidate, was quickly declared the winner of the run-off election and soon sworn in as President.

Post-Run-off Election

The run-off election revealed the true state of Zimbabwe's democracy. It was non-existent so far as multipartism was concerned. The Harmonized Elections of March 29 2008, which combined presidential, senatorial,

House of Assembly and local elections, up to the point of the end of polling were given pass marks on a rather low bar for credible democratic elections. Those elections were adjudged to be an improvement over all elections held over the past decade. Although the Harmonized Elections benefited from improvements attributed to the SADC mediation led by the former President of South Africa, Thabo Mbeki, those elections were called somewhat prematurely before the completion of negotiations that would have engendered constitutional change and improvement to the electoral environment of Zimbabwe. There were some positive improvements to the electoral management structure of the Zimbabwean EMB, and some less high profile procedural changes, such as the posting up of counting of votes results outside the polling station which made a difference regarding the transparency of the counting process at the polling station.

Alas, the gains achieved with respect to the preparation of the Harmonized Elections began to fade with the lack of transparency with the counting of the presidential votes and the counting of the V-11 forms at the Constituency Command Centres. The election management quality deteriorated fast after this point. The results of the March 2008 elections were not released on a timely basis, the late request by the ruling party, ZANU-PF, for recount in 23 constituencies did not accord with the interpretation of the rules. The ZEC slowly stifled and then quickly strangled the confidence of stakeholders in its ability to conduct democratic elections to acceptable standards.

Despite avoidable blemishes that occurred along the preparatory route of the Harmonized Elections, stakeholders and international observers grudgingly gave those elections 'pass' marks. However, there could be no such concession with respect to the run-off presidential elections of June 2008. It was clear to many stakeholders that the ZEC, the ruling party and the incumbent President, all deliberately trampled on the multiparty democratic script. That approach was followed without regard for the democratic rights to campaign in the run-off election. It was obvious to the curious onlookers and confirmed by stakeholders that the run-off election campaign was farcical. All the pillars of democratic elections were removed—freedom to hold political rallies, that is to say, freedom to speak, to move about, and to assembly; widespread violence against opponents by the ruling party, and the strong perception that the ZEC was partisan in favour of the ruling party.

Where Does Zimbabwe Go From Here?

With the debacle that was the run-off election, the results of which were not accepted by many stakeholders in Zimbabwe, and by the international community, regional diplomacy stepped in to engineer a temporary solution to the political impasse, if not an electoral one. The diplomatic initiative launched by the SADC and supported by the African Union was spearheaded by Thabo Mbeki, former President of South Africa. He failed to produce a proper democratic solution and instead settled for a power-sharing arrangement between ZANU-PF and the MDC-T. The power-sharing arrangement sought to substitute itself for the legitimate government that should have emerged after the run-off election. The proposed solution was in line with a similar arrangement worked out between the Government and opposition in Kenya earlier in 2008. Perhaps the situation in Zimbabwe was different from that in Kenya. The Zimbabwean strongman, President Mugabe had displayed little flexibility and was probably too mired in his past campaign rhetoric that the opposition would never take power in Zimbabwe. An agreement between the parties ZANU-PF and MDC-T was reached on 15 September 2008, creating the posts of President and Prime Minister supported by two deputy presidents and two deputy premiers respectively. There would be a Cabinet of 31, made up of 15 nominated by ZANU-PF, 13 by MDC-T and 3 by MDC-M. The House of Assembly and the Senate were modified slightly. The power-sharing arrangement became stuck because Mr. Mugabe and the ZANU-PF claimed all the influential cabinet posts, and so the arrangement was not implemented until 14th February 2009–despite subsequent efforts by Mr. Mbeki, the mediator. Although the main problem of the allocation of portfolio of important Government Ministries was apparently solved by the time the Inclusive Government was formed in February 2009, the political environment remained extremely fragile. There were arrest of opposition supporters, including one who was designated a Deputy Minister, and several human rights and civil society activities. For several months after the formation of the Inclusive Government in which Mr. Morgan Tsvangerai was Prime Minister and Mr. Biti of the MDC-T was the Finance Minister, its future prospects looked uncertain. However, some early measures by the Inclusive Government through the Finance Minister were successful in stabilizing the currency situation and modest financial assistance by African Institutions was attracted to Zimbabwe.

Case Study III

Political Succession in Malawi 2004-09

Background

Since the resumption of multi-party democratic elections in 1994 in Malawi, two subsequent national elections in 1999 and in 2004 have been held in that country. The Malawian electoral environment has been disturbed since the lead up to the 2004 elections due to the inability of the then ruling political party, the United Democratic Front (UDF), to properly manage the issue of political succession within that party. Since then other issues affecting the electoral environment arose, particularly the perception among stakeholders that the Electoral Commission was not be independent and so a new Commission was installed in 2006. The questionable conduct of the voter registration exercise for the 2009 elections also came under close scrutiny. However, the real source of tension in the country was the political rivalry between the incumbent President Mutharika and his party, the Democratic Progressive Party (DPP) and the former President Muluzi and his political party, the United Democratic Front (UDF).

The Constitution

The Head of State:

The President is the Head of State and Government, as well as the commander in Chief of the armed forces. The President is directly elected concurrently with the National Assembly. The President is restricted to two terms of office and presidential candidates must be over 34 years of age and the nominations must be endorsed by 10 registered voters in each district. To win a candidate requires a simple majority of valid ballots cast.

Tenure of office

The President will hold office for five years from the date that his or her oath of office is administered, but shall continue in office until his or her successor has been sworn in.

The First Vice-President and the Second Vice-President will hold office from the date of the administration of the oath of office to them until the end of the President's term of office unless their office should come to an end sooner in accordance with the provisions of the Constitution.

The President, the First Vice-President and the Second Vice-President will serve in their respective capacities a maximum of two consecutive terms (The constitution of Malawi clearly stipulates in section 83 (3) that the President and Vice-president shall serve a maximum of 2 consecutive terms.)

Election of the President and the Vice-President

The President is elected by a majority of the electorate through direct, universal and equal suffrage.

Every presidential candidate will declare who will be his or her First Vice-President if he or she is elected at the time of his or her nomination.

The First Vice-President will be elected concurrently with the President and the name of a candidate for the First Vice-President will appear on the same ballot paper as the name of the Presidential candidate who nominated him.

Where the President considers it desirable in the national interest so to do, he or she may appoint a person to the office of Second Vice-President.

Political parties

Malawi Congress Party (1961-1994)

The Malawi Congress Party (MCP) was originally known as the Nyasaland African Congress, but became the MCP under Hastings Banda, its (and the country's) first president.

It won all of the seats in the legislature in the 1961 Nyasaland elections, and led the country to independence as Malawi in 1964. When Malawi became a republic in 1966, the MCP was formally declared to be the only legal party. All adult citizens were required to be party members. They had to carry "party cards" in their wallets at all times. The MCP lost its monopoly on power in a 1993 referendum, and was roundly defeated in the country's first free elections the next year.

Unlike other former single parties in Africa, the MCP remains a major force in Malawi. It is strongest in the central region populated by ethnic Chewa and Nyanja people.

At the general elections held on 20 May 2004, its candidate for president, John Tembo won 27.1% of the vote, and the party won 60 out of 194 seats.

United Democratic Front (1994-2004)

The United Democratic Front (UDF) claims to be a liberal party in Malawi and is mainly strong in the southern region populated by ethnic Yao. The party is a member of Liberal International, which it joined at the latter's Reykjavík Congress in 1994. Bakili Muluzi, who was president of Malawi from 1994 to 2004, is the chairman of the UDF.

In the general election held on 20 May 2004, the UDF's candidate for president, Bingu Wa Mutharika, won 35.9% of the vote and managed to win 49 out of 194 seats.

Democratic Progressive Party (2005-2009)

The Democratic Progressive Party (DPP) was formed in February 2005 by Malawian President Bingu wa Mutharika after a dispute with the United Democratic Front. The party is named after the major Taiwanese political party, Democratic Progressive Party, a funder of political groups in Malawi, before the end of diplomatic ties between the nations.

There were allegations that members of the former governing UDF did not adequately tackle corruption.

The Main Political Party Leaders—

Bingu wa Mutharika

Bingu Wa Mutharika was appointed Minister of Economic Planning and Development in 2002, and was then nominated by Muluzi as his successor. Mr. Mutharika had been hand-picked by the outgoing President Muluzi as the UDF candidate after Parliament refused to accept an amendment to the constitution allowing Mr. Muluzi to stand for a third term. Perceived as a relative outsider, his nomination surprised many UDF members and led to several defections. Wa Mutharika won about 36% of the vote in the presidential election of May 20, 2004, ahead of John Tembo and Gwanda Chakuamba.

After taking office, Wa Mutharika came into conflict with Muluzi, the Chairman of the UDF, over his campaign against corruption. The dispute between them had been an important feature of Bingu wa Mutharika's time in office, and it had been claimed that political conflict was interfering with the country's governance.

On February 5, 2005, wa Mutharika announced his resignation from the UDF, saying that he had no support in the party because of his stand against corruption. After Mutharika formed the DPP in 2005, over 70 Members of Parliament joined the new party (DPP); the opposition, including the UDF, has sought to have these MPs expelled from their seats for switching parties.

There had previously been talk of expelling Bingu from the party, and there had also been an alleged assassination plot against him by party members in early January 2005. In October 2008, the DPP's national governing council unanimously chose wa Mutharika as the party's candidate for the 2009 election.

While serving as President, wa Mutharika also held the portfolio of agriculture and food security in the Cabinet, and he additionally took over the education portfolio.

Wa Mutharika highlighted his economic achievements in his re-election bid. Inflation and interest rates fell and harvests had been generally good under his rule. The government had forecast 8 percent growth in 2009, slightly higher than the International Monetary Fund's projection of 7.7 percent.

Elson Bakili Muluzi was the candidate of the opposition UDF in the May 1994 presidential election, the country's first multiparty election. He won the election with 47% of the vote, defeating Malawi's leader since independence, Hastings Kamuzu Banda. Muluzi was hailed a hero in Malawi for ousting Kamuzu Banda, a victory that appeared to mark the end of authoritarian rule in the country of 13 million people.

He was re-elected in June 1999, taking 52.4% of the vote and defeating challenger Gwanda Chakuamba. In 2002 he proposed an amendment to Malawi's constitution that would have allowed him to run for a third term, but this was abandoned due to demonstrations against him. He therefore stepped down after the May 2004 election, in which UDF candidate Bingu wa Mutharika was elected to succeed Muluzi as President.

The anti-graft body briefly arrested Muluzi in 2006 on 42 counts of corruption. But all the charges, except for one involving $11 million, were dropped for lack of evidence. Malawi's Anti-Corruption Bureau (ACB) said it plans to prosecute Muluzi over $11 million in donor money it says was siphoned into his private account. But Muluzi denies any wrongdoing

For the May 2009 Presidential Election, Mr. Muluzi lost his battle with the Electoral Commission and subsequently with the High Court to be a presidential candidate and the ordinary interpretation of the Constitution that the president may serve two consecutive terms prevailed.

The Electoral Commission

The Electoral Commission which consists of a Chairman who will be a Judge nominated in that behalf by the Judicial Service Commission and such other members. Members of the Electoral Commission, not being less than six, will be appointed in according to the Act of Parliament.

A person will not be qualified to hold the office of a member of the Electoral Commission if that person is a Minister, Deputy Minister, a Member of Parliament or a person holding public office.

Except for the first multi-party elections in 1994, when the President was obliged to get the approval of the Council, it does not appear that the President is obliged to consult with stakeholders when appointing Commissioners.

High-Level Mission

The Chairperson of the African Union Commission (AUC) dispatched a high-level mission to Malawi between 20th-26th February 2009 to undertake consultations, among other things, with all the stakeholders, particularly the incumbent President, former President and other parties to assess and determine the current political situation in Malawi. The Mission was headed jointly by H.E. Mr. Joaquim Chissano, former President of Mozambique, and H.E. Mr. John Kufuor, former President of Ghana.

The Mission held several sessions of consultations with H.E. Dr. Bingu Wa Mutharika, President of Malawi, former President Dr. Bakili Muluzi, leader of the United Democratic Front (UDF) and the Electoral Commission/ The High-level Mission appealed for calm and urged stakeholders to take measures to reduce the political tension. The High-level Mission pointed to certain difficulties that could threaten the peace, security and stability of Malawi—these included the need to:

- Create an environment for free and fair elections;
- Adhere to the rule of law;
- A level playing field for political parties contesting the elections;
- Deal with electoral complaints expeditiously;
- Promote a culture of tolerance, dialogue and peace; and
- Facilitate equal access to public resources for political parties.

Further Developments

The former President, Dr. Muluzi, leader of the UDF Party who sought to be the Party's presidential candidate was not allowed to stand as he had previously served two consecutive terms as President of Malawi. Dr. Muluzi took the matter to the High Court, which dismissed his action, albeit on a technical point. He has indicated that he will appeal to the Supreme Court. However, in the meanwhile, Dr. Muluzi has publicly indicated that his party would endorse the candidacy of Mr. John Tembo of the Malawi Congress Party (MCP), as it is unlikely that the appeal would be heard in good time to allow him to campaign for the forthcoming elections.

Stakeholders were dissatisfied with the lack of equal access to the publicly owned media, particularly by the opposition parties.

The Chairman of the African Union, H.E. Mr. Ping, visited Malawi in May 2009 shortly before the May 19th elections to try to calm the political tension that flowed from Mr. Muluzi's failed attempt to contest the election.

The 2009 elections were held in May and the incumbent President wa Mutharika won by a landslide gaining more than 2 to 1 ratio of the votes cast over his nearest rival candidate John Tembo. Prior to the election the Supreme Court had rule against Muluzi's attempt to run for a third term.

Lessons Learned

The Malawi experience demonstrated that an incumbent President's persistent attempts to influence political succession in a Member State of the African Union can be thwarted by peaceful means. Dr. Muluzi was determined to influence the political succession in Malawi, for having failed to amend the Constitution in 2002 to allow him to contest the presidency for a third term, he hand picked wa Mutharika to succeed him in 2004. After Muluzi fell out with wa Mutarika in 2005, many political moves were made by Muluzi's Party to remove Mutarika from power. Muluzi's final move was to challenge the ruling of the Electoral Commission of Malawi that, having already served two consecutive terms as President, he was not eligible to contest a third term. The Supreme Court of Malawi decided in favour of the Commission's ruling. The people of Malawi showed their overwhelming support for Dr. wa Mutarika at the polls in 2009 general elections, and settled the issue of political succession for the time being in Malawi.

The democratic means are the best way to settle the thorny issue of political succession in the Member States of the African Union.

Discourse

Compacts

Evolution of the Compacts Family

Although attempts to conceptualize the formalization of the relationship between government and CSOs have been in the making since the early 1990s, it was only when the Deakin Commission Report of 1996 made some positive recommendations that the conceptualization was given real impetus. The basic thrust of the Deakin Report was that partnerships should be established between the voluntary sector and public authorities on the basis of agreed basic principles.[170] In 1997, a Compact Working Group was set up under the management of the National Council for Voluntary Organizations. The outcome of that compact project was four compacts between the voluntary sectors and the authorities of England, Scotland, Wales and Northern Ireland concluded in 1998. Similar approaches followed in 1999 by Canada, Denmark in 2000, and Germany in 2003. Other European countries, including Croatia, Estonia, Hungary and Poland, followed in a similar vein. In the United States of America, the National Council of Non-Profit Associations promoted a move towards convening in October 2006 a Non-Profit Congress with the aim of passing a Declaration of America's non-profits. The three-fold purpose of the congress was to develop a common identity based on shared values; agree a unified vision and message, and speak with a collective voice.[171]

---

[170] See *Meeting the Challenge of Change: Voluntary Action into the 21ˢᵗ Century. The Report of the Commission on the Future of the Voluntary Sector. 1996*

[171] For a useful perspective of the evolution of Compacts see draft report by British Council, March 2006.

Elements of the Compact Concept

The underlying approach as the Deakin Report recommended is the partnership relationship between the voluntary sector and the public sector. The new cooperative effort is also characterized as promoting greater participatory democracy. The emphasis of the UK type compact is on cooperation between government and CSOs, while later type introduced by the emerging democracies of Eastern Europe places importance on the strategies for developing a thriving civic sector organizations.

Another consideration which underpins the compacts is the adherence to practice codes of good conduct in particular areas. Codes of good practice have been introduced in five areas, namely, consultation and policy appraisal, funding and procurement, black and minority organizations, volunteering, and community groups, in England. In Canada, the Accord made provision for two codes, good practice on funding, and good practice on policy dialogue.

Contents of Compact Agreements

Compact agreements have as their principal function the creation of a flexible framework for cooperation between national government (although they may be extended to local government) and the non-profit sector (CSOs). All compact agreements encompass the recognition or identity of the parties to whom they are addressed, the representation of those parties, the relationship contemplated, and the identification of resources to support the implementation of the agreed objective of the cooperation. With good reasons, compact agreements tend to place the onus on government to improve and provide the inspiration for the enhancement of the cooperation between the parties there to. This may very well be due to the fact that there is the belief that governments control the resources within their jurisdiction so far as the voluntary sector is concerned, although that position would appear to derogate from the spirit of cooperation that is being established. The CSOs are always keen to see the partner government fully acknowledging their independence and diversity. In this context, the inclusive nature of compact agreements will mean that some CSOs may adopt advocacy roles that are in conflict with government policy and remain within the frame of the compact.

This aspect of compact agreements might not operate at ease with many AU Member States. However, with the growing partnership arrangements between governments of countries in the APRM and non-governmental entities, it may not be difficult for that functional relationship to develop into more general compact arrangements between governments and CSOs.

Partnership—this element of compacts is the key to their operational success, for it conveys the essential rationale for the new approach. The term connotes a status that is free of rivalry and is not based on the first among equals concept. It conveys the notion of collaboration in decision-making. In order for this approach to work smoothly, there has to be accurate and timely exchange of information on matters relevant to issues with respect to which decisions are to be made affecting both sides. In a similar vein, the working method and the structure of decision-making apparatus of each side should be made known to the other. This approach could be assisted by secondment of personnel from the voluntary sector to work with relevant policy-making departments and government personnel would be seconded to work with CSOs.[172] There is really no reason why these partnerships could not flourish in the AU Member States.

Compacts and Resources

Resources availability and management are also a key element of partnerships created by compact agreements. This is a complex issue. Some jurisdictions find it more convenient to deal with this matter in a code of conduct. In any event, two issues need to be considered, namely, the best practices and procedures for allocating resources by government and CSOs' best practices in using and accounting for these resources. One of the main goals of a compact is to ensure that government's commitment to resource allocation to CSOs is objective and clear, and applies to all relevant departments in a consistent manner. The matter of

---

[172] A Canadian report on relationship with CSOs suggested that special internships and fellowships between the voluntary sector and government was a feasible approach, see for example, The Voluntary Sector Initiative-An Accord between the Government of Canada and the Voluntary Sector, December 2001; http://dsp-psd.communication.gc.ca/Collection/cp32.

long-term strategic funding which is crucial for the sustainability of CSOs is usually a difficult issue to resolve. The bulk of government funding of CSOs usually goes to specific projects and field services and compacts always recognized this. The practices of governance which are relevant here, competitive bidding and accountability for public funds expended, have to be observed by CSOs benefiting under a compact.

Compacts and Accountability

Good practices in governance currently require proper accounting for the expenditure of all public funds. It is not surprising therefore that compacts' arrangements deal prominently with this issue. The actual forms of accountability should be clearly set out in the compact. This approach may include the design of tax return forms for CSOs and competitive bidding procedures. Often CSOs express concern that accountability requirements may impinge upon their independence. Reasonable intervention of this kind by government should not be considered as discriminatory or intrusive, but rather as consistent with good management of public funds. Full accountability is always supported by transparency which is manifested in timely and accurate reporting. Compacts or their accompanying codes of good practice should deal with reporting in a balanced manner thus avoiding excessive demands which could be burdensome to CSOs.

Compacts and Local Governments

While this brief account of the potential for a structured relationship between CSOs and government is concerned with national government, it should be stated that compacts can and do impact at the local level. In England local compacts are fashioned on the national compact but agreed between CSOs and public bodies for a local or county area. The concept of local compacts has taken hold in England to the extent that by 2009 99% of local authority areas had either published their compact or were in the process of negotiating one.[173] Compacts, at the level of local government, can strengthen governance, and as the Nigerian Country Review under

---

[173]   UK Local Government Association-99% of Local Authority has a Local Compact-see website: http://www.lga.uk.

the APRM showed, local government will form part of the inclusivity in APRM member states in the future.

Settlement of Disputes

The framework for any compact family agreement should include procedures for resolving differences that might arise out of the interpretation or application of a particular compact. But in practice, to date many compacts do not contain provisions for the settlement of disputes. In England the compact provides that disputes may be dealt with by negotiation by the parties or by mediation, or by the Parliamentary Commissioner for Administration.

Training

Compacts usually provide for training of officials who will service the partnership, and also for the wide dissemination of information about the compact and its contents.

Implementation of Compacts

Inevitably, the implementation of compact agreements requires that suitable structures be put in place by each side to facilitate smooth application. From governments' viewpoint, the cooperation to galvanize the partnership with CSOs needs to be managed by mechanisms or senior officials in order to ensure consistency by all arms or agency of government. The CSOs may also experience difficulty in establishing and supporting a cooperation mechanism unless the framework was included in the compact. Large umbrella networks might be well placed to support the cooperation mechanism.

Since compacts are aimed at strengthening the working relationship between governments and CSOs, there is scope for compacts to take hold in the AU Member States. The emergence of the APRM process, coupled with the ECOSSOC as an umbrella organization for CSOs in the AU, will facilitate the development of arrangements on the African continent similar to compacts in Europe and North America.

Case Studies On:
The African Peer Review Mechanism
The Country Review System and Its Achievements

Introduction

The African Peer Review Mechanism (APRM) is a dynamic structure created as a voluntary governance self-monitoring system as an off-shoot of the New Partnership for Africa's Development (NEPAD). The APRM has enormous potential to improve the performance of participating States through the process of participatory self assessment reinforced by a review process which enables a forum constituted by all other participating States to consider support (where necessary) to the reviewed State. Among the key features of the Mechanism are the voluntary nature and the do-it-yourself procedure by the participating States. Each State freely decides whether or not to join the APRM and one the main pillars of the review process is the self-assessment by the participating State concerned. In theory, the APRM entails reviewing the working of government in which all stakeholders would contribute. It requires the removal of the veil from sensitive areas of government operations, and allows transparency the freedom to prevail. The issue of whistleblowers and their protection has been raised in some countries during the self-assessment process. Can the APRM prevent some of Africa's perennial problems such as disputed elections or blunted political succession? It is still early days in the life of the APRM, the Kenya experience of 2007 elections came after Kenya was one of the first participating countries to submit to review process. Further, one of the architects of the NEPAD and the APRM, former Nigerian President Obasanjo sought to engineer a third term in 2007 which some felt was contrary to the spirit of the APRM.

The APRM Process

The structure and process of the APRM were discussed briefly above (at pages-217 to 221). This Discourse is concerned mainly with individual country's self-assessment and review. In order to put the procedures in perspective, a cursory glance needs to be taken of the continental, as well as the country structures, that are required to effect a successful country review process.

The structures at the continental level are:

a.   The Committee of Participating Heads of State and Government (APR Forum). It considers and makes recommendation with respect to review reports on the member states and authorizes the publication of the APRM reports. The APR Forum selects the members of the African Peer Review Panel of Eminent Persons.

b.   APR Panel is the APRM's executive arm and as such directs and manages its operation. It is in charge of the country review processes and offers guidance and oversight tasks with respect to country teams. The Panel may be considered as the guardian of the integrity of the review processes. The members of the Panel are between 5-7 persons selected from Africans who have distinguished themselves in the fields of political governance, macro-economic management, public financial management and corporate governance, and are of high moral stature and committed to the ideals of Pan Africanism. Potential members of the Panel are nominated by participating countries and short-listed by a Committee of Ministers. In appointing the members of the Panel, the APR Forum takes account of regional, gender and cultural balance.

c.   The Secretariat supports the APR Panel in its operation. The Secretariat, through its executive director ensures that secretarial, technical, coordinating and administrative support services are provided to the APRM process. The Secretariat prepares the background documents for peer review teams and tracks the performance of individual countries with respect to the APRM process. It maintains a database on political and economic development in participating countries.

APR Structures at the National Level:

a) The APR Focal Point is a national mechanism designed to communicate, coordinate and liaise between national and continental structures. There is flexibility regarding the form and profile of the focal point and the participating country is free to make it choice, but preference would be for the focal point to be made up of high-level officials who report to the Head of State or Government and to whom national stakeholders have access.

b) Under the APRM each country is required to establish a national coordinating structure, such as a national governing council, in which the main stakeholder groups are represented. This entity is responsible for conducting the country's self assessment through wide consultations with the key stakeholders in the public and private sectors. There is a measure of flexibility as to how the self assessment is done. It may well be that precedence will emerge that serve to tighten up this procedure to meet minimum standards, but that stage may be some way off.

The Review Process

As set out in the base document of AHG/235 (XXXVIII) July 2002 Annex II and discussed above, the peer review process has five main stages, namely, country self assessment review and report, country review mission, compilation of a country report, submission to the APR Forum and publication of the report.

Submission to APRM Reviews

Many of the 30 participating countries have submitted to the APRM system of review and are at varying stages of the review process. Among the earliest submission to review were Ghana, Kenya, Mauritius and Rwanda. These will be examined with a hint of comparison in mind. However, the main thrust of this examination is the quest to discover the level of inclusivity in carrying out the self assessment, the participation of civil society, the level of cooperation of government with the continental review team and the inclusivity of inputs in the plan of action agreed to by the reviewed country. Many other countries which have either also completed their first review process, or in the process of doing so, will be selected at random, but with regional distribution in mind, including Ghana, Kenya, Mauritius, Nigeria, and Rwanda.

APRM Case Study I

Ghana

Ghana APRM Process[174]

Ghana acceded to the APRM on March 9 2003 and just over a year later in May 2004 received a support mission which carried out a fact-finding exercise from 24-29 May 2004. It examined the processes and mechanisms that were being put in place to undertake the country's self-assessment undertaking. The Support Mission advised on a preliminary Programme of action and noted the various technical committees which were being set up to carry out the peer review exercise in Ghana.

Ghana's National APR Structure

Shortly after acceding to the APRM in 2003, Ghana established a Ministry of Regional Cooperation and NEPAD, which was mandated to ensure that Ghana was ready for the peer review. The Ministry appointed an independent National ARPM Governing Council (NAPRM-GC), to act as Ghana's National Focal Point with respect to the APRM. The composition of the NAPR-GC consisted of representatives of civil society. The Government created a National APR Secretariat to assist the NAPRM-GC to carry out its mandate. The NAPRM-GC was vested with the task of appointing four separate lead technical institutions, one for each of the four main areas to be reviewed, namely:

---

[174] For a critical assessment of Ghana's country review process see *"Ghana and the APRM: A Critical Assessment* by Adotey Bing-Pappoe, 2007. Africa Governance Monitoring and Advocacy Project (AfriMAP).

- The Centre for Democratic Development—Democracy & Political Governance;
- The Centre for Policy Economic Analysis—Economic Governance;
- Private Enterprise Foundation—Corporate Governance; and
- The Institute for Statistical, Social & Economic Research—Socio-Economic Development.

These lead technical institutions were given the task of preparing the preliminary Country Report in respective areas of expertise. Guidance for the format of this exercise was provided in the APRM Self-Assessment Questionnaire. The Institutions' reports were submitted to the NARM-GC which edited them into one report. The NARM G-C took a pro-active stance and travelled the countryside and conducted sensitization workshops in order to gage the nation's state of governance from a wide section of stakeholders.

The Self-Assessment Exercise

On March 18 2004 the President of Ghana inaugurated the Ghana National APRM Governing Council. The members of the Council were appointed in their individual capacities based on their experience and distinction in their respective fields. There were criticisms of the appointments as individuals and not as representatives groups, also because there were little consultations prior to the appointments. Although not initially, a liaison officer was appointed through whom the Governing Council could engage with the President.

The preparations for the self-assessment report were conducted along two lines of approach, namely, activities by the Governing Council and research activities by the technical research institutes (TRIs). The NAPRM-GC was responsible for conducting public awareness programmes among stakeholders, and to facilitate active participation in validation of the self-assessment report and in the programme of action. The technical research institutes were to deal with the surveys and to report the views of Ghanaians on the nature of political governance, economic management, corporate government, and socio-economic development in Ghana.

Four technical institutes, namely, the Centre for Democratic Development (CDD) for democracy and good political governance; the Centre for Economic Policy Analysis (CEPA) for economic governance and management; the Private Enterprise Foundation (PEF) for corporate governance; and the Institute for Statistical, Social and Economic Research (ISSER) for socio-economic development; were selected to lead the research. Each of these organizations was well known in its field of research. The TRIs worked closely with the NAPRM-GC and with each other. The questionnaire was 'domesticated' to make it more user-friendly. The NAPRM-GC employed a stakeholder liaison officer to engage with the public and with CSOs.

A Country Support Mission from the APRM Panel visited Ghana in May of 2004 to formally commence the Ghana APRM process. On 24 May 2004 the Memorandum of Understanding (MoU) was signed by Minister K. Apraku on behalf of the Republic of Ghana and Dr. Chris Stals signed on behalf of the Panel. A national stakeholder workshop was held immediately after the signing of the MoU at which the adaption of the questionnaire to suite the Ghanaian requirements. In addition, three other consultative meetings were organized, namely, in February 2005 to discuss the national self-assessment report together with the NPoA; the national validation meeting during the Country Review Mission in April 2005; and a validation meeting during the visit of the Chairperson of the APRM Panel of Eminent Persons, Madam Marie-Angelique Savane in Accra June 2005.

The methodology of the technical research institutes followed a general format even if the actual methods varied due to the differences in subject areas. Each of the TRIs used a three-stage process as follows;

• Stage 1. The pre-field methodology involving in-house research or literature review; education awareness programme and the creation of ownership among ordinary Ghanaians; harmonizing and coordinating methodological approaches among technical review teams; identifying stakeholders; recasting the questionnaire into a survey instrument; data gathering and analysis.

- Stage 2. The field methodology involving interviews with government and independent state officials, and civil society groups, and sample survey of ordinary Ghanaians.
- Stage 3. The post-field methodology involved assessment by independent experts appointed by the Governing Council the material produced by the TRIs, and validation by various stakeholders.

In total the TRIs consulted approximately 5,000 people, albeit not using identical methods. To facilitate quality control with respect to democracy and good governance, expert and civil society groups were invited to undertake specialist reviews. In respect of technical focus areas expert individuals were commissioned on a consultancy basis to conduct peer reviews of documents prepared by the technical teams.

Adoption of the Self-assessment Report and Draft Programme of Action

The country self-assessment report and the draft programme of action went through a series of validation meetings and reviews including the following:

- A national validation exercise organized by the NAPRM-GC between 10-13 February 2005 at the Ghana Institute of Management and Public Administration where stakeholders received the draft reports and NPoA presented by the technical review teams;
- Revisions to the country self-assessment draft based on the proceedings of the national validation workshop;
- In-house ministerial review by government officials from the Ministry of Regional Cooperation and NEPAD;
- Review of the draft self-assessment report and programme of action by a government-appointed team of experts at a retreat in Elmina on 18-20 February 2005;
- Review by a team of government ministers;
- Review by a parliamentary select committee on APRM matters; and Review by the Trades Union Congress.

The final consolidated self-assessment report and the draft Programme of action were presented to the government on March 18 2005 and shortly thereafter to the APRM Secretariat in South Africa.

The Country Review Mission.

A 16-member country review team from the APRM Panel and Secretariat visited Ghana after the self-assessment was submitted to the APRM Secretariat. The purpose of the country review mission was to address the identified weaknesses and shortcomings in the areas of governance and development and to discuss the draft programme of action that the country drew up to improve their governance and socio-economic development. The team was led by Dr. C. Stals a member of the panel of eminent persons. The team travelled around the country from 4-16 April 2005 and met a wide range of stakeholders.

The members of the Country Review Mission involved in a number of activities, including:

- Working sessions with the APRM-GC and the technical teams on issues papers prepared by the APRM Secretariat;
- Attending a workshop for Trade Union Congress, academia, and non-governmental organizations to discuss the CSAR and evaluate the extent to which ordinary Ghanaians were involved in the review process;
- Attending meetings with various national bodies such as the Commission on Human Rights, Justice Department, Serious Fraud Office, as well as ministries and departments of government;
- Visiting regional capitals to meet regional stakeholders and assess the level of broad-based participation and the role of regional stakeholders in the review process;
- Attending a workshop with Parliamentarians in Accra;
- Meetings with Ghana's partners; and
- A meeting with the deputy minister for finance and the governor of the Bank of Ghana.

Visit by the Chairperson of the APRM Panel

The Chairperson of the APRM Panel of Eminent Persons Marie-Angelique Savane, and Dr. Stals, visited Accra in June 2005 after the departure of the country review mission had departed, to review the APRM process, particularly to look at the NAPRM-GC's engagement with CSOs and to examine the costing of the NPoA.

The APRM Panel prepared its Ghana Country Review Report on the basis of the self-assessment report it received along with the NPoA, the APRM Secretariat's issues paper and the findings of the country review mission. The report was submitted to the Government on 18 March 2005 and on 19 June 2005, the ARPM Panel submitted the Ghana Country Review Report and the national programme of action to the APRM Forum.

Formally Tabling of the Ghana Review Report

The Ghana APRM Country Review Report was placed before a meeting of the APRM Forum held in Khartoum, Sudan, in January 2006. The Country Review Report and the programme of action were published by the APRM Secretariat in October 2005.

The country's self-assessment process was considered exemplary by some commentators, particularly due to its strong emphasis on civil society participation. The independence of the self-assessment from political manipulation was attributed to the composition of the governing council being composed of a small group of distinguished individuals working through independent research institutions. The Ghana peer review exhibited two significant characteristics, namely, freedom from political manipulation and strong participation of citizens and civil society groups. Nevertheless, some civil society groups in Ghana felt that a more critical view should be taken of the country's performance.[175] Some critics also pointed to the large size of the cabinet and interference in judicial cases.

---

[175] See for example, paper by Adotey Bing-Pappoe, "Ghana and the APRM: A Critical Assessment, June 2007, Africa Governance Monitoring and Advocacy Project (AfriMAP).

APRM Case Study II

Kenya

Kenya's African Peer Review (APR) Process.[176]

The APR of Kenya, correctly or otherwise, will be assessed in the light of the 2007 elections and the tragic aftermath. The APR took place some eighteen months before the elections, it has been argued that the APRM was intended to prevent such occurrences and indeed some human rights activists contended that even if fifty percent of the APR's recommendations had been implemented the post elections violence might have been avoided. These sentiments might have been based on vain hopes rooted in hindsight, but the Kenyan post APR developments have rightly raised the question of how effective is APR process in improving the working of government and the national machinery in important areas such as the preparation and conduct of national elections.

The general APR process as laid down in the base document of 2002 at the July Durban Summit (AHG/225 (XXXVIII) Annex II applies to all African Peer Reviews. The five stages laid down in the base document need to be met as was seen in the case of Ghana above. However, the first, and probably the most important stage is not standardized and so each country with some support and oversight from the member of the Panel who is assigned to the review is free to organize the structure and procedures with respect to this stage, the self-assessment. The danger is

---

[176] For further reading see also: The APRM Process in Kenya, Steve Ouma Akoth, March 2007, Africa Governance Monitoring and Advocacy Project (AfriMAP); also African Peer Review Mechanism: Lessons from Kenya, Bronwen Manby, Pambazuka News 2008-04-15 Issue 362 http://pambazuka. org/en/category/features/47406

for countries to avoid the APR exercise becoming a "state—centric" one, or as occurred in Ghana overlooking an important sector, the informal business sector.

Although the Base document of the APRM list five stages, there are many steps to be covered in some stages, particularly in the first stage. In order to achieve a high level of participation in the self—assessment exercise, the following steps as a minimum may be needed:

- Upon signing or acceding the Memorandum of Understanding (MoU) of 9 March 2003, agreeing to undergo peer review;
- Establishing an APRM National Focal Point;
- Establishing an ARPM National Commission (by whatever name called) to provide oversight to the process;
- Carrying out of awareness programmes about NEPAD and APRM among important stakeholders;
- Undertaking workshops among different stakeholders;
- Making contact, through the Focal Point, with many stakeholders to get views on various governance issues;
- Holding consultative workshops with limited (manageable size) numbers;
- Setting up technical groups of limited numbers-20-25 to discuss specific issues and report back to larger groups;
- At this teething stage, consultation of the APR Questionnaire provided by the APRM Secretariat which contains four thematic areas:

  (i) Democracy and good political governance
  (ii) Economic governance and management
  (iii) Corporate governance
  (iv) Social/economic development

- Reporting back by the thematic groups to a national consultative workshop;
- Formation of a Technical Review Team may be necessary to validate work done at workshops and elsewhere;
- Supporting mission from the Panel may visit at this point;

- Setting up of the APRM National Commission (by whatever name called) which will work with the Questionnaire four thematic areas mentioned above;
- Acting on the advice of the Support Mission and the validation work by the four thematic groups, the National Commission may finalize its self-assessment report and its draft Plan of Action Report.

The foregoing steps may not occur in the order set out above and not all of the may be necessary, depending on the format followed by a particular country which is undergoing review. However, if the majority of these steps were to be followed in a timely manner, the delay encountered in the Kenyan self-assessment exercise would be avoided.

The Kenyan review process did not proceed smoothly. There were several delays and change of personnel along the way. There was uneasiness on the part of civil society groups as the level of engagement of non-governmental entities in the process to the extent that some civil society groups labeled the exercise to "state-centric". The main problem was due to the failure of the government—appointed entities to gain the confidence of the civil society groups as partners in the process of self-assessment. The National Governing Council (NGC) lost some credibility when the Minister responsible dismissed three of its members, including its Chairperson, pursuant to a dubious procedure. The matter was acrimonious and even went to court, although the aggrieved lost the court action.

The national machinery to guide the review through its paces consisted of:

- NEPAD National Steering Committee—nine permanent secretaries of ministries;
- Vice Chancellor of the University of Nairobi;
- A representative of a private university;
- Two representatives of the private sector; and

Two representatives of the non-governmental organizations (NGOs).

A National NEPAD Kenya Secretariat with a chief executive officer was set up.

In February 2004, Minister Nyong'o told the APRM Forum that Kenya was ready to begin the formal review process and Panel member Dr. Graça Machel was assigned to guide the Kenya process.

An APRM Task Force was established at the national level whose terms of reference were:

- To propose a detailed timeline for the process;
- Develop the terms of reference and guidelines for the various structures of the APRM in Kenya, including the National Governing Council which was to oversee the process;
- Set its overall direction; and
- Ensure that the APRM process in Kenya was not solely government driven.

The chairman was the Permanent Secretary in the Ministry of Planning and National Development. Initially, the Task Force comprised government officials from ministries, namely, Ministry of Justice and Constitutional Affairs, Finance, Foreign Affairs, Trade and Industry, Agriculture and the Office of the President and the Central Bureau of Statistics. The Task Force, after two meetings with an all government officials, decided to extend its composition to include as members representatives of the private sector, civil society organizations (CSOs), universities, independent research institutes, and faith-based organizations. The Planning Minister incurred the displeasure of many CSOs when he announced that the government would select to CSOs to take part in the Task Force.

The Kenyan Minister of Planning, Mr. Nyong'o opened the APRM Consultative Forum as part of a public process on July 14 2004. A second Forum meeting was convened a week later to 'domesticate' the Questionnaire but it encountered difficulties when a group of CSOs walked out of the meeting.

The APRM country support mission, headed by Dr. Machel, began work on 26 July 2004. The task of the Mission was to assess Kenya's readiness to undertake the review, as well as to offer technical assistance. The Ministry of Planning had produced a 'road map' for the review which would commence on5 August 2004 and end on February 25 2005. During the

Support Mission's visit to Kenya, Dr. Machel and the Support met CSOs who complained that CSOs had not been given enough time to put their views. Dr. Machel intervened with the Ministry on behalf of the CSOs and succeeded in slowing down the operations. Eventually, a memorandum of understanding was signed whereby Kenya committed itself to complete the self-assessment by the end of March 2005.

The intervention by Dr. Machel and the Support Team did have an impact and when the Kenya APRM National Governing Council was revamped, its chairperson was a CSO representative. The lead agencies chosen to direct research and write the self-assessment report, as well as the development of the Plan of Action met with general approval, including that of the Ministry of Planning and National Development and the APRM Kenya Secretariat.

Considerable amount of work was done to 'domesticate' the Questionnaire to meet the Kenyan needs, so as to facilitate desk research, panel discussions, sampling households surveys, and to hold focus groups discussions.

Nevertheless, Kenya missed the original deadline agreed with Dr. Machel of March 2005 and a further revised deadline for June for the presentation of the self-assessment report. Dr. Machel paid a follow—up visit to Kenya in July 13 to 15 2005 and expressed disappointment at the inability of the Kenyans to meet deadlines. She agreed another deadline of 31 August 2005. There was no doubt that Minister Nyong'o was stirred into action by the second Support Team's expression of disappointment, for on the 20 July 2005 he dismissed the Chairperson and two members of the National Governing Council, whom the Minister blame for the slow pace of performance of the NGC.

Despite the apparent turbulence in the NGC, the initial draft of the Kenyan self-assessment report was produced by the lead technical agencies. The NEPAD Kenya Secretariat and the Ministry of Planning had brought together a team of independent experts to examine critically the initial draft and prepare the final version. A consultative forum attended by delegates from every district assembled in early September 2005 to validate the self-assessment report. This validating exercise was not transparent as the delegates were not given the report but rather only summary presentations of it. The Kenya self-assessment report was, after the validation at the consultative forum, submitted to the APRM Secretariat in South Africa

The Country Review

The country review mission was led by Dr. Machel from 3 to 17 October 2005. The Mission conducted interviews and did research to test the findings of the self-assessment report. They visited all eight provinces in Kenya.

The Panel Report

The Report prepared by Dr. Machel was based on the review mission's findings when she and her team visited Kenya after the self-assessment report was submitted. The Panel Report would have taken into account independent information compiled by the APRM Secretariat.

Presentation of the Report on Kenya to the APRM Forum

The Kenya Country Review Report was presented to the APRM Forum on 30 June 2006 by Dr. Machel in Banjul, Gambia. President Mwai Kibaki presented Kenya's PoA and responded to the panel's report. The APRM eminent person's country review report showed fulsome praises on Kenya's stability but correctly, and alas prophetically, drew attention to the fact that ethnic strife remained a real possibility given prevailing patterns of ethnic politics and regional inequalities. The report drew attention to many of the pressing problems that faced Kenya, including:

- Neglect of the North Eastern Province;
- Managing diversity in nation building;
- Addressing gender inequality and youth unemployment;
- Lack of independence of the judiciary;
- Lack of adequate measures to protect economic, social, and cultural rights which resulted in more than 56% poverty in the country; and
- Existence of persistent corruption in the country.

Weaknesses in the Review Exercise

It is clear from the brief account of the Kenya country review that much more needs to be done in bringing government ministries to work in harmony with non-governmental entities in exercises such as the APR. Much time was lost due to unnecessary bickering between the government agencies and non-government entities throughout the preparation of the self-assessment report preparation

Although the country review report by the panel of eminent persons was considerably hard hitting, it does not appear that the peer Heads of State and Government followed through on the frank recommendations of the APRM panel of eminent persons' report.

The report did not address the weaknesses in the management structure of the Electoral Commission of Kenya.

APRM Case Study III

Rwanda

Rwanda APRM Process[177]

Rwanda was one of the first four countries, along with Ghana, Kenya and Mauritius, to commit to the APR. It signed the Memorandum of Understanding establishing the APRM on 9 March 2003 and undertook to submit to a peer review in February 2004. Rwanda moved quickly to commence its implementation of the peer review process. In March 2004 it set up a National NEPAD Secretariat within the Office of the President of the Republic. The Secretariat was headed by an Executive Secretary who also served as a focal point for NEPAD and the APRM in Rwanda. In March 2004, the National NEPAD Secretariat and the National NEPAD Steering Committee (which was set up by the Government in August 2003) quickly organized a national awareness conference on the ARPM. The conference attracted over 200 participants from various interest groups throughout the country. The conference organized a group of 21 members, the majority of whom came from government offices, to form a technical body to deal with the APRM Questionnaire and translating it into Kinyarwanda. The group of 21 members constituted the four technical thematic teams which dealt with the four areas set out in the APR

---

[177] For more information on Rwanda's APRM process see "Critical Review of the African Peer Review Mechanism Process in Rwanda" by The for Human Rights in the Great Lakes Region (LDGL), Kigali, January 2007; "RWANDAN Self-Assessment Process" EISA 2007 http://www.eisa.org.za/aprm/toolkit/countries-rwanda-assess.htm; also "Rwanda's APR Programme of Action (PoA) Implementation" Progress Report (June-December 2006) APRM National Commission.

Questionnaire and formulated initial responses to questions contained therein. These four technical teams met at a retreat in April 2004 to review the progress that was made with respect to the self-assessment preliminary report.

An APRM coordination office was set up within the National NEPAD Secretariat in April 2004. The technical review teams reported on progress on the self-assessment to a meeting of APRM participants who added to the recommendations prepared by the technical review teams.

An APRM support mission led by Mme Marie-Angélique Savané of the panel of eminent persons visited Rwanda from 21-24 June 2004. The mission reviewed the self-assessment report, heard from government officials, civil society and private sector and gave the 'green lights' to the national plan for completion of the initial self-assessment exercise. The mission was concerned about the preponderance of government inputs and weight in the initial self-assessment report and recommended that the National APRM Commission should be re-constituted in a manner that was more independent of government. The mission's recommendation was accepted and a new commission was constituted on the 24 June 2004. The new commission was a much larger body with government representatives, the legislature, judiciary, civil society and the private sector.

The new APRM National Commission on 24-26 July 2004 to formulate its strategy. In the mean time, the National NEPAD Secretariat co-opted the services of the South African Institute of International Affairs (SAIIA) to assist with a one-day training course on awareness for civil society increased participation in the self-assessment work.

The APRM National Commission organized a validation conference for the self-assessment draft report on 17 December 2004. The conference was attended by some 83 participants from the National Commission, government, civil society, the private sector, the church, and international organizations. The conference went off smoothly although the report was not circulated before the meeting. The recommendations from the conference were recorded and were subsequently incorporated in the report by the technical review teams.

The validated draft self-assessment report was then submitted for technical review by the African Institute for Political Analysis and Economic Integration (AIPA) based in South Africa. The AIPA formulated proposals on the report which were integrated into the report with the help of the Rwandan branch of the Organization for Social Science Research in Eastern and Southern Africa, OSSREA, before it was submitted to the continental APRM Secretariat in South Africa in March 2005.

The APRM country review mission, led by Ms. Dorothy Njeuma, a member of the APRM panel of eminent persons, commenced soon after the submission of the self-assessment report to the APRM Secretariat on 18 to 30 April 2005. The mission met with members of government, public officials, the APRM National Commission, members of civil society, private sector, and others. They then made comments on the self-assessment and submitted their own report to the Government of Rwanda. The Rwandan Government examined the report of the panel of eminent persons and responded to the comments of the APRM country review mission on 11 June 2005.

The draft of the Rwandan country review report and the PoA for corrective action of the failings identified were submitted to the third summit of the APRM Forum in Abuja, Nigeria, and received preliminary discussions, before it was returned to the APRM Panel and the Rwandan Government to finalize the PoA. The final Rwandan APRM country review report prepared by the panel of eminent persons and the APRM Secretariat, along with the PoA agreed with the government, was eventually submitted for review by the fifth summit of the APR Forum and the African Union, held in Banjul, Gambia, 2006 where it was formally adopted.

It was published in Kigali on 13 July 2006.

An Assessment of the Rwandan APR

Although the APR exercise went off relatively quickly and smoothly, there were difficulties along the way. The main problems, in the context of the APR, may be listed as follows:

- State "centricism" held sway in the organization, structure and contribution with respect to the country self-assessment report preparation;
- Stakeholders felt that restricted autonomy in administration and management in the conduct of the APRM process impacted negatively on the exercise;
- The consultations with non-governmental entities did not seem to the stakeholders concerned to have filtered through to influence direction or impact on the substantive issues;
- The governmental agencies and their representatives were given a head start in being given copies of the Questionnaire before non-governmental stakeholders;
- Moreover, civil society representatives complained that generally not enough time was allowed to deal with questions on the questionnaire, and that was the case even when the training workshop was held for civil society representatives in October 2004;
- There was an imbalance between the level of governmental representatives and non-governmental representatives on the APRM National Commission, and similarly in the executives of the ad hoc technical sub-committees which was dominated by civil servants;
- The Questionnaire appeared not to have been "domesticated" enough to meet Rwanda's needs, as many stakeholders complained that significant numbers of participants found the questionnaire difficult to understand and to respond to meaningfully;
- Although some stakeholders were critical of the fact that Rwanda had to seek outside help for technical review of its self-assessment report (in this case the AIPA of South Africa, nevertheless it is commendable that Rwanda recognized the need for outside assistance; after all this was the first country self-assessment in the first round of APRM review for that country.

Lessons Learned

The government authorities and non-governmental bodies that took part in the APRM review and especially in the country self-assessment exercise learned many things about how the government works. After all, the

APR is perhaps the largest process and mobilization of participants in the country, apart from national legislative elections and national population census. Mobilization of people and expertise was perhaps the essential factor in the success of the APRM process in Rwanda. The shortcomings listed above indicate lessons to be learned, but there are others which may summarized thus:

- The mobilization of prospective stakeholder participants could have been easier had the media been fully motivated and made aware of the true dimensions of the APRM process;
- The non-governmental stakeholders need to have greater access to government-controlled relevant information required for the APRM process;
- Representatives of CSO's need to be brought on board in good time and be exposed to proper training for the country self-assessment exercise, and be supplied with relevant documents, such as the APRM Questionnaire in a timely manner;
- Gradually, the preponderance of government-related agencies and their representatives should be reduced and make way for more meaningful involvement of non-governmental stakeholders; and
- The budget for an APRM process needs to be adequate in order that the full mobilization of participating stakeholders can be done on a timely basis.

APRM Case Study IV

Mauritius

Mauritius' APRM Process[178]

For Mauritius the APRM process has been a long one. Mauritius was among the first four countries, along with Ghana, Kenya and Rwanda, selected to be reviewed after signing up for the African Peer Review Mechanism. The Mauritian national self-assessment process was launched in early 2004 and soon saw relatively fast progress so that by March 2005 a preliminary draft self-assessment report was in place. However, by mid-2005 the exercise came to a halt for a variety of reasons. One principal reason for the halt was that a change of Government took place in Mauritius about that time. A re-launch of the APRM process took place in June 2007 and was in progress at the time of writing.

Soon after Mauritius signed the Memorandum of Understanding (MOU) establishing the APRM on 9th March 2003, the Government began identifying structures that would manage the APRM process. In October 2003, it announced that the process would be managed by the National Economic and Social Council (NESC). The NESC is a statutory body composed of government representatives, business, labour and civil society. The NESC was to serve as the focal point for the APRM process in Mauritius. The focal point was charged with the responsibility of liaising between the national stakeholders and the APRM Secretariat, as

---

[178]   For further reading see 'The African Peer Review Mechanism in Mauritius-Lessons from Phase 1-2007, Sheila Bunwaree, Africa Governance Monitoring and Advocacy Project (AfriMAP). Also Dr. Arvin Boolell: African Peer Review Mechanism (APRM) Country Review for Mauritius, http://te-in.facebook.com/note.php?note_id=116790149384.

well as being responsible initially for preparing the APR self-assessment report and a preliminary national programme of action (PoA). The NESC consisted of 23 councilors drawn from four sectors, but with about half of them government appointees. The Council was structured in three commissions, namely, economic affairs; infrastructure, physical resources, environment and sustainable development; and social affairs and human resource development. Each commission had between 8 and 12 members and is chaired by a commissioner chosen by the councilors.

There was an Executive Committee of the Council, consisting of the chairperson, the vice-chairperson, the three commissioners and the Secretary-General of the NESC. The Executive Committee administered the operations of the NESC, including the preparation of budget proposals for approval of the NESC. The reach of the NESC was such that every institution or organization in Mauritius was believed to fall within the jurisdiction of the NESC. Perhaps it was that perception that contributed to the selection of the NESC as the focal point of the APR process.

In its capacity of focal point, the NESC appointed a National Coordinating Structure (NCS), consisting of representatives of various ministries, the private sector, the media, labour organizations, political parties, parliamentarians, professional associations, and non-governmental organizations, among others. All the members of the NESC were also members of the NCS. Other organizations and individuals were invited to join in by letters. The objective of the NCS was to promote national dialogue in order to develop a national self-assessment. The NCS was responsible for developing, through validating, the self-assessment report, as well as helping to draft the national PoA.

The NCS held three formal meetings between May 2004 and March 2005 and many members of the NCS attended a sensitization workshop in June 2004 during an APR Secretariat's country support mission to Mauritius.

The APR Secretariat in South Africa sent the NESC a draft memorandum of understanding in January 2004 for the technical assessment mission and the draft guidelines for countries to prepare for and participate in the APRM. An advance mission from the APRM visited Mauritius in February 2004. The work on the APRM process was divided between NESC and the NCS with the NESC being responsible for the management of the self-assessment and the NCS for the more strategic matters. Mauritius joined the APRM in earnest in 2004 and received the APR Questionnaire and rules of procedure guiding the reviews. In May 2004, the NSC began to examine to APR Questionnaire and decided that government ministries would collect the responses from their departments and submit them to the NESC, private sector bodies, and other CSOs would send their responses directly to the NESC. The NESC also decided that the self-assessment report which NESC would prepare would be prepared and validated by all the members of the NCS.

An APR country support mission visited Mauritius in June 2004. The mission was led by Mourad Medelci, a member of the APR Panel of Eminent Persons. On 29 June 2004, a sensitization workshop was held with all members of the NSC and attended by a wide range of stakeholders, including heads of government ministries and departments, representatives of the private sector, trade unions, academia, political parties and CSOs. The workshop was addressed by the delegation from the APRM. During the visit, on June 30 2004, a memorandum of understanding was signed by Mourad Medelci on behalf of the APR Panel and by the then Minister of Foreign Affairs, International Trade and Regional Cooperation, Jayen Cuttaree, on behalf of the Government of Mauritius.

Subsequent to the visit of the APR country support mission, the NESC began to collect responses to the APR Questionnaire from stakeholders. The response was disappointing, except from government ministries. The NESC hired a consultant from the University of Mauritius to help draft the self-assessment report based on the submission received. The consultant produced a report based on the thematic areas of the APR, namely, democracy and political governance, economic governance and management, corporate governance, and socio-economic development.

The stage was set for the completion of the first draft of the self-assessment report which was completed in March 2005. The NCS convened a validation workshop on the 31st March 2005. The NESC presented the draft report. In presenting the draft report, the NESC conceded that important gaps had to be filled before it could be submitted to the APR Secretariat.

In the light of these developments, the non-governmental bodies were called upon for further inputs to consolidate the draft. NESC called a meeting of the CSOs in April 2005 to gather further responses. By the end of April 2005, NESC sent the draft to the APR Secretariat as work in progress. The informal submission of the somewhat incomplete self-assessment report caused a measure of confusion.

Halt to the APRM Process

After the submission of the incomplete self-assessment report, the review process effectively came to a halt. General elections were set for July 2005 and those elections resulted in a change of Government, which took some time to take full charge of the reins of government, including the APRM process. However, in June 2006 a new of NESC, Mr. Mohamad Vayid, was appointed. In May 2007, the new Chairman of the NESC announced that the APRM in Mauritius would be re-launched on 6th June 2007. On 20 July 2009, at the Conference Centre of Grand Bay, the Minister of Foreign Affairs, Regional Integration and International Trade, Dr. the Hon. Arvin Boolell, officially launched the consultations of the African Peer Review Mechanism (APRM) country review team with Mauritian stakeholders. According to reports, the self-assessment report was completed and sent to the APR Secretariat in February 2009. It is expected that Mauritius will be peer reviewed in January 2010.

An Assessment-Why Did the First Attempt Fail?

For most African countries, including Mauritius, the APRM exercise is, perhaps next to a general legislative elections and population census, is the largest process aimed at mobilizing the opinion-makers or participation of citizens in the nation. It calls for not only awareness but motivation to participate constructively in the exercise. It calls for access to relevant information by governmental and non-governmental national entities. It requires a modest amount of resources to keep the activities going, once started. It needs lots of political will to drive it along without monopolizing the ability to make inputs. Most important, the APRM exercise needs effective structures that are autonomous. Mauritius has many of these elements, or at least so it was thought, but they did not hang together sufficiently well to forge success in the first attempt at producing a credible self-assessment report in a timely manner.

The performance of civil society and non-governmental organizations was not distinguished, nor, for that matter was that of the representatives of governmental ministries and departments. To the uninvolved interested observer, a touch of complacency ran through the attempts at implementation of the exercise. For whatever shortcomings that might have attended the Mauritian process, there were similar comparisons with respect to other APRM processes in the other three countries, Ghana, Kenya and Rwanda, that started out with the APRM at the time Mauritius. It might have been a matter of degree of the problems to be overcome and the determination to achieve the objective of the APRM.

However, in critical areas of the APRM process, Mauritius was unable to overcome the challenge; in particular the focal point did not fully grasp its pivotal role in the mobilization of participation of non-governmental stakeholders. The contributions of non-governmental stakeholders in general came across as lacking in quality contribution to the exercise. The APRM Questionnaire might have been more difficult than expected, but other countries like Nigeria, having had somewhat similar difficulties, promptly set about 'domesticating' it to suite their local needs, according to the various local languages. The problem of poor access to information and a touch of "state-centricism" have been the common concern of non-governmental stakeholders in this phase of the implementation of the APRM process.

APRM Case Study V

Nigeria

The Peer Review Process in Nigeria[179]

Commencement of the APRM Process

Nigeria signed the APRM Memorandum of Understanding (MoU) on March 9 2003. Its implementation of the APR process was slow with the preparatory period stretching over a period of two years, 2004 and 2005, and when the self-assessment exercise did get on the way in 2006, it was slowed down as the incumbent President's, or at least some members thereof, wanted to amend the Constitution to facilitate a third term for the incumbent President Obasanjo. The constitutional controversy diverted the nations' attention from the self-assessment exercise which was not completed until late 2007 after the presidential elections of that year.

Initial Review Structures under President Obasanjo

The structures created to manage the APR process were an APRM National Focal Point, National Coordinator and the National Focal Point Secretariat. In addition there were the APRM National Working Group and Steering Committee.

---

[179] For further reading on Nigeria's APRM process see "*The African Peer Review Process in Nigeria,* by L. Adele Jinadu, July 2008, Open Society Initiative for West Africa (OSIWA); also *The African Peer Review Mechanism (APRM): An Assessment of Concept and Design,* by Ravi Kanbur, Cornell University January 2004. www.people.cornell.edu/pages/sk145

About the Nigerian National Focal Point

- President Obasanjo, in March 2003 appointed the Secretary to the Government of the Federation (SGF) as APRM National Focal Point;
- The SGF had daily access and reported directly to the President;
- The National APRM Secretariat was located in the SGF's office;
- The National Focal Point facilitated the commencement of the APRM process in the country;
- It was charged with the overseeing and coordinating the operations of the in-country APRM structures and processes;
- Assisted in mobilizing resources for the self-assessment process and the national plan of action (NPoA);
- Kept the President informed about the APRM process in the country; and
- Liaise with the APR Panel, the continental APRM Secretariat and international partners on matters relating to the APR process in the country.

About the APRM National Coordinator & the APRM National Focal Point Secretariat:

- The APRM National Focal Point Secretariat assisted the SGF in the discharge of his functions;
- The Secretariat was staffed by mainly public servants from the presidency and the federal civil service;
- The APRM National Coordinator advised, reported and was responsible to National Focal Point on APRM matters;
- The Coordinator was responsible for ensuring that the APRM National Focal Point and Secretariat was well served with adequate human, fiscal and infrastructure facilities and resources to carry out their tasks;
- The in-coming President Yar'Adua in 2007 made changes to the senior personnel dealing with the APRM, as well as some structural changes which were aimed at strengthening the APRM national framework.

About the APRM National Working Group and National Steering Committee:

- President Obasanjo, in 2004 appointed a 50-member APRM National Working Group (APRM-NWG);
- The NWG was aimed at broadening the base for stakeholders' inputs in the national APR process;
- The composition of the NWG included representatives of the presidency, the private sector, academia, the media, labour, civil society organizations (CSOs), and non-governmental (NGOs);
- The breakdown of the various sectors represented in the NWG was as follows—20 per cent government; 8 per cent National Assembly/political parties; 18 per cent private sector organizations; 10 per cent media; 28 per cent NGOs/CSOs; 10 per cent professionals and organized labour, and 6 per cent youth organizations;
- The NWG was also responsible for providing guidance, direction and oversight to ensure the credibility of the process,;
- The NWG was also charged with the responsibility of ensuring that the process was carried out professionally and competently;
- Its functions also included the organization of sensitization of activities on a nation-wide scale to popularize the APRM and to ensure that the country accepted ownership of the process;
- The NWG was mandated to engage the national research institutions to conduct the country technical assessment of the 4 APRM thematic areas;
- Liaise with the continental APRM Secretariat in South Africa, the National Focal Point, on the country APR process; and
- The NWG was to prepare the country for and facilitate the visit, including the in country work of the country review mission from the continental APRM Secretariat.
- The National Steering Committee (NSC) had 14 members was set up in consultation with the APRM-NWG;
- The NSC mandated to:

    - regularly review the APR process in the country;
    - receive and assess reports from the NWG and stakeholders concerning the APR process in the country;
    - serve as a final clearing house for APRM policy matters;

- liaise with the continental APRM Secretariat, through the National Focal Point; and
- report to the President on the progress of the APR process in the country.

The NWG operated through sub-committees at certain levels and set up four such entities to carry out oversight of the review process in each of the four APRM thematic areas, namely, democracy and political governance; economic governance and management; corporate governance; and socio-economic development.

The NWG and the In-coming President 2007

President Yar'Adua reconstituted the NWG in 2007. Its membership was expanded to 250, particularly to encourage popular participation and national ownership and sustainability. The expanded NWG included the secretaries of state governments (SSGs) of the 36 states, women, people with disabilities and faith-based organizations. A new chairperson was elected.

The NSC was also re-constituted into a 42-member body and the Chairperson of the NWG also became the Chairperson of the NSC. The composition of the new NSC was 38 members of the APRM-NWG who were chosen by other members of the APRM-NWG; two members representing the government (the permanent secretary-political in the office of the SGF, and the permanent secretary in the office of the head of the civil service of the federation); and two co-opted members.

Other National Supporting Structures

The foregoing main national structures were supported by the following;

- Technical research institutes (TRIs) which were replaced by lead research organizations (LROs) which undertook the country self-assessment survey;
- APRM Coordinators with respect to:
  -Democracy and political governance/socio-economic development;
  -Economic governance and management/corporate governance; and

-Statistics, to advise on the country self-assessment process.

- An APRM monitoring and evaluating team, made up of a core team at the national level, and zonal teams, comprising non-state stakeholders, in each of the country's six geopolitical zones.
- APRM advocacy and sensitization task team, made up of stakeholders from the print and electronic media, and mandated to widely disseminate the APRM to the Nigerian public and mobilize support for it.

APRM Process and Methodology in Nigeria

Nigeria's interpretation of the APR process places the questionnaire with respect to the four thematic areas (democracy and political governance; economic governance and management; corporate governance; and socio-economic development) at the centre of the methodology of the process. However, Nigeria took the view that the questionnaire needed to be 'domesticated' in order for it to be properly implemented. In July 2004, the National Focal Point held an in-country pre-test of the questionnaire. The procedure consisted of distributing the pre-test questionnaire to a sample of respondents, drawn from state, and non-state stakeholders who were asked to complete the questionnaire. When the results were revealed at consultative workshop in December 2004, only about 30 per cent of those who were given the pre-test questionnaire had completed it, and many responses were sketchy. The workshop decided that the questionnaire should be simplified and the TRIs were asked to ensure that the questionnaire conform to the multi-sector (economic, political and social) reforms, with 1960 as a baseline. Gender was to be a crosscutting issue in the four thematic areas. The TRIs were to settle on a common methodology to be used for the survey of all four thematic areas, taking account of the lessons learned from other countries which had undergone peer review. It was agreed that the questionnaire would be so managed that specific target audiences among the relevant stakeholder groups (including foreigners), while sensitizing Nigerians generally, and that the assistance of professional associations, such as the Nigerian Economic Association, the Nigerian Political Science Association, and the Nigerian Medical Association.

In 2004 certain organizations were invited to be the technical research institutions (TRIs) to conduct research for and prepare the draft country self-assessment report (CSAR). Although the organizations were of good standing and drawn from state and non-state entities, because the National Focal Point the selections without proper consultations with NWG and without advertising the positions, the apparent lack of transparency in selection process attracted strong criticisms.

APRM Country Support Mission March 2005

A Country Support Mission visited Nigeria from 21 to 24 March 2005 to assess the progress that was made. The mission was led by Ambassador Kiplagat, a member of the panel of eminent persons. The mission met with the National Focal Point, Chief Ufot Ekaette, and with the TRIs, as well as with various state and CSOs' representatives. The mission also had an open forum at which APR process was presented. At the end of the mission, the Ambassador and Chief Ekaette signed a memorandum setting out the various stages for the implementation of the APRM in Nigeria. The support mission recommended that NWG be expanded to include more civil society groups and that the chair should be not come from government.

Sensitization Activities

With the assistance of partners, particularly UNDP and the Department of International Development (DFID), a series of awareness workshops and seminars were held in Nigeria to raise the level of understanding the APRM. For example, a two-day workshop was held in Ota, Ogun State in mid-September 2005 to discuss inputs in the country report. A further 10 national technical workshops were held at Ota between September and December 2005 regarding the monitoring the implementation of APR process. Each two-day workshop was attended by different sectors-media, federal legislators, speakers and deputy speakers of Nigeria's legislatures, trade union leaders, civil service, federal and state judiciary, and the private sector. The workshops covered in-depth presentations concerning, among other things, the concept, principles and structures of the APRM, the self-assessment report and the national plan of action, the challenges of monitoring and evaluating the ARPM in Nigeria and the implementation of the NPoA after the review was completed.

Activities of the NFP

The National Focal Point convened a series of meetings from February going back to November 2005 with the TRIs to finalize the structure and form of the questionnaire and the survey methodology. There was a meeting between the NFP Secretariat and the TRIs in February 2005 on the questionnaire; and that meeting was followed by a meeting (retreat) with the TRIs on the methodology on 9-10 March 2005. At the retreat, a number of topics were discussed and agreed, including the following:

- The domestication of the questionnaire, including gender mainstreaming, youth, the physically challenged, and other marginal groups in the four thematic areas;
- The methodology of the survey;
- The sampling frame;
- Techniques of field work, including the appropriate modalities for engaging the three tiers of government at federal, state, and local government levels, in the country self-assessment process; and
- A work plan for the social survey or country self-assessment phase of this stage of the process.

A further retreat was held on 9TH November 2005 in Abuja with the TRIs on the self-assessment process. At that retreat final agreement was reached on the domestication of the questionnaire and on the methodology and sample frame of the survey. The methodology agreed included the following:

- Desk research—focus on relevant literature on APRM-related governance issues in Nigeria since 1960;
- Self-administration of the APRM questionnaire by randomly sampled/selected respondents;
- Elite/decision-maker interviews—to capture elite/decision-makers' perceptions of governance issues in the country;
- Focus group discussions—to capture the views of non-elite and local opinion leaders through issues-based discussion on governance issues; and

• Mass household survey—to capture mass households' perceptions of governance issues in the APRM questionnaire.

It was agreed at the November 2005 retreat that samples for the 'domesticated' questionnaire administration, elite/decision-maker interview, mass household survey, and the focus group discussion would be taken from one local government area (LGA) from each of two of the three senatorial districts in each state. One of the local government areas selected would be in the senatorial district in which the state capital is located, while the second LGA would be selected on the basis of either being the farthest from the LGA chosen from the state capital, or on the basis of other relevant demographic or geographical differences or communal ones. In each selected LGA, two communities would be selected for sampling in such a manner as to reflect cultural, population, and rural/urban diversities, among others. The sampling or working universe would be selected, on the basis of stratified random sampling, from the population 18 years and over in each LGA.

The retreat had difficulty agreeing that the services of the National Bureau of Statistics (NBS) should be co-opted to take part in the mass household survey.

It took another retreat which was held on December 5-6 2005 under the chairmanship of Ambassador Kiplagat, a member of the APR Panel of eminent persons, to resolve the outstanding issues from the November 2005 retreat. It was decided at the December 2005 retreat that the TRIs should focus on only three of the self-assessment research tasks, namely, desk research, elite interviews, and focus group discussions, while the NBS would conduct the mass household survey. However, the TRIs could not agree fees with the NFP and their inability to submit activity-based budgets and work plans by the deadline of 13 December 2005 led to the dismissal of the TRIs on the 19 December 2005.

New Lead Research Organizations

The TRIs were replaced by five new lead research organizations (LROs) in March 2006. Their mandate was to conduct the country self-assessment survey, one for each APR theme, and the NBS to conduct the household survey. The NFP also appointed three consultants/experts as thematic coordinators for the APR process. The task of these thematic coordinators was to coordinate the survey by the LROs, harmonize their report into a consolidated CSAR and produce the NPoA. The coordinators were also to advise the APRM National Focal Point Secretariat on the advance of the country's governance self-assessment process. The thematic coordinators were to ensure that the LROs carry out their tasks competently.

The End in Sight

The LROs worked on the self-assessment report between June and December 2006, continuing into 2007 and by April of that year, each LRO had completed a draft of the self-assessment report and a draft of the national plan of action for the theme which was assigned them. The drafts were consolidated into a single report by the coordinators and submitted to the NFP in June 2007.

Four new research organizations were recruited by the NFP Secretariat to review the draft the self-assessment report to ensure that it was professionally done in accordance with the APRM guidelines. Each of these expert organizations was contracted to review the thematic area in which it had the expertise. The expert research organizations finished their exercise by the end of October 2007

Validation of the CSAR

The full self-assessment draft report was not made available to the public, but an executive summary was widely publicized. The national coordinator claimed that 40 million copies would have been published but that was not verified. However, in November 2007 the NFP mobilized four teams each of about 50 members of the NWG to undertake a nationwide validation exercise of the draft CSAR and preliminary NPoA. The validation of the CSAR was based on the published executive summary only.

The four validation teams held meetings in 14 of the 36 states of Nigeria, and representatives of 22 states were invited to attend their nearest meeting place geographically. The validation meetings in each group of states visited lasted for two days. The validation meetings had a set format, namely, day one would see presentations on the draft CSAR made to the state ministries, legislature and judiciary; while on day two, presentations would be made to non-state stakeholders, including the media, academics, professional organizations, NGOs, traditional leaders and political parties. In addition special events were sometimes held for the media. Separate validation sessions were held in the Federal Capital Territory, Abuja, in December 2007.

The APRM Country Review Mission

After the conclusion of the validation workshops through out the country in December 2007, the APRM-NWG organized zonal sensitization workshops in the country's six geopolitical zones in January 2008 in preparation for the country review mission (CRM). The workshops were organized by the NSC and the NFP who had set up an organizing committee for the mission. The APRM-NWG appointed centre coordinators to work with the NWG members to ensure the smooth deployment of the CRM in 16 clusters of states.

The CRM visited Nigeria for a month from 3 February to 2 March 2008 under the leadership of Ambassador Kiplagat, a member of the panel of eminent persons. The mission carried out intensive stakeholders' consultations throughout the country. The mission was divided into two teams, each of which visited eight centres, with each centre comprising a cluster of states, including the Federal Capital Territory of Abuja. The teams met with state and non-state stakeholder groups. The CRM also held sector specific meetings in Abuja and held an open forum meeting with non-state stakeholder groups. One of the Teams met with the Senate and the other met the House of Representatives. The CRM also met representatives of Nigeria's development partners, leaders of the diplomatic community, and members of the judiciary. The CRM held its wrap-up session with the NFP and the APRM-NWG on February 29 2008.

The CRM was of the view that Nigeria's CSAR was credible. It found that the APRM-NWG had done a good job in sensitizing the various stakeholders and communities of the importance of the APR process.

The End of the Review Process

The CRM indicated that their report, the ARPM country review report, and the modified NPoA, would be sent to Nigeria by the end of March 2008 and that Nigeria would be expected to react to the country review report and modified NPoA by the end of April 2008, so that the APRM Secretariat could send them to member states of the APRM Forum by the third week of May. The country review report, with Nigeria's comments annexed, and the finalized NPoA agreed between the Nigerian Government and APRM Secretariat would then be considered by heads of state and government of the participating states during the APR Forum held in the margins of the AU summit in Egypt in July 2008. This schedule was followed and the Nigerian review opened at the APR Forum Summit in Sharm El Sheik, Egypt, on 29th June 2008. At the Forum, Ambassador Kiplagat, the lead panelist for the Nigerian review, raised certain governance issues with respect to Nigeria, including over-dependence on oil, endemic corruption, and pervasive poverty, management of elections, the management of diversity, and the slow pace of the progress of women. The report noted, however, the achievement of good practices such as the commitment to peace-keeping in Africa, the adoption of the Extractive Industries Transparency Initiative and the publication of assets by President Yar'Adua.

President Yar'Adua acknowledged the challenges posed by pluralism in Nigeria and indicated that steps were being taken to deal with the situation. He stated that measures were being taken to improve the electoral process and to curtail corruption in the country. The President indicated that steps were being taken to include gender mainstreaming in the national development process and to removing any provisions of the Constitution that discriminate against women.

The Forum was unable to complete the Nigeria peer review at Sharm EL Sheik and so an Extraordinary Summit was agreed to dispose of that peer review report and other outstanding matters. At an Extraordinary Summit of the APR Forum held in Cotonou, Benin, October 25-26 2008, the Nigeria and Burkina Faso peer reviews were completed.[180]

---

[180] See The APRM Monitor Nos. 6 October 2008 and 7 June 2009, Partnership Africa Canada info@pacweb.org

Weaknesses in the Nigerian APR Approach

The general guidelines, among other things, require the APRM process is to be credible and free from political manipulation by anyone, and particularly the government of the day. In the nature of the APR process overall weakness will be measured by the transparency of the exercise and the opportunity for non-state stakeholders to freely make their contribution, particularly to the self-assessment process. Against this background, the Nigeria review process exhibited the following weaknesses:

- The selection of the secretary to the government of the Federation as the National Focal Point;
- The location of the NFP/APRM Secretariat within the presidency;
- The original 50-member APRM-NWG did not include some groups as specially designated organizations representing women, or other marginalized groups as specific categories apart from NGOs/CSOs;
- The 50-member APRM-NWG was classified by the APRM country support mission in March 2005 as being predominantly of the executive and not sufficiently representative of civil society; this situation was largely remedied in November 2007 when the new NWG was expanded to 250;
- The nomination of members to the APRM-NWG, as well as to the APRM-NSC was not always done through a transparent procedure;
- The federal structure of the Nigerian State created some difficulties at first and consequently states and local government entities were not treated as stakeholders in their own right until towards the end of 2007;
- Failure to consult state governments prior to the signing of the APRM Memorandum of Understanding, or to adequately brief them about it afterwards;
- 'Federalizing' the APR coordinating structure, in particular the devolving responsibilities to states for implementing the NPoA will require much political skill;
- Although there had been a broad but vague recognition of a number of state and non-state stakeholders in Nigeria, the criteria

for selection for the purposes of contribution to the APR process were never attempted, and remain unclear, leaving the selection largely in the hands of the executive;

- Although there were no specific complaints about access, or lack of it, to specific bits of information, the lack of a freedom of information law must have inhibited access to some categories of information, for example, oil revenues flow;
- The self-assessment exercise took more than two and a quarter years to complete, partly due to the controversial political succession arguments in the country;
- The role of the judiciary and the legislature appeared to be somewhat de-emphasized during the validation exercise at both federal and state levels;
- The key business and industrial sectors of banking and oil was not prominently represented on the reconstituted APRM-NEG;
- The uniform services were under-represented on the APRM-NWG membership;
- The executive summary of the CSAR did not clearly indicate whether or not only federal government policies were in focus;
- The executive summary did not indicate whether or not regional crisis like the Niger Delta impacted on the country's human and general development; and
- The CSAR executive summary did not indicate the role and place of the local government council in the political and economic governance of Nigeria.

Perceptions of the APRM Process

At the time of writing 30[181] AU had signed up to the APRM process and peer reviews had been launched in fifteen of those countries[182]. Peer reviews at the level of Heads of State and Government had been conducted in 12

---

[181] The latest accession was by Cape Verde in June 2009.
[182] These were: Algeria, Benin, Burkina Faso, Ethiopia, Ghana, Kenya, Lesotho, Mali, Mauritius, Mozambique, Nigeria, Rwanda, South Africa, Tanzania and Uganda.

countries.[183] These case studies looked at 5 of the fifteen countries which submitted to the peer review, namely, Ghana, Kenya, Mauritius, Rwanda and Nigeria, of these countries only Mauritius was yet to complete the review process.

The APRM process holds great potential for open government in the Member States of the African Union. Like the challenge of holding genuine periodic democratic elections, the APRM process will take plenty of time to produce satisfactorily balanced self-assessment reports throughout the Union. The five processes examined herein have thrown some common problems, albeit in different degrees of intensity. The common experiences may be summarized as follows:

- The APRM Questionnaire has proved to be troublesome and had to undergo considerable 'domestication', for example, in Nigeria;
- The initial national self-assessment structures often proved unbalanced with too much governmental inputs and too little non-state contributions, or otherwise inadequate inputs, due to their flawed composition;
- The lack of sufficiently broad non-state participation base, coupled, in some cases, with lack of quality contributions;
- Inadequate awareness/sensitization programmes with respect to the APRM process, particularly regarding the validation of inputs in the draft self-assessment report;
- Underestimated time frame for the country assessment report-allowances for general elections interval apparently not sufficiently taken into account-Mauritius and Nigeria;
- Failure to take sufficient account of the three-tier (federal, states and local government) structure of federalism in Nigeria in the design of the APRM questionnaire;
- Failure to publicize (lack of transparency) the full draft self-assessment report instead of an executive summary for the purposes of use at validation workshops;

---

[183] These were: Ghana (January 2006), Rwanda and Kenya (June 2006), Algeria and South Africa (July 2007), Benin (January 2008), Uganda (July 2008), Nigeria (July and October 2008), Burkino Faso (October 2008), Lesotho, Mali, and Mozambique (July 2009).

- Failure to publicize the submissions of the member of the panel of eminent persons and those of the Head of State or Government being reviewed to the APRM Forum; and
- Failure of some reviewed countries to implement in a timely manner the agreed national plan of action.

Prognosis for APRM Process

There is little doubt that the APRM process has considerable potential to encourage the culture of open government in the Member States of the AU. The notion of country self-assessment in the Member States of the AU which is a voluntary act has created waves. At the time of writing, 30 of the 53 countries of the AU had signed up for the APRM 15 of which had submitted to the country review process and of which twelve reviews had been completed. It is clear that some Member States had not fully appreciated what was involved in the exercise, particularly the country self-assessment process. As it turned out, it was a struggle for many countries that had undergone the review process, and only made it with considerable support from the assigned member of the eminent person and the APRM continental Secretariat. However, the peer review mechanism means subtle peer pressure not to shy away from the undergoing the peer review.

It is clear that some practices will be difficult to shed by governments of the Member States of the Union. For example, most governments that had submitted to the review process to date had considerable difficulty in opening up information channels to non-state stakeholders. The true test will come when a second review is due to be carried out. Already, at the time of writing, the Kenyan Government deferred the second APRM review due to governance difficulties faced by the Unity Government. Perhaps Kenya was a special case in the light of political troubles experienced in 2007 and 2008 and optimistically the second round of review in other countries is eagerly awaited to see what improvements have been achieved.

EPILOGUE

Introduction

It May be bold or perhaps even foolhardy of anyone to prognosticate with respect to the course of democratic elections in a particular country in the Union much less regarding the membership of the entire Union. Many countries of the Union experienced a somewhat checkered record in holding democratic elections since achieving their independence and particularly during the first decade of the 21ˢᵗ Century. The list of countries with interrupted democratic elections was very long; suffice it to name a few, Burundi, Chad, Côte d'Ivoire, Democratic Republic of Congo, Kenya, Guinea, Lesotho, Liberia, Malawi, Madagascar, Mauritania, Niger, Sierra Leone, Somalia, and Zimbabwe. At the time of writing, many States of the Union have strayed from the path of holding democratic elections, including Côte d'Ivoire, Guinea, Guinea Bissau, Madagascar, and Mauritania. The first decade of the 21ˢᵗ Century ended with yet another disputed election, this time in Côte d'Ivoire where the incumbent President, Laurent Gbagbo, refused to hand over the presidency to the victorious candidate, Alassane Ouattara.[184]

---

[184] The Côte d'Ivoire presidential election was held on 31ˢᵗ October 2010 and no candidate got the 50% plus one vote to claim victory and so a run-off election was held on 28 November 2010. The Electoral Commission declared candidate Alassane Ouattara the winner with 54% of the votes and the incumbent Gbagbo with 46% of the votes. The Constitutional Council subsequently reversed the position awarding Gbagbo 51% of the votes and Ouattara 49% of the votes and thus declaring Gbagbo the victor and had him sworn in as President for another term of office. The United Nations, ECOWAS and the African Union, as well as other stakeholders and many counties, including the USA and the European Union recognized Ouattara as the legitimate winner of the run-off election, but Gbagbo refused to step down. Gbagbo's behaviour attracted sanctions by the European Union and several countries at the very end of the first decade and there is no doubt

Notwithstanding the foregoing observations, there had been cases of successful elections in Africa. Some countries succeeded in holding three or more successive national elections, these include Botswana (although the ruling party never lost power), Mauritius, Namibia, Ghana, South Africa and Tanzania.[185] Many countries adhered to the two-term constitutional rule requiring the Head of State to step down after serving two consecutive terms in office. Many incumbent presidents had that rule changed to benefit the incumbent of the day; these include Algeria, Namibia and Uganda. Others have tried and failed to secure the necessary constitutional change including, former President Chiluba of Zambia, former President Muluzi of Malawi, and former President Obasanjo of Nigeria.

The aim of the *Epilogue* to this work is to highlight some of the electoral issues which may profoundly influence the direction of the development of democratic elections in the Member States of the African Union in the near future.

Competitive Elections in the Member States of the African Union

Many of the primary stakeholders in national elections in the Member States of the AU appeared to be shy of truly competitive elections, fought vigorously but within the rules, code of conduct, and the spirit of democratic principles. All political parties and candidates entered national electoral contest hoping to win, but they also know that in a scenario of democratic elections there was the possibility of losing and they should be prepared to deal with that eventuality.

Many critics of the one-party era in Africa pointed to the lack of competitive democratic elections as one of the key weaknesses of that system. The rise of the dominant party system in many countries, whether based on ethnic or religious or linguistic dominance was once again threatening the genuineness of competitive elections in many countries of the Union.

---

that the matter would be resolved most likely in favour of Ouattara early in 2011.

[185] See for example, short note by Denis Kadima, Electoral Institute of Southern Africa, in *id21 insights Issue #74*.

The diminution of elective competitiveness in the rising dominant party scenario in the first decade of the 21st Century was due in part to the ruling party's and government's grip on the public resources which were often used and abused for the incumbents' political purposes. This development was not good for democratic elections. As could be seen in Botswana, Namibia, South Africa and Zimbabwe opposition parties found it hard to survive as the ruling parties controlled the access to public resources.

The trend towards the creation and perpetration of dominant political parties may be difficult to curb, but it can be mitigated through stronger rules on incumbency abuse of public resources and greater support from local and outside partners for the opposition. If the present trend of dominant-party syndrome continues, the sad but realistic result will be the demise of many opposition parties in many countries of the Union, and that cannot be a good democratic prospect to contemplate.

The Full Potential of DEAU/DEAF

The future role of the Democracy and Electoral Assistance Unit (DEAU) and Fund (DEAF) is promising. The foresight of the OAU /AU in setting up these entities is commendable. There can be no doubt that with the unsteadiness of democratic elections at present in many Member States of the Union, there is an urgent need for a central body to be in a position to have oversight of developments throughout the continent. However, a central body as the DEAU will have to tread carefully as regional institutions such as the Regional Economic Communities (RECs) and the Pan-African Parliament (PAP), rightly guard their sphere of competence jealously. Much more is needed than observing elections, because if the people who conduct elections are not properly trained or have not imbibed deeply in the culture of fairness and non-partisanship credibility in election organization and conduct will not be improved discernibly in the near future. The length of time that the DEAU and DEAF took to get off the ground—six years from the decision in 2002 until their inauguration in May 2008, may be an indication of the level of importance or the lack of urgency which the AU placed on them. However, the DEAU and DEAF have a wonderful challenge to meet on many fronts, particularly in democratic elections and related matters such as constitutions and democratic elections in general.

Enhancement of the Central AUC Role

In the first year of its existence the DEAU organized eleven AU election observation missions and a couple of run-off elections. It also revised a number of the procedures in organizing AU election observation missions with a view to making missions operate more effectively. The DEAU's initial work plan included bringing the EMBs of the Member States of the AU together to foster closer working relations between the DEAU and the EMBs, and also between the EMBs themselves. The initial work plan also included the raising of electoral processes standards, offering of technical assistance to national EMBs, creation of a master database of African EMBs, African election experts, and CSOs dealing with elections, and training of election observers.

The Democracy and Electoral Assistance Fund (DEAF) attracted more than US$ 2 million in its first year.

The Partners of DEAU—The initial partner of DEAU was the International Foundation for Electoral Systems (IFES) under an African Union Support Program, funded by USAID. IFES was the executing agency for USAID under the Support Program.[186] The IFES Chief of Party joined the Program about a year before the staff of DEAU was in place and helped to prepare the ground for the staff and their initial work plan. The UN was the next on stream with a short-term capacity-building consultant from November 2008—February 2009. The European Union made a significant contribution to the DEAF and other contributions towards the continental meeting of EMBs, as well as cooperation in election observations. The International Institute for Democracy and Electoral Assistance (IDEA) came on stream with a substantial program of assistance to the DEAU in BRIDGE Training Course for national EMBs and other help with a continental conference on elections.

Actual and Potential Threat to the DEAU Achieving its Goals—The greatest setback for the DEAU was the scaling back of its status from what was recommended in the Feasibility Study from Level P5 for the head of DEAU and Level P 3 for the senior officers to the current Level P3 for

---

[186] The IFES Chief of Party for the Support Program is the author.

the head of DEAU and Level P2 for the Election Officers. This placed the DEAU in an embarrassingly low status in the hierarchy of the Political Affairs Department where in an important matter such as elections in the AU, the Head of DEAU was four tiers down from the Commissioner who is head of the Department. This position could be contrasted with similar electoral positions in the UN, EU and the Commonwealth Secretariat where a more senior status reflected the political importance of elections in the scheme of things in those organizations. This rather low status of the DEAU affected every aspect of its operations from the way decisions were taken with respect to electoral matters in the Department to the way partners perceived the role of DEAU. In practice, the status of DEAU overlooked the fact that the tasks recommended for the DEAU in the Feasibility Study and which were accepted for the higher levels of staff, were being carried out without any obvious modification. This matter should be reviewed as a matter of urgency.

Wasteful Competing Competence

The perceived threat of overlapping competence which characterized so many of Africa's institutions from the RECS to the Programs of NEPAD and those of the AU, and the multiplicity of continental court systems recently led to the single Protocol which created the African Court of Justice and Human Rights. The concern is that the Pan-African Parliament might soon rival the African Union Commission (AUC), meaning the DEAU in AU election observation.[187] The simple case in favour of the AUC continuing to be the primary body to observe AU-wide elections was based on the fact that:

- The AUC was not likely to be seen as tainted by potential conflict of interest which by its very nature the PAP observers might face from time to time;
- The AUC, as the successor to the OAU's observation role, combined with the AU's experience had over 160 observer

---

[187] In 2010 DEAU, through the Department of Political Affairs of the AUC agreed with the PAP to merge their election observation efforts by jointly sending observation missions under the auspices of the AUC.

missions in total and thus was in a strong position to continue to
develop observation techniques;

- The AUC, through the DEAU, had a dedicated body to identify
weaknesses in election organization through the recommendations
of observation missions and to offer technical assistance to the
EMBs concerned to take immediate remedial measures; and

- The AUC, through the DEAU and DEAF, had the mechanism to
mobilize funds to finance electoral activities, including election
observations.

Dispute Settlement within Member States of the AU—This matter was
fully treated above. It remained to be highlighted only because it was so
important that every aggrieved person deserved to be satisfied that there was
a reliable mechanism in place that could ensure that justice was meted out
to him/her. The several mechanisms available to an EMB were discussed
above, but often in the AU countries during the period under review it was
not the absence of mechanisms rather it was how they were administered
that caused the dissatisfaction. An example of the implementation of
complaints procedures in a transparent and efficient manner was seen in
Liberia during and after the national elections in 2005. There the Senior
Legal Adviser to the Electoral Commission conducted the hearing into
each complaint filed with the Commission. The hearings were conducted
in open, observers and members of the public attended and the evidence
from and on behalf of the complainant and the defendant was taken in
public. The findings and verdict were delivered in public. The transparency
was there for all to see and the proceedings were held in a timely manner.
Some disputed results of the elections went to the courts for resolution
and they too were dealt with in a timely manner. With determination
and a bit of assistance where needed, even a small jurisdiction as Liberia's
demonstrated that electoral complaints and disputes could be resolved
satisfactorily.

Incumbency in the Member States of the African Union—The excesses and
abuses of the incumbent leadership and the ruling party of the day must
be tackled in order to roll back the unfair advantages accruing to the
Head of State and governing party over opposition parties. In electoral
terms, these advantages manifested themselves as abuses when used for
party campaign purposes instead of for the sole purposes of executing

official duties. Thus incumbency abuses occurred whenever a President or Prime Minister uses public resources for party campaign purposes, whether the resources were in the form of funds, motor vehicles, houses, public servants, or the announcement of investments on the heels of a national election. Incumbent abuses were not confined to the improper uses of public resources, but seeking to improperly influencing voters, for example, placing the incumbent President or Prime Minister in a voting place or allowing a President or Prime Minister, or any other Minister of Government to visit a polling place in any capacity other than as a candidate should not be allowed. In many Member States of the AU incumbency rules were covered in the election regulations or in a code of conduct for political parties, including the ruling party. However, some of these improper incumbency practices were so entrenched in some of the Member States of the Union that perhaps only action Union-wide by the DEAU might serve to chip them away. In this connection, the strict rules dealing with the party in power in India during the 2009 elections should serve as a reminder how incumbency might be dealt with. The rule stated that the Party in power whether at the Centre or in the State or States concerned, shall ensure that no cause is given for any complaint that it has used its official position for the purposes of its election campaign and in particular:

- The Ministers shall not combine their official visit with electioneering work and shall not also make use of official machinery or personnel during the electioneering work;
- Government transport including official aircraft, vehicles, machinery and personnel shall not be used for the furtherance of the interest of the party in power;
- Public places such as maidans for the holding of election meetings, and the use of helipads for air-flights in connection with elections shall not be monopolized by itself. Other parties and candidates shall be allowed to use such places and facilities on the same terms and conditions on which they are used by the party in power;
- Rest houses, bungalows or other Government accommodation shall not be monopolized by the party in power or its candidates and such accommodation shall be allowed to be used by the other parties and candidates in a fair manner but no party or candidates shall use or be allowed to use such accommodation (including

premises appertaining thereto) as a campaign office or for holding any public meeting for the purposes of election propaganda;

- Ministers and other authorities shall not sanction grants/payments out of discretionary funds from the time elections are announced by the Commission;
- From the time elections are announced by the Commission, Ministers and other authorities shall not-

    (a) Announce any financial grants in any form or promises thereof; or

    (b) (Except civil servants) lay foundation stones of projects or schemes of any kind; or

    (c) Make any promise of construction of roads, provision of drinking water facilities etc., or

    (d) Make any ad-hoc appointments in Government or in Public Undertakings, *which* may have the effect of influencing the voters in favour of the party in power;

- Ministers of the Central or State Government shall not enter any polling station or place of counting except in their capacity as a candidate or voter or authorized agent.

Integrity of the Electoral Process in the Member States of the African Union—the integrity of the electoral process lies primarily with the EMB and its staff. They must protect the integrity of the electoral process by not allowing improper outside influence with respect to any of its activities. Where there is responsibility, there must be control, and unfortunately that is not always the case with election organization. An EMB always has the responsibility to deliver free and fair elections to the stakeholders, but often it does not have full control over the sum total of the electoral tasks necessary to complete an election cycle. For example, many EMBs proper in the Member States of the African Union during the period under review did not have competence to deal with the delimitation of electoral districts, and some did not have authority over the issuance of national identity cards, the possession of which was a condition precedent to registration as a voter; still other EMBs proper were not responsible for the registration of voters, while some EMBs did not have the primary responsibility for voter education. If an EMB was expected to fully protect the integrity of the electoral process, then it should have a good measure of control over its electoral processes.

The Growth of Dominant Political Parties—The phenomenal growth of the dominant was discussed above. To the extent that these political parties had a tendency to stifle opposition parties and hence the promotion of healthy democracies, their growth should be arrested. Some ideas were advanced above as to how the harsh effects of the dominant parties may be mitigated, for example by strengthening the rules against incumbency abuses, but on a longer term basis other measures such as a review of the electoral system in place with a view to introducing a more political party-friendly electoral system, which may dilute the impact of the dominant parties.

Political Succession in the African Union—Perhaps there was no greater threat to democracy in many Member State of the African Union during the first decade of the 21ˢᵗ Century than the succession at the Head of State level and or the leadership of the ruling party level. Despite the firm stance of the African Union against the change of government in any Member State by unconstitutional means,[188] at the time of writing there were several such cases.[189] In addition, botched elections in Kenya and Zimbabwe resulted in unity governments which many commentators held was nothing more than resistance to peaceful and smooth political succession. The issue had also surfaced in Côte d'Ivoire where open national conflict erupted and where national elections were long overdue.[190]

---

[188] See for example, OAU Decision AHG/Dec. 141 (XXXV), adopted by the Thirty-Fifth Ordinary Session of the Assembly of OAU Heads of State and Government in Algiers, 12-14 July 1999 and Decision 142 (XXXV) also adopted at the same Session, both of which are against 'unconstitutional change of government'.

[189] Guinea, Guinea Bissau, Mauritania and Madagascar,

[190] Disputed elections and run-off elections were held towards the end (November 2010) of the decade, some five years late because of conflict. For an account of the conflict see Paul Collier's "Wars, Guns & Votes" chapter 7 'Meltdown in Côte d'Ivoire' p.155, Vintage 2009

There are cases where, as David Sebudubudu pointed out, the constitution had in the post-democratization era been used as a tool to engineering political succession.[191] He pointed to the controversies caused in Malawi, Namibia and Zambia when outgoing presidents sought to change the constitution to secure a 'third term'. In his paper, Sebudubudu pointed out that it was not only succession of the state president which was a political issue but succession in the party leadership as well. He pointed to the cases of Botswana, Kenya, Malawi, Namibia, Nigeria, Uganda, South Africa and Zimbabwe illustrated that the African continent was yet to resolve the issue of succession. He expressed the view that the leadership of the party became an issue because of its links to the office of head of state.

In dealing with the unseating of the President of South Africa, Thabo Mbeki, Mr. Thoko Mpumlwana, Deputy Chairperson of the Electoral Commission of South Africa, pointed out that the bitter leadership succession struggle within the ruling African National Congress in South Africa, which resulted in the incumbent President being removed from office by his own party was indicative of the fact that the main challenge was not just the party change-over but the general political of leadership succession.[192] He cited the case of Malawi where similar intra-party struggle which like South Africa led to the creation of breakaway parties. Mr. Mpumlwana threw light on some of the constraints on smooth political succession when he indicated that when there is a prospect of party changeover, resistance does not only come from party leaders, but from senior civil servants, military and police officials.

The difficulty in fixing the political succession issue was that it belonged more to the realm of 'high' politics, as well as to constitutionalism, than to just elections. Nevertheless, unless something was done about it soon, the political succession would threaten the stability of many states in the AU. Perhaps alongside the OAU Declarations against unconstitutional

---

[191]   See David Sebudubudu of the University of Botswana in *Comparative Politics in Africa*, p.4.

[192]   Mr. Thoko Mpumlwana, *the Electoral Process and the Democratic Changeover of Political Power between Parties* in Challenges of Democratic Succession in Africa.

change of governments, a positive declaration should be made addressing the internal party democracy with respect to electing the leadership of political parties in the Member States of the African Union.

Publicly Owned Media—There were codes of conduct for the media, including the publicly owned media, in many Member States of the Union. These codes of conduct deal mainly with fair, or even, or equitable or equal access by all parties, although the main objective was to ensure some form of level playing field for opposition parties. The publicly owned media were singled out for special treatment as often they were controlled by the incumbent government and the governing party, but the privately-owned media also had an obligation whenever they reported on election or carried election advertisements, in keeping with their journalistic professional standards, to be objective and truthful. Codes of conduct usually applied to the public media, but may also apply to the private media, although many EMBs shied away from enforcement against private media because of fear of being accused of seeking to muzzle the media. Sometimes, in order to guard against excesses by the private media during electoral campaigns national associations of journalists drew up their own codes of conduct for election purposes. This approach could go a far way in curbing 'hate' speeches during election campaigns, and create a level playing field for election contestants.

Professionalism in Electoral Administration in EMBs of Member States of the African Union—The EMBs of the AU in general would benefit considerably from improved professionalism in electoral administration. Professionalism encompasses greater compliance with the electoral law, regulations, procedures, manuals and directives relating election organization than obtained in many EMBs during the past decade of the 21st Century. Professionalism with respect to electoral administration extends to a keen appreciation of the principles of good electoral practices and the need to develop and deliver high-quality electoral services to all stakeholders. A professional electoral administrator should possess full knowledge of certain factors that are the key to good electoral management, in particular:

- Efficiency, which embodies the conduct of electoral activities in a sustainable and cost-effective manner and the best use of funds and other resources;
- Impartiality, which includes non-partisanship behaviour towards stakeholders and the creation of a level playing field with respect to all contestants in an election;
- Independence, which includes the ability to work without being under any outside influence, particularly that of the government or ruling party;
- Transparency, which points to EMBs and staff being open and facilitating the flow of information to stakeholders on a timely basis; and
- High quality services to stakeholders, particularly voters including those with disability.

The BRIDGE Training Course for EMBs in some Member States of the Union which was conducted by International IDEA and DEAU of the AU helped to strengthen professionalism of EMBs' staff, although no evaluation was done regarding the impact on EMBs during the decade under review.

Rationalization of Regional Integration Groupings—During the first decade of the 21st Century, there were 14 regional integration groupings, eight of which were recognized as Regional Economic Communities (RECs) and, as such, were further regarded as pillars of the African Economic Community (AEC). But the Abuja Treaty envisaged only five regional economic communities, one in each of the five regions of the African Union. Many AU Member States belonged to multiple regional groupings due to political and strategic considerations and they showed scant regard to comply with the Abuja Treaty. Since the early 1980s, the OAU/AU Commission with the help of the United Nations Economic Commission for Africa (UNECA) and the World Bank tried to rationalize these regional groupings without success, despite undertaking studies which showed significant benefits that would accrue to Member States and to the AU as a whole from rationalization. All attempts to rationalize regional integration groupings failed during the period under review. Yet from a purely legal and economic point of view it would be relatively easy to reduce the 8 RECs and 6 non-RECs to 5 RECs by the designation of a dominant REC in each of the five regions and allowing the dominant institution to take over the functions of the other institutions operating within the region concerned. This approach would be similar to the failed approaches tried in the West African and Central African Regions in the 1990s. The Members States concerned could exercise their sovereignty to withdraw or demote the status of the less dominant regional institutions. The political and strategic dimensions seemed to be the unbridgeable ones and the solution with respect to these two factors cannot be measured in legal or economic terms.

The rationalization of regional groupings would not necessarily have any adverse effects on the development of democratic elections in AU; indeed by strengthening the economic potential of Member States, the rationalization of regional groupings could enhance the stability of the Member States.

Training of EMBs' Staff—The topic was treated at length above, but it is so important that a few parting thoughts ought to be shared. The key to improving the quality of conducting registration of voters and polling in the African Union lies in vastly improving the quality of training for temporary field officers. The numbers are usually relatively large regardless of the size of the electorate. The workers are usually temporary; and scarce resources often mean that training time may be measured in days rather than weeks; therefore the training programmes need to be well planned and effectively delivered.

The standard of performance of registration officers would be helped if there were common performance standards for registration officers, polling officers and returning officers throughout the Union, even if performance standards were at first set and operated regionally.

Similarly, electoral training providers should be expanded from almost exclusively nationally based to regional and even continental-wide where specialized training is concerned. This may not be as far-fetched an idea as it may seem at first, as a bit of this happens at present with voter registration equipment acquisition and training.

The APRM Process

The African Peer Review Mechanism (APRM) is a voluntary process which is open to States which have signed or acceded to the Memorandum of Understanding (MOU) on the APRM. This is one of the truly great innovations in the AU family of nations and, along with the creation of DEAU, augurs well for governance and democratic elections in Africa. The country self-assessment exercise opens the way for open government in countries that sign up for the review process. It has the potential to foster closer working relations between non-state and state bodies to work together when assessing the achievements, as well as the shortcomings, of the State. This opens the way for AU Member States which are Parties to the APRM to create new relationships like *compact arrangements* between governments and NGOs/CSOs.

The country review which is conducted by a member of the eminent persons panel holds out the potential for experienced experts of integrity and impartiality to report on the state of governance within the country being reviewed. The fact that the highest authorities of State and Government are present at the presentation of the report to their peers at the APRM Forum with the right to respond and indicate how identified weakness will be remedied, ought to commend itself to all regimes that aspire to improve the lot of their people.

Many stakeholders in Kenya have felt let down by the APRM process in that country in so far as the APR process was completed more than one year before the 2007 national elections which ended in disaster for the country failed to bring about improved governance. On the other hand, there are stakeholders who have indicated that had the Government implemented even half of the recommendations contained in the Country Review Report, the post-2007 election violence would not have occurred.

At the time of writing, 30 countries had joined the APRM, 15 of which had submitted to peer reviews, and 12 had completed the peer review process.[193]

---

[193] See Discourse 4 within for a fuller discussion of the APRM.

Annex 1

References and Further Reading

African Union: Guidelines for Electoral Observation and Monitoring Missions, 2002.

Bakary, Tessy Prof. Political Science Department, University Laval Quebec, African Union Commissioned Study on Election Observation Missions' Reports, 2007.

Ballington, Julie, ed. *The Implementation of Quotas: African Experiences* International IDEA, Stockholm, 2004.

Barker, Christine—*"Compacts between Government and Civil Society Organizations in the UK."* Seal, Winter, 2004.

Bentley, Julia—*"Survival Strategies for Civil Society Organizations in China"*, in the International Journal of Not-for-Profit Law. January 2004.

Bevis, G.G. et al.—*"Civil Society Groups and Parties: Supporting Constructive Relationships"*. Prepared for the Bureau for Democracy, Conflict and Humanitarian Assistance-USAID.

British Council: Draft Report—*"Assessment of the Experience of Other Countries in Developing, Preparing and Implementing Compacts of Cooperation between the Non-profit and Public Sectors"*. April 2006.

Bryan, Shari, & Baer, Denis, ed. *Money in Politics: A Study of Party Practices in 22 Countries* 2005 National Democratic Institute.

Clayton, Andrew et al— *"Civil Society Organizations and Service Provision"*. Civil Society and Social Movements Programme Paper No. 2000.

Cartner, Holly, Executive Director, Europe and Central Asia Human Rights Watch, comments on the 2005 Bill in Russia, as it affected CSOs; in Human Rights News November 2005.

Collier, Paul, "Wars, Guns & Votes", Vintage 2009

Compact Agreements: *Introduction to Compact*-see www.thecompact.org.uk.

Council of Europe: *"Fundamental Principles on the Status of Non-Governmental Organizations in Europe"* 2002, reached at multilateral meetings held in Strasbourg.

Dundas, Carl W. *Improving the Organization of Elections: A 2006 Perspective*, Ian Randle Publishers, Kingston & Miami, 2006.

Dundas Carl W. *Compendium of Election Laws, Practices and Cases of Selected Commonwealth Countries* Vol. 1 & 2, Parts 1 & 2, Commonwealth Secretariat, London, 1996-98.

International IDEA, Electoral Justice, The International IDEA Handbook, 2010, SE 103 34 Stockholm.

Ebobrah, Solomon, T. *The African Charter on Democracy, Elections and Governance: A New Dawn for Enthronement of Legitimate Governance in Africa?* Open Society Institute. Africa. Governance, Monitoring, & Advocacy Project.

Geanakoplos, John, *Three proofs of Arrow's Impossibility Theorem* Cowes Foundation, Paper 1116, Yale University, 2005.

Gordy, Eric—: *Community Revitalization through Democratic Action (CRDA) and Civil Society in Serbia*—USAID.

Medetsky, Anatoly—The 2005 Bill *"Amendments to General Laws of the Russian Federation"*, Moscow Times, 9 November 2005.

Mpumlwana, Thoko, *The Electoral Process and the Democratic Changeover of Political Power between Parties* in Challenges of Democratic Succession in Africa—delivered at the International Conference organized by the Institute of Human Rights and Promotion of Democracy: Cotonou, Benin 2009.

Norris, Pippa, and Mattes, Robert, *Does Ethnicity Determine Support for the Governing Party* Afrobarometer, paper No. 26 2003.

Salamon, L.M. et al—*Global Civil Society, An Overview.* The Johns Hopkins University, Institute for Policy Studies, Center for Civil Society Studies.

Salih, Mohamed, ed. *African Political Parties: Evolution, Institutionalization and Governance,* Pluto Press, 2003.

Sebudubudu, David, *Comparative Politics in Africa,* University of Botswana, p.4

Soesastro, Hadi, Fmr. Executive Director of the Center for Strategic and International Studies in Jakarta, *"Civil Society and Development: the Missing Link".* 1999.

Tabarrok, Alexander, *Arrow's Impossibility Theorem,* Department of Economics, Ball State University Muncie, IN 47306, 2005.

Terlinden, Ulf, *African Regional Parliaments/Parliamentary Bodies as Engines: Integration's Current State and Challenges* at roundtable on 'the interface between Regional Parliamentary bodies and the Pan-African Parliament, August 2005.

The Pew Forum on Religion and Public Life: *"The Faith-Based Initiative Two Years Later . . ."* 2005.

US Congressional Executive Commission on China, 2004 comments on the *"New Chinese Regulations on Foundations".*

Thompson, Dennis F. "Just Elections" University of Chicago Press 2002.

Van Dusen, Nathan— *"Liberian Elections Commission, Civil Society Rise to the Challenge"*, IFES, September 2005.

Voter Registration in Africa, A Comparative Analysis, ed. Astrid Evrensel, EISA 2010.

World Bank: *"Engaging Civil Society Organizations in Conflict-Affected and Fragile States-Three African Case Studies*—2005.

Annex 2

Declaration of Principles for International Election Observation

a)   Genuine democratic elections are an expression of sovereignty, which belongs to the people of a country, the free expression of whose will provides the basis for the authority and legitimacy of government. The rights of citizens to vote and to be elected in periodic, genuine democratic elections are internationally recognized human rights. Genuine democratic elections are central for maintaining peace and stability, and they provide the mandate for democratic governance.

(b)   In accordance with the Universal Declaration of Human Rights, the International Covenant for Civil and Political Rights and other international instruments, everyone has the right and must be provided with the opportunity to participate in the government and public affairs of his or her country, without any discrimination prohibited by international human rights principles and without any unreasonable restrictions. This right can be exercised directly, by participating in referenda, standing for elected office and by other means, or can be exercised through freely chosen representatives.

(c)   The will of the people of a country is the basis for the authority of government, and that will must be determined through genuine periodic elections, which guarantee the right and opportunity to vote freely and to be elected fairly through universal and equal suffrage by secret balloting or equivalent free voting procedures, the results of which are accurately counted, announced and respected. A significant number of rights and freedoms, processes, laws and institutions are therefore involved in achieving genuine democratic elections.

(d)   International election observation is: the systematic, comprehensive and accurate gathering of information concerning the laws, processes and institutions related to the conduct of elections and other factors concerning the overall electoral environment; the impartial and professional analysis of such information; and the drawing of conclusions about the character of electoral processes based on the highest standards for accuracy of information and impartiality of analysis. International election observation should, when possible, offer recommendations for improving the integrity and effectiveness of electoral and related processes, while not interfering in and thus hindering such processes. International election observation missions are: organized efforts of intergovernmental and international nongovernmental organizations and associations to conduct international election observation.

(e)   International election observation evaluates pre-election, election-day and post—election periods through comprehensive, long-term observation, employing a variety of techniques. As part of these efforts, specialized observation missions may examine limited pre-election or post-election issues and specific processes (such as, delimitation of election districts, voter registration, use of electronic technologies and functioning of electoral complaint mechanism). Stand-alone, specialized observation missions may also be employed, as long as such missions make clear public statements that their activities and conclusions are limited in scope and that they draw no conclusions about the overall election process based on such limited activities. All observation missions must make concerted efforts to place the Election Day into its context and not to over-emphasize the importance of Election Day observers. International election observation examines conditions relating to the right to vote and to be elected, including, among other things, discrimination or other obstacles that hinder participation in electoral processes based on political or other opinion, gender, race, colour, ethnicity, language, religion, national or social origin, property, birth or other status, such as physical disabilities. The findings of international election observation missions provide a factual common point of reference for all persons interested in the elections, including the political competitors. This can be particularly valuable in the context of disputed elections, where impartial and accurate findings can help to mitigate the potential for conflicts.

(f)   International election observation is conducted for the benefit of the people of the country holding the elections and for the benefit of the international community. It is process oriented, not concerned with any particular electoral result, and is concerned with results only to the degree that they are reported honestly and accurately in a transparent and timely manner. No one should be allowed to be a member of an international election observer mission unless that person is free from any political, economic or other conflicts of interest that would interfere with conducting observations accurately and impartially. There criteria must be met with effectively over extended periods by long-term observers, as well as during the more limited periods of Election Day observation, each of which periods present specific challenges for independent and impartial analysis. International election observation missions should not accept funding or infrastructure support from the government whose elections are being observed, as it may raise a significant conflict of interest and undermine confidence in the integrity of mission's findings. International election observation delegations should be prepared to disclose the sources of their funding upon appropriate and reasonable requests.

(g)   International election observation missions are expected to issue timely, accurate and impartial statements to the public (including providing copies to electoral authorities and other appropriate national entities), presenting their findings, conclusions and any appropriate recommendations they determine could help improve election related processes. Missions should announce publicly their presence in a country, including the mission's mandate, composition and duration, make periodic reports as warranted and issue a preliminary post-election statement of findings and a final report upon the conclusion of the election process. International election observation missions may also conduct private meetings with those concerned with organizing genuine democratic elections in a country to discuss the missions may also report to their respective intergovernmental nongovernmental organizations.

(h)   The organizations that endorse this Declaration and the accompanying Code of Conduct for International Election Observers pledge to cooperate with each other in conducting international election observation missions. International election observation can be conducted, for example, by: individual international election observer missions; ad hoc joint international election observation missions; or coordinated international election observation missions. In all circumstances, the endorsing organizations pledge to work together to maximize the contribution of their international election observation missions.

(i)   International election observation must be conducted with respect for the sovereignty of the country holding the elections and with respect for human rights of the people of the country. International election observation missions must respect the laws of the host country, as well as national authorities, including electoral bodies, and act in a manner that is consistent with respecting and promoting human rights and fundamental freedoms.

(j)   International election observation missions must actively seek cooperation with the host country electoral authorities and must not obstruct the election process.

(k)   A decision by any organization to organize an international election observation mission or to explore the possibility of organizing an observation mission does not imply that the organization necessarily deems the election process in the country holding the elections to be credible. An organization should not send an international election observation mission to a country under conditions that make it likely that its presence will be interpreted as giving legitimacy to a clearly undemocratic electoral process, and international election observation missions in any such circumstances should make public statements to ensure that their presence does not imply such legitimacy.

(l)   In order for an international election observation mission to effectively and credibly conduct its work basic conditions must be met. An international election observation mission therefore should not be organized unless the country holding the election takes the following actions:

(i)   Issues an invitation or otherwise indicates its willingness to accept international election observation missions in accordance with each organization's requirements sufficiently in advance of elections to allow analysis of all of the processes that are important to organizing genuine democratic elections;

(ii)   Guarantees unimpeded access of the international election observer mission to all stages of the election process and all election technologies, and the certification processes for electronic voting and other technologies, without requiring election observation missions to enter into confidentiality or other nondisclosure agreements concerning technologies or election processes, and recognizes that international election observation missions may not certify technologies as acceptable;

(iii) Guarantees unimpeded access to all persons concerned with election processes, including:

- electoral officials at all levels, upon reasonable requests,
- members of legislative bodies and government and security officials whose functions are relevant to organize genuine democratic elections,
- All of the political parties, organizations and persons that have sought to compete in the elections (including those that qualified, those that were disqualified and those that withdraw from participating) and those that abstained from participating.
- News media personnel, and
- All organizations and persons that are interested in achieving genuine democratic elections in the country;

(iv) Guarantees freedom of movement around the country for all members of the international election observer mission;

(v) Guarantees the international election observer mission's freedom to issue without interference public statements and reports concerning its findings and recommendations about election related processes and developments;

(vi) Guarantees that no governmental, security or electoral authority will interfere in the selection of individual observers or other members of the international election observation mission or attempt to limit its numbers;

(vii) Guarantees full, country-wide accreditation (that is, the issuing of any identification or document required to conduct election observation) for all persons selected to be observers or other participants by the international election observation mission as long as the mission complies with clearly defined, reasonable and non-discriminatory requirements for accreditation;

(viii) Guarantees that no governmental, security or electoral authority will interfere in the activities of the international election observation mission; and

(ix) Guarantees that no governmental authority will pressure, threaten action against or take any reprisal against any national or foreign citizen, who works for, assists or provide information to the international election observation mission in accordance with international principles for election observation.

(x) As a prerequisite to organizing an international election observation mission, intergovernmental and international nongovernmental organizations may require that such guarantees are set forth in a memorandum of understanding or similar document agreed upon by governmental and/ or electoral authorities. Election observation is a civilian activity, and its utility is questionable in circumstances that present severe security risks, limit safe deployment of observers or otherwise would negate employing credible election observation methodologies.

(m) International election observation missions should seek and may require acceptance of their presence by all major political competitors.

(n) Political contestants (parties, candidates and supporters of positions on referenda) have vested interests in the electoral process through their rights to be elected and to participate directly in government. They therefore should be allowed to monitor all processes related to elections and observe procedures, including among other things the functioning of electronic and technologies inside polling stations, counting centres and other electoral facilities, as well as the transport of ballots and other sensitive materials.

(o) International election observation missions should:

(i) establish communications with all political competitors in the election process, including representatives of political parties and candidates who may have information concerning the integrity of the election process;

(ii) Welcome information provided by them concerning the nature of the process;

(iii)   Independently and impartially evaluate such information; and

(iv)   Should evaluate as an important aspect of international election observation whether the political contestants are, on a nondiscriminatory basis, afforded access to verify the integrity of all elements and stages of the election process. International election observation missions should in their recommendations, which may be issued in writing or otherwise be presented at various stages of the election process, advocate for removing any undue restrictions or interference against activities by the political competitors to safeguard the integrity of the electoral processes.

(p)   Citizens have an internationally recognized right to associate and a right to participate in governmental and public affairs in their country. These rights may be exercised through nongovernmental organizations monitoring all processes related to elections and observing procedures, including among other things the functioning of electronic and other electoral᾽ technologies inside polling stations, counting centers and other electoral facilities, as well as the transport of ballots and other sensitive materials. International election observation missions should evaluate and report on whether nonpartisan election monitoring and observation organizations are able, on a nondiscriminatory basis, to conduct their activities without undue restrictions or interference. International election observation missions should advocate for the right of citizens to conduct nonpartisan election observation without any undue restrictions or interference and should in their recommendations address removing any such undue restrictions or interference.

(q)   International election observation missions should identify, establish regular communications with and cooperate as appropriate with credible domestic nonpartisan election monitoring organizations. International election observation missions should welcome information provided by such organizations concerning the nature of the election process. Upon independent evaluation of information provided by such organizations, their findings can provide an important complement to the findings of international observation missions, although international election observation missions must remain independent. International election observation missions therefore should make every reasonable effort to consult with such organizations before issuing any statements.

(r) The intergovernmental and international nongovernmental organizations endorsing this Declaration recognize that substantial progress has been made in establishing standards, principles and commitments concerning genuine democratic elections and commit themselves to use a statement of such principles in making observations, judgments and conclusions about the character of election processes and pledge to be transparent about principles and observation methodologies they employ.

(s) The intergovernmental and nongovernmental organizations endorsing this Declaration recognize that there are a variety of credible methodologies for observing election processes and commit to sharing approaches and harmonizing methodologies as appropriate. They also recognize that international election observation missions must be of sufficient size to determine independently and impartially the character of the election process in a country and must be of sufficient duration to determine the character of critical elements of the election process in the pre-election, election day and post-election periods—unless an observation activity is focused on and therefore only comments on one or a limited number of elements of the election process. They further recognized that it is necessary not to isolate or over-emphasize election day observations, and that such observations must be placed into context of the overall electoral process.

(t) The intergovernmental and nongovernmental organizations endorsing this Declaration recognize that international election observation missions should include persons of sufficient diverse political and professional skills, standing and proven integrity to observe and judge processes in the light of: expertise in electoral processes and established electoral principles; international human rights; comparative election law and administrative practices (including use of computer and other election technology); comparative political processes and country specific considerations. The endorsing organizations also recognize the importance of balanced gender diversity in the composition of participants and leadership in the composition of participants and leadership of international election observation missions, as well as diversity of citizenship in such missions.

(u) The intergovernmental and international nongovernmental organizations endorsing this Declaration commit to:

(i) familiarize all participants in their international election observation missions concerning the principles of accuracy of information and political impartiality in making judgments and conclusions;

(ii) Provide terms of reference or similar document, explaining the purposes of the mission;

(iii) Provide information concerning relevant national laws and regulations, the general political environment and other matters, including those that relate to the and well being of observers;

(iv) Instruct all participants in the election observation mission concerning the methodologies to be employed; and

(v) require all participants in the election observation mission to read and pledge to abide by the Code of Conduct for International Election Observers, which accompanies this Declaration and which may be modified without changing its substance slightly to fit requirements of the organizations, or pledge to abide a pre-existing code of conduct of the organization that is substantially the same as the accompanying Code of Conduct.

(v) The intergovernmental and international nongovernmental organizations endorsing this Declaration commit to use every effort to comply with the terms of the Declaration and the accompanying Code of Conduct for International Election Observers. Any time that an endorsing organization deems it necessary to depart from any terms of the Declaration or the accompanying Code of Conduct in order to conduct election observation in keeping with the spirit of the Declaration, the organization will explain in its public statements and will be prepared to answer appropriate questions from other endorsing organizations concerning why it was necessary to do so.

(w) The endorsing organizations recognize that governments send observer delegations to elections in other countries and that others also observe elections. The endorsing organizations welcome any such observers agreeing on an ad hoc basis to this declaration and abiding by accompanying Code of Conduct for International Election Observers.

(x) This Declaration and the accompanying Code of Conduct for international election observers are intended to be technical documents that do not require action by the political bodies of endorsing organizations (such as assemblies, councils or boards of directors), though such actions are welcome. This Declaration and the accompanying Code of Conduct for International Election Observers remain open for endorsement by other intergovernmental and international nongovernmental organizations. Endorsements should be recorded with the United Nations Electoral Assistance Division.

Code of Conduct for International Election Observers

International election observation is widely accepted around the world. It is conducted by intergovernmental and international nongovernmental organizations and associations in order to provide an impartial and accurate assessment of the nature of election processes for the benefit of the population of the country where the election is held and for the benefit of the international community. Much therefore depends on ensuring the integrity of international election observation, and who are part of this international observation mission, including long-term and short-term observers, members of assessment delegations, specialized observation teams and leaders of the mission, must subscribe to and follow this Code of Conduct.

Respect Sovereignty and International Human Rights

Elections are an expression of sovereignty, which belongs to the people of a country, the free expression of whose will provides the basis for the authority and legitimacy of government. The right of citizens to vote and to be elected in periodic elections is an internationally recognized human right, and requires the exercise of a number of fundamental rights and freedoms. Election observers must respect the sovereignty of the host country, as well as the human rights and fundamental freedoms of its people.

Respect the Laws of the Country and the Authority of Electoral Bodies

Observers must respect the laws of the host country and the authority of the bodies charged with administering the electoral process. Observers must follow any lawful instruction from the country's governmental, security and electoral authorities. Observers must maintain a respectful attitude toward electoral officials and other national authorities. Observers must note if laws, regulations or the actions of state and/or electoral officials unduly burden or obstruct the exercise of election-related rights guaranteed by law, constitution or applicable international instruments.

Respect the Integrity of the International Election Observation Mission

Observers must respect and protect the integrity of the international election observation mission. This includes following this Code of Conduct, any written instructions (such as a term of reference, directives and guidelines) and any verbal instructions from the observation mission's leadership. Observers must: attend all of the observation mission's briefings, training and debriefings; become familiar with the election law, regulations and other relevant laws as directed by the observer mission; and carefully adhere to the methodologies employed by the observation mission. Observers also must report to the leadership of the observation mission any conflicts of interest they may have and any improper behavior they see conducted by other observers who are part of the mission.

Maintain Strict Political Impartiality at All Time

Observers must maintain strict political impartiality at all times, including leisure time in the host country. They must not express or exhibit any bias or preference in relation to national authorities, political parties, candidates referenda issues or in relation to any contentious issues in the election process. Observers also must not conduct any activity that could not be reasonably perceived as favoring or providing personal gain for any competitor in the host country, such as wearing or displaying any partisan symbols, colors, banners or accepting anything of value from political competitors.

Do Not Obstruct Election Processes

Observers must not obstruct any element of the election process, including pre-election processes, voting, counting and tabulation of results and post Election Day processes. Observers may bring irregularities, fraud or significant problems to the attention of election officials on the spot unless this is prohibited by law, and must do so in a non-obstructive manner. Observers may ask questions of election officials, political party representatives and other observers inside the polling stations and may answer questions about their own activities, as long as observers do not obstruct the election process. Observers may ask and answer questions of voters but may not ask them to tell for whom or what party or referendum position they voted.

Provide Appropriate Identification

Observers must display their identification provided by the election observation mission, as well as identification required by the national authorities, and must present it to election officials and other interested national authorities when requested.

Maintain Accuracy of Observations and Professionalism in Drawing Conclusions

Observers must ensure that all of their observations are accurate. Observers must be comprehensive, noting positive as well as negative factors, distinguishing between significant and insignificant factors and identifying patterns that could have an important impact on the integrity of the election process. Observers' judgments must be based on the highest standards for accuracy of information and impartiality of analysis, distinguishing between subjective factors from objective evidence. Observers must base all conclusions on factual or verifiable evidence and not draw conclusions prematurely. Observers must keep well-documented record of where they observed, the observations made and other relevant information as required by the election observation mission and must turn in such documentation to the mission.

Refrain from Making Comment to the Public or the Media before the Mission Speaks

Observers must refrain from making any personal comments about their observations or the conclusions to the news media or members of the public before the election observation mission makes a statement, unless specifically instructed otherwise by the observer mission's leadership. Observers may explain the nature of the observer mission, its activities and other matters deemed appropriate by the observer mission and should refer the media or other interested to those individual designated by the observer mission.

Cooperate with other Election Observers

Observers must be aware of other election observer missions, both international and domestic, and cooperate with them as instructed by the leadership of the election observation mission.

Maintain Proper Personal Behavior

Observers must maintain proper personal behavior and respect others, including exhibiting sensitivity for host-country cultures and customs, exercise sound judgment in personal interactions and observe the highest level of professional conduct at all times, including, including leisure time.

Violations of this Code of Conduct

In a case of concern about the violation of this Code of Conduct, the election observation mission shall conduct an inquiry into the matter. If a serious violation is found to have occurred, the observer concerned may have their observer accreditation withdrawn or be dismissed from the observation mission. The authority for such determination rests solely with the leadership of the election observer mission.

Pledge to Follow this Code of Conduct

Every person who participates in this election observation mission must read and understand this Code of Conduct and must sign a pledge to follow it.

Pledge

I have read and understand the Code of Conduct for International Election Observers that was provided to me by the international election observation mission. I hereby pledge that I will follow the Code of Conduct and that all my activities as an election observer will be conducted completely in accordance with it. I have no conflict of interest, political, economic nor other, that will interfere with my ability to be an impartial election observer and to follow the Code of Conduct.

I will maintain strict political impartiality at all times. I make my judgments based on the highest standards for accuracy of information and impartiality analysis, distinguishing subjective factors from objective evidence, and I will base all my conclusions on factual and verifiable evidence.

I will not obstruct the election process. I will respect national laws and the authority of election officials and will maintain a respectful attitude toward electoral and other national authorities. I will respect and promote the human rights and fundamental freedoms of the people of the country. I will maintain proper personal behavior and respect others, including exhibiting sensitivity for host country cultures and customs, exercise sound judgment in personal interactions and observe the highest level of professional conduct at all times, including leisure time.

I will protect the integrity of the international election observation mission and will follow the instructions of the observation mission. I will attend all briefings, trainings and debriefings required by the election observation mission and will cooperate in the production of its statements and reports as requested. I will refrain from making personal comments, observations or conclusions to the news media or the public before the election the election observation mission makes a statement, unless specifically instructed otherwise by the observation mission's leadership.

Annex3

Draft Specimen Electoral Assistance Procedure under the Democracy and Electoral Assistance Unit (DEAU) and the Democracy and Electoral Assistance Fund (DEAF)

Background

The Democracy and Electoral Assistance Unit (DEAU) and the Democracy and Electoral Assistance Fund (DEAF) were conceived in Durban, South Africa in 2002 by the Council of Ministers of the Organization of African States (OAU). Separate feasibility studies were undertaken into the DEAU and the DEAF in the years subsequent to 2002 and 2006 the Executive Council of the African Union approved the DEAU to which the DEAF became an integral part. The principal aim of the DEAU is to, among other things; promote democracy and democratic elections; to develop effective election observation missions; and to develop a framework for electoral assistance.

The DEAF has as its principal goals provision of financial resources to support requests for technical assistance to the DEAU; to support national electoral processes that facilitate holding of regular free and fair elections at acceptable standards; and to enhance the capacity of the AU to support national and regional initiatives to build and sustain democratic processes.

The DEAF is managed by the AU's Finance, Budget and Administrative Department. The focal point for the DEAF is the Commissioner of

Political Affairs. The DEAF operates in a transparent and accountable manner under strict reporting, monitoring, and evaluation requirements.

A Trust Forum of ten members will provide external oversight to the Political Affairs Department with respect to the distribution of the resources of the DEAF.

Nature of Electoral Assistance

• Technical support through the provision of expertise that a given electoral management body (EMB) lacks, such as electoral legislative specialists, election systems experts, or electoral districts delimitation specialists;
• Material aid, such as provision of equipment for processing data, or enhancing voter identification techniques;
• In appropriate, but unusual, cases, financial aid to particular budgetary election processes.

Prioritization of Cases for Consideration

• States emerging from conflicts and are seeking to organize multiparty democratic elections;
• States who are facing extremely difficult economic situation (even if there is no conflict or post-conflict factor involved) and require assistance to prepare for and conduct democratic elections;
• Independent electoral bodies (EMB) which specify particular electoral needs—where an EMB makes more than one request, it will be asked to rank them in terms of urgency, and where there are several requests for assistance by EMBs from the different regions, regard should be had to achieving a fair distribution of technical assistance throughout the five Regions of the AU;
• Civil society organizations within member states that play a significant role national elections organization.

Types of Electoral Assistance offered by DEAU

The DEAU will offer electoral assistance to national electoral management bodies (EMBs) at their request in the following areas:

- Review of electoral systems and advice and assistance with information programmes to enable stakeholders to buy into any changes on a timely basis, as well as assistance with the implementation of any changes resulting from the review;
- Review of all relevant electoral legislation, including constitutional provisions dealing with elections, with a view to reforming (modernizing) the electoral legislative scheme in the requesting country or EMB to achieve good practice;
- Review of the boundaries of electoral districts/constituencies with a view to ensuring fair boundaries, assisting with a timely awareness programme for stakeholders to participate in the exercise, and assisting with the construction of the delimitation exercise;
- Registration of voters—where appropriate, up-to-date technology in data collection and voter identification in compiling voter registers;
- Political party legislation, including formation, funding, code of conduct, campaign financing and party coalitions and alliances;
- Registration of parties and candidates for the purposes of contesting elections;
- Defining the role of stakeholders in election organization and conduct;
- Management of election logistics;
- Training programmes for all levels of elections officers;
- Designing voter/civic education programmes for EMBs;
- Assisting with pilot studies in electronic voting and counting of votes; and
- Assisting EMBs to undertake comprehensive post-election audits in the requesting country.

Procedure for Requesting Assistance from DEAU

- All requests for assistance should be addressed to the DEAU;
- In the case of assistance to a national EMB requests should be made by the EMB under the hand of the Chairman, or by the Member State concerned through the Ministry of Foreign or the relevant portfolio Ministry;

- In the case of requests for assistance by CSOs of a member state, the application should be made by the head of the organization.

Form and Content of Requests

Every request for assistance to the DEAU shall:

- Be in writing, dated and bear the logo or other official stamp of the EMB, organization, or Ministry concerned, and be under the hand of the appropriate official;
- State concisely but clearly the need for assistance and the nature of the assistance sought from DEAU;
- Where the EMB or the Member State is incapable or unsure of the need or the scope there of, indicate so to the DEAU and ask for an assessment mission to visit the country to clarify the need;
- Where multiple needs are contained in a request, rank the priority of the needs;
- Be made in electronic form, or by letter or both; oral request, unless and until confirmed in one of the foregoing forms will not be acted upon;
- Requests should be made in a timely manner in order to allow for the proper processing and assessment thereof;
- In proper cases, the request may embody the project outline with appropriate accompanying explanations.

Treatment of Requests

- All requests should be dated and recorded in a register of requests and given a number;
- Every request shall be scrutinized and placed in a prioritized category and the region of AU from which it originates;
- The DEAU shall undertake an evaluation of the request, taking account of all relevant facts available, and the demand on resources required to meet the request;
- Taking account of relevant factors, including the need or otherwise for DEAU to send an evaluation mission to assess the need in situ, and funds availability, a priority assessment would be undertaken

before the request would be submitted for approval by the Director of the Political Affairs Department.

Evaluation of Requests for Electoral Assistance

Evaluation of requests for assistance from DEAU may take several forms, and employ different methodologies as follows:

- Where the staff members of DEAU are familiar with the facts on which the request is based, or the institutional records of the AU-DEAU have sufficient factual records on the matter, an in-house evaluation can be undertaken;
- In proper cases, a fact finding mission can be undertaken by the staff of DEAU;
- Where appropriate, an assessment mission may be mounted examine facts and assess needs;
- An important aspect of the evaluation requests will be the estimated cost of the project—this will be undertaken by the DEAU.

Annex 4

Electoral Systems in Use in the African Union

Country	Electoral System for National Assembly	Electoral System for President
Algeria	List PR	TRS
Angola	List PR	TRS
Benin	List PR	TRS
Botswana	FPTP	-
Burkina Faso	List PR	TRS
Burundi	List PR	-
Cameroon	PBV, List PR &FPTP	FPTP
Cape Verde	List PR	TRS
Central African Republic	TRS	TRS
Chad	PBV, List PR, & TRS	TRS
Comoros	TRS	TRS & FPTP
Congo (Brazzaville)	TRS	TRS
Congo, Democratic Republic	List PR (constituency-based PR)	TRS
Côte d'Ivoire	FPTP & PBV	TRS
Djibouti	PBV	TRS

Egypt	TRS	[Election by the Legislature, plus confirmation by referendum]
Equatorial Guinea	List PR	FPTP
Eritrea		
Ethiopia	FPTP	
Gabon	TRS	TRS
Gambia	FPTP	TRS
Ghana	FPTP	TRS
Guinea (Conakry)	Parallel (List PR & FPTP)	TRS
Guinea-Bissau	List PR	TRS
Kenya	FPTP	TRS
Lesotho	MMP (FPTP& List PR)	-
Liberia	TRS	TRS
Libyan Arab Jamahiriya		
Republic of Madagascar	FPTP & List PR	TRS
Malawi	FPTP	FPTP
Mali	TRS	TRS
Mauritania	TRS	TRS
Mauritius	BV	-
[Morocco	List PR]	
Mozambique	List PR	TRS
Namibia	List PR	TRS
Niger	List PR & FPTP	TRS
Nigeria	FPTP	TRS
Rwanda	List PR	FPTP

Sao Tome and Principe	List PR	TRS
Senegal	Parallel (PBV & List PR)	TRS
Seychelles	Parallel (FPTP & List PR)	TRS
Sierra Leone	FPTP	TRS (55% needed to avoid run-off)
Somalia		
South Africa	List PR	-
Sudan	FPTP & List PR	TRS
Swaziland	FPTP	-
United Republic of Tanzania	FPTP	TRS
Togo	TRS	TRS
Tunisia	Parallel (PBV & List PR)	FPTP
Uganda	FPTP	TRS
Zambia	FPTP	FPTP
Zimbabwe	FPTP	TRS

Annex 5

Types of Embs in the African Union

Countries . . .	Type of Electoral Management	Name of EMB . . .	Size & term of office . . .
Algeria	Governmental	Ministry of Interior	N/A
Angola	Independent	National Electoral Commission	11 members, term of service unspecified
Benin	Independent	Permanent Administrative Secretariat; National Autonomous Electoral Commission	4 members who serve for 5 years; 25 members who serve for the election period only.
Botswana	Independent	Independent Electoral Commission	7 members who serve for maximum of 10 years
Burkina Faso	Independent	Independent National Electoral Commission	15 members whose term is 5 years
Burundi	Mixed	Ministry of the Interior; Independent National Electoral Commission	N/A [To be checked on]

Cameroon	Mixed	Ministry of the Territorial Administration and Decentralization National Electoral Observatory	N/A 12 who serve for 3 years
Cape Verde	Mixed	Central Support Services for Elections; National Elections Commission	N/A 5 members who serve for term of 6 years
Central African Republic	Mixed	Ministry of Territorial Administration; Independent Mixed Electoral Commission	N/A 30 members whose term of office is unspecified
Chad	Mixed	Ministry of Interior; Independent National Electoral Commission; Constitutional Council	N/A; 31 members serving for electoral period only; 9 members who serve for 9 years.
Comoros	Independent	Independent National Electoral and Accreditation Commission	27 members whose term is unspecified.
Congo (Brazzaville)	Mixed	Ministry of the Interior; National Commission for the Organization of Elections.	N/A; 9 members who term of appointment is unspecified.

Congo, Democratic Republic of (DRC)	Independent	Independent Electoral Commission	21 members (transition)
Côte d'Ivoire	Mixed	Ministry of the Interior and Decentralization; Independent Electoral Commission.	N/A; 31 members who serve for 6 years.
Djibouti	Mixed	Ministry of the Interior & Decentralization; Independent National Electoral Commission.	N/A; 13 members for term of 5 years
Egypt	Governmental	Ministry of Interior	N/A
Equatorial Guinea	Mixed	Ministry of Interior; Central Elections Board.	N/A; Not less than 13 for election period only.
Eritrea	Independent	Election Commission	5 members for unspecified period
Ethiopia	Independent	National Electoral Board	7 for term of 6 years
Gabon	Mixed	Ministry of Interior; Bureau of the National Electoral Commission.	N/A; 7 members who serve for election period only.
Gambia	Independent	Independent Electoral Commission	5 members who serve for 7 years
Ghana	Independent	Electoral Commission	7 members whose term is not limited.

Guinea (Conakry)	Independent	National Autonomous Electoral Commission	22 serve for 5 years {to be checked}
Guinea—Bissau	Independent	National Electoral Commission	8 members who serve for 4 years.
Kenya	Independent	Electoral Commission	22 members who serve for 5 years. [Expected to be changed shortly]
Lesotho	Independent	Independent Electoral Commission	3 members whose term is 5 years.
Liberia	Independent	National Elections Commission	7 whose term is for 7 years.
Libyan Arab Jamahiriya	-	-	-
Madagascar	Mixed	Ministry of Interior and of Administrative Reform; National Advisory Electoral Commission.	N/A; 7 members whose term is 5 years.
Malawi	Independent	Electoral Commission	7 members whose term is 4 years.

Mali	Mixed	Ministry of Territorial Administration; Independent National Electoral Commission; Constitutional Court.	N/A; 15 unlimited term; 9 members who serve for 7 years.
Mauritania	Independent	Independent National Electoral Commission	15 members who serve for transitional period. {To be monitored in light of coup.}
Mauritius	Independent	Electoral Commissioner; Electoral Supervisory Commission.	1 unspecified term; Chair and up to 7 members for 5 years.
[Morocco	Governmental	Ministry of Interior	N/A]
Mozambique	Independent	National Election Commission	19 members who serve for 5 years.
Namibia	Independent	Electoral Commission	5 members who serve for 5 years.
Niger	Independent	Independent National Electoral Commission	30 members for electoral period only
Nigeria	Independent	Independent National Electoral Commission	13 members whose term is 5 years.
Rwanda	Independent	National Electoral Commission	7 members for a term of 3 years.

Sao Tome and Principe	Governmental	Electoral Technical Cabinet	N/A
Senegal	Mixed	Ministry of Interior-Directorate General of Elections; Autonomous National Election Commission.	N/A; 12 members whose term is 6 years.
Seychelles	Independent	Office of Electoral Commissioner	1 member whose term is 7 years.
Sierra Leone	Independent	National Electoral Commission	5 members who serve for unspecified term.
Somalia	Independent	National Electoral Commission	7 members for a term of 5 years.
South Africa	Independent	Independent Electoral Commission	5 members for 7 years.
Sudan	Independent	National Elections Commission	9 members for 6 years
Swaziland	Independent	Elections and Boundaries Commission	5 members for 12 years.
Tanzania United Republic of	Independent	National Election Commission	7 members for a term of 5 years.
Togo	Mixed	Ministry of Interior, Permanent Administrative Secretariat; Independent National Electoral Commission.	N/A; 9 members whose term is unspecified.
Tunisia	Governmental	Ministry of Interior	N/A

Uganda	Independent	Electoral Commission	7 members for a term of 7 years.
Zambia	Independent	Electoral Commission	5 members for term of up to 7 years.
Zimbabwe	Independent	Zimbabwe Electoral Commission	7 members for term of 5 years.

Annex 6

Declaration on Democracy, Political, Economic and

Corporate Governance

NEPAD/HSGIC/03-2003/APRM/MOU/Annex 1

Preamble

1. We, the participating Heads of State and Government of the member
    states of the African Union (AU), met in Durban, South Africa, at
    the inaugural Assembly of the African Union and considered the
    report of the New Partnership for Africa's Development (NEAD)
    Heads of State and Government Implementation Committee
    established at the Organization of African Unity (OAU) Summit in
    Lusaka, Zambia, in July 2001.
2. In the general context of our meeting, we recalled our shared
    commitment underlying the establishment of NEPAD to eradicate
    poverty and to place our countries, individually and collectively,
    on a path of sustainable growth and development and, at the same
    time, to participate actively in the world economy and body politic
    on equal footing. We affirm this pledge as our most pressing duty.
3. In reviewing the report of the NEPAD Heads of State and
    Government Implementation Committee and considering the
    way forward, we were also mindful of the fact that, over the years,
    successive OAU Summits have taken decisions aimed at ensuring
    stability, peace and security, promoting closer economic integration,
    ending unconstitutional changes of government, supporting human
    rights and upholding the rule of law and good governance. Among
    these decisions are:

a. The Lagos Plan of Action, and the Final Act of Lagos (1980);
b. The African (Banjul) Charter on Human and Peoples' Rights (1981);
c. The African Charter for Popular Participation in Development (1990);
d. The Declaration on Political and Socio-Economic Situation in Africa and the Fundamental Changes Taking Place in the World (1990); and
e. The African Charter on the Rights and Welfare of the Child (1990);
f. The Abuja Treaty establishing the African Economic Community (1991);
g. The 1993 Cairo Declaration Establishing the Mechanism for Conflict Prevention, Management and Resolution;
h. The Protocol on the Establishment of an African Court on Human Rights;
i. The 1999 Grand Bay (Mauritius) Declaration and Plan for the Promotion and Protection of Human Rights;
j. The Framework for an OAU Response to Unconstitutional changes of Government (adopted at the 2000 OAU Summit in Lome, Togo, and based on the earlier decision of the 1999 Algiers OAU Summit); and
k. The Conference on Security, Stability, Development and Cooperation (CSSDCA) Solemn Declaration 2000; and
l. The Constitutive Act of the African Union 2000.

4. We, member states parties to the aforementioned instruments, reaffirm our full and continuing commitment to these and other decisions of our continental organization, as well as the other international obligations and undertakings into which we have entered in the context of the United Nations. Of particular significance in this context are the Charter of the United Nations and the United Nations Universal Declaration on Human Rights and all conventions relating thereto, especially the Convention on the Elimination of All Forms of Discrimination against Women and the Beijin Declaration.

5. Africa faces grave challenges and the most urgent of these are the eradication of poverty and the fostering of socio-economic development, in particular, through democracy and good governance. It is to the achievement of these twin objectives that the NEPAD process is principally directed.

6. Accordingly, we the participating Heads of State and Government of the member states of the African Union have agreed to work together in policy and action in the pursuit of the following objectives:

- Democracy and Good Governance
- Economic and Corporate Governance
- Socio-Economic Development
- African Peer Review Mechanism.

Democracy and Good Political Governance

At the beginning of the new century and millennium, we reaffirm our commitment to the promotion of democracy and its core values in our respective countries. In particular, we undertake to work with renewed determination to enforce:

- The rule of law;
- The equality of all citizens before the law and the liberty of the individual;
- Individual and collective freedoms, including the right to form and join political parties and trade unions, in conformity with the constitution;
- Equality of opportunity for all;
- The inalienable right of the individual to participate by means of free, credible and democratic political processes in periodically electing their leaders for a fixed term of office; and
- Adherence to the separation of powers, including the protection of the independence of the judiciary and of effective parliaments.

8. We believe in just, honest, transparent, accountable and participatory government and probity in public life. We therefore undertake to

combat and eradicate corruption, which both retards economic development and undermines the moral fabric of society.

9. We are determined to increase our efforts in restoring stability, peace and security in the African continent, as these are essential conditions for sustainable development, alongside democracy, good governance, human rights, social development, protection of environment and sound economic management. Our efforts and initiatives will also be directed at seeking speedy peaceful solutions to current conflicts and at building Africa's capacity to prevent, manage and resolve all conflicts on the continent.

10. In the light of Africa's recent history, respect for human rights has to be accorded an importance and urgency all of its own. One of the tests by which the quality of a democracy is judged is the protection it provides for each individual citizen and for the vulnerable and disadvantaged groups. Ethnic minorities, women and children have borne the brunt of the conflicts raging on the continent today. We undertake to do more to advance the cause of human rights in Africa generally and, especially to end the moral shame exemplified by the plight of women, children, and the disabled and ethnic minorities in conflict situations in Africa.

11. In Africa's efforts at democracy, good governance and economic reconstruction, women have a central role to play. We accept it as a binding obligation to ensure that women have every opportunity to contribute on terms of full equality to the political and socio-economic development in all our countries.

12. To fulfill these commitments we have agreed to adopt the following action plan:

13. In support of democracy and the democratic process

We will:

• Ensure that our respective national constitutions reflect the democratic ethos and provide for demonstrably accountable governance;

• Promote political representation, thus providing for all citizens to participate in the political process in a free and fair political environment;

- Enforce strict adherence to the position of the African Union (AU) on unconstitutional changes of government and other decisions of our continental organization aimed at promoting democracy, good governance, peace and security;
- Strengthen and, where necessary, establish an appropriate electoral administration and oversight bodies, in our respective countries and provide the necessary resources and capacity to conduct elections which are free, fair and credible;
- Reassess and where necessary strengthen the AU and sub-regional election monitoring mechanisms and procedures; and
- Heighten public awareness of the African Charter on Human and Peoples' Rights, especially in our educational institutions.

14. In support of Good Governance

We have agreed to:

- Adopt clear codes, standards and indicators of good governance a the national, sub-regional and continental levels;
- Accountable, efficient and effective civil service;
- Ensure the effective functioning of parliaments and other accountability institutions in our respective countries, including parliamentary committees and anti-corruption bodies; and
- Ensure the independence of the judicial system that will be able to prevent abuse of power and corruption.

15. To promote and protect human rights

We have agreed to:

- Facilitate the development of vibrant civil society organizations, including strengthening human rights institutions at the national, sub-regional and regional levels;
- Support the Charter, African Commission and Court on Human and People's Rights as important instruments for ensuring the promotion, protection and observance of Human Rights;
- Strengthen co-operation with the UN High Commission for Human Rights; and

- Ensure responsible free expression, inclusive of the freedom of the press.

Economic and Corporate Governance

16. Good economic and corporate governance including transparency in financial management are essential pre-requisites for promoting economic growth and reducing poverty. Mindful of this, we have approved eight prioritized codes and standards for achieving good economic and corporate governance.

17. These prioritized codes and standards represent those "fundamental" internationally, regionally, and domestically accepted codes and standards that all African countries should strive to observe within their capacity capabilities. In other words, they are the codes and standards that need to complied with as a minimum requirement, given a country's capacity to do so.

18. We believe the eight prioritized and approved codes and standards set out below have the potential to promote market efficiency, to control wasteful spending, to consolidate democracy, and to encourage private financial flows—all of which are critical aspects of the quest to reduce poverty and enhance sustainable development. These codes and standards have been developed by a number of international organizations through consultative processes that involved the active participation of and endorsement by African countries. Thus, the codes and standards are genuinely global as they were agreed by experts from a vast spectrum of economies with different structural characteristics. They are the following: a. Code of Good Practice on Transparency in Monetary and Financial Policies; b. Code of Good Practices on Fiscal Transparency; c. Best Practices for Budget Transparency; d. Guidelines for Public Debt Management; e. Principles of Corporate Governance; f. International Accounting Standards; g. International Standards on Auditing; and the h. Core Principles for Effective Banking Supervision.

19. We have also approved other key codes and standards in transparency and financial management. These include: a. Principles for Payment Systems; b. Recommendations on Anti-money laundering; and c. Core principles for securities and insurance supervision and regulation.

Socio-Economic Development

20. We believe that poverty can only be effectively tackled through the promotion of:

- Democracy, good governance, peace and security;
- The development of human and physical resources;
- Gender equality;
- Openness to international trade and investment;
- Allocation of appropriate funds to social sector; and
- New partnerships between governments and the private sector, with civil society.

21. We affirm our conviction that the development of Africa is ultimately the responsibility of Africans themselves. Africa's development begins with the quality of its human resources. We, therefore, undertake to work towards the enhancement of our human resources through the provision of more and better education and training, especially in Information and Communications Technology (ICT) and other skills central to a globalizing world; and better health care, with priority attention to addressing HIV/AIDS and other pandemic diseases.

22. The marginalization of women remains real despite the progress of recent years. We will, therefore, work with renewed vigour to ensure gender equality and ensure their full and effective integration of women in the political and socio-economic development.

23. Globalization and liberalization does not mean that there should no role for government in socio-economic development. It only means a different type of government. We, therefore, undertake to foster new partnerships between government and the private sector; a new division of labour in which the private sector will be the veritable engine of growth, while governments concentrate on the development of infrastructure and the creation of a macro-economic environment. This includes expanding and enhancing the quality of human resources and providing the appropriate institutional framework to guide the formulation and execution of economic policy.

24.   The regional economic communities remain the building blocks for Africa's economic integration. We will, therefore continue to strengthen them in every way practicable and to relate their evolution more closely to the development of the African Union.

25.   We welcome the strong international interest in and support for NEPAD. It is our intention to build on this promising foundation, working with our development partners and the wider international community to:

Forge new forms of international co-operation in which the benefits of globalization are more evenly shared;

Create a stable international economic environment in which African countries can achieve growth through greater market access for their exports; the removal of trade barriers, especially non-tariff barriers and other forms of protectionism; increased flows of direct foreign investment; debt cancellation; a meaningful increase in ODA; and the diversification of their economies. Africa's prosperity will be a multiplier in world prosperity.

26.   NEPAD is founded on a hardheaded assessment of the political and socio-economic realities in Africa today. We do not, therefore, underestimate the challenges involved in achieving NEPAD's objectives, but we share a common resolution to work together even more closely in order to end poverty on the continent and to restore Africa to a place of dignity in the family of nations.

27.   No African country is a replica of another and no African society is a mirror image of another. However, we believe that the variety within our oneness can be enriching. It is part of the purpose of this Declaration to mobilize all those enriching qualities to build African unity, in respect of the specific of our countries.

African Peer Review Mechanism

28.   We have separately agreed to establish an African Peer Review Mechanism (APRM) on the basis of voluntary accession. The APRM seeks to promote adherence to and fulfillment of the commitments

contained in this Declaration. The Mechanism spells out the institutions and processes that will guide future peer reviews, based on mutually agreed codes and standards of democracy, political, economic and corporate governance.

Annex 7

Base Instrument of the African Peer Review Mechanism (APRM)

38TH Ordinary Session of the Assembly of Heads of State and
Government of the OAU: African Peer Review Mechanism
8 July 2002
Durban, South Africa
AHG/235 (XXXVIII)

Annex II

THE NEW PARTNERSHIP FOR AFRICA'S DEVELOPMENT
(NEPAD)

THE ARFICAN PEER REVIEW MECHANISM (APRM)

1.   The African Peer Mechanism (ARPM) is an instrument voluntarily
      acceded to by Member States of the African Union as an African
      self-monitoring mechanism.

Mandate of the APRM

The mandate of the African Peer Review Mechanism is to ensure that
the policies and practices of participating states conform to the agreed
political, economic and corporate governance values, codes and standards
contained in the Declaration on Democracy, Political, Economic and
Corporate Governance. The APRM is the mutually agreed instrument for
self-monitoring by the participating member governments.

Purpose of the APRM

2   The primary purpose of the APRM is to foster the adoption of policies, standards and practices that lead to political stability, economic growth, sustainable development and accelerated sub-regional and continental economic integration through sharing of experiences and reinforcement of successful and best practice, including identifying deficiencies and assessing the needs for capacity building.

Principles of the APRM

3.   Every review exercise carried out under the authority of the Mechanism must be technically competent, credible and free of political manipulation. These stipulations together constitute the core of the Mechanism.

Participation in the African Peer Review Process

4.   Participation in the process will be open to all member states of the African Union. After adoption of the Declaration on Democracy, Political, Economic and Corporate Governance by the African Union, countries wishing to participate in the APRM will notify the Chairman of the NEPAD Heads of State and Government Implementation Committee. This will entail an undertaking to submit to periodic peer reviews, as well as to facilitate such reviews, and be guided by agreed parameters for good political governance and economic and corporate governance.

Leadership and Management Structure

5.   It is proposed that the operations of the APRM be directed and managed by a Panel of between 5 and 7 Eminent Persons. The members of the Panel must be Africans who have distinguished themselves in careers that are considered relevant to the work of the APRM. In addition, members of the Panel must be persons of high moral stature and demonstrated commitment to the ideals of Pan Africanism.

6. Candidates for appointment to the Panel will be nominated by participating countries, shortlisted by a Committee of Ministers and appointed by Heads of State and Government of the participating countries. In addition to the criteria referred to above, the Heads of State and Government will ensure that the Panel has expertise in the areas of political governance, macro-economic management, public financial management and corporate governance. The composition of the Panel will also reflect broad regional balance, gender equality and cultural diversity.

7. Members of the Panel will serve for up to 4 years and will retire by rotation.

8. One of the members of the Panel will be appointed Chairman by the Heads of State and Government of the participating countries. The Chairperson will serve for a maximum period of five years. The criteria for appointment to the position of Chairperson will be the same as for other members of the Panel, except the candidate will be a person with a proven leadership record in one of the following areas: Government, public administration, development and private sector.

9. The Panel will exercise the oversight function over the review process, in particular to ensure the integrity of the process. Its mission and duties will be outlined in a Charter, which will also spell out reporting arrangements to the Heads of State and Government of participating countries. The Charter will secure the independence, objectivity and integrity of the Panel.

10. The Secretariat may engage, with the approval of the Panel, the services of African experts and institutions that it considers competent and appropriate to act as its agents in the peer review process.

11. The Panel will be supported by a competent Secretariat that has both the technical capacity to undertake the analytical work that under pins the peer review process and also conforms to the principles of the APRM. The functions of the Secretariat will include: maintaining extensive database information on political and economic developments in all participating countries, preparation of background documents for the Peer Review Teams, proposing performance indicators and tracking performance of individual countries.

Periodicity and types of Peer Review

12. At the point of formally acceding to the peer review process, each State should define a time-bound Programme of Action for implementing the Declaration on Democracy, Political, Economic and Corporate Governance, including periodic reviews.

13. There will be four types of reviews:

- The first country review is the base review that is carried out within eighteen months of a country becoming a member of the APRM process;
- Then there is a periodic review that takes place every two to four years;
- In addition to these, a member country can, for its own reasons, ask for a review that is not part of the periodically mandated reviews; and
- Earl signs of impending political or economic crisis in a member country would also be sufficient cause for instituting a review. Such a review can be called for by participating Heads of State and Government in a spirit of helpfulness to the Government concerned.

APRM Process

14. The process will entail periodic reviews of policies and practices of participating states to ascertain progress being made towards achieving mutually agreed goals and compliance with agreed political, economic and corporate governance values, codes and standards as outlined in the Declaration on Democracy, Political, Economic and Corporate Governance.

15. The peer review process will spur countries to consider seriously the impact of domestic policies, not only on internal political stability and economic growth, but also on neighboring countries. It will promote mutual accountability, as well as compliance with best practice.

16. Bearing in mind that African countries are at different levels development, on joining the Mechanism, a country will be assessed (the base review) and a timetable (Programme of Action) for

effecting progress towards achieving the agreed standards and goals must be drawn up by the state in question, taking into account the particular circumstances of that state.

Stages of the Peer Review Process

17.   Stage one will involve a study f the political, economic and corporate governance and development environment in the country to be reviewed based principally on up-to-date background documentation prepared by the APRM Secretariat and material provided by national, sub-regional, regional and international institutions.

18.   In stage two, the Review Team will visit the country concerned where its priority order of business will be to carry out the widest possible range of consultations with the Government, officials, political parties, parliamentarians and representatives of civil society organizations (including the media, academia, trade unions, business, & professional bodies).

19.   Stage three is the preparation of the Team's report. The report is prepared on the basis of the briefing material prepared by the APRM Secretariat and the information provided in the country by official and unofficial sources during the wide-ranging consultations and interactions with all stakeholders. The report must be measured against the applicable political, economic and corporate governance commitments made and the Programme of Action.

20.   The Team's draft report is first discussed with the Government concerned. Those discussions will be designed to ensure the accuracy of the information and to provide the Government with an opportunity both to react to the Team's finding and to put forward its own views on how the identified shortcomings may be addressed. These responses of the Government will be appended to the Team's report.

21.   The Team's report will need to be clear on a number of points in instances where problems are identified. Is there the will on the part of the Government to take the necessary decisions and measures to put right what is identified to be amiss? What resources are necessary to take corrective measures? How much of these can the Government itself provide and how much is to come from external

sources? Given the necessary resources, how long will the process of rectification take?

22. The Fourth Stage begins when the Team's report is submitted to the participating Heads of State and Government through the APRM Secretariat. The consideration and adoption of the final report by the participating Heads of State and Government, including their decision in this regard, marks the end of this stage.

23. If the Government of the country in question shows a demonstrable will to rectify the identified shortcomings, then it will be incumbent upon participating Governments to provide what assistance they can, as well as to urge donor governments and agencies also to come to the assistance of the country reviewed. However, if the necessary political will is not forthcoming from the Government, the participating states should first do everything practicable to engage it in constructive, offering in the process technical and other appropriate assistance. If the dialogue proves unavailing, the participating Heads of State and Government may wish to put the Government on notice of their collective intention to proceed with appropriate measures by a given date. The interval should concentrate the mind of the Government and provide a further opportunity for addressing the identified shortcomings under a process of constructive dialogue. All considered, such measures should always be utilized as a last resort.

24. Six months after the report has been considered by the Heads of State and Government of the participating member countries, it should be formally and publicly tabled in key regional and sub-regional structures such as the Pan-African Parliament, the African Commission on Human and Peoples' Rights, the envisaged Peace and Security Council and the Economic, Social and Cultural Council (ECOSOCC) of the African Union.

This constitutes the Fifth and final stage of the process.

Duration of the Peer Review

25. The duration of the review process per country should not be longer than six months, commencing on the date of the inception of Stage

One up to the date the report is submitted for consideration of the Heads of State and Government.

Funding of the Peer Review Mechanism

26.   Funding for the Mechanism will come from assessed contributions from participating member states.

Review of the APRM

27.   To enhance its dynamism, the Conference of the participating countries will review the APRM once every five years.